Making Ukraine Soviet

Library of Modern Russia

Advisory Board:
Jeffrey Brooks, Professor at Johns Hopkins University, USA
Michael David-Fox, Professor at Georgetown University, USA
Lucien Frary, Associate Professor at Rider University, USA
James Harris, Senior Lecturer at the University of Leeds, UK
Robert Hornsby, Lecturer at the University of Leeds, UK
Ekaterina Pravilova, Professor of History at Princeton University, USA
Geoffrey Swain, Emeritus Professor of Central and East European Studies at the University of Glasgow, UK
Vera Tolz-Zilitinkevic, Sir William Mather Professor of Russian Studies at the University of Manchester, UK
Vladislav Zubok, Professor of International History at the London School of Economics, UK

Building on Bloomsbury Academic's established record of publishing Russian studies titles, the *Library of Modern Russia* will showcase the work of emerging and established writers who are setting new agendas in the field.

At a time when potentially dangerous misconceptions and misunderstandings about Russia abound, titles in the series will shed fresh light and nuance on Russian history. Volumes will take the idea of 'Russia' in its broadest cultural sense and cover the entirety of the multi-ethnic lands that made up imperial Russia and the Soviet Union. Ranging in chronological scope from the Romanovs to today, the books will:

- Reconsider Russia's history from a variety of interdisciplinary perspectives.
- Explore Russia in its various international contexts, rather than as exceptional or in isolation.
- Examine the complex, divisive and ever-shifting notions of 'Russia'.
- Contribute to a deeper understanding of Russia's rich social and cultural history.
- Critically reassess the Soviet period and its legacy today.
- Interrogate the traditional periodizations of the post-Stalin Soviet Union.
- Unearth continuities, or otherwise, among the tsarist, Soviet and post-Soviet periods.
- Reappraise Russia's complex relationship with Eastern Europe, both historically and today.

- Analyse the politics of history and memory in post-Soviet Russia.
- Promote new archival revelations and innovative research methodologies.
- Foster a community of scholars and readers devoted to a sharper understanding of the Russian experience, past and present.

Books in the series will join our list in being marketed globally, including at conferences – such as the BASEES and ASEEES conventions. Each will be subjected to a rigorous peer-review process and will be published in hardback and, simultaneously, as an e-book. We also anticipate a second release in paperback for the general reader and student markets.

For more information, or to submit a proposal for inclusion in the series, please contact:

Rhodri Mogford, Publisher, History (Rhodri.Mogfrod@bloomsbury.com).

New and forthcoming:

Fascism in Manchuria: The Soviet-China Encounter in the 1930s, Susanne Hohler
The Idea of Russia: The Life and Work of Dmitry Likhachev, Vladislav Zubok
The Tsar's Armenians: A Minority in Late Imperial Russia, Onur Onol
Myth Making in the Soviet Union and Modern Russia: Remembering World War II in Brezhnev's Hero City, Vicky Davis
Building Stalinism: The Moscow Canal and the Creation of Soviet Space, Cynthia Ruder
Russia in the Time of Cholera: Disease and the Environment under Romanovs and Soviets, John Davis
Soviet Americana: A Cultural History of Russian and Ukrainian Americanists, Sergei Zhuk
Stalin's Economic Advisors: The Varga Institute and the Making of Soviet Foreign Policy, Ken Roh
Ideology and the Arts in the Soviet Union: The Establishment of Censorship and Control, Steven Richmond
Nomads and Soviet Rule: Central Asia under Lenin and Stalin, Alun Thomas
The Russian State and the People: Power, Corruption and the Individual in Putin's Russia, Geir Hønneland et al. (eds.)
The Communist Party in the Russian Civil War: A Political History, Gayle Lonergan

Criminal Subculture in the Gulag: Prisoner Society in the Stalinist Labour Camps, Mark Vincent
Power and Politics in Modern Chechnya: Ramzan Kadyrov and the New Digital Authoritarianism, Karena Avedissian
Russian Pilgrimage to the Holy Land: Piety and Travel from the Middle Ages to the Revolution, Nikolaos Chrissidis
The Fate of the Bolshevik Revolution, Lara Douds, James Harris, and Peter Whitehead (eds.)
Writing History in Late Imperial Russia, Frances Nethercott
Translating England into Russian, Elena Goodwin
Gender and Survival in Soviet Russia, Elaine MacKinnon (trans. and ed.)
Publishing in Tsarist Russia, Yukiko Tatsumi and Taro Tsurumi (eds.)
New Drama in Russian: Performance, Politics and Protest, Julie Curtis (ed.)
The Culture of Samizdat: Literature and Underground Networks in the Late Soviet Union, Josephine von Zitzewitz
Making Ukraine Soviet: Literature and Cultural Politics under Lenin and Stalin, Olena Palko

Making Ukraine Soviet

Literature and Cultural Politics under Lenin and Stalin

Olena Palko

BLOOMSBURY ACADEMIC
LONDON • NEW YORK • OXFORD • NEW DELHI • SYDNEY

BLOOMSBURY ACADEMIC
Bloomsbury Publishing Plc
50 Bedford Square, London, WC1B 3DP, UK
1385 Broadway, New York, NY 10018, USA
29 Earlsfort Terrace, Dublin 2, Ireland

BLOOMSBURY, BLOOMSBURY ACADEMIC and the Diana logo
are trademarks of Bloomsbury Publishing Plc

First published in Great Britain 2021
This paperback edition published in 2022

Copyright © Olena Palko, 2021

Olena Palko has asserted her right under the Copyright,
Designs and Patents Act, 1988, to be identified as Author of this work.

Series design by Tjaša Krivec

Cover image: Ukrainian writers and poets at the Fifth Plenum of the Union of Soviet Writers of Ukraine,
Stalino, December 21–23, 1950. © Central State Archive of Literature and Arts of Ukraine (TsDAMLMU)

All rights reserved. No part of this publication may be reproduced or transmitted in any form or by any
means, electronic or mechanical, including photocopying, recording, or any information storage or
retrieval system, without prior permission in writing from the publishers.

Bloomsbury Publishing Plc does not have any control over, or responsibility for, any third-party websites
referred to or in this book. All internet addresses given in this book were correct at the time of going
to press. The author and publisher regret any inconvenience caused if addresses have changed or sites
have ceased to exist, but can accept no responsibility for any such changes.

Every effort has been made to trace copyright holders and to obtain their permissions for the use of
copyright material. The publisher apologizes for any errors or omissions and would be grateful if notified
of any corrections that should be incorporated in future reprints or editions of this book.

A catalogue record for this book is available from the British Library.

Library of Congress Cataloging-in-Publication Data
Names: Palko, Olena, author.
Title: Making Ukraine Soviet : literature and cultural politics under Lenin and Stalin / Olena Palko.
Description: London ; New York : Bloomsbury Academic, 2020. |
Series: Library of modern Russia | Includes bibliographical references and index.
Identifiers: LCCN 2020030974 (print) | LCCN 2020030975 (ebook) |
ISBN 9781788313056 (hardback) | ISBN 9781350230927 (paperback)| ISBN 9781350142701 (ebook) |
ISBN 9781350142718 (epub)
Subjects: LCSH: Ukraine–History–1921–1944. | Ukraine–Politics and government–
1917–1945. Ukraine–History–Revolution, 1917–1921. | Soviet literature–History and criticism. |
Ukrainian literature–20th century–History and criticism. | National characteristics,
Ukrainian. | Communism–Ukraine. | Social change–Ukraine–History–20th century. |
Tychyna, Pavlo Hryhorovych, 1891–1967 Criticism and interpretation. |Khvyl'ovyi?,
Mykola, 1893-1933–Criticism and interpretation.
Classification: LCC DK508.813 .P35 2020 (print) | LCC DK508.813 (ebook) |DDC 947.708/4–dc23
LC record available at https://lccn.loc.gov/2020030974
LC ebook record available at https://lccn.loc.gov/2020030975.

ISBN:	HB:	978-1-7883-1305-6
	PB:	978-1-3502-3092-7
	ePDF:	978-1-3501-4270-1
	eBook:	978-1-3501-4271-8

Series: Library of Modern Russia

Typeset by Integra Software Services Pvt. Ltd.

To find out more about our authors and books visit www.bloomsbury.com
and sign up for our newsletters.

Contents

Illustrations	viii
Acknowledgements	ix
Note on transliteration and translation	xi
Abbreviations	xii
Introduction	1
Part One Competing projects of Ukraine	17
1 *'Above Kyiv there is a Golden Hum'*: The National Revolution in Kyiv	19
2 In search of 'a blue Savoy': The Bolshevik revolution in Kharkiv	49
Part Two Debating Soviet culture in Ukraine	77
3 Towards Soviet literature in Ukrainian	79
4 Defending Soviet Ukrainian literature	97
Part Three Fitting in the Soviet canon	115
5 *'Ukraine or Little Russia'*: The battle for cultural autonomy in 1926	117
6 State appropriation of literature during the first Five-Year Plan	147
Epilogue	185
Notes	192
Bibliography	231
Index	252

Illustrations

1. Map of Soviet Ukraine, 1921 — xiv
2. Pavlo Tychyna, self-portrait, 1922 — 21
3. National Amateur Choir Chapel named after Mykola Leontovych, 1920 — 45
4. Mykola Khvyl'ovyi, Kharkiv, 1925 — 54
5. Mykola Khvyl'ovyi and Valeriian Polishchuk, Kharkiv, 1925 — 59
6. A meeting between the writers from Kyiv and Kharkiv. Kyiv, 1923 — 66
7. Soviet Ukrainian writers in Kharkiv, 1925 — 90
8. *Hart* writers Valeriian Polishchuk, Pavlo Tychyna and Oleksa Dosvitnii before travelling to Western Europe, 1924 — 92
9. Writer Valeriian Polishchuk. Undated — 94
10. Soviet Ukrainian writers, 1920s — 100
11. Ukrainian writers. Undated — 104
12. Ivan Dniprovs'kyi, Iurii Ianovs'kyi, and Mykola Khvyl'ovyi. Undated — 108
13. Soviet Ukrainian writers (Pavlo Tychyna, Mykola Kulish, Volodymyr Sosiura and others), 1920s — 127
14. Soviet Ukrainian writers near Viis'kove village, 1926 — 135
15. Ukrainian artists in Moscow, 1929 — 154
16. Ivan Dniprovs'kyi, Mykola Kulish, and Hryhorii Epik. Undated — 166
17. Soviet Ukrainian writers in Artemivs'k, 1928 — 168
18. Soviet Writers, members of the VUSPP, 1932 — 169
19. Tychyna's poem *Partiia Vede* in *Pravda* — 181
20. Ivan Mykytenko, Petro Panch, Oleksandr Korniichuk, and Pavlo Tychyna before travelling to the International Congress of Writers for the Defence of Culture in Paris, 1935 — 183

Acknowledgements

This book grew out of my doctoral thesis written and defended at the University of East Anglia. First and foremost, I would like to thank my academic advisors Matthias Neumann and Francis King, as well as Tony Kemp-Welch, for their intellectual advice, guidance and feedback on my work as well as for always providing constant reassurance and unfailing encouragement. I am truly indebted to them for the support they have provided during the course of my studies and their encouragement to turn my thesis into a book. My study and research at UEA, however, would not be possible without the support of Cathy Carmichael; if it were not for her, I would have never come to England in the first place. In addition, I would also like to thank Peter Waldron and Matthew Pauly for their comments and helpful advice in identifying areas of improvement in the thesis. The book would not have been as it is without their timely advice. In addition, I would like to thank Sonia Combe, my advisor during my research stay at the Centre Marc Bloch in Berlin, for her invaluable advice; and Béatrice von Hirschhausen for her help, feedback and support during perhaps the hardest period of my life. My studies and research at UEA were made possible by a number of scholarships: UEA's Faculty of Arts and Humanities doctoral studentship, Global Society Supplementary Grant from the Open Society Foundation, and financial assistance for attendance at advanced Western educational institutions for advanced learning and training from James C. Temerty.

It has taken two additional years to turn my PhD thesis into a book. During this time, I benefited immensely from the hospitable and stimulating academic environment at the Department of History of the University of Basel, where I had the pleasure of being a URIS fellow. I am most grateful to Benjamin Schenk for welcoming me to the department. Those wonderful six months provided me with an excellent opportunity to re-evaluate my thesis and start thinking about it as a possible book. Most of the present text, however, was written at Birkbeck during my first year there as a Leverhulme Early Career fellow. My sincere gratitude goes to Orlando Figes, Jessica Reinisch, Filippo de Vivo and, of course, Jan Rueger for their valuable support and encouragement, as well as allowing me time to finish the manuscript.

This book would not be possible without Thomas Stottor at I.B. Tauris, who took an early interest in my project, as well as the Bloomsbury editorial team – Rhodri Mogford and Laura Reeves who saw it to completion. I am also grateful to my anonymous reviewers – their lengthy and detailed comments ensured that this book became better than it would have been otherwise.

There are a number of people I would like to thank on a personal level for their support, encouragement and assistance during my time in England, especially Graham Harris, Sam Foster, Mark Vincent, Nada Ali, Irina Sirbu and Matt Laube. My deepest thanks go to my husband Borja, who has been a continual source of inspiration and support. He did his best to take care of our twin boys born in the process of completing the manuscript, thus allowing me time to focus on it. Finally, I would like to thank the rest of my family for their constant support, encouragement and, most importantly, for their unconditional belief in my abilities. I would like to dedicate this book to my father, who passed away before seeing this project completed.

Note on transliteration and translation

This book follows the Library of Congress's system of transliterating Ukrainian and Russian texts and names, excluding cases where a commonly accepted English translation exists (e.g. Gorky and Mayakovski). To make it simpler for the readers, I have also used *i* instead of a Ukrainian *ï* throughout the body of the text. For the sake of consistency, I have used the Ukrainian transliteration of Ukrainian names and geographical places (e.g. Kyiv, Kharkiv, Odesa and Donbas).

I have given quotations in the English translations and have used Michael M. Naydan's translation of Pavlo Tychyna's (Pavlo Tychyna, *The Complete Early Poetry Collections of Pavlo Tychyna* [Lviv: Litopys, 2002; London, 2017]). All other translations which are not included in this collection are my own.

As for Khvyl'ovyi's prose, all quotes are referenced from the following texts:

- Mykola Khvylovy, *The Cultural Renaissance in Ukraine*. Translated by Myroslav Shkandrij (Edmonton: CIUS, 1986);
- Mykola Khvylovy, *Stories from the Ukraine*. Translated by George S. N. Luckyj (New York: Philosophical library, 1960);
- Mykola Khvylovy, 'Woodcocks'. Translated by Yuri Tkacz in *Before the Storm: Soviet Ukrainian Fiction of the 1920s* (Ann Arbor: Ardis, 1986).

Quotes from short stories not included in these translated collections are my own.

Abbreviations

Cheka	*Chrezvychainaia Komissia po Bor'be s Kontrrevoliutsiei i Sabotazhem,* Extraordinary Committee for combating counter-revolution, Sabotage and Speculation
DVU (or *Derzhvydav*)	*Derzhavne Vydavnytstvo Ukrainy,* the State Publishing House of Ukraine
GPU	*Gosudarstvennoie Politicheskoie Upravleniie,* State Political Directorate
IKSOOO	*Ispolnitel'nyi Komitet Soveta Ob'edinennykh Obshchestvennykh Organizatsii,* Executive Committee of the Council of United Community Organisations
Komsomol	*Komunistychynyi Soiuz Molodi* (Ukr.), *Kommunisticheskii Soiuz Molodiozhi* (Rus.), Young Communist League
KP(b)U	*Komunistychna Partiia Bil'shovykiv Ukrainy,* the Communist Party of Bolsheviks of Ukraine
Liknep	(Ukr., *likbez* in Russian) eradication of illiteracy
Narkomos	(Ukr., *Narkompros* in Russian) *Narodnyi Komisariat Osvity* (Ukr.), *Narodnyi Komissariat Prosveshcheniia* (Rus.), Peoples Commissariat for Education
NEP	*Novaia Ekonomicheskaia Politika,* New Economic Policy
Prolitfront	*Proletars'kyi Literaturnyi Front,* Proletarian Literary Front
Radnarkom	(Ukr., *Sovnarkom* in Russian) *Rada Narodnykh Komisariv,* Council of Peoples Commissars
RKP(b)	(*VKP(b)* in 1925–52) *Rossiiskaia Kommunisticheskaia Partiia Bol'shevikov,* the Russian Communist Party of Bolsheviks
RSDRP	*Rossiiskaia Sotsial-Demokraticheskaia Rabochaia Partiia,* Social-Democratic Labour Party
RSFSR	*Rossiiskaia Sovetskaia Federativnaia Sotsialisticheskaia Respublika,* Russian Soviet Federative Socialist Republic
SVU	*Spilka Vyzvolennia Ukrainy,* the Union for the Liberation of Ukraine
TsDAMLMU	*Tsentral'nyi Derzhavnyi Arkhiv-Muzei Literatury i Mystetstv Ukrainy,* the Central State Archives Museum of Literature and Arts of Ukraine

TsK KP(b)U	*Komitet Komunistychnoi Partii Bil'shovykiv Ukrainy,* the Central Committee of the Communist Party of Bolsheviks of Ukraine
TsK RKP(b)	*Tsentral'nyi Komitet Vserossiiskoi Kommunisticheskoi Partii Bol'shevikov,* Central Committee of the All-Russian Communist Party of Bolsheviks
TUP	*Tovarystvo Ukrains'kykh Postupovtsiv,* Society of Ukrainian Progressivists
UAPTs	*Ukrains'ka Avtokefal'na Pravoslavna Tserkva,* the Ukrainian Autocephalous Orthodox Church
UNR	*Ukrains'ka Narodna Respublika,* the Ukrainian People's Republic
UNTs	*Ukrains'kyi Natsional'nyi Tsentr,* the Ukrainian National Centre
UPSR	*Ukrains'ka Partiia Sotsialistiv-Revoliutsioneriv,* the Ukrainian Party of Socialist Revolutionaries
USDRP	*Ukrains'ka Sotsial-Demokratychna Robitnycha Partiia,* the Ukrainian Social-Democratic Labour Party
UkrSSR	(Ukrainian SSR) *Ukrains'ka Sotsialistychna Radians'ka Respublika,* the Ukrainian Socialist Soviet Republic (1919–37); *Ukrains'ka Radians'ka Sotsialistychna Respublika,* the Ukrainian Soviet Socialist Republic (1937–91)
UVO	*Ukrains'ka Viis'kova Orhanisatsiia,* the Ukrainian Military Organisation
VAPLITE	*Vil'na Akademiia Proletars'koi Literatury,* Free Academy of Proletarian Literature
VAPP	*Vserossiiskaia Assotsiatsiia Proletarskikh Pisatelei,* the All-Russian Association of Proletarian Writers
Vseukrlitkom	*Vseukrains'kyi Literaturnyi Komitet,* the All-Ukrainian Literary Committee
Vsevydav	*Vseukrains'ke Vydavnytstvo,* the State Publishing House of Ukraine
VUAN	*Vseukrains'ka Akademiia Nauk,* the All-Ukrainian Academy of Sciences
VUAPP	*Vseukrains'ka Asotsiatsiia Proletars'kykh Pys'mennykiv,* the All-Ukrainian Association of Proletarian Writers
VUFKU	*Vseukrains'ke Foto-kino Upravlinnia,* the All-Ukrainian Photo-Cinema Administration
VUSPP	*Vseukrains'ka Spilka Proletars'kykh Pys'mennykiv,* All-Ukrainian Union of Proletarian Writers
VUTsVK	*Vseukrains'kyi Tsentral'nyi Vykonavchyi Komitet,* the All-Ukrainian Central Executive Committee
ZUNR	*Zakhidno-Ukrains'ka Narodna Respublika,* the Western Ukrainian National Republic

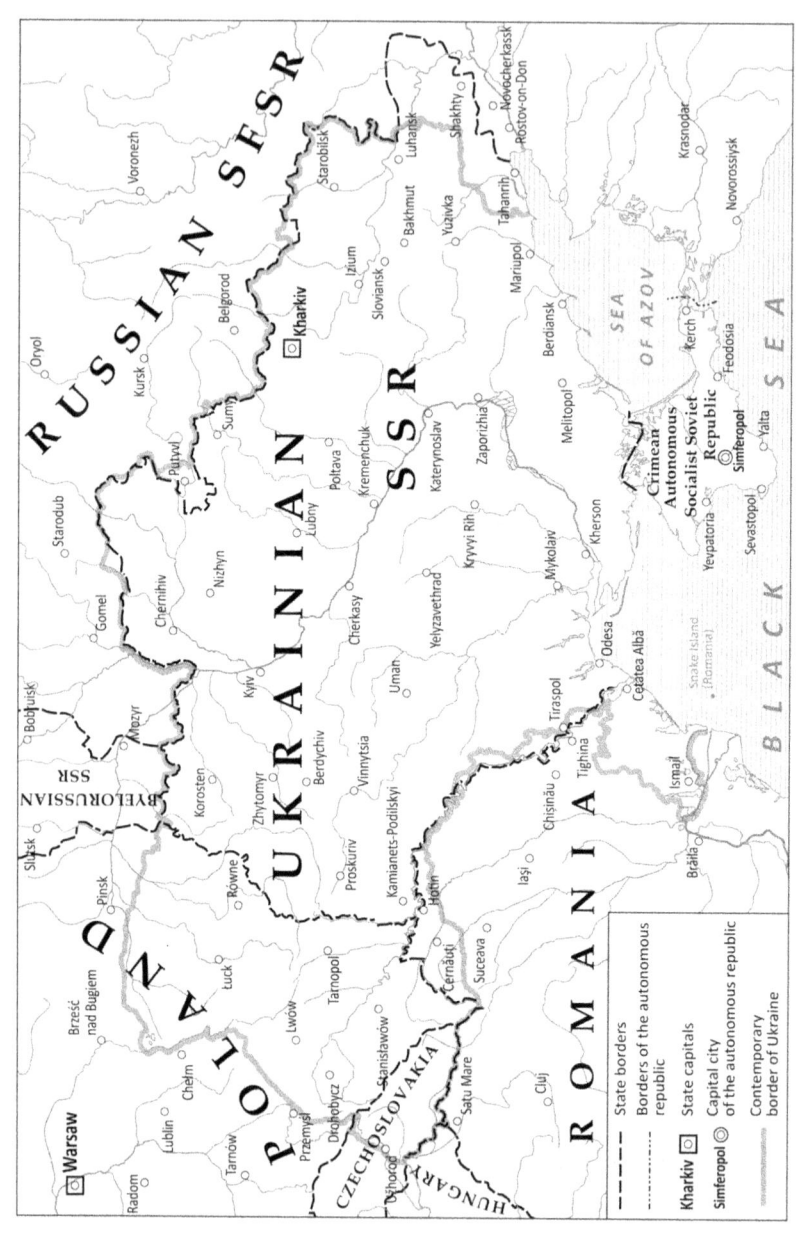

Figure 1 Map of Soviet Ukraine, 1921. © Dmytro Vortman.

Introduction

On 9 February 1929, a delegation from Soviet Ukraine, which included its most prominent writers, artists, actors, film and theatre directors, arrived at the Kursky train station in Moscow. Despite unexpectedly cold weather, the mood among these Ukrainians was sanguine, as this was the delegation's first official visit to the Soviet capital and a new experience for many of its members. The poet Dmytro Zahul confessed that he had visited many European cities but never even been to Russia before, similar to the recognized leader of this current generation of Ukrainian artists Mykola Khvyl'ovyi, also visiting Moscow for the first time. At the train station, the delegates were warmly welcomed by Platon Kerzhentsev, the head of the Russian Department of Agitation, Propaganda and Press (Agitprop), who would not leave their side until the end of the visit a week later. The programme of the Ukrainian week in Moscow was intense. It included literary evenings, meetings with readers and publishing directors, art exhibitions and theatre outings, a private tour through the Kremlin and a visit to Lenin's mausoleum. The highlight was an afternoon meeting with Stalin in Maxim Gorky's apartment on 12 February.

In all respects, this was an unprecedented event – the first official meeting of the two Soviet cultures at the highest official level. At the opening event, the Russian Commissar for Education, Anatoly Lunacharsky, regretfully admitted how little cooperation and exchange there was between the two Soviet literatures: 'Strange to think! It is much easier for us to get acquainted with English literature than with the Ukrainian one that is so much closer to us.'[1] The speaker of the Ukrainian delegation, a writer called Ivan Mykytenko, joined Lunacharsky in remarking that it took twelve years for such a meeting to occur: 'During this time we have already developed ties with French, German, English and even Turkish writers.'[2] Indeed, many Russian writers visited Kharkiv: Gorky, Vladimir Mayakovski and Boris Pilnyak, to name just a few. Yet there was little institutional collaboration between the two literatures, translation into Russian was almost non-existent and, as a result, little was known about contemporary Ukrainian literature beyond its borders. Overall, cultural life in these two Soviet republics developed in parallel to each other, with little or no interaction between the two. The Ukrainian week was, thus, even more important. As admitted by the Ukrainian Commissar for Education, Mykola Skrypnyk, in February 1929 self-standing Soviet Ukrainian culture was recognized and acknowledged at the highest Union level.[3]

During the 1920s, writers and artists in Soviet Ukraine were engaged in constructing a new cultural and political identity that was both Soviet and Ukrainian. These cultural figures came of age during the First World War, they were inspired by the revolutions of 1917 and fought on the battlefields of the civil war; many anticipated a soviet regime and developed loyalty to the Soviet authorities. They subsequently joined the Communist Party of Bolsheviks of Ukraine (KP(b)U) seeking to build a strong self-standing Soviet Ukraine. Those writers dedicated themselves to creating revolutionary literature in Ukrainian and constructing a modern, urban Soviet Ukrainian identity. In this book, the process of constructing Soviet Ukrainian culture in the 1920s is studied through the life and works of two Ukrainian writers: the poet Pavlo Tychyna (1891–1967) and the prose author and public intellectual Mykola Khvyl'ovyi (1893–1933).

This book investigates the complex and multifaceted process of Ukraine's cultural Sovietization. During the 1920s, different political projects for creating an alternative socialist government and a Soviet Ukraine were put to the test. The first was developed and executed by the Ukrainian communist movement, particularly the *Borot'bysty*, the former left-wing members of the Ukrainian Party of Socialist Revolutionaries (UPSR), who after their merger with the KP(b)U in 1920 had contributed greatly to strengthening a separatist political horizon in the party. Another project was implemented by the KP(b)U members with a clear centripetal orientation towards Moscow, advocating in favour of preserving established historical relations between the centre and the periphery and constructing an all-Russian (all-Soviet) political and cultural space. Consequently, these two political cultures, or ideological horizons, in the KP(b)U endorsed different cultural projects in Soviet Ukraine. Firstly, there was a project of Soviet Ukrainian culture curated from Kharkiv by the cultural wing of the *Borot'bysty* and Ukraine-minded Bolsheviks. Secondly, the idea of an all-Union Soviet culture, to which Ukraine's cultural figures would contribute equally with representatives from other Soviet republics, was vigorously promoted.[4]

These differing political orientations were also reflected in the way the artistic map of the Soviet Union was perceived. Whereas the promoters of the Soviet Ukrainian cultural project aimed at a decentralized artistic map with numerous cultural centres spread across the various Soviet republics, the contributors to the all-Soviet culture saw Moscow as the only true centre and the peripheries as provincial. These competing visions crystallized during the Literary Discussion of 1925–8, when Khvyl'ovyi, as spokesperson for the cultural opposition, called upon Soviet Ukrainian writers to 'flee as quickly as possible from Russian literature and its styles'.[5] The writers' trip to Moscow in February 1929 proved to be the extent of this autonomous vision for Soviet Ukrainian culture. Not only did Soviet writers not regard Moscow as a reference point for their literary activities, they embarked on their trip to Russia as if it were a foreign country, highlighting the physical and ideological borders between the two.[6]

Yet the biggest difference between these two cultural projects was in their understanding of a national culture and its future under socialism – the ultimate goal both factions pursued. The promoters of the all-Union Soviet canon followed Marx and Lenin in their belief that nations, nation-states, national cultures and languages would disappear under socialism. In the 1920s, the Soviet authorities undertook to defend, sponsor and promote national identities; yet they did so while coveting a universal and homogeneous socialist culture. There was no contradiction, however. National cultures would gradually yet necessarily wither away, while the promotion of native languages was instrumental in raising the cultural level of the popular masses and bringing them closer to socialism.

However, the defenders of Soviet Ukrainian culture saw it as a value in itself. In this book, Soviet Ukrainian culture is defined with reference to both political dynamics and cultural tropes. At the level of institutional dynamics and cultural politics, its promoters aimed for political and cultural autonomy for Soviet Ukraine and often were affiliated – ideologically, if not always institutionally – with Ukraine-minded communists and left radicals from the *Borot'bysty* party. In this regard, Soviet Ukrainian cultural agents rejected cultural and political hierarchy and opposed 'Moscow', which they regarded as both a centre of artistic domination and political control. They strived for an independent cultural development that would reflect equally their socialist values and national preoccupations. On an artistic level, agents of Soviet Ukrainian culture opposed the didactic and socially useful view on literature promoted by the Bolshevik leaders. Despite rejecting types of 'mass culture' produced by certain Soviet literary organizations in both Moscow and Kharkiv, they wished to create 'high culture' for educated proletarians. In the 1920s, this opposition was framed as '*kul'tura*' vs. '*khaltura*', a culture of lasting values versus hackwork.

Although the creators and advocates of the two soviet cultural projects used the Ukrainian language as their medium, their intention behind the promotion of Ukrainian were different. Whereas the Ukrainizers in Kharkiv saw Ukrainian as a prerequisite for creating a modern, urban-based culture with equal appreciation of traditional social structure (specifically the Ukrainian-speaking peasantry) and pre-Soviet cultural trends, centrally oriented art officials used the Ukrainian language (the language of the largest ethnic group in the republic) as a necessary concession to achieving certain strategic goals. In this regard, the Ukrainian language was yet another symbolic marker of national identity on a par with folklore, dress, food, historical heroes and events, and classic literary works.[7] In the end, the party officials pursued Sovietization albeit through the means of controlled and limited Ukrainization.[8]

It is important to admit, however, that Ukrainian culture (no matter the ideological position) was being created in a multi-ethnic context with other national languages being endorsed as a part of Soviet *korenizatsiia*.[9] The promoters of Soviet Ukrainian culture were cognizant and conscious of this diversity. The history of VAPLITE – the literary organization established by Khvyl'ovyi in 1925 as the flagship of the new cultural project – suggests that one of the hallmarks of this cultural project was its inclusivity. The first clause of the VAPLITE statute highlighted that the organization was open to all proletarian writers in Ukraine no matter the language of their work.[10] The discussion in this book, however, focuses primarily on the Ukrainian variant of the Soviet Ukrainian culture, which was a result of at least two reasons. First, it was primarily Ukrainian inasmuch as it concurred with the process of constructing a national identity while overcoming a century-long legacy of Russification and provincialism. Second, it was Ukrainian in the view of the party officials who often rejected and opposed this autonomist project as nationalist and anti-Russian.

Contemporary Soviet art and party officials were well aware of the language's ideological significance. In 1925, the leading literary critic Volodymyr Koriak stated that Soviet writers were expected to put an end to 'Ukrainian literature' and 'Ukrainian poets' and start creating a universal 'proletarian culture in the Ukrainian language'.[11] In line with Stalin's famous formula, Koriak advocated for the Soviet culture to be national only in a form that is created in Ukrainian to ease the spread of socialist content among the Ukrainian-speaking population. However, the promoters of a separatist cultural approach believed that socialism could be achieved 'only through channels national both in content and form', as emphasized by the Ukrainian Commissar for Education Hnat Mykhailychenko in 1919.[12] This book utilizes Koriak's definition to distinguish two visions of literature created by pro-Soviet writers during the 1920s – Soviet Ukrainian literature and Soviet literature in Ukrainian.

It must be said, however, that no clear and obvious divide actually existed between these differing Soviet writers. These two cultural projects were implemented simultaneously and, as this book intends to show, the evolution of each and every writer was non-linear, with frequent changes between the ideological camps. This distinction, therefore, is instrumental in highlighting how a complex process of negotiation between these two competing visions of Soviet literature eventually led to the unification of Ukraine's various artistic currents and the formation of a unified Soviet canon of socialist realism.

Moreover, during the 1920s, there was nothing close to a unified view on what should actually constitute Soviet Ukraine's literary canon, or even uniform understanding of the form and content of this Soviet Ukrainian culture.[13] As the following chapters will show, there were different literary currents in Soviet Ukraine, each of which, despite their acknowledged adherence to the revolution and/or proletarian orientation, varied in their views on artistic direction, the purpose of literature, the question of audiences, engagement with current affairs and the limits of party intervention. All of these differences were reflected in the institutional diversity of letters in Soviet Ukraine. In addition, the vision of Soviet Ukrainian literature varied between generations, ideological preferences and the language and ethnic origin of its contributors. Hence, the formation of a literary tradition in Soviet Ukraine required compromises between and assimilation of different interest groups, which was achieved through institutional unification in the early 1930s.

The unified Soviet canon that emerged in the early 1930s was, therefore, an amalgamation of at least two different Soviet cultural projects: Soviet Ukrainian culture and Soviet culture created in the Ukrainian language. The ongoing debates and negotiations between the two political and cultural orientations in the KP(b)U, among public intellectuals, artists and art officials are the focus of this book.[14] At the same time, the study explores those cultural, and often political, alternatives, which Soviet Ukraine had lost once the interaction between political actors and art creators was forced into a strictly defined channel, determined by a centralist cultural strategy.

The context of the study

Alternative visions of Soviet culture were enabled by many internal and external factors. First, young writers and artists were inspired by the potential of the 1917 revolutions that exposed the urgency of both national and social concerns exemplified by the rivalry between the Ukrainian People's Republic (*Ukrains'ka Narodna Respublika, UNR*), formed on 20 November 1917 and proclaiming its independence on 22 January 1918, and the Bolshevik-led Soviet Republic in Ukraine, which existed under various names from December 1917. A new generation of artists and writers was born amidst these revolutionary upheavals. Their orientation towards the future and their critical attitude towards the past initiated a new chapter of revolutionary and proletarian culture.[15] This new post-revolutionary artistic and literary corpus existed side by side with old-line intellectuals attempting to adapt to the new political reality. The wealth of national literature produced in the decade that followed the 1917 revolutions was mainly the result of creative cooperation between these two groups: young utopians and 'old' classics.[16] Unlike their Russian fellows, artists and writers in Ukraine at the time also searched for national identity, and, as such, emphasized the national dimension of the emerging revolutionary culture, with both class and nation featuring equally on their agenda.[17]

In addition, a separatist vision of Soviet culture was enabled by relative pluralism in the political sphere. During the 1920s, there were ongoing negotiations between central and local elites about the extent of Soviet Ukraine's autonomy and the status of the KP(b)U.[18] Unsurprisingly, this led to separatist claims in the cultural sphere, when the new generation of artists, inspired by the revolution and emboldened by strong Ukrainian voices in the party leadership, provocatively demanded to break the eternal dependency on Russian cultural patterns. Throughout the mid-1920s, many public intellectuals and party leaders, who were both Ukrainians and communists, objected to Soviet Ukraine's 'colonial status', either in political, economic or cultural matters.[19]

The difference between these two understandings of Soviet Ukraine was encapsulated in the dichotomy of 'Ukraine or Little Russia?' (*Ukraina chy Malorosiia?*) as defined by Khvyl'ovyi at the peak of the Literary Discussion in 1926. As it suggests, two types of national identity were being constructed at the time: 'Ukraine' as an autonomous and comprehensive identity-building project or 'Little Russia' (or, using another frequent polemic trope of the time, '*khokholiandia*', a country of '*khokhly*' – a pejorative exonime used to define Ukrainians, or even 'slavic India', as the writer Oleksa Slisarenko defined it) – a subordinate partial cultural denomination, suggesting Ukraine to be only a branch of the single Russian nation, an imperial periphery.

The strength of these political and cultural debates in Soviet Ukraine resulted from the ambiguity of the central Soviet government's own cultural policies.[20] In 1925, the government reasserted its non-intervention in the literary sphere, seeking compromise between proletarian and non-Soviet writers (the so-called fellow travellers (*poputnyky*)). Literary groups of different ideological orientations competed for state funding and published their almanacs in state-supported publishing houses. Nonetheless, from 1921, culture became widely recognized as the third front, a locus of struggle, 'an arena in which power (hegemony) could be won or lost'.[21] Despite its declared pluralism and tolerance, Soviet cultural strategy from very early on aimed at the Sovietization of intellectual, social and cultural life. Katerina Clark dubbed this latent state interference as a 'quiet revolution'.[22]

The potency of Soviet Ukrainian culture was attributed in large part to *korenizatsiia* and *Ukrainizatsiia* as its local variant.[23] The new Soviet nationalities policy, adopted at the Twelfth Russian Communist Party of Bolsheviks (RKP[b]) Congress in April 1923, called for reorganizing the Soviet Union 'in such a way as fully to reflect not only the common needs and requirements of all the nationalities of the Union, but also the special needs and requirements of each individual nationality'.[24] The rationale behind the new nationalities policy was that by engaging and promoting national cadres into local party organs (party entrenchment) and facilitating the development of national cultures and languages, the Communist Party would be able to curb any manifestation of 'bourgeois' local nationalism and strengthen the trust of the border republics towards the Soviet centre and its initiatives.[25]

Recently, the Soviet nationalities policies were the subject of numerous studies, most of which analyse the intentions and political objectives of the party centrally.[26] This book suggests yet another layer to our understanding of these policies by separating two different approaches to its implementation, each of which had its own agents, sets of short-term and long-term objectives, end goals and strategies. The different understanding of the nationalities policies is reflected in the terminology used throughout this book: *korenizatsiia* in Ukraine – to correspond to the central perspective – and *Ukrainizatsiia* – to reflect its national perception. While *korenizatsiia* implied cultural and linguistic concessions, the accomplishment of the *Ukrainizatsiia*'s objectives relied heavily on economic and political decentralization. This two-layered understanding of the nationalities policies – as defined by the central authorities and promoted by Ukrainian communists in Kharkiv – suggests that there was no paradox as to why anti-*Ukrainizatsiia* measures were launched as early as 1926, the year when *korenizatsiia* was only just gaining momentum.[27] That said, *korenizatsiia* could also be, as defined by Martin, a strategy of the 'affirmative action empire' designed to promote and support local languages and cultures, along with other markers of national identity. Its success, however, depended on eliminating other alternative identity-building projects, in this case, *Ukrainizatsiia*.

In Soviet Ukraine, the combined intentions of the central and local nationalities specialists triggered a wave of publications in the Ukrainian language and contributed to the creation of a Ukrainian urban environment.[28] After only a few years, Kharkiv, the former provincial city and new capital of Soviet Ukraine, experienced its own cultural renaissance, attracting many young artists from all over Ukraine who were creating innovative, modern and original cultural products.[29] At the same time, nationalities policies coupled with broad education campaigns and a programme for tackling illiteracy provided writers with an audience for new proletarian literature. While social modernization created a demand for Soviet culture, state promotion of national languages and cultures as a spin-off of the *korenizatsiia* campaign led to widespread literacy in native languages and, eventually, an increased interest in cultural products in those languages.[30]

The following chapters will examine these two visions for Soviet literature: Soviet Ukrainian literature, anticipated and enhanced by artists and art officials for whom Kharkiv as the Soviet Ukrainian capital remained the main reference point, as opposed to the Soviet literature in the Ukrainian language promoted by the Moscow-oriented literary forces and political elites. The eventual merger of these cultural projects occurred both 'naturally', through the weakening and diffusion of the Soviet Ukrainian cultural strategy, and 'unnaturally' through external pressure, most commonly defined as the state's *diktat* and control.[31] By analysing literary politics in interwar Soviet Ukraine, as well as the ideological and aesthetic evolution of Ukraine's writers, this book argues that the precursors for cultural Sovietization in Ukraine were gradually developing throughout the 1920s, whereby the creation of the Union of Soviet Writers in 1934 became the final step in the complex process of cultural Sovietization and the unification of artistic forces in Ukraine.[32]

Theoretical framework

According to conventional narratives, the 1920s in Ukraine became known as the 'executed renaissance' (*rozstriliane vidrodzhennia*).[33] This paradigm, first articulated by literary critics within the Ukrainian diaspora following the Second World War, rests on the view that the decade was marked by a unique period of cultural flowering in Ukraine, which was violently interrupted by Stalin's terror. Seen from this perspective, the generation of the 1920s is defined by an inherently anti-Soviet stance and strong national orientation. This Ukraine-centred perspective leads to a partial assessment of the 1920s and rejects those internal developments in Soviet Ukraine, which eventually contributed to artistic and institutional unification in the 1930s. While not seeking to undermine the determinant role of this artistic milieu in establishing modern Ukrainian culture, this study argues that during the 1920s, these same artists also contributed to another important current – Soviet culture. This culture was distinctly Soviet, created by artists with strong ideological positions and in accordance with the party line; Ukrainian, to embrace the objectives of the new preferential Soviet nationalities policy of *korenizatsiia*; and mass-oriented, tasked to reach the republic's working class and engage it in cultural production.

At the same time, this book challenges the model of diffusion widespread in studying Soviet culture, according to which all cultural trends originated in Moscow from where they filtered down to the other Soviet republics. This model cements the view that Russian cultural trends were superior and that literary developments and negotiations in Moscow determined cultural developments in the periphery. This study challenges this hierarchy in Soviet cultural production, arguing that throughout the 1920s Soviet Ukraine pursued its own trajectory of cultural development, which ran parallel to that of Russia.[34] Soviet Ukrainian writers constantly rejected any comparison to their Russian counterparts, popular among contemporary literary critics. For instance, Khvyl'ovyi, as leader of the 1920s artistic generation, painfully and even aggressively reacted to being dubbed the 'Ukrainian Pilnyak' (a reference to the popular Russian writer Pilnyak), which, for him, suggested a subordinate status for Soviet Ukrainian literature.

The study also builds on the paradigm of internal transnationalism, introduced by Mayhill C. Fowler who applied it to the study of differing manifestations of Soviet culture across the Soviet Union.[35] Accordingly, there were different, yet interrelated cultural processes unfolding simultaneously in different regions of the Soviet Union. Hence, cultural development in Soviet Ukraine, at least until the introduction of the first Five-Year Plan, occurred independently of Moscow. This book, however, intends to show that there was no unified view on what the Soviet Ukrainian cultural project actually was. During the 1920s, there were constant negotiations and debates on the nature of this project with many of its leading representatives changing their allegiance depending on the political climate. Moreover, throughout this decade, the Soviet Moscow-centred cultural project had also started putting down roots in Ukraine. The two cultural projects were therefore interrelated not only transnationally, but also nationally within the borders of Soviet Ukraine.

Case studies and biographical approach

This book examines two different aspects in the historical development of Soviet Ukrainian culture. Firstly, it assesses the position of fellow travellers in Soviet Ukraine and the possible ways for them to accept Soviet culture. As shown in the case of Tychyna, the tangled process of their self-Sovietization did not live up to the expectations of the Soviet Ukrainian cultural managers. Some fellow travellers settled for Soviet Ukrainian culture, whereas others from the very beginning oriented themselves towards Moscow and contributed to the all-Soviet cultural canon. Secondly, the process of defining the category of 'Soviet Ukrainian culture' among the communist faction of Ukraine's literary corpus will be explored. The study of Khvyl'ovyi exposes the heterogeneity of the proletarian front in the republic and suggests the reasons for the eventual decline of the separatist Ukrainian cultural project. These two men of letters have been chosen due to their high creative merit and importance for Ukrainian literature and the cultural politics of the time, as well as their non-linear ideological evolution, that cannot be easily labelled pro- or anti-Soviet. Through the study of their literary and public activity, the entangled relationship between the arts and politics as well as between the centre and provinces is explored.

The cases of Khvyl'ovyi and Tychyna present different examples of artistic pursuits and forms of political engagement. Khvyl'ovyi was a communist by conviction. A card-carrying party member since 1919, he fully embodied revolutionary literature in Ukraine and elaborated the artistic current of revolutionary romanticism. In his early prose, he developed a glorious myth of the revolution and the civil wars. Later, however, he underwent the painful process of negotiating his 'revolutionary romanticism' with the centralizing tendencies of the RKP(b) and KP(b)U. In his pamphlets, written during the Literary Discussion of 1925–8, Khvyl'ovyi elaborated on the autonomist cultural position, he opposed massovisation of Soviet culture and promoted high-quality literature. His demands soon assumed a clear political aspect, insisting on more political power for Soviet Ukraine. On the other hand, Tychyna had established himself as a poet of the UNR and representative of Ukrainian modernism. During the civil war years, he occasionally supported different factions but eventually agreed to side with the Soviet cultural paradigm, and adopted a simplistic and functional view on literary work contributing to the emerging Soviet mass culture. Eventually, he became a party eulogist holding several important state offices (including the Minister of Education and the Chairman of the Ukrainian Parliament). The year 1933 was decisive for both protagonists: on 13 May, Khvyl'ovyi committed suicide in an act of symbolic dissociation from the policies of the Communist Party. By contrast, on 21 November, Tychyna ascended to the heights of Soviet literature and politics after his eulogy, *Partiia Vede* [The Party Leads] was published in the Moscow newspaper *Pravda* to mark the sixteenth anniversary of the October Revolution.

To a certain degree, the cases of Khvyl'ovyi and Tychyna represent different interpretations of being a Ukrainian in the formative Soviet decades. While committed to constructing an autonomous Soviet Ukrainian literature, Khvyl'ovyi and his fellow writers aimed at a modern, urban, forward-looking national identity. Their Ukrainianness was shaped during the period of revolutionary strife; they aimed at a new independent cultural tradition with only limited reference to the past, as well as dreaming of an independent socialist Ukraine. They believed that the construction of socialism was compatible with and could only be achieved within a national state. They contributed to cultural production that rejected any political hierarchy and references to their Russian fellows; the Ukrainian culture they strived to create was in opposition to the all-Soviet canon. Defining and defending their vision of a socialist Ukrainian culture often required confrontation with the party line. For a long time, they tried to fit and adapt their separatist vision of Soviet Ukrainian culture within the centralizing tendencies of the authorities. Yet their aspirations were crushed by the tightening of the political and cultural controls. In line with this book's argument, Khvyl'ovyi was a Soviet Ukrainian writer insofar as he promoted an independent literary canon and defended a proletarian 'high culture'.

In contrast, the late Tychyna – like other Ukrainian Soviet writers – was, using Serhy Yekelchyk's definition, a Stalin's Ukrainian,[36] who came to represent Soviet literature in Ukrainian. Their patriotism manifested itself through rediscovering the pre-revolutionary Ukrainian national tradition, yet in a revisited meaning emphasizing compliance and accord with Russians and Russian culture.[37] They incorporated national patrimony into their artistic work, yet without crossing the line of what was defined as ideologically sound and party-minded literature. In short, Tychyna was one of the cultural agents of the 1930s onwards who had reconciled his Ukrainianness with the Soviet *diktak* and contributed to the process of cultural production that complemented but did not undermine the all-Soviet culture. To paraphrase Yekelchyk's conclusion, Ukraine's writers during High Stalinism learned how to produce a revised and acceptable version of Ukrainian literature – or Soviet literature in Ukrainian – that emphasized ideological ties to Russia and accepted its cultural predominance.[38] Tychyna's life and creative writing during late Stalinism and thereafter suggest how the Ukrainian culture and identity had changed after the party consolidated its control over cultural matters. Although the cultural agents under Stalinism abandoned the idea of a Ukrainian autonomy, they continued to define their cultural difference, but in a compliant, non-challenging and non-political way. While Khvyl'ovyi's modern and urban Ukrainian culture failed, folk-inspired rural culture came to represent 'Ukrainian' during High Stalinism and beyond.[39]

The Soviet canon of late Stalinism, however, is beyond the scope of this study.[40] The case of Tychyna is helpful inasmuch as it exemplifies a non-linear process of embracing the centralization of cultural controls, coming to terms with the party line, negotiating and reconciling one's position under close party supervision. Although this book aims to present intellectual biographies of both writers, Khvyl'ovyi features more prominently; first, due to his important role in the cultural and political affairs of the debate and, second, in agreement with the study's focus on lost cultural and, by extension, political, alternatives – an autonomous Soviet culture that was created and eventually failed in Soviet Ukraine.

This study uses a biographical approach to discuss the process of cultural Sovietization in Ukraine. The study is not, however, intended as a historical portrayal of the individual lives of its two protagonists. While recognizing the limitations of the biographical perspective (especially the impossibility of examining a life of an individual as a coherent thread unrolling in a logical and chronological order, defined by Pierre Bourdieu as a 'biographical illusion'[41]), this approach is used as a window to examine the complex problem of reciprocal accommodation and negotiation between local intellectuals and party officials, literature and politics. Rather than offering a personal account of the ideological and artistic evolution of these writers, the study provides a starting point for considering the broader question of interrelations between the Soviet Ukrainian and Soviet cultural projects. More broadly, it suggests how the interaction between literature and politics influenced the consolidation of the Soviet regime and its legitimation in Ukraine. Chronologically, the study focuses on the period between 1917, the year of both the national and Bolshevik revolutions in Ukraine, and 1933, the key year for both protagonists, symbolizing the ultimate loss of cultural alternatives and the adoption of socialist realism as a single artistic method. Their life stories beyond this period are sketched to provide the background to their ideological evolution or to explore their intellectual legacy in both Soviet and independent Ukraine.

Use of primary sources

The biographical approach, chosen to answer the main research question, defines the focus on sources relating to the lives and creative work of its two protagonists. However, this is somewhat undermined by a lack of trustworthy archival evidence due to the regime's policy of eliminating Khvyl'ovyi's name from public remembrance after 1933 and erasing or modifying any evidence surrounding Tychyna's pre-1933 activities. The way the protagonists were evaluated during Soviet times also defines the number of available documents. For example, in the Central State Archive of Literature and Arts of Ukraine (TsDAMLMU) there is only one file, consisting of twenty-one pages, on Khvyl'ovyi, which includes several copies from newspapers, photographs and documents, mainly connected to the writers' suicide and funeral in May 1933. In comparison, the archive holds a multivolume personal collection comprising 148,000 documents on Tychyna. This includes various items such as autographs of his verse and poetry, personal and official correspondence, diaries, drafts of his speeches, papers and photographs. Despite the abundance of sources in the archives, many of the documents available reveal very little due to Soviet censorship and the poet's self-censorship. As such, they are of limited use for today's historian. Instead, Tychyna's and Khvyl'ovyi's personal correspondence with different cultural figures shed light on these writers' uncensored beliefs, doubts, concerns and attitudes.[42]

Autobiographical writings – including those produced for job applications or party membership, regular party inspections, and purges of party ranks, party questionnaires (*ankety*), and diaries – constitute another valuable group of primary sources. The overarching characteristic of these documents is defined by their intentional character. These pieces contributed to creating an unblemished image of a revolutionary, a Bolshevik, and a state official, and were composed, arguably, to fit one's life story to this 'ideal' image. Most autobiographical writings of the period represented a gradual process of shaping the protagonists' revolutionary personae, and were used to excuse any possible 'defects' in their pre-Bolshevik/Soviet lives.[43]

There are two frequently cited documents on Khvyl'ovyi's early revolutionary years: a fragment from an autobiography and a short autobiographical note written for a *troika* [the NKVD three-men commission] during a regular KP(b)U purge in 1924.[44] These sources reflect the process of fashioning Khvyl'ovyi's Bolshevik persona and the struggle with his ideological inconsistencies. As for Tychyna, the archives abound in numerous autobiographical writings, prepared mostly for party membership applications or career promotions. These official accounts of Tychyna's life present a polished image of a spotless state functionary and a Communist Party member.[45] The main challenge in using autobiographies is the question of how to regard these sources: do they present the true 'inside' and aspirations of their authors or, conversely, do they tell us more about power and ideology, which compel a person to write with a censor in mind?[46]

Other party documents used for this biographical study present similar concerns. This includes interrogation and surveillance files, secret reports (*svodki*), speeches and official correspondence, compiled by the secret services.[47] Although these sources are used throughout the book, their reliability, defined by Andrea Graziosi, as 'compilations of compilations' with all sorts of distortions and biases,[48] remains questionable. The overall question here is whether the party documents tell us more about the intelligentsia or about the intention of the party instigating the compiling, selecting and filing of these primary sources in order to create and cement a required image of those being scrutinized. One may agree with István Rév that the documents in the archives are 'largely fabrications: misinformation, blatant lies, overdramatization, or their opposite: trivialisations of dramatic events'.[49] In view of their limitations, all the above types of primary sources are used and checked against other sources.

This research embraces 'the linguistic turn', paying attention to the role of language (and literature) in shaping the mentality of the period.[50] It focuses on the fiction, imaginative narratives, political and social essays, and poetry from the 1920s often used by the two writers not only to fashion their public personae but also, although in a disguised manner, to express their beliefs and feelings about the society they lived in and contributed towards. Using works of fiction and poetry as a primary source allows it to build upon and particularize the meaning of non-fictional sources. Besides, imaginative literature can be used to trace the writers' ideological evolution and attitudes towards the Soviet regime. In this respect, Tychyna's intimate poetry and poetry with social content (*hromadians'ka liryka*) and Khvyl'ovyi's self-referential, 'autothematic'[51] creative writings are used to fill the blank spots in both writers' biographies. Tychyna's early poetry in full reflects the perturbations of the civil war years, whereas Khvyl'ovyi's early prose recounts the writer's negative attitude towards the ideological shifts of the post-revolutionary years. Their literary works are also important in order to understand the process of shaping the writers' public personae. Nonetheless, prose and poetry are used as primary sources with caution to avoid speculations around the lives of their authors. They complement and help to verify the existing sources and enrich our understanding of the protagonists, as well as of the political and cultural shifts of the period.

Note on historiography

The existing secondary literature on Khvyl'ovyi and Tychyna offers a variety of ideologically loaded assessments of their personae, literary activity or public engagement. Often, the way the writers are evaluated depended on the interpreter's personal convictions, or an uncritical evaluation of the entire period of the 1920s in either Soviet diaspora or national historiographies. Khvyl'ovyi, acclaimed in the early 1920s as 'one of the most outstanding writers of the proletarian age',[52] vanished from the Soviet cultural narrative after his suicide in 1933.[53] In the Soviet Union, within a short period of time, his life long activities were labelled counter-revolutionary, his writings were removed from libraries and his name disappeared from official literary criticism. Until the early 1980s, his name in the Soviet Union could only be used in connection with '*khvyl'ovizm*' – a general term used to define class enemies. The same approach was also used for his entry in the Great Soviet Encyclopaedia (1935).[54] Moreover, Khvyl'ovyi's image as the leader of a 'national deviationist group of writers' was introduced outside Soviet Ukraine: in an English edition of a reference volume about Soviet Ukraine (1969), Khvyl'ovyi was mentioned only through his 'manifestation of local nationalism'.[55] As observed by a diaspora literary scholar, Mykola Ohloblin (Hlobenko), 'In the press, there was no more mentioning of Khvyl'ovyi. Only *khvyl'ovizm* was left as a dangerous hint, but soon even it was overshadowed by more widespread labels of "the most dangerous for the peaceful life in Ukraine" *petliurivshchyna*, nationalism. Behind the curtain (abroad) it was considered good style not to mention him at all.'[56] The first attempts to re-evaluate Khvyl'ovyi were made only in the late 1980s, when his nationally oriented communist affiliation fused with the political perspective of national communists, trying to wrest control over Soviet Ukraine from Moscow during the all-Soviet crisis.[57]

Tychyna, in contrast, became a part of the Soviet literary canon and was studied extensively. From the late 1920s onwards, he was the focus of critics' attention who, in eager rivalry, lauded Tychyna for joining the ranks of Soviet poets.[58] Among the major scholars of this later period were Leonid Novychenko, Semen Shakhovs'kyi and Stanislav Tel'niuk, whose studies combined a biographical approach with literary criticism.[59] Needless to say, scholarship from this era portrayed Tychyna as an unblemished communist poet and a devoted state official. A reappraisal of Tychyna's literary and ideological evolution was first attempted by Vasyl' Stus in his censored study *Fenomen Doby (Skhodzhennia na Holhofu Slavy)* ['The Phenomenon of the Age (Ascending to the Golgotha of Fame)'] (1970-1). According to Stus, himself a poet at odds with the regime, 'In the history of world literature perhaps there is no other example of a poet who devoted half of his life to high poetry and another half – to a relentless fight with his own genius.'[60]

Both protagonists merited varied receptions among the Ukrainian diaspora with debates on their contributions to Ukrainian literature and politics flourishing from the early 1930s. Unsurprisingly, the main point of discussion was their collaboration with the Bolshevik party, which was presented either as something they were compelled to do in order to pursue their literary activity or as a voluntary association, including their betrayal of the Ukrainian cause and cooperation with the enemy. The way these writers were evaluated within the diaspora depended significantly on the ideological background of the observer. Among Ukrainian right-wing groups, both received differing appraisals, with Khvyl'ovyi depicted as representing an ongoing national opposition to the Bolshevik authorities. One such evaluation was voiced by the leader of the Ukrainian nationalists in Western Ukraine, Dmytro Dontsov, who claimed that Khvyl'ovyi was one of those 'divided souls that were unable to cope with the problem: to what extent they are Ukrainians, and to what extent they are subject to Russia'.[61] In particular, Khvyl'ovyi was praised for his repeated calls to distance Ukraine from the Russian Communist Party and Moscow. As a result, he was seen as a leader of a 'modern nationalism of the 1930s',[62] as *khvyl'ovizm* was defined. By contrast, Tychyna's post-1933 literary and political activity was seen as a definite and, more importantly, sudden break with his literary genius;[63] a betrayal of his earlier beliefs and a disreputable surrender to the party line. At around the same time, attempts were made to excuse Tychyna's degeneration into a 'grapho-maniac' and a 'party fool' by introducing the idea of histrionic 'shields' and 'masks', worn by the poet in order to rescue himself from Stalin's terror and the purges. Consequently, an attempt was made to reread Tychyna's post-1933 poetic contribution to discern 'grains of truth' behind alleged allegories and metaphors.[64]

Appraisals of the Soviet writers in Ukraine also depended heavily on the general ideological orientation of these emigrants. The third post-Second World War wave of Ukrainian emigration strengthened the nationalistic attitude of the diaspora. This ideological 'turn to the right'[65] consolidated the idea of a united, independent Ukrainian state as the ultimate goal of the national struggle, which, consequently, rejected leftist sentiments of any kind. The reorientation of the way in which the whole generation of the 1920s was regarded had, nevertheless, a dual outcome. On the one hand, Ukrainian communists or artists who cooperated with the regime after the October Revolution were seen as definite and inexcusable traitors to the nationalist cause, leading to an undermining of their overall contribution to Ukraine's history, politics and culture.[66]

On the other hand, this reorientation brought about a significant development in the historiography of the 1920s. A new paradigm of the 'executed renaissance' was introduced, evaluating the entire generation of the 1920s through their commitment to the nationalist cause. This approach hindered historians and literary critics from unbiased evaluation of the activity and creative works of those writers. Firstly, those who chose to view this entire interwar generation of Ukrainian artists and cultural workers as martyrs of the Soviet regime praised intellectuals based not on their merit but on the year of their death. The gist of this paradigm was, according to Halyna Hryn, the idea that 'national and moral criteria can be brought to bear in the evaluation of authors and their works.'[67] Secondly, the moral right of those Ukrainian intellectuals, who one way or another survived the terror, to continue their creative or public activity after the majority of their peers had been executed, was questioned. For example, Tychyna or Maksym Ryl's'kyi, who not only survived the terror but also attained privileged positions in Soviet cultural and political life, became targets for this sort of criticism for decades to come.[68]

After Ukraine gained independence in 1991, the 'executed renaissance' paradigm, along with the national communist perspective, merged with another approach – to 'nationalise' Ukrainian early Soviet intellectuals, and present them as part of a national opposition to the Communist regime.[69] This contributed to the utopian view that the whole history of Ukraine should be seen as a struggle to build an independent and united country. As Mark von Hagen observed, the narrative of history in independent Ukraine replaced the familiar dogmatic approach of Marxism – Leninism and dialectical materialism with a national teleology.[70] Accordingly, the intellectual and political history of Ukraine was rewritten in a way that made nationalists and separatists out of nearly all prominent Ukrainians. Among modern Ukrainian historians and literary scholars, Khvyl'ovyi has become one of the most researched Ukrainian writers, whose life and writings have been adjusted to the 'new dogma of an eternal and unchained nation, whose history was defined by the struggle against a "national oppressor" for Ukrainian independence and unity'.[71]

This nationalistic approach attempts to rehabilitate and to excuse both protagonists for being communists by finding reasons for their decisions to serve the party. In order to cope with the obvious dilemma of Tychyna and Khvyl'ovyi being a talented poet and writer, respectively, in spite of their affiliation with the party, an attempt was made to push the concept of Khvyl'ovyi's 'permanent inner ambivalence' – which originated partly from his romantic nature and partly from his idealistic belief in Bolshevik populism[72] – and Tychyna's 'genius histrionics'.[73] Native Ukrainian historiography and literary criticism, therefore, promotes further the 'either … or' paradigm, with little or no reference to the complicated process of inner ideological evolution, which each and every representative of the 1920s generation underwent.[74] Similarly, there is no attempt to trace the evolution of Ukrainian modernism (the most important literary current since the end of the nineteenth century) into socialist realism.[75]

Book outlines

The book is divided into three parts. Part One covers the lives of the two protagonists during the revolutionary period of 1917–21, when two revolutions coincided on Ukraine's territory: the national and the Bolshevik ones. This early period was also defined by the rivalry between the two forms of statehood – the UNR and the Soviet Republic in Ukraine that lasted with varied success until November 1921, when the Red Army succeeded in occupying almost the entire territory of Ukraine. Chapter 1 recounts the story of the national revolution and the civil war as experienced by Tychyna in Kyiv, when power in the city changed hands thirteen times in just three years. Tychyna's modernist poetry gives an intimate insight into these extraordinary years. He glorified the national revolution and anticipated the establishment of an independent Ukraine. With time, however, he apprehended the end of the national revival and discerned a new victor emerging from the battlefields of the civil war. Chapter 2 introduces the October Revolution as seen from the new Soviet capital of Kharkiv. The chapter tells a story of soviet power through the eyes of Khvyl'ovyi, who, already at the frontline, internalized the revolutionary slogans of universal emancipation and came to Kharkiv to become a writer and build a new Soviet Ukraine. He ardently accepted the revolution and depicted it most vividly in his creative writing. Nonetheless, as the civil war ensued he started questioning the ideological commitments of those in power. Through Khvyl'ovyi's personal life and textual analysis of his early prose, the origins of proletarian literature in Ukraine are examined.

Part Two focuses on different understandings of Soviet culture in Ukraine and the incessant political debates between the two competing horizons in Ukraine's Communist Party, especially around the implementation of the *korenizatsiia* policy. The distinction between *korenizatsiia* – representing the central perspective on the national question; and *Ukrainizatsiia* – the perspective of Ukrainian communists – is introduced. Both these camps contributed to the development of competing projects of Soviet Ukrainian culture, exemplified by the political and literary commitments of Tychyna and Khvyl'ovyi. In Chapter 3, Tychyna's gradual reorientation towards the Soviet cultural canon is scrutinized. His poetry, especially his 1920 collections *Zamist' Sonetiv i Oktav* [Instead of Sonnets and Octaves] and *Pluh* [The Plough], is examined to pinpoint the poet's ideological shifts towards accepting the new political and cultural orientation and artistic tropes, initiating his eventual submission to Soviet literary standards. Tychyna would ultimately come to represent the lost alternatives of modernism in Ukrainian literature. Chapter 4 investigates the complex process of elaborating and implementing the project of Soviet Ukrainian culture. Here, Khvyl'ovyi's numerous pamphlets written during the Literary Discussion of 1925–8 are scrutinized to draft political, ideological and aesthetic contours of a separatist Soviet Ukrainian cultural project. Already in 1926, Khvyl'ovyi called his followers to 'flee away from Moscow', underlining the political component of the Literary Discussion. In this chapter, Khvyl'ovyi presents those alternative visions of Ukrainian revolutionary, proletarian and Soviet culture lost during the 1920s.

Part Three is dedicated to the process of ideological unification in Soviet Ukraine, leading eventually to the triumph of a centralist political and cultural perspective throughout the Soviet Union. Chapter 5 discusses the first major political crisis of 1926 and the clash between Ukraine's two ideological camps at the KP(b)U, leading to the weakening of the separatist political perspective, the policy of *Ukrainizatsiia* as defined locally, and, eventually, the decline of the autonomist project of Soviet Ukrainian culture. Stalin's criticism of the Ukrainian Commissar for Education, Oleksandr Shums'kyi, at the party plenum in June had serious repercussions for Ukraine-minded party members and cultural elites. As the party took direct control over the implementation of *Ukrainizatsiia*, little room remained for cultural and political debates. The campaigns against Shums'kyi and Khvyl'ovyi for their national, political and cultural views unleashed nationality-based persecutions in Soviet Ukraine, long before this became a common practice Union-wide. Chapter 6 examines the period of the first Five-Year Plan, seen as the most decisive period in defining Soviet power and culture. By the end of the 1920s, the centre of political and cultural life had shifted to Moscow, with Soviet Ukraine becoming politically peripheral and culturally provincial. From 1928–32, attempts to preserve the autonomy of Soviet Ukrainian culture were initiated, whereas 1933 is regarded as the pinnacle of the decade-long political battle on the cultural front of Soviet Ukraine. Khvyl'ovyi, an ardent promoter of the autonomous cultural project, committed suicide, while Tychyna confirmed his position in the Soviet literary pantheon by publishing his eulogy to Communist power in Ukraine. The Epilogue drafts the contours of cultural development in Soviet Ukraine in the 1930s, following the disbanding of the early literary organizations and the creation of the Union of Soviet Writers.

Part One

Competing projects of Ukraine

Part One of this book examines the ideological and political rivalry between the supporters of a national and a socialist Ukraine, and the parallel cultural projects endorsed by these contradictory, and often mutually exclusive, projects of state-building. On the one hand, national leaders in Kyiv initiated a separatist project of Ukraine, with their demands ranging from an autonomous Ukraine within a free federative Russia, up to complete independence in early 1918. In the cultural sphere, those national governments wished to overcome the imperial legacy of Ukraine's Russification and introduced numerous initiatives to provide a basis for national cultural awakening. Following the imperial ban on Ukrainian-language publications, a number of newspapers, literary journals and almanacs, as well as publishing houses, were launched. The most popular literary and artistic movement of the time was modernism, with poetry enjoying a dominant position.

On the other side, having seized power in Petrograd, the Bolsheviks turned their attention to Ukraine. In December 1917, the Soviet government was established in Kharkiv striving to extend its authority across Ukraine. The Bolsheviks aimed at a proletarian dictatorship that could not be achieved without a cultural domination of the working class. A new proletarian culture was required that would reflect its leading position. The cultural projects initiated during and after the Bolshevik revolution aimed at an international proletarian culture often insensitive to national differences. While promoting international culture, those projects were mostly Russia-oriented and Russian-speaking.

There was yet another party, however. In the revolutionary period of 1917–20, leftist groups and movements in Ukraine, unhappy with the Russia-oriented Bolshevik programme and moderate stand of the national leaders, joined forces to promote a national way to socialism. Representatives of Ukrainian communist parties believed that socialist revolutions would result in creating national republics; unlike the Bolsheviks, they sought a national form of proletarian culture in Ukraine that would be created in the Ukrainian language.

Through the analysis of the literary movements and artistic currents that had originated and been strengthened during and shortly after the revolution, the following chapters examine the origins of the divisions in Ukraine's literature that would later result in a competition between the two incarnations of Soviet literature in Ukraine – Soviet literature in Ukrainian and Soviet Ukrainian literature. Chapter 1 examines Tychyna's experience of the chaotic civil war years as reflected in his early poetry. The chapter traces the evolution of Tychyna from being a poet of the national revolution to embracing the proletarian discourse. Tychyna's life and creative activity during this period suggest a difficult process of adaptation for those members of the national intelligentsia who found themselves under the new regime, whose values they did not necessarily share. Chapter 2 looks at Khvyl'ovyi's prose written during the civil war period, highlighting the important difference in Ukraine's revolutionary literature when compared to that of Russia. While Ukrainian writers shared many concerns and grievances similar to their Russian counterparts– over-romantization of the revolution, a bleak view on the post-revolutionary everydayness and criticism of the party's early centralization and bureaucratization – they were also preoccupied with the national question. Those national concerns penetrated Ukrainian revolutionary literature and set Ukrainian writers against their Russian fellows, as well as against certain Ukrainian writers who embraced the centralization of cultural and political life.

1

'Above Kyiv there is a Golden Hum':
The National Revolution in Kyiv

' ... not Tychinin, but Tychyna'

Tychyna is conventionally regarded as one of Ukraine's most gifted poets. His oeuvre consists of multiple volumes of poetry written between 1908 and 1967. He wrote his first poems before the First World War under the influence of modernism and gained fame for his poetic responses to the national revolutionary upheavals of 1917–20. During the civil war, the poet was forced to find his way amidst excruciating power struggles and finally adapt to the expectations of the victorious party. Within a decade, he had become a poet laureate and high-ranking official in the Soviet government of Ukraine. His successful career as a Soviet bureaucrat and the large print runs of his 'ideologically sound' poetry in Ukrainian suggest an uneasy compromise between the central authorities and Ukraine's intellectuals, whereby cultural agents used their position to continue defining their cultural difference without challenging the party's hegemony.

Tychyna's rise to the heights of the Soviet hierarchy could hardly have been predicted from the start, however. He was born in 1891 in the village of Pisky in Chernihiv province (*gubernia*), Left-bank Ukraine, into the poor family of a priest's assistant [*psalomshchyk* or *diak*] and a literacy teacher for a local church. Unsure on how to provide education for their nine children, his parents decided to send the nine-year-old Pavlo to the provincial capital of Chernihiv, where he successfully auditioned for a church choir and was soon promoted to soloist at the famous choir of the Chernihiv Trinity Monastery. As a choral singer, Tychyna also studied in a local religious school, *bursa*, and, on completing his education, entered Chernihiv seminary.

Chernihiv, although a provincial city, was an important cultural centre on the Russian Empire's frontier. Its prominence dated back to medieval Kyivan Rus', when the city had been second only to Kyiv. Chernihiv experienced its second renaissance as part of the Hetmanate, a Cossack state that existed on the territory of modern Ukraine from 1649–1775, before its autonomy was finally abolished by Catherine the Great. The city's reputation for high-cultural heritage and intellectualism was connected to the work of the late seventeenth-century archbishop Lazar Baranovych, who transformed Chernihiv into an important religious, educational and publishing centre. The Great Reforms of Tsar Alexander II once again prompted the city's cultural growth, especially the *zemstvo* reform of 1864 that provided for the creation of elected institutions of local self-governments.[1] A *zemstvo* was established in Chernihiv in September 1865 with many Ukrainian activists, being otherwise barred from public duties, joining this progressive organ of self-governance. The Chernihiv *zemstvo* was responsible for opening Ukrainian-language schools, while its statistical committee carried out ethnographic studies of the region. Moreover, under its auspices, a 'Museum of Ukrainian Antiquities' was opened in 1902, the first museum in the empire to have 'Ukrainian' in its name.[2]

Continued liberalization under the tsarist regime in the 1860s and 1870s led to the founding of the *Hromada* group in Chernihiv, part of a wider cultural and semi-political clandestine movement that united the Ukrainophile intelligentsia and contributed to the Ukrainian national revival in Imperial Russia. This was granted a significant boost by enlightenment societies for mass education (*prosvity*), which were opened throughout the *gubernia* after 1905, providing Ukrainian-language literacy courses.[3] At the turn of the century, many prominent Ukrainian intellectuals, academics and artists lived and worked in Chernihiv. Among them were the leading literary figure and modernist Mykhailo Kotsiubyns'kyi; the writer, ethnographer, member of the Ukrainian populist (*narodnyky*) movement and the editor of the four-volume Ukrainian Dictionary (*Slovar' ukrains'koi movy*, 1907–9) Borys Hrinchenko; the poet and translator Volodymyr Samiilenko; the symbolist poet, theatre director and political activist Mykola Voronyi; the historian and head of the Chernihiv Archival Commission Vadym Modzalevs'kyi; and the academics, educators and political activists Oleksandr and Sofia Rusovs.

This was the cultural milieu that sixteen-year-old Tychyna joined as a student of the Chernihiv theological seminary. Creatively gifted, he conducted the seminary's choir, wrote poetry and studied drawing with the famous modernist painter Mykhailo Zhuk, who at the time also lived and worked in Chernihiv. It was Zhuk who introduced the young Tychyna to Kotsiubyns'kyi, who hosted weekly literary salons attended by many talented youths.[4] Tychyna often came together with his close friend Vasyl' Ellans'kyi, later known as the poet 'Ellan' and the communist party activist Blakytnyi, the future composer and founder of the Ukrainian state folk chorus Hryhorii Veriovka, the poet Arkadii Kazka and the future playwright Ivan Kocherha, all of whom would come to play important roles in the creation of Soviet Ukrainian culture. To Kotsiubyns'kyi, Tychyna was indebted for having discerned his talent and for publicizing his early poetry. Indeed, Tychyna would later acknowledge that Kotsiubyns'kyi had been his greatest influence during these formative years.[5] One of his first poems, *Vy Znaiete Iak Lypa Shelestyt'?* [*You Know How Linden Rustle?*], was published in 1912, under Kotsiubyns'kyi's recommendation, in the prestigious literary journal *Literaturno-Naukovyi Visnyk* [The Literary-Scholarly Herald].[6] Kotsiubyns'kyi also recommended Tychyna to the Russian realist writer Gorky, who would later speak fondly of his earlier work.[7]

In 1913, having spent twelve years in Chernihiv, 22-year-old Tychyna decided to move to Kyiv. According to imperial law, absolvents of theological schools could not study in a public university. Had he remained unaffiliated, Tychyna could have also been legally conscripted into the imperial army.[8] Consequently, 'Pavlo Tychinin' (a Russified spelling of his surname used to register him at birth and in official

Figure 2 Pavlo Tychyna, self-portrait, 1922. © Central State Archive-Museum of Literature and Arts of Ukraine, courtesy of TsDAMLMU.

documentation up until 1917[9]) enrolled at the newly created private Kyiv Commercial Institute.[10] Whilst there, he studied alongside his childhood friend Blakytnyi; the Soviet Ukrainian writer Iurii Smolych and the world-renowned film director Oleksandr Dovzhenko belonged to this same cohort.

To support himself financially, Tychyna worked as a technical secretary in the editorial houses of several Ukrainian periodicals such as the daily *Rada* [Council], edited and financed by the conservative activist Ievhen Chykalenko, and the monthly pedagogical journal *Svitlo* [the Light]. These Ukrainian-language newspapers started appearing after the 1905 revolution, when the ban on Ukrainian-language printing, introduced in 1863 and further reinforced in 1876, was finally lifted.[11] Among other Ukrainian periodicals being published at this time in Kyiv were the monthly journal *Literaturno-Naukovyi Vistnyk*, founded in Lviv in 1898 by Mykhailo Hrushevs'kyi and moved to Kyiv in 1907; the monthly journal of literature, literary criticism and politics *Ukrains'ka khata* [The Ukrainian Hut]; an educational periodical for children and adolescents, *Moloda Ukraina* [Young Ukraine]; and *Zapysky* [Notes] of the Ukrainian Scientific Society. None of these periodicals could hope for state support with most being privately funded by two wealthy philanthropists: the industrialist and manager of his family's sugar-refining company Vasyl' Symyrenko and Chykalenko, a wealthy landowner known for saying 'Love Ukraine not only to the depth of your heart, but also to the depth of your pocket.'[12]

In the lead up to the First World War, these Ukrainian-language periodicals were closed down with the declaration of martial law in July 1914.[13] Tychyna, now unemployed, moved back to Chernihiv, where he found employment in the *zemstvo*'s statistical office.[14] The war also impeded his studies at the Commercial Institute, which was evacuated eastwards to Saratov in Russia. Those students who decided to remain in Kyiv continued their education by correspondence, expected to only return to Saratov for the exam period. Needless to say, during the war, travelling over a thousand kilometres from Kyiv to Saratov was neither cheap nor convenient.[15] Tychyna withdrew from the Institute in 1915 and reapplied to study at the philology department of the newly established Ukrainian State University in 1917.[16]

Events in Petrograd during the spring of 1917 shook Ukraine.[17] Following the abdication of Nicholas II, a Provisional Government was formed in Petrograd and began replacing imperial bureaucrats throughout the empire with their own administration.[18] The Provisional Government was only intended to serve as a caretaker administration until elections could be held for an All-Russian Constituent Assembly that would decide the future of the empire. In Kyiv, civic and political activists formed the Executive Committee of the Council of United Community Organisations (*Ispolnitel'nyi Komitet Soveta Ob'edinennykh Obshchestvennykh Organizatsii*, or *IKSOOO*), consisting of various political parties and national associations.[19] The majority of these groups belonged to the Russian Constitutional Democratic Party (*kadety*), the Russian Socialist Revolutionary Party (SRs), or were high-ranking military officers whose presence and authority had been reinforced since the start of the war. Kyiv's Ukrainian population was represented in the IKSOOO by the only existing Ukrainian national organization at the time – the Society of Ukrainian Progressivists [*Tovarystvo Ukrains'kykh Postupovtsiv, TUP*], a semi-clandestine, non-partisan political and civic organization formed in 1908. All these political factions supported the Provisional Government.

Before spring 1917, Ukrainian life in Kyiv was almost non-existent with Ukrainians only composing around 16 per cent of the city's total population, while almost 50 per cent were Russians.[20] Since education in Ukrainian was non-existent, Russian was the language of instruction with schools having long been the tool of imperial Russification. The educated Ukrainian-speaking intelligentsia, therefore, existed as a cultural minority while the Ukrainian-language press had disappeared with the ban of 1914. On 1 March 1917, for instance, a general meeting of the TUP, called by Chykalenko to discuss the rumours about the revolution in Petrograd, was attended by only twenty-seven people.[21] Indeed, little had changed since 'the heyday of the Ukrainian Intelligentsia' on 30 August 1903, when Kyivan intellectuals travelled to Poltava to celebrate the unveiling of the monument to the poet Ivan Kotliarevs'kyi, whose travesty of Virgil's *Aeneid*, written wholly in the Ukrainian vernacular, had marked the beginning of modern Ukrainian literature. Chykalenko later recalled that if the train carrying delegates from Kyiv had crashed, this would have meant the end of the Ukrainian movement for a long time. Almost the entirety of Kyiv's intelligentsia was able to travel in just two carriages.[22]

The February Revolution provided the impulse for the revival of political and cultural life in Ukraine that had been briefly suspended with the outbreak of the war. On 4 March 1917, Ukrainian national leaders in Kyiv established the *Tsentral'na Rada* (Central Council) claiming its status as Ukraine's autonomous self-government. The core of the Rada's members comprised Ukrainian activists from the pre-war TUP, as well as the revived Ukrainian Social-Democratic Workers' Party (*Ukrains'ka Sotsial-Demokratychna Robitnycha Partiia*, USDRP), the newly founded Ukrainian Socialist-Revolutionary Party (*Ukrains'ka Partiia Sotsialistiv-Revoliutsioneriv*, UPSR) and the Ukrainian Socialist-Federalist Party (*Ukrains'ka Partiia Sotsialistiv-Federalistiv*, UPSF). Its leaders included intellectuals, academics, writers and public activists, many of whom had just returned to Kyiv, inspired by the promise of a Ukrainian national revolution. Hrushevs'kyi, the former professor at L'viv University in Austrian Galicia, who at the time was an exile in Moscow, was elected *in absentia* as Rada's president.[23]

At this early stage, the demands of the Rada's national leaders did not extend beyond national-territorial autonomy for Ukraine within a democratically transformed Russia. In a letter of greeting to the head of the Provisional Government in Petrograd, Prince L'vov, and the Minister of Justice Alexander Kerensky dated from 7 March 1917, the Ukrainian leadership congratulated the new government on its formation and expressed their hope that it would allow local autonomy for Ukraine.[24] In its first declaration, 'To the Ukrainian People' issued on 9 March 1917, the Rada called for Ukrainians 'themselves to forge the better future [...] in the family of free peoples'. Until the status of Ukraine was defined by the All-Russian Constituent Assembly, the Rada was instructed to instead focus on cultural development by promoting the Ukrainian language and education.[25]

The formation of the Ukrainian Rada was met with great enthusiasm. As one contemporary recalled: 'On the streets and the squares of Kyiv, even inside the building of the Central Rada there were continuous meetings and debates; Ukraine became the most democratic country in the world!'[26] Nonetheless, not everyone regarded the Rada as a legitimate centre of authority. The Ukrainian leadership wished for an all-Ukrainian *viche*, a popular assembly, which would transform it into a true representative of the population and prove that the Ukrainian national cause had a genuine grassroots support. Inspired by a manifestation of some 25,000 soldiers and students gathered under the blue-and-yellow national flag of Ukraine in Petrograd on 12 March – which yet had gone unnoticed by the Ukrainian general public – the Rada's leaders decided to hold a 'dress-rehearsal' on the streets of Kyiv. The opportunity for this came on the 'Day of the Revolution' held on 16 March and organized by the IKSOOO and Kyiv city council to celebrate the beginning of Russia's democratic transformation.[27] Some 250,000 people were reported to have congregated on Kyiv's streets, many of whom carried both the red (revolutionary) and blue-and-yellow Ukrainian flags.[28]

Encouraged by this visible expression of Ukrainian national feeling during the IKSOOO's celebration, the Ukrainian leaders called for a Ukrainian Freedom Day (*Sviato Svobody*) to be held on 19 March.[29] To their own astonishment, an estimated 100,000 people, one sixth of the city's entire population, attended the event carrying blue-and-yellow flags and banners stating 'A free Ukraine for a free Russia' and 'Autonomy to Ukraine'. Hrushevs'kyi recalled that 'the entirety of Kyiv went out onto the streets: ones to demonstrate, others to observe'.[30] It was a true celebration of the Ukrainian national awakening; many came attired in national costumes and Cossack outfits while 'Ukraine has not perished yet', a song that would soon become the national anthem, was performed on every street corner. The demonstration had proven, as Hrushevs'kyi summarized, that 'Ukrainianness was not a fiction in the heads of some romantics or maniacal intelligentsia; it was a living energy with a true power to mobilise the masses into action.'[31]

The political upheaval of the February Revolution transformed Kyiv into a revolutionary capital. Tsarist-era censorship was abolished, and Ukrainian-language periodicals started appearing again. On 25 March 1917, *Rada* resumed publication as *Nova Rada* [New Council] while the monthly journal *Literaturno-Naukovyi Visnyk* was also revived in July 1917. The imperial police were also abolished removing restrictions on public gatherings and demonstrations. Unsurprisingly, these changes breathed new life into the national literary and cultural scene. The war and the revolution created cultural mobility and brought a new generation of artists to the fore. In Kyiv, younger writers from all corners of the former empire mixed with their older peers with the single desire of reviving Ukrainian culture:

> Some returned from the front, where they had been agitators, Ukrainizers of the army, newspaper editors, lecturers; others from other towns, as far away as Vladivostok. This was a bustling, lively, youthful element, which had gained confidence during revolutionary activity and which was fired with a passion to work. Kiev, the centre of revolutionary events in Ukraine at the time, absorbed this youth into itself like a sponge; people who knew the language and could be trusted were needed everywhere, so almost everyone got several jobs and worked literally day and night.[32]

Tychyna was one of those youth who were quick to respond to the political upheaval in Kyiv joining the editorial boards of *Nova Rada* and *Literaturno-Naukovyi Visnyk* as head of their news division and poetry section, respectively. He also worked as assistant choirmaster at Kyiv's only permanent Ukrainian-language theatre company managed by Mykola Sadovs'kyi. Being an eyewitness of the Ukrainian manifestation in Kyiv on 19 March, he was astonished by the power, enthusiasm and patriotism of the people gathered on Kyiv's streets. In a highly patriotic poem *Hei, Vdarte v Struny, Kobzari* [Hey, Strike the Strings, Kobza Players!], which appeared in *Nova Rada* on 30 March, he conveyed the joy of transforming Kyiv into a centre of Ukrainian awakening:

> Hey, strike the strings, kobza players!
> Inspire hearts with songs!
> Ukrainian flags are overhead
> Like sun above the steppes (O.P.)

Tychyna also anticipated the Rada's future steps, especially the Ukrainization of the army. In *Hei, Vdarte v Struny*, he portrayed jubilant crowds cheering the procession of the Khmel'nyts'kyi regiment, the first Ukrainian military unit in the Russian Army created on 16 March. These were the first combatants out of approximately 300,000 soldiers who swore allegiance to the Rada in summer 1917. Tychyna glorified those recruits:

> Hey, scatter plentifully the path with flowers,
> Ring the bells!
> Ukrainian army is on the field
> Marching, wrapped in glory (O.P.)

In a letter to his brother Ievhen dated April 5, Tychyna expressed the joy associated with the emerging Ukrainian Revolution, 'this festival that had started but would not finish'. He also wrote of the newly opened *prosvity*, about Ukrainian schools in Kyiv and Ukrainian newspapers. Inspired by this rebirth of the Ukrainian political life, Tychyna requested that his brother address his reply to 'Tychyna, not Tychinin' [a Ukrainian variant of his surname].[33]

'Above Kyiv there is a golden hum'

The Central Rada strove to become the supreme representative body for post-imperial Ukraine. Inspired by the success of the manifestation in Kyiv, the Ukrainian leadership called for an All-Ukrainian National Congress intended to transform the Rada into a representative national body. Leaflets with information about the upcoming congress were circulated among the participants of the Kyiv demonstration and its full programme appeared in one of *Nova Rada*'s earlier issues, published on 28 March. Approximately a thousand delegates, reflecting Ukraine's regional, national and social diversity, attended the National Congress, convened on 6–8 April 1917.[34] In line with the Rada's previous declarations, the National Congress passed a resolution demanding national-territorial autonomy for Ukraine that would 'guarantee the needs of the Ukrainian people and other people living on Ukraine's land'.[35]

Soon thereafter, in early May 1917, the First All-Ukrainian Military Congress took place in Kyiv, representing those Ukrainianized military units, which pledged support to the Rada. Altogether, around 900 delegates, representing Ukrainian military units stationed on all fronts, the Baltic and Black Sea fleets and military garrisons based in Ukraine and Russia, participated in the Congress where they passed a resolution 'On Ukrainian Autonomy', encouraging the Rada to immediately declare the national-territorial autonomy for Ukraine.[36] Armed with the support of these military units, a delegation from the Rada left for Petrograd on 13 May 1917 to present a case for Ukraine's autonomy to the Provisional Government. Those demands were largely ignored in Petrograd, however;[37] the evasive reply being that no decisions could be made until after the establishment of an All-Russian Constituent Assembly.[38]

Nevertheless, the Ukrainian leadership proceeded with their agenda. Backed by numerous local councils of soldiers and peasant deputies, the Rada decided to declare autonomy unilaterally. The First Universal [a legal act-declaration], issued by the Rada on 10 June 1917, proclaimed that 'without seceding from all of Russia [...] let the Ukrainian people have the right to manage its own life on its own soil'.[39] The First Universal also envisaged the creation of a democratically elected all-Ukrainian people's assembly with the sole right to draft laws for Ukraine. However, these were to still be confirmed by the All-Russian Constituent Assembly. On 13 June, the Central Rada formed a governmental cabinet – the General Secretariat, with Volodymyr Vynnychenko, a member of the USDRP's executive committee and prominent modernist writer, as its head.

These early steps in Ukrainian state-building were immortalized in one of Tychyna's greatest poems, *Zolotyi Homin* [The Golden Harmony], inspired by the First Universal. *Zolotyi Homin* referred to the bells ringing in the churches of St Sophia and Lavra in Kyiv to celebrate the declaration of Ukraine's autonomy, when thousands of people gathered in St Sophia Square to listen to the Universal. This poem quickly became the hymn of the national revolution and a eulogy to the newborn nation: 'I am a strong nation. I am young!'

> Heaps of rocks crashing down on my chest
> I took them off so easily
> Like eider down ...
> I am the unquenchable Beautiful Fire,
> The Spirit Eternal. [...]
> I am young!
> Young!

Zolotyi Homin was full of allusions to Ukrainian folklore and religious symbols. One of the poem's references is to Apostle Andrew (Andrew the First-Called, as he is known in the Orthodox tradition), who, the legend has it, in the first years of Christianity brought the message from God and blessed the Kyivan hills where a great city was to emerge. For Tychyna, the events of spring-summer 1917 became a fulfilment of this prophecy:

Above Kyiv there is a golden hum,
Both doves and the sun! [...]
It was the Apostle Andrew,
Illuminated,
Wounded in the heart with God's grace,
Blessing Ukraine with a cross
For all the years disgrace.

This unilateral declaration of Ukraine's autonomy shocked both the Provisional Government in Petrograd and the Russian population of Kyiv.[40] Events in Ukraine even precipitated division within the Provisional Government. To avoid further confrontations, a delegation headed by Kerensky arrived in Kyiv on 28 June 1917 to negotiate Ukraine's territorial status.[41] This resulted in a compromise that laid the foundation for the Second Universal, issued on 3 July, reiterating that Ukraine had no aspirations to separate from Russia until after the decision of the All-Russian Constituent Assembly 'in order that we and all her peoples might jointly strive toward the development and welfare of all Russia and toward the unity of her democratic forces'.[42] Instead, the Provisional Government, without acknowledging the Rada itself, recognized the authority of its General Secretariat over five out of nine provinces, where ethnic Ukrainians constituted the majority: Kyiv, Chernihiv, Poltava, Podolia and Volhynia.[43]

'Black wings over the doves and sun – Black wings'

The events in Petrograd in late October 1917 once again reversed the political trajectory in Ukraine. On 25 October, the Bolsheviks overthrew the Provisional Government and started developing plans on how to broaden their success to the former imperial borderlands. As in Petrograd, their immediate targets were the Provisional Government's local administrations. The Ukrainian leaders, who also considered the Provisional Government as their primary adversary, supported the Bolshevik activists, who provoked a revolt on the streets of Kyiv.[44] After three days of fighting, a truce was agreed, according to which the military and local administration of the Provisional Government were withdrawn from the city, with the Rada assuming their powers in Ukraine.[45]

After the fall of the Provisional Government, all power in Ukraine was handed over to the Central Rada. Exploiting this prerogative further, on 7 November, the Rada adopted its Third Universal. 'Without separating ourselves from the Russian Republic and maintaining its unity', a separate Ukrainian People's Republic and government – the General Secretariat – was proclaimed.[46] The Third Universal also included a number of important political and social decisions: abolishing existing private landownership, introducing an eight-hour workday and state control over production, and granting national minorities the right to national-personal autonomy.[47] All these initiatives were to be legalized by a Ukrainian Constituent Assembly – not to be confused with the All-Russian Constituent Assembly – the elections for which were scheduled for 9 January 1918.[48]

The proclamation of the UNR was celebrated with a military parade on St Sophia Square in Kyiv.⁴⁹ A member of the Central Rada and future UNR Minister Mykyta Shapoval recalled the mood on Kyiv's streets in June 1917: 'What an unforgettable day! Grey November sky over Kyiv observed as the waves of people arrived in St Sophia Square, as the Ukrainian army and the Central Rada marched through the streets, as the Ukrainian revolutionary anthem resounded over old Kyiv […] all saluting the Ukrainian republic.'⁵⁰ Tychyna, by now recognized as 'the poet of the national Revolution', continued to respond enthusiastically to every new step in national state-building. The coverage of the military parade on the pages of *Nova Rada* was accompanied by his poem – *Oi, shcho v Sofiis'komu Zahraly Dzvony* [Oh in Sophia the bells struck]. This patriotic ode emphasized the jubilation from the promise that 'from now on – there will be no master in the free Ukraine'. A similar mood permeated the early 1917 *Duma pro Triokh Vitriv* [A Duma on Three Winds], in which the revolutionary upheaval was associated with the long-anticipated sun in early spring and a wind of change.

The shift from autonomism to separatism in Ukraine's political discourse, however, did not correspond to the Bolshevik vision for the territory's future. Tychyna, despite saluting the formation of the national state, apprehended: 'Black wings over the doves and sun – Black wings.' The cooperation between the Bolsheviks and the Ukrainian nationalists was short-lived. Both governments competed over the influence of local soviets (councils) of workers' and soldiers' deputies, which since February 1917 started to spontaneously form in the mostly industrial centres and garrisons of radicalized soldiers along the frontline. In Ukraine, the first soviet was elected in Kharkiv on 2 March 1917, and a day later in Kyiv. By mid-1917, there were already 252 soviets on Ukraine's territory. Most of them were situated in the east of Ukraine (180 soviets or 71 per cent in the industrial Donbas area), big cities, such as Kharkiv, Kyiv, Katerynoslav, and Poltava, and in the frontline areas. Initially, the soviets on Ukraine's territory were dominated by the all-Russia socialist parties – the SRs and the Mensheviks. As 1917 wore on, some of them sided with the Ukrainian government, while others pledged their support directly to the Bolsheviks in Petrograd.⁵¹

In Ukraine, however, the Bolsheviks started from a marginal position. In 1917, the regional organizations of the RSDRP(b) in Ukraine numbered some 23,000 members, with two-thirds of them being concentrated in the industrial and Russian-speaking Donbas area.⁵² In Kyiv, their public support was especially meagre, as illustrated by the results of the elections to the city council on 23 July 1917. The Bolshevik party list gained only 9,256 votes in comparison to those 34,057 votes cast for the Ukrainian list (coalition of the USDRP and UPSR) and 25,495 for the Russian bloc.⁵³

Such political metrics can be easily explained by Kyiv's demographic and social-economic make-up. Unlike major industrial centres in the east, Kyiv consisted mostly of the middle class – merchants, artisans, clerks, and those occupied in liberal professions – who did not share the sentiments expressed in the Bolshevik's proletarian discourse. At the same time, however, Kyiv had been dominated by Russians since imperial times. Russians not only constituted half of Kyiv's population – 49.4 per cent (against 18.6 per cent Jews, 16.4 per cent Ukrainians and 9.1 per cent Poles),⁵⁴ but the city was also a centre of Russian monarchism, kindled by the local Russian nobility and high-ranking imperial officers.⁵⁵ One of the major Russian-language newspapers, *Kievlianin*, founded and edited by a Russian conservative monarchist Vasily Shulgin, was subsidized by the tsarist government and was well known for its anti-Ukrainian narrative. After the defeat of the Provisional Government, these conservative Russian circles, however, agreed to support the new Ukrainian authorities, whom they saw as a more legitimate centre of power, when compared to the Bolsheviks.

Nonetheless, the popularity of the Russian Bolsheviks gradually increased in Kyiv. The results of the elections of the All-Russian Constituent Assembly, held on 25 November 1917, are often used to prove that 'the Ukrainian populists scored a decisive electoral victory throughout most of the Ukraine'.⁵⁶ Indeed, the elections showed that the project for Ukraine, elaborated by the nationally oriented parties, enjoyed considerable support throughout the territory: the national parties gained 75 per cent of the votes against just 10 per cent for the Bolshevik share of the poll.⁵⁷ In Kyiv, the Ukrainian Socialist bloc (UPSR, *Selians'ka Spilka* [Peasant Union], and USDRP) together received 77 per cent of the vote. If one compares these results to the elections for the Kyiv city council from earlier that year, another conclusion comes to mind. While the support of the Ukrainian socialist parties rose to 70 per cent (from 34,057 in July to 46,764 in November), the Bolsheviks gained almost three times more votes than in July, 32,576 against 9,256 respectively.⁵⁸ This increase in popularity can be attributed, first, to their successful anti-war propaganda and, second, to the weakness of the Ukrainian government and its inability to offer any feasible alternatives for those Kyivans who could not fully identify with Ukrainian nationalist demands.

In Russia, the Bolsheviks gained power by taking control of the soviets and securing control of the country through the Second All-Russian Congress of Soviets of Workers' and Soldiers' Deputies, held immediately after the overthrow of the Provisional Government in late October 1917. This same scenario was repeated in Kyiv where they hoped to gain a majority at the All-Ukrainian Congress of Soviets of Workers' and Soldiers' Deputies, summoned from 4–6 December 1917. The Ukrainian leaders, well aware of the Bolshevik's intentions, encouraged those Ukrainian soviets loyal to them to attend the Congress. As a result, most of the soviets pledged support to the Ukrainian government, prompting the defeated Bolsheviks to retreat eastwards to Kharkiv. Here, they convened an alternative congress, at which they proclaimed an autonomous Ukrainian People's Republic of Soviets under a parallel government – the People's Secretariat of Ukraine; a separate Communist Party of Bolsheviks of Ukraine (KP(b)U) was formed in April 1918. At the same time, an ultimatum, signed by Lenin and Trotsky, was sent to the Rada demanding the legalization of Bolshevik military units, and threatening war if this demand was unmet.⁵⁹ The UNR leaders rejected the ultimatum, precipitating an armed conflict.⁶⁰

'Be damned together with war! Raven-black wind … '

The Soviet-Ukrainian war turned out to be disastrous for the Ukrainian government. The UNR could only counter the organized Red Army with some irregular units of 'Free Cossacks' and volunteers. This resulted in the UNR quickly losing control over

Left-bank Ukraine, where the Bolsheviks gained significant support from local Red Guards and pro-Soviet forces. On 11 January under Bolshevik fire, the Rada's Fourth Universal finally declared Ukraine's independence: 'From this day forth, the Ukrainian People's Republic becomes independent, subject to no one, a Free, Sovereign State of the Ukrainian People.'[61] By this point, however, the declaration made little practical difference, the General Secretariat was too weak to defend its territory. On 9 February 1918, Red Army units under the leadership of Mikhail Muraviov and Vladimir Antonov-Ovseyenko entered Kyiv, and the UNR was forced to retreat westwards to Zhytomyr. The capture of Kyiv was followed by extreme terror. In the first weeks of Bolshevik rule, between 2,000 and 5,000 'class enemies', mostly Russian aristocracy, military elites and the supporters of the Ukrainian government, were executed in the city.[62]

On numerous occasions, Tychyna reflected on those turbulent weeks in Kyiv. *Pam'iaty Trydtsiaty* [In Memory of the Thirty] is the most revealing testimony of the violence committed by the Red Army. The poem was written to commemorate the thirty young cadets captured during the unequal Battle of Kruty and later executed in Kyiv. Fighting took place on 29–30 January 1918, when around 500 students tried to stop the offensive of 4,000 soldiers headed by Muraviov near a railway station 130 km north-east of Kyiv.[63] *Pam'iaty Trydtsiaty* was first published in *Nova Rada* on 21 March, immediately after the cadets' ceremonial funeral in Kyiv.

> Deep in the Mound of Askold
> Their bodies have been laid –
> Thirty staunch Ukrainians,
> Young, glorious, unafraid ...
> Here in the Mound of Askold
> The bloom of the Ukraine! –
> Our fate it was by bloody paths
> This destiny to gain.[64]

Tychyna glorified those first fallen fighters for the Ukrainian state. In the poem *Viina I* [War I], he tried to further soothe the pain of this great loss: 'Do not grieve / for whoever dies for Ukraine dies not!' Unsurprisingly, *Pam'iaty Trydtsiaty* was never included in any of Tychyna's poetry collections or reprinted during the Soviet era. Similarly, the Battle of Kruty was 'censored' from Soviet history textbooks until Ukraine gained independence in 1991.

Within a few months, Ukraine's capital witnessed astounding military and political reversals. The Bolshevik occupation of Kyiv lasted only three weeks. In search of allies, the nationally oriented Ukrainian political elites turned to the Central Powers, inviting their former enemies to occupy Ukraine. By the end of February 1918, there were almost half a million German and Austro-Hungarian soldiers on Ukrainian territory. By the end of April, they had occupied it entirely, returned the Ukrainian authorities back to power in the capital and forced the Bolsheviks to retreat back to Russia.[65] The Central Powers, however, had little trust in the left-leaning UNR. A coup was organized, which brought the conservative government of Pavlo Skoropads'kyi to power.[66] Skoropads'kyi, known as a 'Russian general of Little Russian extraction',[67] ruled as a dictator opposing the Rada's domestic agenda. Shortly after the coup, he reversed its socialist programmes, reinstated private property and launched campaigns against left-wing Ukrainian activists. In return for their military support, the Central Powers required Skoropads'kyi's government to honour the UNR's earlier pledge to deliver substantial quantities of grain, food and raw materials to them. The main burden fell on the peasants, who could not comprehend how or why the Germans had come to be in control. Later, Tychyna recalled that 'Everything ceased to exist – the language, the arts, science, – only *salo*, flour, sugar, and iron ore, looted and in wagons, was sent to Germany.'[68]

For a poet who had survived the succession of bloody military reversals in Kyiv, everyday reality became a painful experience of rejecting those earlier anticipated revolutionary values. Caught amidst this chaos, Tychyna ventured to 'find an herb / to heal human madness' (*Viina II* [War II]). But there was none: 'Be damned together with war! / Raven-black wind … ' (*Po Blakytnomu Stepu* [Along the azure steppe]). In Kyiv, the civil war brought all of the Ukrainian leadership's aims and ambitions to naught. The discrepancy between the expectations and outcome of the revolution, which, instead of sovereignty, brought hatred and fratricidal wars for years to come, were captured in a short poem *Odchyniaite Dveri …* [Open the Doors …]:

Open the door –
The bride is coming!
Open the door –
The azure blue!
Eyes, hearts, and chorales
Paused,
Waiting …
The door was opened –
A dark, stormy night!
The door was open –
All the roads in blood!
In unweepable tears,
In darkness
Rain

Consequently, Tychyna foresaw 'There will never be paradise / In this blood-spattered land' (*Skorbotna Maty III* [Sorrowful Mother III]).

The year of 1919 marked a period of complete chaos and anarchy in Ukraine. In late December 1918, UNR forces overthrew Skoropads'kyi's conservative government and once again, albeit for only a few months, consolidated their position in Kyiv. Although a new Directory of the UNR was established, it had no concrete plans on how to govern the country. As the wider Russian Civil War spread to Ukrainian territory, this weak government was forced to compete with the Bolsheviks and the Whites, while, in the countryside, peasant leaders (*otamans*) took advantage of the existing power vacuum to declare self-rule and seize control over the land. On 5 February 1919, Bolshevik troops entered Kyiv for the second time; the weakened directory had no legitimacy or ability to oppose them and were once again forced to retreat westward in search of foreign allies.

' ... a party member or not'

The events of spring 1917 initiated irreversible political changes throughout the former Russian Empire. Yet the revolution also provided a stimulus for an extraordinary cultural revival in Ukraine; it released enormous creative energy uniting the 'old' intelligentsia together with the new generation of writers who 'suddenly emerged from what was often social obscurity into a prominent position of intellectual leadership'.[69] They embraced values that were simultaneously universal and national, and in so doing, became important supporters of the Ukrainian government's state-building initiatives. During the Ukrainian revolution, politics, culture and scholarship became closely intertwined with Hrushevs'kyi and Vynnychenko occupying the highest political posts, while poets, like Tychyna, eagerly provided support, popularizing each and every government initiative in their patriotic verse.

Cultural and literary activities in Kyiv continued despite the succession of governments and changes of authorities. No matter the ideological underpinning, every government was 'culture-minded', with a particular focus on the development of the Ukrainian language, literature and scholarship. The short-lived Skoropads'kyi's government, despite setbacks in the social sphere, was perhaps the most expansive in their cultural policies. In the brief period between April and December 1918, several cultural institutions were established, among them the State Ukrainian Archive, the National Art Gallery, the Ukrainian History Museum, the Ukrainian National Library, the Ukrainian National Academy of Sciences and the Ukrainian State Publishing House, providing economic bases for Ukraine's cultural revival. Despite the subsequent years of political anarchy, these institutions remained and provided the outlet for Ukrainian culture. At the same time, writers and artists, among those who still remained in the capital, tended to seek accommodation with each and every new government, extending the conditions of normality as best they could. As a result, although literature could not keep pace with the constant change in leadership, creative life in Kyiv did not vanish altogether. Writers joined literary groups, collecting their forces to keep Ukraine's cultural milieu alive, while several journals and newspapers continued to appear with relative frequency.

During 1914–19, Ukrainian literature was dominated by modernism. Initiated by Voronyi's 'modernist manifesto' of 1901, it united those writers and poets who defended the autonomy of art and devoted themselves to the pursuit of 'pure art', 'l'art pour l'art' (art for art's sake), rejecting the social themes and reflections of current affairs. The symbolist school was the main modernist literary current of the time, represented by, among others, Tychyna, Zahul, Hryhorii Chuprynka and Iurii Mezhenko. Against Voronyi's teachings, these writers became engaged in the politics of the day. As the example of Tychyna suggests, they were deeply involved in the revolutionary events in Ukraine, trying to fuse symbolist and modernist conventions with patriotic concerns to the point that Zahul even stated that 'only a national culture can exist'.[70]

In March 1918, these writers formed a literary group called *Bila studia* [White Studio], consisting of Tychyna, Iakiv Savchenko, Slisarenko, Mykhailo (Mykhail') Semenko, Zahul, Les' [Oleksandr] Kurbas, Petro Kovzhun and Anatol' Petryts'kyi. This coterie published *Literaturno-krytychnyi al'manakh* [The Literary-Critical Almanac], the first issue of which appeared in December 1918. To this collection, Tychyna contributed the poem *Enharmoniine* [Enharmonic]. In January 1919, the symbolists formed another literary and artistic group by the name of *Muzahet* [Musagetes]. *Muzahet* was backed by the Directory of the UNR and, with the promise of financial support, set up a monthly literary journal under the same name. The defeat of the Ukrainian government in February 1919, however, adjusted their objectives and the overdue issue of *Muzahet* did not appear until May. This first issue, which was also the only one that the group managed to publish, opened with three poems by Tychyna – *Mizhplanetni Intervaly* [Interplanetary Intervals], *Pluh* [The Plough] and *I Bielyi, i Blok* [And Bely and Blok].[71]

Somewhat aside from the symbolists, stood a smaller group known as *neoklasyky* [neoclassicists], or academists who gathered around the Ukrainian Academy of Sciences. This 'cluster of five' (*piatirme hrono*) was composed of such prominent poets as Ryl's'kyi, Pavlo Fylypovych, Iurii Klen (pen name of Oswald Burkhard) and Mykhailo Drai-Khmara, centred around the professor of Ukrainian literature, poet, translator, classicist and literary historian Mykola Zerov. Although they never established a formal organization or programme, *neoklasyky* were united in their dedication to high art, universal themes and Ukraine's orientation towards Western European culture.[72]

Yet there were also those writers for whom the revolution brought the promise of purging Ukrainian literature of traditional 'bourgeois' norms. One such group was the futurists, who gathered around the poet Semenko. The futurists eagerly responded to the revolution, believing that, as anticipated, it represented the beginning of a new era in history, liberated from conservative values that would see the individual set free. Other groups of Kyivan writers anticipated the beginning of proletarian literature. In 1918, one such leftist group, which included Mykhailychenko, Vasyl' Chumak, Andrii Zalyvchyi and Ellan-Blakytnyi, established *Borot'ba* [The Struggle]. It also published the literary almanacs *Zshytky Borot'by* [Chapbooks of Struggle] and *Chervonyi Vinok* [The Red Wreath]; the latter continued to appear in Odesa during the Denikin occupation.

The boundaries between those literary trends and schools were porous, however. Despite ideological differences, these writers all wished for Ukraine's cultural revival and often collaborated on various projects and contributed to the same literary almanacs.[73] For instance, symbolist Tychyna collaborated with the *Borot'ba* group; the Neoclassicist Zerov edited a critical-bibliographical monthly *Knyhar* [The Bookseller], providing a detailed account of post-revolutionary literary life; and the futurist Semenko edited the state-sponsored journal *Mystetstvo* [Art] with contributions from all the above-mentioned authors.

Tychyna's first collection of poetry *Soniachni Klarnety* [The Clarinets of the Sun], published at the end of 1918, was the biggest literary sensation of the civil war period. It included poems written between 1914 and 1918, as well as those pieces of writing previously published in *Nova Rada*. *Soniachni Klarnety* brought Tychyna immediate fame. According to Iurii Lavrinenko, the collection was a 'congenial aesthetic *universal* of the country that in the tellurian [*teliurychnyi*] mass upheavals of the national revolution of 1917 woke up to overcoming the internal and external slavery, to a new life'. The critic put Tychyna's collection in line with Alexander Bloc's 1918 monumental patriotic odes *The Twelve* and *The Scythians,* the greatest examples of the poetry inspired by the revolution in Russian literature.[74] The collection received high critical acclaim. As intended, *Soniachni Klarnety*, with its unique 'fusion of folksongs and poetry, or rather the transformation of folksongs into poetry',[75] brought new life into Ukrainian symbolism. The contemporary literary critic Serhii Iefremov noted that it opened a new 'fresh, exciting, and deep' page in the history of Ukrainian literature.[76] According to the critics, Tychyna's talent disproved all those 'grumblings about the inherent crudity of the Ukrainian language'.[77] Instead, his work raised the Ukrainian language up to a new standard, showing that it could be used not only for realistic novels, but also for highly symbolic modernist poetry.[78] Shortly after the publication of *Soniachni Klarnety*, Tychyna became known as 'the most prominent Ukrainian poet of the twenties'[79] or even 'of the entire twentieth century'.[80]

'We will overcome everything … '

The second Bolshevik takeover of Kyiv in February 1919 briefly stabilized politics in Ukraine. The expansion of Soviet power westwards initiated heated debates within the socialist camp about a possible cooperation with the Bolsheviks. Left Socialist-Revolutionaries, who after the split in the summer of 1918 created a separate Ukrainian Party of Socialists-Revolutionaries (Communists) (*Ukrains'ka Partiia Sotsialistiv-Revoliutsioneriv [Komunistiv]*), or simply the *Borot'bysty*, became especially susceptible to Bolshevik propaganda. Among its founders, and most famous representatives, were Mykhailychenko, Shums'kyi, Blakytnyi, Panas Liubchenko and Zalyvchyi, who would soon occupy important positions in Soviet Ukraine. These Ukrainian Marxists and socialists supported the idea of 'soviet power', that is, that Ukraine should be a republic of soviets, in which power was exercised by these workers' and peasants' councils. They also welcomed the Red Army's arrival on the streets of Kyiv: this 'true revolutionary army of proletariats and peasants, those makers of the social revolution, who were committed to drown servitude and social injustice in their own blood'.[81] Yet they dreamed of an independent Ukrainian communist state, and not one ruled by a single hierarchical party where all the important decisions were taken in Moscow.[82] Consequently, they opposed the Bolshevik party, whose pan-imperial attitudes differed little from the former highly centralized tsarist regime. Some went as far as to assert that the Bolshevik party in Ukraine united 'all sorts of Russian nationalist elements from the Black Hundreds to the revolutionary intelligentsia in Ukraine […] joining forces with the Bolsheviks to help reconstruct a "united and indivisible Russia"'.[83] In this regard, Lenin's Bolshevism was nothing more than a renewed Russian imperialism.[84]

Ukraine's independence was the *Borot'bysty*'s primary goal, which, however, could only be achieved through means of a socialist revolution. As argued in February 1919, 'the best solution to the national question would be to reach socialism; thus, the primary goal of each and every revolutionary socialist party [in Ukraine], despite their national affiliation, should be strengthening the achievements of the socialist revolution, which will eventually result in national emancipation'.⁸⁵ They rejected outright the idea of a messianic role for the Russian working class and opposed those Moscow-oriented and Russian-speaking communists who had no link with Ukraine's predominantly Ukrainian-speaking peasant population. Instead, the *Borot'bysty* believed that the revolution in Ukraine would have its own trajectory and a different social basis in the semi-proletariat and poor peasantry that needed to be co-opted into the revolutionary struggle. Hence, their major task was to translate the Russian revolution 'into the language of local conditions'.⁸⁶

The *Borot'bysty* had been represented in the Central Rada and the Ukrainian government; they also gained a significant following in Ukraine, especially among the Ukrainian-speaking workers and peasants. Until its self-liquidation in 1920, the *Borot'bysty* were the only party with considerable leverage against those pro-Moscow-oriented Bolsheviks, competing with the former for support of Ukraine's toiling population and the right to become a vanguard of the proletarian revolution in Ukraine. Indeed, before their self-liquidation in 1920, the *Borot'bysty* outnumbered the Bolsheviks: there were around 15,000 members of the *Borot'bysty* party with broad representation in central and western *gubernias*, while the Bolsheviks numbered 11,087 members with 2,439 candidate members concentrated mostly in urban areas in the south and east of Ukraine.⁸⁷

After 1919, Tychyna, although not in the party, began to involve himself in state cultural initiatives, joining the State Publishing House (*Derzhvydav*) and the editorial board of the state-sponsored periodical *Mystetstvo*. This affiliation was not ideological, although it is difficult to speculate on Tychyna's convictions during this period due to the scarcity of primary sources and the prudence with which the poet omitted any public expression of his views. This cooperation was most probably initiated by Tychyna's childhood friend Ellan-Blakytnyi, a leader of the *Borot'bysty* party whose representatives had, by this time, joined the Soviet government and gained control over its Commissariat for Education. Blakytnyi, on repeated occasions, helped Tychyna survive through the civil war years, offering him various employment opportunities and procuring financial support from the new Soviet government, believing that he lacked revolutionary temper and stamina and that his nervous disposition could not endure moments of extreme tension without some ideological guidance.⁸⁸

Through Blakytnyi, Tychyna joined a small section of writers, who gathered under the *Borot'bysty*-controlled All-Ukrainian Literary Committee, *Vseukrlitkom*. He contributed to their almanacs and submitted pieces to the *Borot'bysty* press. Two of his poems, *Na Maidani* ... [On the Square ...] and *Iak Upav* ... [When he fell ...], for instance, appeared in the newspaper *Borot'ba*, edited by Blakytnyi, on 23 February and 25 February 1919, respectively. This not only provided Tychyna with a small income, but also helped secure his status as a revolutionary poet. In time, *Iak Upav* ... and *Na Maidani* ..., later included into the 1920 collection *Pluh* [The Plough], became conventional poetic references to the October events in Ukraine.⁸⁹ Nonetheless, by analysing the wording of these verses, another contextualization comes to mind. For example, *Na Maidani* ... opens with the stanza suggesting to elect a shepherd for a leader, an *otaman* in Ukrainian:

> In front of the church on the square,
> The Great Revolution is on.
> 'Hey, shepherd!' cries shatter the air.
> 'For leader, you've enough brawn.'

Iak Upav ..., in turn, depicts the death of a soldier during combat who is then laid to rest with shouts of *Slava!*:

> He fell from his horse
> Onto the white snow
> 'Hurrah! Hurrah!' Rolled up to him
> and lay at his feet.

Despite their overt revolutionary message, these two stanzas include allusions to the Ukrainian national, and not the Bolshevik, revolution: there were no *otamans* in the Bolshevised military units, while '*Slava*' was never used during the funerals of Red Army soldiers.

The authorities of the Soviet government were re-established, and the territory once claimed by the UNR became fully incorporated into the Ukrainian Soviet Republic. The Bolsheviks in Moscow, having learned the hard lessons of neglecting the Ukrainian question, conceded to a separate soviet republic. Despite this, all major decisions were continued to be made in Moscow with the Ukrainian Bolshevik party having hardly any power over the state's political and economic matters. Nonetheless, Soviet Ukraine retained its formal independent statehood and as such had its own attributes, including a border-defined territory and government, and its own symbols: a flag, a coat of arms and an anthem.

Already in early 1919, the Ukraine's Commissariat for Education (*Narkomos*) announced a competition to select a revolutionary anthem for the newly formed Ukrainian Socialist Soviet Republic (UkrSSR).[90] Tychyna joined a jury committee as a *Vsevydav* representative. Not only did he evaluate the submissions, but also offered his own text for the committee's consideration. This propaganda piece, written in spring 1919, was the complete opposite of *Zolotyi Homin*, a conventional hymn of the national Ukrainian revolution, composed in summer 1917. Instead of the inner musicality and metaphorical abundance, the anthem of the Bolshevik socialist revolution consisted of simple agitation rhymes:

> We will overcome everything, we are capable of everything,
> The darkness we will turn away!
> To make a brother out of a slave –
> This is a slogan of proletariat!
> To unchain the un-free world –
> This is our behest! [...]
> We rouse, awaken, call – hammer, whistle and funnels,
> We are, we were, and we will be, same as the sun above us!
> We are striding, we are walking,
> And the bourgeois world we are destroying! (O.P.)

However, the question of how sincere Tychyna actually was while composing this propaganda verse remains open to debate. One of the pieces in the 1920 collection, *Zamist' Sonetiv i Oktav*, does suggest another side of his singing praise to the Bolsheviks, admitting that:

> The most profound, the loftiest and at the same time, the simplest content is composed of two or three notes – that's a true hymn.
>
> Not for contests, and not for awards, write a contemporary 'Christ is Risen'

Tychyna's text did not win the competition. Instead, Voronyi's rendition of *L'Internationale* was announced a de facto anthem of Soviet Ukraine.[91] Tychyna's revolutionary hymn was, instead, recited frequently in front of the Red Army soldiers dispatched to fight the Volunteer Army commanded by General Anton Denikin, another of the Bolshevik's major rivals during the civil war.[92]

The Bolsheviks, while competing with the nationalist governments on Ukraine's territory, were waging a far bigger war. The major anti-Bolshevik player on the post-imperial scale was the Whites or those conservative generals, such as Denikin, who wished to reconstruct a 'united and indivisible Russia' and favoured the return of the tsar. These generals, with support from the intervening Allied Powers, quickly took control of the former imperial peripheries. In Ukraine, the White movement was led by General Denikin, whose Volunteer Army entered Kyiv on 31 August 1919. Almost simultaneously, the Directory of the UNR, reinforced by the military forces of the West Ukrainian National Republic (ZUNR), arrived in the city from the west. The Ukrainian army, however, discouraged by the fact that neither the Whites nor the Allies expressed interest in Ukrainian statehood, quickly withdraw from the capital.

As a committed monarchist, Denikin aimed to restore the pre-revolutionary social order. Naturally, he had no sympathies for either the Ukrainian nationalists or the Bolsheviks, banning the use of the Ukrainian language, and arresting Ukrainian intellectuals and Bolshevik supporters. Ukrainian activists and socialists alike feared persecutions by the White Army and were forced underground. Dreading arrests and military conscription, Tychyna, together with other *Borot'bysty*, found refuge in the crypts of Kyiv's Baikove cemetery where they remained for several months.[93] The Denikin regime, although short-lived, took a heavy toll on Ukrainian cultural affairs. Among those brutally executed were the *Borot'bysty* poet Chumak and the Commissar for Education Mykhailychenko. Tychyna dedicated a poem in honour of the latter's death, calling for people to rally together for the common victory: 'We take an oath: in the hour of victory – to fight to the death – but we'll vanquish the enemy!' Another of Tychyna's poem was dedicated to the Red Army that re-took Kyiv on 16 December 1919. The poem glorified Mykhailychenko and Chumak as the 'red martyrs' of 'the new era':

> Do hope ... Hide the truth in your purse.
> Above Ukraine – the hand of Taras ...
> New days are at dawn in Kyiv, –
> These are the days of Mykhailychenko and Chumak (O.P.)

Even after the Whites had been ousted, Ukraine's political situation remained turbulent. The UNR leaders continued to seek political alliances against the Bolsheviks. In May 1920, the Directorate's erstwhile Chairmen Symon Petliura, returned to Kyiv with the backing of the Polish army as part of the Soviet-Polish war. Ironically, Tychyna's poetry, inspired by the struggle for the Ukrainian state in 1917, was anonymously distributed from Soviet agitation trains during the Bolshevik anti-UNR and anti-Polish campaigns during the summer of 1920. *Rondeli* [Rondels] called for mobilization and unification of the world proletariat against the common enemy:

> We'll shout to the world about our pain!
> So that from our planet to the stars –
> All the proletarians everywhere would hearken
> To what we fight for, here, in the field!
> The poplars mobilise

This UNR military campaign did not gain significant public support, and the general anti-Bolshevik uprising failed to materialize, despite the hopes and efforts of the Ukrainian leaders. The government in Kyiv only lasted until 13 June when they abandoned the city to the Bolsheviks for the final time.

The Bolshevik victory brought the long-awaited promise of normality to Kyiv. The Ukrainian intelligentsia, exhausted by the years-long war, economic chaos and social disorder, was now ready to come to terms with the victors. As previously mentioned, it is hard to trace the evolution of Tychyna's ideological convictions. His diaries or personal documents reveal little about the poet's early life.[94] Nevertheless, a diary entry from 1 August 1920 suggests that he himself was ready to accommodate the new authorities and was even considering joining their ranks: 'In recent days, I have been thinking quite often: a party member or not.'[95]

'Should I, too, kiss the slipper of the Pope?'

The civil wars took a heavy toll on Ukrainian cultural life. Despite the efforts of those intellectuals who had remained in Kyiv throughout and attempted to continue their activities as usual, the wartime atmosphere was hardly conducive towards encouraging cultural development. As one witness to those years in Kyiv remarked: 'Those who might express interest in the literary activities during our national revolution and wars can simply be told, "there was none." There were years subsumed by a drive to create a [Ukrainian] state … People … fought with arms and words, but no one wrote. Only publicists wrote. Writers and poets were silent. *Inter arma silent musae*.'[96] In fact, remarkably, some outlets, such as *Chas* [The Time], *Drukar* [The Publisher] and *Krynytsia* [The Well], continued with their publishing activities while promoting literary activities in the city.

In spite of the unfavourable conditions, in 1920, Tychyna managed to publish two further poetry collections. The second of these *Pluh* [The Plough] included poems written in 1918–20, most of which had previously been published in various periodicals. The first volume *Zamist' Sonetiv i Octav* [Instead of Sonnets and Octaves] featured short prosaic aphoristic reflections on the recent experiences in a war-torn Kyiv. Both collections exposed the poet's inner doubts and reservations caused by the disastrous turmoil of the civil wars. Controversially, *Pluh* even proposed a possible solution to Ukraine's fraternal wars. Tychyna introduces a metaphor of 'a million million muscular arms' as a reference to the victorious proletariat approaching the bright socialist future, presenting them as the heralds of the 'beauty of the dawning day'. By contrast, *Zamist' Sonetiv i Octav* presented the tormented poet as struggling to come to terms with the ever-changing authorities. The two collections merited different receptions. While *Pluh* was widely celebrated as Tychyna's 'decisive "yes" to the Socialist revolution',[97] *Zamist' Sonetiv i Octav* was censored shortly after the first edition, and only republished in the late 1980s.

When placed together, however, both collections show that the period 1919–20 was not about making decisive choices; it was the time of reconciling with and comprehending the idea(s), which made the terror and cruelty of the civil war possible. Tychyna was disoriented, especially since he himself used to glorify revolution, which, however, had revealed the worst side of the human nature. Thus, his revolutionary dreams crumbled:

> We expected a hero, but the swineherd has come, –
> Who then made a victim so brutally out of us? (O.P.)

He questioned:

> Who then brought you to such derision?
> Who has stabbed you with a knife in your heart? [...]
> Who has brought this bloody trial on you?
> Who then made a victim so brutally out of us? (O.P.)

Those, who promised to lead, brought weapons and fratricidal war with them:

> They took axes to warm them up in blood,
> and brother stepped against brother to bereave, to share ...
> And blood was shed over the fields and groves,
> because those who slashed were our kin and our own. (O.P.)

The poet's confusion soon came to embody his tormented country:

> There stands Kyiv tormented a hundredfold
> and I, crucified two hundred times

Nevertheless, he still believed that 'Ukraine will raise its own Moses – / it has to be.' He justified himself and his role in that struggle: 'poet, to love your homeland isn't a crime / when you do it for the good of all.'

'The beauty of the dawning day,' glorified in *Pluh*, was still gruesome. Tychyna, like many of those who had lived through the civil war, became disenchanted with the revolution; its universal values were compromised by all the crimes committed in its name. More painfully, all his contemporaries now shared in this guilt, especially those poets who had cherished the revolutionary idea and translated it to the masses. Tychyna explained: 'the creators of the revolution are, for the most part, lyric poets'. But those who came to preach were useless since 'the one who said, "to kill is a sin" the next morning lies with a bullet in his head'. Tychyna denounced any possible justification for such terror, challenging the notion that 'The great idea demands sacrifices. But is it a sacrifice when a beast eats a beast?' Tychyna did not differentiate among those involved in red terror: 'Damnation to all, damnation to all, who've become beasts!'

There must have been a good reason as to why these two complementary collections appeared in the same year: while *Pluh* suggested the possibility of accepting 'the new day', *Zamist' Sonetiv i Octav* pondered on the cost of such determination. Writing in *Pluh*, Tychyna glorified locomotives and industrial innovations, while positing in *Zamist' Sonetiv i Octav* that those technological advances come at a cost of dehumanization: 'airplanes and the perfection of technology – what good is it when people don't look each other straight in the eye?' He questioned the conviction that revolutionary transformation would justify the countless loss of human lives and one's humanity. He determined, '[E]verything can be justified by a lofty purpose – but not the emptiness of the soul'. Similarly, while encouraging every village to join the fight and find its own *Marseillaise*, he condemned the war: 'they shoot the heart, they shoot the soul – they pity nothing.' Hence, the universal idea of revolution was doomed, having lost its purity and become smeared with blood: 'without music socialism can't be established by any cannons'.

Pluh with its glorification of the 'new day' marked Tychyna's departure from symbolism, from his devotion to folklore, religious motifs, the inner musicality of his language and the manifold sounding of his lyrics. Instead, new heroes and values came to the fore, as revealed through *Pluh*'s central poem, *Psalom Zalizu* [Psalm to Iron]. The poem describes a town devastated by war just before the establishment of the new Soviet order. Tychyna captured the moment when communists marched through the town. Unlike Saint Andrew the Apostle, who, according to the legend, had blessed the Kyivan hills on which he prophesized the foundation of a great Christian city, or a sorrowful mother who mourned her hasty sons (the images of Tychyna's early poetry), those communists now summon workers 'to smash the capitalists'.

The 'new renaissance' came to glorify 'steel, iron and a factory whistle', while Tychyna's 'Madonna of Mine, Immaculate Virgin, exalted in eternity' becomes superfluous. Hence, *Pluh* was not only an expression of support for the new social order and their creators – the communists (*Psalom Zalizu* was the first explicit reference to the Communist Party in Tychyna's poetry to date), but also a 'farewell to his Madonna',[98] his previous aesthetic credo:

Lean over, Madonna, against the side
Of the last house in the village.
Smile – and then leave through the ploughed fields,
Flicking away bullets like bees.

The ambiguity reflected in these two collections, fully corresponded to the author's personal confusion about the social and political developments of the time. He was hesitant, he questioned the party (perhaps, ironically): 'Join the party, where they look upon a human being as a world treasure, and they all are as one against the death penalty'. The concluding piece from *Zamist' Sonetiv i Octav* best presents his disillusionment with all those futile ideas and their standard-bearers:

> It's still not a revolution just to play Scriabin for the prison guards.
> The Eagle, a Trident, a Hammer and Sickle ... each acts as your own.
> But a rifle has killed our own.
> Our own lies at the bottom of our soul.
> Should I, too, kiss the slipper of the Pope?

For many critics, the concluding line (*Should I, too, kiss the slipper of the Pope?*) marked Tychyna's final breakdown.[99] Tychyna, nonetheless, continued to search for answers, as is obvious from his later poem *Na Mohyli Shevchenka II* [At Shevchenko's Grave ... II]: 'and there was no one to ask: / whom should we expect to save Ukraine?'

Pluh and *Zamist' Sonetiv i Octav* were warmly welcomed by critics who represented different literary and ideological orientations, those who regarded Tychyna as a herald of modernism and those who anticipated his joining the ranks of proletarian literature. Blakytnyi was among those who glorified Tychyna's shift towards accepting the proletarian discourse. In 1921, he named Tychyna the most talented contemporary poet, 'the beauty and pride of the new Ukrainian poetry'. He regretted to note, however, that he was 'not yet a complete Communist'; fortunately, as *Pluh* had demonstrated, Tychyna was 'striding forward, consciously catching up with the revolution, with the new life'.[100]

Blakytnyi's anticipation was shared among those young proletarian writers in Kharkiv who declared their support for the Soviet government. One such group, *Zhovten'* [October], consisting of Khvyl'ovyi, Volodymyr Sosiura, Maik Iohansen and Koriak, even dedicated the first issue of their almanac to Tychyna. The dedication, printed on the book's cover page, read: 'To Pavlo Tychyna. Dear Comrade, please accept from us this book as a proof of our candour and red respect [*chervona povaha*]. We know You and we love You. We hope, and we believe – You are with us. With warm and communist greetings, the Kharkiv group of proletarian writers and the *Vseukrlitkom*.'[101] An entry in Tychyna's diary from around the same time suggests that he did not appreciate the gesture: 'How shallow we all are! To regard that signature from *Vseurklitkom* with the communist (October) greetings as an attempt to lure me to their camp – what a narrow-mindedness! [...] What do they want from me?!'[102]

Both of Tychyna's collections from 1920 were characterized as 'pro and contra of the [October] revolution' by Soviet literary scholarship.[103] While *Zamist' Sonetiv i Octav* was quickly forgotten, *Pluh* became Tychyna's milestone. Semen Shakhovs'kyi characterized *Psalom Zalizu* as 'the biggest victory of the Soviet ideology; Tychyna's major step forward towards overcoming his [ideological] hesitations, towards formulating the true thoughts of the people'.[104] Bilets'kyi called *Pluh* a 'book of iron tunes, a book with a sound of fanfares rather than organs, a book, where a breeze becomes a wind and later a storm, unfurled by millions of muscular hands'.[105] The significance of this collection was aptly underlined by the contemporary critic Volodymyr Iurynets in a review from

1926: 'For a long time, Tychyna has been trying to occupy a position of a by-stander, an uninvolved observer, searching for positive and negative features in both rivalling camps. In the end, being unable to endure this splendid isolation, he throws himself into the current of life. *Psalom zalizu* and *Kosmichnyi orkests*[106] are the milestones in his transformation.'[107] By contrast, Iefremov feared that Tychyna 'was facing a danger of exchanging eternal values for profits [secured by] literary associations and party-mindedness'.[108] Instead of being pleased by this mostly positive reception, the poet himself was deeply confused. On 23 August 1920, Tychyna noted that: 'People show their admiration for my poetry. And this is not for the first time. How can I understand this: either I have pleased everyone (then I am not a poet) or ... (interrupted)?'[109] The poet was aware of the incessant feuds in the literary world when men of letters took sides and ardently confronted each other's ideological convictions. In this situation, when the war was fought not only on the battlefield, but also on the pages of literary almanacs, one's literary merit started to be measured by the level of their involvement into ideological debates. With this in mind, Tychyna's diary entry suggests that approval of the ideological rivals could be interpreted as a sign of little commitment to and uncertainty of his ideological stand.

' ... good that I am alive and who cares about the rest'

By late 1920, Ukraine's haphazard political power struggle had come to an end. Tychyna remembered that 'in Kyiv in those years [1919–20] everyone found it difficult. During only four years ... at a rough estimate – we survived a dozen and a half changes of authorities (German invasion, the Denikin Army, and the White Poles, needless to mention all the interim and recurrent forays of different barbarous gangs!).'[110] The war was over, yet the country was devastated. Ukraine's economy, already damaged by the war effort, was ruined. 'War Communism' – an emergency economic programme aimed at assisting the Bolshevik military targets by means of nationalization of industries, compulsory labour conscription and forced grain requisitioning – only exacerbated the chaos. Throughout this period, as aptly characterized by Lynn Viola, 'three of the four horsemen of apocalypse – war, famine and disease – stalked the Russian [and Ukrainian] land in an all too literal orgy of death and destruction.'[111]

In Kyiv, the economic situation was particularly bad. The city had been left shattered by the civil war and was now plagued by shortages of food and fuel. Moreover, as a centre of the national revolution and a middle-class stronghold, Kyiv could hardly expect mercy from the new authorities. Many of its former inhabitants had abandoned it, with the survival of those who remained being at serious risk. At the end of 1920, the Kyivan intelligentsia found itself lacking many of its traditional sources of income: most theatres, cinemas and museums had been destroyed, while newspapers and publishing houses – the economic base of intellectual life – were closed down in line with the Bolshevik's decree on 'hostile newspapers'.[112]

The Kyiv University and the Academy of Sciences – both products of the Ukrainian revolution – were also treated with utmost suspicion. Most universities were transformed into institutes for adult learning, providing crash courses for undereducated working class and military workers. Other educational institutes, modelled on the Kyiv State University, were also opened to provide social and professional education for future teachers of labour schools along with party-run schools. Indeed, having a job there could and did provide a Kyivan intellectual with some state protection. Yet pay was minimal and what limited funding did exist was eaten up by inflation and devaluation by the time it reached Kyiv from Kharkiv. For several months in 1921, members of the Ukrainian Academy of Sciences (VUAN) received 'advances', instead of salaries, of some 6,000 *karbovanets*, an amount which could not even buy a pound of bread a day.[113]

Professor Volodymyr Vernads'kyi, the founder of VUAN and its first president, recalled formidable practical problems during this difficult time:

> at home the temperature was 3–5°C, I used to thaw out on the meetings at the Academy, where there was at least some heating. Kyivans are in apathy and desperate. Cold, and devastation, and soaring prices, and it is impossible to leave. It is not getting any better, only worse. One may easily lose heart while observing everything that is going on. The mood everywhere is heavy and despondent. Life is becoming more difficult. Those who can, leave Kyiv with their families.[114]

The historian Natalia Polons'ka-Vasylenko recalled that during 1920–1 most intellectuals were forced into manual labour, turning 'into gardeners and lumbermen'.[115]

Most importantly, the city was starving. Food supplies were averted well short of the city's borders to the industrial centres and the Red Army under 'war communism' regulations. Some official supplies of rations were organized, yet these were sparse and irregular with many being paid for their work with food. Victor Petrov, also known under his pen name 'Domontovych', remembered how he often passed by the head office of *Knyhar* at lunchtime, because the staff were paid for their day's work with bowls of soup.[116] Tychyna reflected in his diary: 'Last year at least there was a cross on the grave of Lesia Ukrainka [a Ukrainian poet], this year it was taken as fire wood' (May 1920).[117] 'On my way from the office, I saw a woman with a sign "I am starving"' (July 1920).[118]

Everyday life for the city's intellectuals soon became so desperate that the authorities were obliged to intervene. Indeed, despite a keen distrust of the old intelligentsia, it was clear to the Bolshevik leaders that the revolution could not survive without a controlled collaboration. The Bolsheviks were dependant on their skills and knowledge; they needed the services of educated professionals, especially if they wished to revive the ruined economy.[119] In addition, due to extensive communication with the West, the deteriorating living conditions of the intelligentsia was also becoming known abroad, harming the positive outlook that the Soviet government was trying to develop in preparation for the much-coveted European revolution.

All these factors combined led to a softening in Bolshevik attitudes towards the local intelligentsia. Starting in 1919, the Soviet government introduced an official supply of rations to those occupied in intellectual activity, known as the academic ration (*akademichnyi paiok*). On 31 August 1920, the Soviet Ukrainian Government (*Radnarkom*) issued a decree 'on improving the material situation of scholars, specialists and distinguished art and literature workers' to provide minimum living conditions for those covered by the scheme.¹²⁰ In addition, the creation of semi-official writers' and artists' trade unions was initiated, aiming to promote the material interests of the intelligentsia while encouraging them to accept the values of the Bolshevik revolution.¹²¹ One such organization was the Union of the Workers of Arts (*Profesiina Spilka Robitnykiv Mystetstva, Robmys*) established in January 1921. Later that same year the All-Ukrainian Committee of Assistance to Scholars (*Vseukrains'kyi komitet spryiannia vchenym*) was formed, with the registered number of 3,362 scientific workers in 1923 and 1924, to whom the Soviet government provided various forms of assistance such as food rations, social care and state pensions.¹²²

While hunger, depravation and epidemics in Kyiv were becoming unbearable, many became attracted by the better-supplied countryside where they offered their skills and knowledge in exchange for food. For instance, the Kyivan poets Zerov, Petrov and Klen accepted an offer from a headmaster at a provincial school to teach in Baryshivka some 80 km from Kyiv.¹²³ Tychyna, also wishing to escape the poverty-stricken capital, embarked on a tour of Ukraine with the Ukrainian Republic Capella (choir) headed by the composer Kyrylo Stetsenko. Tychyna left a detailed diary depicting harsh conditions in the provinces.¹²⁴ During the tour, the undernourished poet fell seriously ill and returned to Kyiv to convalesce. It was at that time that Tychyna fell under the governmental assistance scheme and received a personalized ration card to help him through his recovery.¹²⁵ The great value of the poet to the new Soviet regime can be confirmed by the fact that he was among the few Ukrainian intellectuals who received a personal protection card (*okhoronna hramota*) from the Soviet government that for years protected its recipients from civic duties and requisition of personal property. This document was given to Tychyna on 2 January 1922 to 'guaranty that this person who is especially valuable for the socialist building and development of a proletarian culture, and his property stands under the special protection of state authority'.¹²⁶

By the end of 1920, Tychyna had, most probably, accepted the Bolshevik's victory, but still could not reconcile the 'red terror' used to eradicate any perceived anti-Soviet opposition during and immediately after the civil war. Sheila Fitzpatrick points out that the civil war also represented 'a class war' in which the Bolsheviks had targeted and executed hundreds of thousands of alleged counter-revolutionaries. Terror became a natural and predictable outcome of the revolution, with the Cheka, the newly created Extraordinary Commission for combating counter-revolution, being an instrument of terror and class vengeance.¹²⁷ The Bolshevik terror made an impact on the intellectual sphere. Arrests were frequent, and many of those arrested were quickly executed. Among those killed in the bloodshed of the Bolshevik violence were a modernist painter Oleksandr Murashko and a famous composer Mykola Leontovych, both of whom had previously supported the Ukrainian government and participated in their cultural activities. In January 1921, Leontovych was shot dead by a Chekist in his family home in Podillia. Tychyna, who knew Leontovych from the time he spent with Stetsenko touring the region, echoed this event in a poem *Zelene Podillia* [Green Podilia]. He appealed to the humanity of those in control: 'Let this bloody cup pass from Ukraine, let the harmony and equality be among the people.' Tychyna, while mourning the composer's assassination, expressed revulsion towards his own accord with the regime. In a diary entry referring to Leontovych's death, he wrote: 'How awful!

Figure 3 National Amateur Choir Chapel named after Mykola Leontovych, 1920 (Tychyna *top centre*). © Central State Archive-Museum of Literature and Arts of Ukraine, courtesy of TsDAMLMU.

Awful that he was killed and that I am clutching at life. So to say, good that I am alive and who cares about the rest. How awful.'[128] To commemorate the composer, Tychyna organized and directed a choir – The Choir-Studio, which he named after him, and toured with its members until 1923.

Another ordeal of the time was the famine of 1921–2, an expected outcome of the years-long civil war, the extensive Bolshevik grain requisitioning that followed and the government's ineffectiveness at easing the situation. During the hungry years of 1921–2, around forty million people were starving across the former empire, eight million of whom were in the south of Ukraine. The motif of starvation is pervasive in Tychyna's early poetry. Some of his poetry offers the most horrific accounts of the scale of individual dehumanization induced by the famine. In the poem *Holod* [Famine] (1921), later published in the collection *Viter z Ukrainy* [The Wind from Ukraine], the author depicted a desperate mother questioning the (in)sanity of a neighbouring woman who ate her children from hunger. She is searching for a relief to her own children: 'go to sleep, go to sleep, – may you go to sleep forever … Life!' In another striking poem *Zahupalo v Dveri Prykladom* [One Banged on the Door with a Rifle Butt], a demented mother was caught in the act of cooking her own son. Yet she tried to rationalize her deed: 'Am I not his mother? Or didn't I, you tell me, want to eat?'

'You're quite a force, and one day You'll make a communist'

In such dreadful conditions, when mere survival was at stake, writers were forced to make hard political decisions. Literature could not enjoy the privilege of autonomy. The establishment of the Soviet regime divided the intellectual milieu between those who supported the Bolshevik party and those who rejected it. In Kyiv, active supporters of the revolution were few and represented mostly those cultural elites associated with the *Borot'bysty* party. Yet they had mostly left Kyiv when the Soviet bureaucratic institutions were moved to the new capital in Kharkiv. Similarly, many of those who actively opposed the Bolsheviks left Ukraine together with the retreating UNR forces, joining Ukrainian intellectual communities in Prague, Berlin or Munich while the majority who remained attempted to adapt to the post-revolutionary conditions. Some fell silent and went into 'internal exile'; some passively resisted the party while continuing to work in the existing scholarly or cultural institutions. Some, however, saw a promise in the new situation and started seeking ways for collaboration with the new regime.

At first, Tychyna was among those intellectuals who sympathized with the Bolshevik party; he took jobs at state-supported institutions and sporadically published propagandistic pieces in official periodicals. However, as his literary output from 1921–4 suggests, Tychyna was becoming more attuned to the party leadership and willing to contribute to the Bolshevik's propaganda narrative. On numerous occasions, he glorified the party and its leaders, anticipated the future communist order and harshly criticized the dissenters. His poetry from 1921–4 corroborated the fact that Tychyna had come to terms with the regime and even reconciled with the terror that had brought its leaders to power: 'Well, what of it that blood has flooded the universe? Future generation will arise – the union of bodies and souls. We do what we do, and the new world – it will be ours!' (*Zhyvemo Komunoiu, X* [We Live as a Commune, X, 1920]). Similar resoluteness permeates his poem *Prometei* [Prometheus] written in either 1921 or 1922:

> I will go create the life anew –
> Even if over the corpses –
> Alone!
> This is how it should be. (O.P.)

Tychyna also foresaw a place for himself in the new pantheon. The triptych *Lysty do Poeta* [Letters to the Poet] drew a line under his previous ideological inconsistencies: 'You're quite a force, and someday You'll make a communist.'

Despite not being a party member, he fully engaged himself in the ideological battle against the anti-Soviet opposition. Tychyna, who only a while ago had glorified the national revolution, soon stood among the most ardent critics of the anti-Bolshevik Ukrainian political émigrés. His collection *V Kosmichnomu Orkestri* [In Cosmic Orchestra], published by *Vseukrlitkom* in Kharkiv in 1921, boldly warned 'Europe' against the advances of the first proletarian state from the East:

Who are those who began to laugh in Europe,
Who began to wail
That here we're dying of hunger
but won't surrender to our enemies?
[...]
Yes, yes, we're bloating without bread.
Our hope – the children – are dying.
But hunger is the language of the revolution.
And what if the workers of the world
Strike you from behind your back?

The same collection included a squib on political émigrés, 'who betrayed the Republic and dishonestly escaped abroad'. Those Ukrainian leaders were held liable for the outbreak of the civil war in Ukraine, as suggested by *V Tsariakh Znaishly Svoiu Opiku i Ridniu* [In Tsars you Found your Support and Kinship]:

You still have hope? So perish, die like dogs in taverns,
So your bones putrefy and become mouldy!
Why did you dupe the ignorant and blind?
Why did you set brother against brother?

With self-assured pride, Tychyna confirmed his transformation: 'I've reached my height and strength / I've seen the light in the distance' (*Za Vsikh Skazhu* [I will Speak for All], 1922). He became one of those makers of history and creators of the new Soviet Ukrainian republic: 'We'll move forward – history won't wait. Proletarians! Call to each other in the struggle – The Inter-Republic, the Republic is approaching!'

How can one explain such a radical shift in individual perspective? Perhaps under those circumstances anyone could submit and produce verses to attain the party's approval and hence a chance for survival. And yet, the level of submission could be different. In the case of Tychyna, his transformation was particularly striking but was most likely the result of a deeply ingrained sense of confusion. The Ukrainian national government, which he had supported wholeheartedly, had failed, while the Bolsheviks had brought stabilization and offered much-needed financial support during the most turbulent period of the poet's life. Entries from his diary elucidate possible reasons for this self-reinvention. One such entry from 9 March 1922 reads: 'I don't want to lie, I cannot. I want to live, live at this moment!'[129] Another from that same year suggests how frightened he was for his life: 'I am getting mad at nights. I will still face enough affliction, sorrows, tears and deaths. But now I want to live, because only in such a way I can blossom.' As for his new poetical method, he added: 'I won't find a brave, wise Madonna. And yet the bourgeois (*mishchans'ka*) one I don't want.'[130] It remained unclear, however, whether the 'proletarian Madonna' was the one he was looking for. Later, many critics and biographers linked Tychyna's actions, including his submission to the party, to the primitive fear for his own life.[131] Many contemporaries remembered that Tychyna was paranoid and never expressed his political or ideological views since he feared being placed under surveillance.[132] Ironically, this fear eventually helped him assume the identity of the person he would be for the rest of his life.

Tychyna's transition from the heights of symbolism to propaganda eulogy came as a surprise to many. His new persona was regarded as a betrayal of the national revolution, of his earlier lyrical impressionism and subjective poetry. Unsurprisingly, the greatest reproach came from those Ukrainian critics who had fled abroad. According to Ivan Koshelivets', Tychyna's *Pluh* marked the poet's political turn to the Soviets, and the beginning of an epic transformation of 'a genius poet into an excellent grapho-maniac [*graphoman*]'.[133] Those who praised Tychyna enthusiastically back in 1918 harshly criticized his poems written between 1921 and 1924, often ascribing them to his ideological confusion. In 1924, Khvyl'ovyi, a leader of the Kharkiv group of Ukrainian writers, expressed his concerns about Tychyna's literary evolution in a letter to Zerov. Khvyl'ovyi disagreed with Zerov's assumption that Tychyna 'has come to an end (*perevivsia*)'. Instead, he believed that the poet was 'at his turning point'. Indeed, Khvyl'ovyi continued, some of his latest poetry, 'especially those which smell of *agitka*' were repelling. But he expressed hopes that it was only a temporary matter, since Tychyna was easily swayed by political agendas. Thus, 'we need to be more cautious with him, otherwise *the result might be not the one we expect*.'[134] Here, Khvyl'ovyi spoke on behalf of those artists and art officials in Kharkiv who promoted a national form of proletarian culture and opposed its massovisation and subjugation to the party agenda. They awaited Tychyna, the great poet, among their ranks and regretted to see the degradation of the poet's talent.

What Khvyl'ovyi feared most was that Tychyna, despite his talent and great potential, would become a marionette in the hands of the party propagandists who would continue using him for producing agitation rhymes in support of the central party agenda. Khvyl'ovyi, who by this time had established himself as a leader of the generation of Ukrainian writers who sought to create Soviet Ukrainian literary culture that bypassed Moscow's political and cultural influence, cherished Tychyna greatly, even dedicating one of his early poems to him. As a cultural manager, Khvyl'ovyi wished to see Tychyna become a leading contributor to the new body of literature being created in Soviet Ukraine, which was meant to be both Soviet and Ukrainian. Yet Tychyna lived in Kyiv and had little understanding of the peculiarities inherent to Ukraine's political and cultural revival. Ultimately, he had sided with the political forces, which had brought about the long-awaited peace, unaware that in Kharkiv the battle for the status of Soviet Ukraine and its culture had only just begun.

2

In search of 'a blue Savoy': The Bolshevik revolution in Kharkiv

'I wanted to be a Ukrainian communist'

Mykola Khvyl'ovyi (real name Fitil'ov) was born to a teachers' family in 1893 in the town of Trostianets' in Kharkiv *gubernia* it. His father was descended from a family of impoverished Russian nobility and had sympathized with the *Narodniki*, a middle-class Russian populist movement committed to transforming the empire through enlightening the *narod* – mostly the peasants – on the virtues of a more just, socialist society. Khvyl'ovyi shared his father's interest in the Russian revolutionary movement of the 1860s, and was equally inspired by the works of Nikolai Dobroliubov, Vissarion Belinsky and Dmitrii Pisarev.[1] Later on, however, he recalled his father as 'a complete scatterbrain' and 'a dreamer', who also had a drinking habit.[2] For this reason, the family soon broke up, and his mother took a teaching job elsewhere to provide for her five children. Khvyl'ovyi, however, stayed with his mother's relatives, the family of an impoverished landowner, who encouraged the young Khvyl'ovyi to pursue further education. With his uncle's support, Khvyl'ovyi entered a gymnasium in Bohodukhiv, but was soon asked to leave due to his links to a 'so-called Ukrainian revolutionary circle'.[3] Having been subsequently blacklisted by the authorities for his continued agitation against the regime, Khvyl'ovyi, not wishing to endanger his relatives and hoping to escape possible persecutions, left for Donbas where he scraped a living doing odd jobs at different industrial sites.

In 1914, he was drafted into the Imperial Russian Army at the age of twenty-one and sent to the front the following year as a private. What followed was 'three years of marches, hunger, terrible horror that I would not dare to describe; three years of squared Golgotha on the distant fields of Galicia, Carpathians, Romania and so on and so forth'.[4] He would later recall the grim and dehumanizing realities of war: 'fighting, marches, lice, infantry "straps", – all this I withstood physically, but morally it shattered me. It was the time of spiritual decay. I could not dream of any ideological work, because all I saw was an endless marching line, starvation, the cannons roar, and a grey mass of faceless people. Only in 1916 [...] I finally met some "living" people (*zhyvi liudy*), only then I finally remembered that I am a person after all, and not a loaded rifle.'[5]

By early 1917, Russia was losing the war: morale was low while desertion and fraternization with enemy forces were the norm. At home, high inflation and severe food shortages had resulted in Nicholas II losing the support of both the army and the people. Popular demonstrations against the tsar became widespread. Consequently, news of the monarchy's abolition, and the establishment of the Provisional Government in Petrograd, was enthusiastically received at the frontline. Soviets (councils) of soldiers' deputies were established in the garrisons to control the situation and maintain discipline until the election of a constituent assembly scheduled for November that year. During the February Revolution, Khvyl'ovyi was in Romania. Here he became associated with the Ukrainian SRs, at the time an important force in the Central Rada and served on his division's soldiers' committee. He welcomed the Rada's initiative to create Ukrainian military units within the Russian Army and also participated in organizing *prosvity* [enlightenment societies for literacy, cultural and basic political education] and various peasants' unions to demand the socialization of land.[6] As 1917 wore on, however, he, alongside many other soldiers stationed at the front, started to side with the Bolsheviks, whose demands for immediate peace began to grow in support.

Khvyl'ovyi embraced the revolution wholeheartedly. As observed by O. Gan [Pavlo Petrenko], one of his earlier biographers, the writer 'with distinct expansive ardour threw himself into the abyss of political struggle, which was seething in Ukraine. An enthusiast of the Ukrainian national affairs […], full of political extremism, he became an ardent adherent of a future Ukrainian state, in which questions of national and social emancipation would finally be resolved.'[7] For him, two different revolutionary movements had arisen in Ukraine and Russia. The revolutionary upheaval in Ukraine spurred by the events in Petrograd was yet more profound than in Russia, aimed at achieving both social justice and national liberation. Symbolically, in early 1917, Khvyl'ovyi, a combatant and member of the soldiers' committee, arrived at the congress of soviets in Romania with two ribbons pinned to his collar: one red and one yellow and blue. He offered a simple explanation for his dual political views: 'I wanted to be a Ukrainian Bolshevik.'[8]

The Bolsheviks in Ukraine

Politically, the Bolsheviks in Ukraine started from a marginal position. In 1917, the regional organizations of the RSDRP(b) in Ukraine numbered some 22,000 members, with two-thirds of them being concentrated in the industrial and Russian-speaking Donbas area.[9] These local Bolsheviks were institutionally tied to the Russian Bolshevik party, (RKP[b]) and did not have any independent authority of their own. In addition, they operated with significant military support of the Red Army from Russia. The course of the civil war changed matters. Since December 1917, the nationalist Ukrainian and the Russian Soviet governments were engaged simultaneously in negotiating separate peace treaties with the Central Powers. A treaty between the UNR and its former enemies was signed on 9 February 1918, whereby Germany and Austro-Hungary agreed to provide military support to the new Ukrainian government against

Bolshevik Russia in return for foodstuffs.¹⁰ Hence, when Russian representatives signed the Treaty of Brest-Litovsk with the Central Powers on 3 March 1918, they conceded to conclude peace with the UNR and withdraw their forces from the territory of Ukraine.¹¹ Bound by the treaty's clauses, Russian Bolsheviks could not openly wage war against the German-backed Ukrainian government, whereas a nominally independent Soviet government on Ukraine's territory could engage both the Ukrainian and German occupying armies in combat without breaching the treaty.¹² Although regarded as a tactical concession by many, a separate Soviet Ukrainian government could yield benefits for the Soviet's wider foreign strategy. Thus, on 7 March 1918, the creation of the Ukrainian Socialist Soviet Republic was proclaimed at the All-Ukrainian Congress of Soviets, gathered in Kharkiv.¹³

A separate Soviet republic required a separate leadership. The need to react more quickly to political and military reversals on the ground became even more urgent in spring 1918, when the Bolsheviks had been ousted from power in Ukraine and driven underground by the German and Habsburg occupying forces. On 18–20 April 1918, Bolsheviks from Ukraine met in Taganrog to discuss the possibility of a separate party. The main concerns of the Taganrog meeting were the status of the Communist Party in Ukraine: was it a separate organization or a branch of the Russian Bolshevik party; and should the peasants, who constituted most of Ukraine's population, be seen as a revolutionary class?

Already at Taganrog, two different ideological camps within the Bolsheviks in Ukraine took shape. The so-called Katerynoslav group, headed by Fedor Sergeev (Artem) and Emanuel Kviring, represented the industrial south-eastern provinces. This group rejected the idea of a separate party outright, arguing that Ukraine's revolutionary forces, weakened by the civil war and the Central Powers' military occupation, would not be able to restore Soviet power without the help of the Russian Bolsheviks. Hence, Ukraine's Bolshevik organization should remain part of the all-Russia Bolshevik party. By contrast, the Kyiv group, headed by Georgii Piatakov, promoted the idea for an autonomous Ukrainian Bolshevik party, which would become the vanguard of the oppressed people in Ukraine, especially the revolutionary peasantry. A similar position was articulated by Skrypnyk, an old communist and Lenin's close ally, who was sent to Ukraine to mediate between the two groups. Skrypnyk, who headed the Soviet government in Ukraine between December 1917 and April 1918, sided with those supporting a separate communist party. Unlike Piatakov, who envisaged the central committee of a Ukrainian Bolshevik party as acting under the command of the central committee of the Russian Communist Party, Skrypnyk advocated a Ukrainian party, with its own independent central committee, which would cooperate with the RKP(b) only through an international organization, the envisaged Third International.¹⁴ Of these three proposals, Skrypnyk's one gained the majority of votes at Taganrog, and a separate Communist Party of Bolsheviks of Ukraine – KP(b)U – was established.¹⁵

The creation of the Ukrainian Socialist Soviet Republic and its Communist Party put the Ukrainian radical socialists in a situation when they needed to decide on political alliances. The Ukrainian political left was losing ground; following the German-initiated coup that brought the conservative government of Skoropads'kyi to power, the new government reversed the Rada's socialist programs and launched campaigns against the leftist activists. Many of these remained faithful to the Directory of the UNR, organizing or joining paramilitary and militia units to fight against the German army. One such volunteer unit of Free Cossacks (*vilne kozatstvo*), was formed by Khvyl'ovyi, who had recently returned from the front.[16] Under Khvyl'ovyi's command, the unit actively engaged the UNR and German armies led by the commander of the Armed Forces of Ukraine General Count Fedor Keller.[17] The weakening UNR soon adopted emergency measures to dissolve all Free Cossacks units and an order was issued for Khvyl'ovyi's arrest, which he managed to miraculously escape. Following this incident in early 1919, Khvyl'ovyi, as he later admitted, 'fully accepted the Bolshevik ideology' and joined the party and the Red Army.[18]

Khvyl'ovyi's decision to favour the Bolsheviks reflected a general realignment of forces in the Ukrainian socialist camp. Radicalized socialists, aware of the danger of division among the communist forces during the civil war, sought reconciliation with the Bolsheviks, albeit remaining suspicious of the pro-Russian orientation of the newly established KP(b)U's majority. The *Borot'bysty* expressed their readiness to cooperate with the Bolsheviks, take part in Soviet institutions and share government responsibilities. At first, the Bolsheviks were wary of their fellow revolutionaries, especially those national communists, whom the Bolshevik Larik (Ievgen Kasianenko) labelled 'the worst enemy of the communist revolution in Ukraine'.[19] At its Third Congress (1–6 March 1919), the KP(b)U leadership confirmed its stand against cooperation with the other, nationally oriented, pro-Soviet parties, and refused to allow their representatives to join the Soviet government in Ukraine.[20]

Yet the longer the civil war in Ukraine dragged on, the more concerted effort was made to secure grassroots support and co-opt the support of other leftist parties in the struggle against the common enemy. By early April, the Bolsheviks started to reluctantly consider the possibility of allowing representatives of the left-wing Ukrainian SRs into their government. On 10 May 1919, in view of the advancing Russian Volunteer Army of Denikin, the Bolsheviks finally accepted the repeated demands of the *Borot'bysty* and invited Ukrainian communists to join the Soviet government, where they were given secondary ministerial positions in education (Mykhailychenko, later replaced by Shums'kyi), justice (Mykhailo Lebedynets') and finance (M. Lytvynenko). Nevertheless, in a telegram sent to the head of Soviet government in Ukraine, Khrystian Rakovs'kyi, Lenin instructed him to keep them 'under close Bolshevik supervision'.[21]

Engaging non-Bolsheviks, however, could offer only a temporary solution to the lack of loyal Soviet cadres, hardly any of whom become trustworthy representatives of Bolshevik ideology in the long run. These tactical agreements would not suffice if the Bolsheviks wished to consolidate their power and establish political and social systems that would last beyond the civil war. To achieve this, they needed to change the way the party was perceived in Ukraine. Instead of a Moscow-led occupying military force, it needed to become the embodiment of the revolutionary and national liberationist ideals. By the end of the civil war, it was obvious that the national question in the peripheries of the former empire could not be underplayed and that the party needed to ensure a broad social representation. To attract the 'best' elements of the Ukrainian revolutionary intelligentsia – and their social constituencies – to the Bolshevik project, the party needed to offer a plausible alternative to the 'bourgeois nationalism' of the Ukrainian governments and national communists.

First, they had to be seen to avoid 'chauvinistic' behaviour in Ukraine. The language question was among the most urgent to tackle, since in their first attempts at ruling Ukraine, the Bolsheviks had pursued Russification tactics reminiscent of the former tsarist government. Hence, linguistic and cultural concessions were among the firsts to be agreed upon. The adverse consequences of the republic's earlier 'forced Russification' were highlighted in the draft constitution of the Ukrainian SSR, adopted by the Third All-Ukrainian Congress of Soviets in March 1919.[22] This turn in the national policy in Ukraine was marked by the RKP(b) central committee resolution of late 1919 'On Soviet Rule in Ukraine'. This resolution, adopted after the victory over Denikin's White forces, proclaimed that the RKP(b) was committed to 'removing all barriers to the free development of the Ukrainian language and culture'. The Bolsheviks in Ukraine were instructed to treat the existing nationalist tendencies 'with utmost patience and tact, countering them with a word of comradely explanation of the identity of interests of the toiling masses of Ukraine and Russia'. Ukrainian was declared 'a weapon of communist education of the toiling people' and a tool in establishing 'the closest contact between Soviet institutions and the native peasant population of the country'.[23]

These concessions to nationalist sentiments were dictated by the logic of the civil war. The Bolsheviks were forced to form alliances with local political forces and engage more of the locals who had the necessary linguistic skills within the party's activities. These tactical steps taken by the Bolsheviks blurred the boundaries between the differing communist forces. Hence, it is unsurprising that Khvyl'ovyi, who joined the KP(b)U in April 1919, explained his predisposition by the fact that 'the Bolsheviks went hand in hand with the Ukrainian parties seeking Ukraine's independence'.[24] At the same time, his decision to join the party was influenced by his brother Oleksandr Fitil'ov who had joined a Bolshevik organization in Moscow after his return from the front, and later died in action fighting the Whites in the south of Ukraine.[25] Whatever the reason, Khvyl'ovyi welcomed the 'decentralised power of soviets' and the chance to actively engage in building a new Ukraine.[26]

Until the end of the civil war, Khvyl'ovyi remained within the Red Army's ranks, participating in the campaigns against the White monarchist armies of Denikin and Pyotr Wrangel. During this wartime service, however, he was mainly occupied in the Red Army political department, where he wrote for the army newspaper and worked on military propaganda while also engaging in party work back in Bohodukhiv. Interestingly, Khvyl'ovyi hardly ever spoke about his military past once the war was over. For example, his fellow writer Hryhorii Kostiuk mentioned in his recollections that 'all those hints and allegations about the active connection of the young Khvyl'ovyi with the revolutionary underground, ... his unique heroism and "devilism," - all these are only inventions and legends.'[27] He also remarked that while being a member of Khvyl'ovyi's narrow circle between 1929 and 1933 (a period in which he faced particularly intensive persecution) he never heard any claims of Khvyl'ovyi's heroic biography even though such assertions (if true) could have saved his reputation among the party leadership. A similar account can be found in the memoirs of Petro Shyhymaga, Khvyl'ovyi's friend from Bohodukhiv: 'I would testify that until Khvyl'ovyi had moved to Kharkiv in 1921, in any way was he engaged in politics. He had never spoken of any meetings, Bolshevik or non-Bolshevik gatherings, neither did he

Figure 4 Mykola Khvyl'ovyi, Kharkiv, 1925. © Central State Archive-Museum of Literature and Arts of Ukraine, courtesy of TsDAMLMU.

participate in any of them. He quietly worked in the department of people's education and for the editorial board of a local newspaper, wrote his essays and published them.'[28]

Perhaps the reason for his silence was the same as to why Khvyl'ovyi never spoke of his 'proletarian' past. As he explained in one of his private letters to Zerov:

I am telling you this so you to know what kind of 'a worker' I am. I feel awkward every time some critic promotes me as a member of the proletariat. As if I am 'boasting' of it. Indeed, I was a worker: from the young age and until the imperialist war, I 'loafed about' at factories and brickworks. But still, am I a worker? Had the time been different, I wouldn't have renounced this 'rank'; but now, when everyone is using this 'title' to obtain some benefits – it simply doesn't feel right to be called this way. All that remains from my time at the factory are my 'proletarian' (unrepresentative) appearance; material standing and my contradictious spirit. The rest is hard to define. There used to be a nice word for it – a commoner (*raznochinets*). But unfortunately, now I cannot use it either.[29]

While still in the Red Army, Khvyl'ovyi started writing feuilletons and propaganda pieces under the pen name Stefan Karol' and *Diad'ko* Mykola (Uncle Mykola).[30] He dreamt of a big literary career and this was perhaps the only 'identity' he wanted to be known for.

' … this big but not grand city'

On 19 December 1919, Kharkiv was proclaimed the capital of the newly established Ukrainian Socialist Soviet Republic. From the Bolshevik perspective, Kyiv, the former UNR capital, was a historic centre of 'bourgeois' Ukraine, with its strong links to traditional Ukrainian culture, recent experience of statehood and, among others, proximity to the border with Poland.[31] While Kyiv remained 'old and historic' (*staryi ta istorychnyi*),[32] Kharkiv was viewed as a young and modern city, a centre of the most industrially developed region in the former imperial south. The decision to make Kharkiv, a border provincial city in eastern Ukraine, a Bolshevik stronghold was justified both politically and strategically. First, since the February Revolution, the Bolsheviks had enjoyed considerable public support in this industrial centre. As seen from the election results to the Constituent Assembly held in November 1917, the Bolsheviks emerged as the most popular party with 27.9 per cent of votes.[33] Yet this level of public support alone does not explain the Bolsheviks as a popular preference among the industrial urban populace. Indeed, in comparison to other industrial centres, Kharkiv lagged far behind other industrial centre such as Luhansk and Iuzovo (later Stalino and Donets'k), where the Bolsheviks captured almost 50 per cent of the vote. What defined Kharkiv as a political capital was its strategic advantage: since imperial times, the city had been well connected to its Russian counterparts by rail, becoming closely integrated into the central Russian economy and easily accessible for Red Army troops, a significant advantage amidst the war.

A capital status provided for rapid cultural, socio-economic and political advances in Kharkiv. It became a dream destination for young artists, writers, political activists and intellectual elites from all over Ukraine, wishing to contribute to the creation of Soviet Ukraine and its new proletarian culture.[34] As observed by one contemporary, Kharkiv was 'the centre and pulse of Ukraine's cultural life, industrial Kharkiv [striding towards] modernity, the new capital, the youngest capital of the Universe'.[35] In only a decade, Kharkiv was transformed from a provincial city into a cultural, political and industrial centre showcasing the potential of the new Soviet regime. In the outline of his future novel, one young writer, Maik Iohansen, expressed his fascination with Kharkiv's growth and modernization:

> Kharkiv theme prevails over others mainly because [its development] proves the creative and life-giving potential of the proletariat that has transformed this place from a gathering of merchants into today's industrial colossus. Instead of an old town with dilapidated shacks and huge junkyards, a new and giant city is being built, which stands on a par, or maybe even surpasses, other European cities. ... I don't even mention those grand changes in the way of life, which took place during this time.[36]

While Kharkiv wanted to establish itself as a centre of a new revolutionary culture, and a symbol of a new industrial age, Kyiv remained a conservative cultural capital. Kyivan writers viewed the new centre 'as energetic but undisciplined and anarchic. At best – unexperienced, at worst – militantly vulgar'.[37] Whereas for the writers of Kharkiv, Kyiv remained an important reference point; to be praised, or even mentioned, by Kyivan 'old' masters meant to be accepted in the world of letters. The value of such 'approval from the old school' can be found in the correspondence between Khvyl'ovyi, a young but already well-established Kharkiv proletarian writer, and Zerov, a Kyivan modernist poet and academic. In his letter from 1924, Khvyl'ovyi wrote: 'Thank you for the offer to publish my works in *Slovo* [a Kyiv publishing house]. At the end of this year I should use my acquaintance with you and publish at least something in Kyiv. I need to do this, because Kyiv is Kyiv. And such professors as Plevako [an editor of the academic edition of the Reader of the New Ukrainian Literature, 1923] etc., I heard, don't want to acknowledge me as a writer based on the fact that I have published everything in Kharkiv, and Kharkiv is only Kharkiv, but Kyiv is Kyiv etc. In a word, an unusual explanation; but, to some extent, I agree with it.'[38]

The 1920s boom was enabled by the favourable ideological climate in the republic, when the Soviet political and cultural elites eagerly joined forces to construct a new proletarian Ukrainian culture and foster a modern Ukrainian urban identity. The *Borot'bysty* were at the forefront of those far-reaching plans. By the end of the civil war, however, it had become much harder for the *Borot'bysty* to justify the need for another communist party, given the steps taken by the Bolshevik leaders to incorporate the national question into their party programme. In addition, the *Borot'bysty* believed that the Bolsheviks were ready to reconcile their centralized policy for Ukraine, as illustrated in Lenin's resolution 'On the question of the attitude towards the working people of Ukraine, now liberating themselves from temporary occupation by the Denikin bands' that was widely publicised in late 1919.[39] Conceding to the sentiments of the national communists, Lenin reassured his Ukrainian counterparts that the RKP(b) had no intention on limiting the independence of the Ukrainian SSR. As for the territories relations with the RSFSR, it was stated that it was 'self-evident and generally recognised that only the Ukrainian workers and peasants themselves can and will decide at their All-Ukraine Congress of Soviets whether the Ukraine shall amalgamate with Russia, or whether she shall remain a separate and independent republic, and, in the latter case, what federal ties shall be established between that republic and Russia'.[40]

Moreover, the *Borot'bysty*'s activities had fallen under increased scrutiny by the Communist International (Comintern), the newly created international forum. In August 1919, the *Borot'bysty* passed their memorandum to the Comintern Executive Committee with demands to accept the party to the organization based on their status of a leading communist party in Ukraine.[41] They explained how different Ukraine was from Russia and that the Bolsheviks attempted to impose Russian domination onto Ukraine thereby threatening the success of the revolution. Their application was rejected, however. On 26 February 1920, the Executive Committee passed a resolution accusing the *Borot'bysty* of retreating from the communist principles and confirming that the KP(b)U had sole right to represent the Ukrainian proletariat at the Comintern. This also raised the question regarding the unification of all communist forces in Ukraine into one party.[42]

The *Borot'bysty* abided by the conditions of membership in the Comintern, according to which each country could only be represented by one communist party. This rule, introduced ostensibly 'to maintain the uniformity of the communist movement in each country', made it almost impossible for the *Borot'bysty* to function separately.[43] At the same time, the Comintern was regarded as an ultimate authority in questions of the future communist movement, and whose decisions were decisive. Conversely, the recommendation for a merger was construed as a possibility to continue promoting the *Borot'bysty*'s vision and agenda within the KP(b)U ranks.[44] At the All-Ukrainian Conference of the *Borot'bysty*, held on 14 May 1920, Shums'kyi expressed his support for the merger: 'We will flow together, flood and overflow the Bolsheviks!' (*My zil'iemosia, rozil'iemosia i zal'iemo bil'shovykiv!*).[45]

For the Bolsheviks, the Comintern's intervention provided the opportunity to legally neutralize the *Borot'bysty* rather than resorting to violent suppression. Despite employing the rhetoric of political compromise, the party's leadership remained suspicious of their rival and never truly believed in their pro-Soviet orientation. In his Draft Resolution on the Ukrainian *Borot'bysty* Party, dated from 6 February 1920, Lenin defined the *Borot'bysty* 'as a party, which, by its propaganda aimed at splitting the military forces and supporting banditism, is violating the basic principles of communism, thereby playing directly into the hands of the Whites and of international imperialism'.[46] It was concluded that the KP(b)U 'must systematically and steadily aim for the dissolution of the *Borot'bysty* in the near future. To this end, not a single misdeed on the part of the *Borot'bysty* should be allowed to pass without being immediately and strictly punished. In particular, information should be collected concerning the non-proletarian and most disloyal nature of the majority of their party members'.[47]

Consequently, the *Borot'bysty* party self-liquidated in March 1920, with around 4,000 former members being admitted into the KP(b)U on an individual basis.[48] In the short-term, this unification of the leading communist parties proved mutually beneficial. The Bolsheviks had eliminated an important political rival, subsumed many of the national communists in the Soviet bureaucracy and governmental institutions, and had been able to exploit their organizational structures and networks for Bolshevik party work. Most importantly, through the *Borot'bysty* the Bolsheviks were granted access to the Ukrainian-speaking countryside. At a KP(b)U meeting held on 17–23 March 1920, Stalin acknowledged the significance of this merger with the

Ukrainian communists: 'Up to now our work in Ukraine was crippled [...] because it was nurtured by the urban proletariat only. We limped on one leg because we had no or only a very weak link with the countryside. [...] Only now, after the merger with our comrades *Borot'bysty*, we will ensure a strong bond between the city proletariat and the village.'[49] In their turn, the Ukrainian communists were granted an opportunity to further promote Ukraine's autonomy and cultural development from within the ranks of the ruling party.

The influence of the former *Borot'bysty* was especially significant in the cultural sphere, which the Bolsheviks had neglected in the frenzy of the civil war. Following the merger, the former *Borot'bysty* Ellan-Blakytnyi and Shums'kyi entered the KP(b)U Central Committee, with the former also acquiring a seat in the Politburo. Panas Liubchenko became the Central Committee Secretary for Culture and editor-in-chief of the party newspaper *Kommunist*.[50] Soon the *Borot'bysty* had also taken control of the *Narkomos* and the *Vseukrlitkom*, a government agency in charge of the arts. In May 1919, the *Narkomos* was handed over to the *Borot'bysty* leader, the poet Mykhailychenko, who was succeeded by Mykhailo Panchenko, Shums'kyi and Hryhorii Hryn'ko.[51] Under the auspices of the *Narkomos*, an All-Ukrainian Publishing House (*Vsevydav*) was established in May 1919. *Vsevydav*, later renamed into the State Publishing House of Ukraine (*Derzhavne Vydavnytstvo Ukrainy*, *DVU* or *Derzhvydav*), and enjoyed a privileged position in distributing printed material on the territory of Soviet Ukraine.

Indeed, throughout the early 1920s, almost all cultural activities in Soviet Ukraine were managed by former *Borot'bysty*. Through their support, *Vseukrlitkom* made daring attempts to gather Ukrainian writers around the first Soviet-sponsored Ukrainian-language literary journal *Mystetstvo* [Art], edited by Blakytnyi and Mykhailychenko from 1919 to 1920; and later around its new publication *Shliakhy mystetstva* [The Paths of Art], published from 1920 to 1923. The former *Borot'bysty* also oversaw the leading Ukrainian monthly *Chervonyi Shliakh* [Red Path] and the party biweekly *Bil'shovyk Ukrainy* [The Bolshevik of Ukraine]. In the summer of 1921, Blakytnyi became the editor of the major daily governmental newspaper *Visti VUTsVK* [VUTsVK News], turning it into a pillar of Ukrainian life in Kharkiv. The newspaper covered republican, all-Union and world news, as well as publicizing official party pronouncements and commentaries. In addition, *Visti* included weekly cultural supplements, *Literatura, Nauka, Mystetstvo* [Literature, Science and Arts], which appeared in 1923–4, and *Kul'tura i Pobut* [Culture and the Everyday Life], 1924–8, which provided a forum for new Ukrainian literature and cultural debates.

In 1921, Khvyl'ovyi, having served 'seven-plus years in the Imperial and the Red Armies',[52] also made his way to Kharkiv where he quickly joined the circle of Ellan-Blakytnyi, who inducted the young writer into the city's artistic and intellectual milieu. A Ukrainian speaker, Khvyl'ovyi easily found a job in the Soviet apparatus, joining the Central Bureau of Political and Educational Work, *Golovpolitosvita*, and taking up work at the editorial house of *Chervonyi Shliakh*. However, these roles, while offering Khvyl'ovyi stable employment, did not fully satisfy him. He wanted to have a literary career and become a poet, like the famous Tychyna to whom he dedicated some of his early poetry. Soon after his arrival in Kharkiv, Khvyl'ovyi published two

Figure 5 Mykola Khvyl'ovyi and Valeriian Polishchuk, Kharkiv, 1925. © Central State Archive-Museum of Literature and Arts of Ukraine, courtesy of TsDAMLMU.

poetry collections – *Molodist'* [Youth] in 1921 and *Dosvitni Symfonii* [Symphonies of the Dawn] in 1922; both went virtually unnoticed. As the contemporary critic Koriak explained: 'Mykola Khvyl'ovyi is ornate (*kucheriavyi*), capricious, incomprehensible for our audience, complicated and refined.'[53]

Khvyl'ovyi, like many other young writers, responded eagerly to the call for dynamic and progressive art; he anticipated a new proletarian culture that would fully reflect on the new reality. In this, he stood on the same side as the Proletkult – a mass movement founded in 1917 in Russia by the Bolshevik Alexander Bogdanov that aimed to ensure a proletarian dictatorship in the cultural sphere that could stand against the alien culture of the bourgeoisie. The organization was characterized by its nihilistic attitude towards the traditions and culture of the past and believed in collective artistic production. Proletkult, as a name suggests, was a cultural organization for the proletariat; the movement strived to protect its pure proletarian essence and adhered to class as the defining principle of their organization.[54] It expanded rapidly during the civil war and by the time of its dissolution in late 1920, gradually grew into a mass organization with half a million followers, boasting thirty-four journals and about 300 organizations across the Soviet territory.[55] Already, in late 1918, the first Proletkult organizations were established in Ukraine, and in May 1919 a branch was opened in Kyiv.[56] The Proletkult's members gained influence in the *Vseukrlitkom* and made *Zori hriadushchoho* [Starts of the Future], a literary almanac established in 1918 by the pro-Bolshevik writers, their official organ after its third issue. However, their activities were impeded by the fact that the Proletkult's leaders were determined to make class their only organizing principle, whereas national Proletkult organizations pushed for broader consideration to national differences within the movement.[57]

To improve the image of Proletkult in Ukraine, a separate organizational committee was formed in Kharkiv in the autumn of 1921, tasked with uniting all Proletkult centres in Ukraine into a single All-Ukrainian Union of Proletarian Creative Forces.[58] Nonetheless, this organization was regarded as yet another national minorities section within the all-Russian Proletkult. According to a Soviet source, Proletkult 'did not only fail to acknowledge Ukrainian national art, culture or language, but referred to the [Ukrainian] Soviet Republic as a "region" [*krai*]'.[59] With so little autonomy, Proletkult could hardly become a platform for Ukrainian proletarian literature. It lost its appeal even among those pro-Soviet Ukrainian writers who were sympathetic to its cause of bolstering the cultural potential of the proletariat. In his 'Theses on the New Proletarian Art', published in 1919, the Commissar for Education and a *Borot'bysty* member Mykhailychenko emphasized the importance of a national way towards 'proletarian culture':

> New proletarian art is the art of labour ... Proletarian culture aims to be mass-oriented, so one can define it using a slogan – culture to the street ... In creating proletarian art, more than the word itself, the language in which this word is being said is important. While red international living language remains its beacon, we need to highlight that the path to it lies only through national languages ... proletarian culture can reach its international essence only through channels national both in content and form.[60]

While unhappy with Proletkult, Ukrainian pro-Soviet writers made several attempts to establish their own 'organization of the October literature' [*zhovtneva literatura*]. Already in late 1921, the group *Zhovten'* [October] was formed, comprising Khvyl'ovyi, Sosiura and Iohansen. The group's manifesto, *Nash Universal* [Our Universal], defined their vision of a new proletarian literature created in Soviet Ukraine. Similar to Proletkult, *Zhovten* rejected previous Ukrainian literature in terms of artistic expression and formal innovations, dedicating itself to instead creating literature that would satisfy the demands of the proletariat, the new victorious social class. Yet unlike its pan-Soviet counterpart, this new movement highlighted the importance of the Ukrainian language, regarded as a link between the workers and 'their thousand-year-long history and their ancestors – the Ukrainian peasantry'.[61] Those were the principles that laid the foundation for a new literary organization – the All-Ukrainian Federation of Proletarian Writers and Artists (*Vseukrains'ka Federatsiia Proletars'kykh Pys'mennykiv ta Myttsiv*) initiated by Khvyl'ovyi in January 1922. This organization saw its task as a 'search for directions to proletarian culture' and 'the education of the masses in a proletarian spirit'.[62] The All-Ukrainian Federation was, however, short-lived, and its only success was a single issue of their journal *Arena*, published in 1922.[63]

'New unknown outset is coming'

In 1923, Khvyl'ovyi published his first prosaic collection entitled *Syni Etiudy* [Blue Etudes]. Unlike his two previous collections, *Syni Etiudy* was an immediate success.

Reviewing the book, Koriak was overwhelmingly positive, describing it as 'Genuinely: Khvyl'ovyi.[64] He is excited and excites us all, he intoxicates and disquiets, irritates, weakens, captivates and fascinates. [...] He scourges anything that is corrupt in the revolution, looks for it everywhere in the name of his beloved idea – Communism, the idea he had accepted wholeheartedly both as an ascetic and a romanticist.'[65] His second collection *Osin'* [Autumn], published in 1924, cemented his fame as 'one of the most outstanding writers of the proletarian age'.[66]

In his early prose, Khvyl'ovyi rejected the Proletkult's approach of 'producing proletarian art'. Instead, he encouraged experimentation with form and style and defended artistic freedom. He called himself 'a romanticist', 'a dreamer', who 'madly adore[s] sky, herbs, stars, thoughtful evenings, soft mornings in autumn with its crimson-feathered woodcocks flying somewhere [...], – all different smells of our mournfully-joyful motley lifetime'.[67] Even more so, Khvyl'ovyi was obsessed with the revolution; he believed in the 'commune behind the hills' which he anticipated 'so desperately, that I can die'. He also admired 'our Ukrainian steppes through which the blue storm of the civil combat flashed by'.[68] This fascination with the revolution and its potential shaped Khvyl'ovyi's own peculiar artistic and literary manner – 'romantic *vitaism*', as he believed, was the only literary style able to render the romanticism of the revolution and its heroes:

> Hence, the time of Romantic *vitaism*, the epoch of civil wars. Hence, its artistic nature is militant 'idealism' (in parentheses) of the young class, the proletariat. Hence, its perspectives are to play the role of a field marshal in the future battles on the barricades.[69]

This romantic *vitaism* was the complete opposite to realism, a widely accepted method of proletarian literature at the time. First, he believed that proletarian literature was not yet ready for realism since the goals of the revolution – the complete awakening of proletariat and its creative potential – had not yet been achieved. Second, realistic methods could not be used to depict the post-revolutionary reality that did not yet correspond to the ideals of the revolution.

Khvyl'ovyi radically influenced post-revolutionary prose by opposing traditional storytelling approaches. His narration was non-linear, tangling his storylines with philosophical reflections, lyrical digressions, first-person interventions and satirical insertions.[70] He easily moves among the stylistic modes, experiments with surrealistic and expressionistic tropes; his prose is ornamentalistic and deeply psychological. To develop his characters, Khvyl'ovyi drew extensively on his own first-hand experience of the civil war. The device of his first-person voice erases the boundaries between the author and his characters, raising doubts in authorial distance from the plot, implying, to some extent, an autobiographical manner to Khvyl'ovyi's writing. Because of this, many literary scholars suggested that Khvyl'ovyi's creative writing is highly self-referential, or 'autothematic', as George Grabowicz put it.[71] His fictional world became 'an objectification of the narrator's internal world, of his feelings and perceptions, forming a vaguely internal landscape and bestowing a lyrical dimension upon most of Khvyl'ovyi's early stories.'[72] Much of his prose, such as *Vstupna novela* [The Introductory Novelette] (1927)[73], *Na ozera* [To the Lakes] (1926) and *Arabesky* [Arabesques] (1927), could hardly even be categorized as fiction.[74]

The autobiographical nature of Khvyl'ovyi's imaginative literature allows us to reflect on the generation of the revolution and the civil war, whose experiences he had known only too well. This chapter draws on Khvyl'ovyi's fictional characters to analyse the evolution of the writer's own understanding of the revolution and the peacetime reconstruction. He created a palette of revolutionary heralds and ordinary people, party functionaries and bureaucrats, both in the time of the revolutionary upheaval and post-revolutionary everydayness. Most of his characters, however, appear in limbo between the bygone revolution and the communist utopia, which is yet to come. As recent scholarship on Soviet youth has shown, for many young militants the regime that emerged out of the revolutionary struggle was a betrayal of the promises of 1917.[75] The following textual analysis of Khvyl'ovyi's fiction provides another angle to examining the attitudes of young communists and revolutionary militants during the civil war and the transitionary period to peacetime that followed.

Khvyl'ovyi introduced and widely promoted a heroic myth of the revolution and the civil wars in Ukrainian literature. Similar to his Russian counterparts, he anticipated the revolution and the changes it would initiate.[76] His revolution was a cardinal shift, a rebellion against triviality, a call for action and purification from old false morality. He described it as being 'without buttons, with elbow room, room to stretch oneself, to draw a lung-filling breath in the wide-open spaces'.[77] His expectations from those turbulent years are condensed in such metaphors as a 'blue Savoy', an 'intangible commune', or a 'commune behind the hills'. Khvyl'ovyi's revolution is universal, boundless in its meaning and scale. See, for instance, his description in *Synii Lystopad* [Blue November] (1923):

> Tomorrow we will open a blue book of eternal lyrics – universal, blue.
> This is the revolution.
>   Could the communards forget about this day? Isn't it a majestic poetry? We plunge into a blue anxious night, our reflections disperse [...]
>   And we are hovering above the earth full of dreams, distant.[78]

In *Chumakivs'ka Komuna* [Chumak's Commune] (1923):

> Do broadcast further: Chumak's commune is saluting into the frost: Long live the World Revolution.
>   And the frost replies: Hurrah! Hurrah! Hurrah![79]

Or in *Syliuety* [Silhouettes] (1923):

> The boyans of the unknown communes are on the road under the glow of the setting sun singing an evening prayer.
>   ... Glory to the revolutionary peaks and joy to the earth.[80]

The same optimism and admiration are granted to a socialist Ukraine. For Khvyl'ovyi, as for many revolutionary contemporaries, the revolution had a modernizing potential that included universal equality, overcoming cultural and social backwardness and mass mobilization. In addition, he believed that the revolution would lead to national awakening and eventually to a separate statehood. These expectations were put into words in Khvyl'ovyi's short stories through the writer's first-person voice:

> And Ukraine is striving upwards ... And I love her – Bolshevik Ukraine – brightly, violently ...[81]
>
> My beloved socialist Ukraine! Steppes, a black kite, and summer sun is moving off the skyline, and right behind, a milky path is singing white, or maybe, crimson songs, cows are mooing, plodding from the pastures – farther and farther. Farms, electric ploughs ... cars, factories, plants ... Ah! And farther and farther.[82]

This was also evident through the words of his characters, as, for instance, in *Liliuli* (1923):

> amidst traffic noise someone opened his sentimental eyes and shouted noiselessly – in despair or in madness, – one cannot tell:
> ... – o my beautiful land beyond the horizon!
> I believe! I believe so profoundly, so unbearably [...]. I believe![83]

Most of his short stories are deeply psychological, bringing to the fore unsystematic individual reflections on the events. It seems that for Khvyl'ovyi there was no insignificant personal experience during those turbulent times. As stated by Iurynets', the key to understanding Khvyl'ovyi's perception of the social (dis)order is his 'adoration of the intemperate, vigorous, mass, *ahistorical* people's element [...] that should be considered as a biological and physiological (*biolohichno-phisiolohichnyi*) experience, and not as a social fact'.[84] Hence, the social and political turbulence of the time serves only as a background for his characters' lived experiences. Overall, Khvyl'ovyi is more interested in the way the revolution had impacted on the lives of the ordinary people, leaving its grand social and ideological achievements aside.

His revolutionary myth originated in the chaotic, heroic and promissory ambience of the civil wars. The irrational belief in the glorious future becomes the attribute of Khvyl'ovyi's romanticists. As with Sten'ka, the main character of the folklore-style story *Lehenda* [The Legend] (1923), these romanticists were ready to abandon triviality, join the revolutionary struggle and sacrifice their lives for the cause of revolution:

> Listen! Listen! I am dying in the name of freedom. I appeal to you: sharpen the knives. Look, look at the glow: that is our liberation blazing; new unknown outset is coming![85]

Most of his characters are driven into revolution by personal motives. In a either sarcastic manner or with earnest sympathy, Khvyl'ovyi presents different reasons for a future communist affiliation. Here, however, ideology does not play a significant part. Except for certain cases, such as Vadym (*Synii Lystopad*), Mariana (*Zaulok* [Blind-Alley], 1923) or Kark (*Redactor Kark*, 1923), the decision to support the Bolsheviks seems irrational, stipulated or even personally loaded. Some were swayed into joining the civil battles by revenge, as, for instance, the deacon from a poor parish, whose seminary was closed down due to the lack of state funding (*Bandyty* [Bandits], 1930); or by revolutionary propaganda, as Veronika (*Syliuety*), who 'herself resembled a variegated placard'.

Khvyl'ovyi's depictions of some of the female characters' motives evoke a particular sense of irony. Oksana, a main character in *Zhyttia* [Life] (1922), 'did not like communists, the whole village did not like them, but in Myshko's eyes there was love, and she started loving communists'.[86] Another example can be found in the anecdote from *Liluli*:

> A spinster is sitting on the veranda, crying. 'Why are you crying?' – then she complains, that she, so to speak, until forty was innocent, like a tear, but now she was seduced by a doctor from one health resort (on this very veranda!) and he spoiled her forever. How horrible! Do you hear: forever! So she decided to head to the capital city and to learn the *kapebeu* [KP(b)U] programme, because who will take her now ... ah? Who needs her?[87]

Whatever the reasons, that 'wild and anxious' revolution had transformed all those 'naked and hungry' people into 'titans and gods'.[88] Those people felt they were involved in a historical change – a creation of a better life and the new world.[89] The shared experience of the civil war contributed to the feeling of a shared belonging, as described by Comrade Uliana, one of the characters of the *Sentymental'na Istoriia* [Sentimental Tale] (1928):

> Heavens! You cannot imagine what a wonderful country it was. Under its sun, not only the inner world of each one of us was transformed and we were made ideal, but we were physically born anew. I swear to you! Even physically we were ideal men and women.[90]

Khvyl'ovyi glorified the revolution's potential to transform people and places. Yet, of greater importance to him was the complicated process of conforming to ideological standards and adapting an entire generation of revolutionary youth and civil war activists to the post-revolutionary reality that was no longer reminiscent of the values they were ready to sacrifice their lives for. Each and every romanticist in Khvyl'ovyi's prose was capable of mastering the revolutionary element because it was close, it felt feasible, it was right there, 'behind the hills'. But as the days ensued, that 'blue Savoy' did not come any closer. With time, the bliss of the revolutionary struggle and the 'commune behind the hills' faded away and the revolutionary heralds woke up into the day, when the cannons fell silent. Khvyl'ovyi's most famous short story *Ia (Romantyka)* [My self (Romanticism)] (1924) presents this particular moment of realizing that the heroic deeds of the revolution were nothing more but violence committed in the name of an illusion.

At the centre of the novel is a provincial Cheka: 'the dark tribunal of the commune'.[91] The Cheka consists of four members: the 'evil genius, my evil will' doctor Tahabat; the 'unhappy communard' Andriusha; the 'faithful guard of the Revolution' *Dehenerat*;

and the nameless head of the revolutionary '*troika*', of this 'new Sanhedrin' *Ia*. *Ia* became perhaps the most tragic character of Khvyl'ovyi's prose. He suffers from a split personality; he is torn between his fanatic self, exacerbated by the civil war, and his other, more human self: 'I am a Chekist, but still I remain a human being.'⁹² This being said, *Ia* embodies the entire generation empowered by the civil war. He stood for countless 'rebellious sons' – hence, nameless – who were about to bring the revolution 'from a distant misty region, from the calm lakes of the intangible Commune'. Instead: 'everything disappears […] and the day darkens'.⁹³

Ia continuously questions his duties, which involve issuing death sentences to numerous 'heterodoxies': 'I, a complete stranger, a bandit, according to one terminology, an insurgent, according to another.'⁹⁴ After another night of sombre decisions, the Chekist recalls the lives he took away:

Six on my conscience?
No, it is not true. Six hundred, six thousand, six million – numberless hosts are on my conscience!
Numberless hosts?!'⁹⁵

At first, the Chekist manages to retain his sanity thanks to his mother, 'the prototype-incarnate of that extraordinary Maria'. His memory of her 'simplicity, silent grief, and boundless kindness'⁹⁶ helps the Chekist harness his fanaticism. Eventually, however, his weak will and hesitations subdue. As the Bolsheviks are about to surrender the town to another military power, the Chekist, in 'extraordinary ecstasy', faces his final duty: to decide the fate of a group of nuns, accused of agitating against the commune. His mother, 'my sorrowing mother with the eyes of Maria', is one of those awaiting a sentence. But the verdict must be executed, and doctor Tahabat agitates: 'Not so loud, you, traitor to the Commune! See that you arrange matters with "mother", same as you have with others.'⁹⁷ Now his loyalty is at stake. In the place 'where sadism presides',⁹⁸ the choice seems obvious. *Ia* is already possessed with his 'evil genius' and he leads his mother to the execution: 'Mother! Come to me, I tell you; for I must kill you!'⁹⁹

On the face of it, the conflict in *Ia (Romantyka)* lies between professional duty and personal attachments. The main character must decide what price he is willing to pay for the sake of those revolutionary ideals, which he had once ardently believed in, for those 'peaceful lakes of the Commune behind the hills'. The image of *Ia* offers a painful confession of a revolutionary, whose 'intangible distance' had been transformed beyond recognition: 'Once more, painfully, I feel like falling to my knees and looking pleadingly at the crude silhouette of the dark tribunal of the Commune.'¹⁰⁰ To enforce a death penalty on his mother is more than fulfilling his duty, it means a final acceptance of the new reality, to join other builders of the socialist future in time, when each and every romantic idea of the revolution became compromised, discredited and devalued.

The publication of this fictional story provoked a scandal after Khvyl'ovyi had presented it at a literary evening in Kyiv.¹⁰¹ Many readers and critics alike were convinced that *Ia (Romantyka)* was based on the author's own experience. Some even went as far as to suggest that he himself was that Chekist who killed his mother in the name of 'the commune behind the hills'.¹⁰² Another, albeit lesser known, short

Figure 6 A meeting between the writers from Kyiv and Kharkiv. Kyiv, 1923. © Central State Archive-Museum of Literature and Arts of Ukraine, courtesy of TsDAMLMU.

story, *Podiaka Pryvatnoho Likaria* [Gratitude of the Private Doctor, 1932],[103] further enflamed the controversy that now surrounded Khvyl'ovyi's past. In this short story, one of the protagonists confesses to killing a doctor from the Hetman's Army during the civil war. While no primary sources to date can confirm the author's involvement in the Bolshevik's wartime repression, he did possess first-hand knowledge of the Cheka's inner workings which he could have used while composing his fiction. During Denikin's offensive in the summer of 1919, Khvyl'ovyi, a member of the Red Army at the time, was rescued from a death sentence by a young female communist and a local Cheka member, Iuliia Umantseva, who would soon become his second wife.[104] His sister, Valentyna Fitiliova, also worked in the Kharkiv Cheka, which she joined as a typist in 1921. Khvyl'ovyi himself never spoke about his wartime experience, preferring to tell fictional stories of those turbulent years, though his characters offer 'only a scrap of the truth and the whole truth – would be the whole revolution', as he evasively explained.[105]

'Maybe this is the end; those sons of a bitch have swallowed our revolution'

When the civil war came to an end in 1921, the Bolsheviks remained the only party able to consolidate their power over the former Russian empire. They found themselves in charge of a huge country, devastated by war and revolution. The civil war and the introduction of 'war communism', a set of radical emergency measures introduced by the Bolsheviks in order to aid the Red Army during the civil war, had led to industrial collapse, overall economic degradation, the famine of 1921–2, urban depopulation and frequent social unrest. Politically, even in Russian society, Bolshevik rule had often little to no legitimacy or public support. Besides the resentful peasantry, agitated by constant grain requisitioning and state monopoly on trade, the proletariat and the Red Army units were ready to turn their backs on the party, as illustrated by the major anti-Bolshevik uprising of sailors, soldiers and workers at the Kronstadt naval base in 1921. While the Bolsheviks had won the civil war, the future of their promised proletarian dictatorship was under threat. The speed of social transformation needed to be adjusted to match the socio-economic conditions of the former empire.[106]

In 1921, Lenin launched the New Economic Policy (NEP): a series of ad hoc initiatives introduced in the hopes of stabilizing the country and reviving the economy. Food requisitioning was brought to an end while wartime state monopolies were eliminated with the population permitted to engage in some elements of a capitalist economy, such as private trade and production. This policy saw a partial return to a market economy and wide acceptance of bourgeois culture. The introduction of NEP, with its retreats in the economic sphere, further party centralization and ideological pluralism disappointed the expectations and aspirations of many revolutionaries and military activists. Indeed, for many, it seemed as if the socialist dream had been postponed indefinitely.

In his early fiction, Khvyl'ovyi exposed the obvious mismatch between revolutionary expectations and the reality of life under the NEP; he also suggested the transformation of Soviet power into a highly centralized and exclusive social order. The Bolsheviks had seized power under the revolutionary slogan 'All Power to the Soviets', yet these non-bureaucratic institutions, soviets and factory committees had proven incapable of exercising power in the newly created Soviet republics and had almost disappeared by the mid-1920s. Instead of a workers' democracy, a centralist bureaucratic institution, a cabinet of ministers (people's commissars) – *Sovnarkom* (and *Radnarkom* in Ukrainian) – had simply replaced the Provisional Government. Sequentially, the elected local Soviets comprising soldiers' and workers' deputies had been superseded by executive committees with permanently appointed staff, giving rise to a state-wide Soviet bureaucracy. While Lenin had called for the abolition of bureaucracy in his famous 1917 April theses, by 1921, the Bolshevik leader was ready to reconcile: 'You can throw out the tsar, throw out the landowners, throw out the capitalists ... but you cannot "throw out" bureaucracy in a peasant country you can only *reduce* it by slow and stubborn effort.'[107]

The Bolshevik party was itself becoming bureaucratic and conservative. With time, instead of a vanguard of the world proletariat, it became, in Khvyl'ovyi's words, 'Your state party',[108] an autocratic institution built around the principles of democratic centralism, permitting relative freedom of democratic debate in return for unity, strict discipline and subordination to the central leadership. The first purge of party ranks was already launched in the aftermath of the Tenth RKP(b) Congress (8–16 March 1921), targeting those 'petty bourgeois' elements 'not trained in the Communist spirit'.[109] As reported at the KP(b)U party congress in December 1921, the party purge resulted in the expulsion of some 22.5 per cent of all the KP(b)U members.[110] Instead, the enrolment of proletarian cadres was prioritized.

Within his fiction, Khvyl'ovyi also criticized frequent abuses of power. Against the expectations of those revolutionaries, the victory in the civil war did not bring about a just socialist society. Instead, the promised dictatorship of the proletariat was replaced by the dictatorship of the Bolshevik party. Soviet power started resembling an arbitrary rule, as Khvyl'ovyi presented in *Kolonii, Vily* [Colonies, villas] (1923): 'The Bolshevik authority, for you to know, is not a backed meadow-mushroom. It means will and freedom. When you are stuffing your jaw, then do not obscure the others' (1923).[111] In *Shliakhetne Hnizdo* (1923), Khvyl'ovyi compared the early Bolshevik society to the 'time of trouble', a reference to the period of Russian history dominated by rival groups of elites and political chaos at the turn of the seventeenth century:

> I do not understand, father Polikarp, what is the matter. My forest, and my meadows, and my land were taken away. Is there a law?
> The person emptied a glass and loudly, to be heard outside the window, to be heard by everyone:
>   - The law, grandpa. The Bolshevik law.
> And then, he leaned forward the grandpa's ear and, looking around, murmured:
>   - Babel pandemonium. Time of Trouble in Rus. This is what it is. Do you understand? That's what it is.[112]

Painfully, Khvyl'ovyi concluded that the revolution 'had slipped into a lavatory bowl filled with excrement' (1926).[113] He was utterly disappointed with the reality and the transformation of the Communist Party and society in general: 'Maybe this is the end; those sons of a bitch have swallowed our revolution' (1923).[114]

'Lenin repeats only once in five hundred years'

The revolution was wholeheartedly welcomed by many revolutionary fanatics, militant youth, political activists and dreamers who believed in the possibility of the new world of tomorrow. Very soon, however, these fanatics witnessed their revolutionary dreams withheld and the old customs reinforced. Khvyl'ovyi represented the generation of those who had anticipated Ukraine's socialist future and felt betrayed by the failure to respond to their ideals. Through his fictional characters, Khvyl'ovyi represented the feeling of those betrayed fanatics, as well as the different ways of coping with the dissatisfactory social atmosphere created by the NEP. While some, frustrated, disenchanted and even traumatized with the experience chose resignation and even suicide, others managed to adapt to the situation and fit in seamlessly with the new regime.

For many revolutionaries and those recently demobilized from the Red Army, it was extremely difficult to return to civilian life under the NEP. Not only did they find themselves adrift in the 'quietness' of everyday life, they also needed to accept a new code of behaviour, to put up with the old routine and adjust to re-established social boundaries and limitations. Khvyl'ovyi exemplifies the difficulty of going back to normal life through the fictional character of Iurko, the main character of the novel of the same name (1922). When the war ended, Iurko was expected to return to his workbench in a factory in Donbas. What he found there, however, was 'twilight, daily routine, and sadness, same as before the revolution'. He cannot bear the post-war humdrum: 'Without revolution, when there is no creativity, life is passing by boringly, monotonously.'[115] He is trying to escape this everydayness; he is seeking the same excitement he felt while on the battlefield: 'Why I am not allowed to go abroad? I can attempt Poincare's life. I was born for explosions [...]. I still hear the cannons.'[116]

For these militant youth, the regime that emerged out of the revolutionary struggle represented an altogether different kind of a socialist society, opposite to the one they envisaged on the fields of the civil wars. Hence, many of them suffered from revolutionary melancholy. They longed for a return to the time of excitement, unlimited freedom, when a bright future felt close and feasible. Khvyl'ovyi renders this feeling of despondency through one of his female characters in *Sentymental'na Istoriia*:

> The thing is that you never played Eva's part and you cannot long for paradise, as myself or as thousands of those broken down by the civil war, do. [...] You have never been on the other side, and you do not know a thing. Only we were driven away from there. That is why we are living in longing.[117]

Although disillusioned and frustrated with the NEP, most, however, had not given up faith in communism as an ideology. Vadym (*Synii Lystopad*) is one such optimist who is continuously idealistic about 'an ever better future'. A former brigade commissar, he is dying from tuberculosis and, although aware of the 'tragedies of our age', he believes in the future triumph of his ideals:

> I, myself am also a romanticist. And the romance is: I am in love with a commune. [...] This requires years, millions of years! Yes, Maria, all is needed as it is. And this all-federative philistinism, and tragedies at hearts of some individuals, and bureaucratism. Finally, we need to stop [...] I am looking at our contemporaneity from the 25th century ... That is why I am so much in love with it. You do not hear this, but I hear how a commune is marching through our houses. Solemnly, it proceeds from one house to another, and only blind men cannot notice this. But my offspring will make a note, I believe. And what are our tragedies against this great symphony towards the future?[118]

Most of Khvyl'ovyi characters are disorientated, sometimes traumatized, often disappointed with and alienated from the socio-political reality. As the euphoria of making revolution wore off, they found themselves groundless, disconnected from time and space. This shared resentment about the present and their anxiety about the future motivated the decision of many young people to put an end to their lives. Unsurprisingly, suicide became common among the most disenchanted to the extent that the authorities started talking about 'the epidemic of self-murder'.[119]

Such suicidal despair was provoked by an idealized remembrance of the past and its unbridgeable distance from the present. Most painfully, many former activists' lives seemed bereft of hope. Like Khvyl'ovyi's young dreamers, they had realized that another chance for a revolution would not come since 'Lenin repeats only once in five hundred years.'[120] Taking their lives, instead, is regarded as a way to prove their former integrity. This was the choice taken by *Redactor Kark*'s titular character, or Mariana (the character in *Zaulok*), who decided to get herself infected with syphilis, since 'this is how a Chekists from the past would act'.[121]

Scholars have noted that the introduction of the NEP created outsiders from those who were previously very much on the inside. Among the most frustrated were perhaps those Red Army soldiers and Bolshevik veterans, who were quickly demobilized and sent back to civilian life. The loss of the privileged status that those militants and activists enjoyed during the civil war contributed to the overall sense of betrayal and exacerbated their disappointment.[122] In the case of juveniles, the decision to commit suicide often stemmed more from concrete experiences of social exclusion and isolation than general disillusionment and pessimism under NEP.[123]

Khvyl'ovyi magnified this feeling of social exclusion and isolation by gathering his uprooted and disenchanted revolutionary romanticists in a sanatorium for 'patients with mental disorder' (*Povist' pro Sanatoriinu Zonu* [A Tale of a Sanatorium], 1924). The topos of a 'sanatorium' has a twofold meaning in this novel. All those confined within the sanatorium's walls failed to comprehend the paradoxical world of the NEP and find their niche in peacetime. Complexity and confusion in the early 1920s make them long for the 'simple arithmetic of the Revolution' – a simplified friend–enemy categorization used to unify all those who fought on the side of the Bolsheviks.[124] By rejecting the NEP, they had become phantom souls whose 'false idealism' is deemed dangerous for new Soviet citizens. As suggested by Khvyl'ovyi, they were now socially superfluous and incompatible with the new socialist society.[125]

At the same time, this confined space can be regarded as a model for socialist society, and the Soviet state itself, where each character presented a type, every interaction contained a statement, and every decision has a universal meaning.[126] Among those revolutionary fanatics trapped in the sanatorium, being unable to fit in in the outside world, are *anarkh* – an anarchist with a 'hairy nature', a former leader of a Ukrainian peasant revolt who 'burned a black banner and bravely unfurled a red-crimson one'; Khlonia – a betrayed Communist idealist; and the typesetter (*metranpazh*) Karno – a mysterious figure and 'provincial Mephistopheles', wild and violent, who is incarcerated for the murder of his wife's lover. They are supervised by Katria, a sanatorium nurse, herself an idealist who dreams of escaping the 'grey sanatorium everydayness' somewhere in Siberia, 'in a remote taiga, at the end of the earth'[127]; and Maia, a secret police officer, who 'gave all she could to that secret police and then not only began to love this job but cannot even live without it'.[128]

The former revolutionaries, *anarkh* and Khlonia, were sent to the sanatorium to find a rational explanation to their frustration with the reality that they had left beyond the sanatorium's walls. Together with their nurse Katria, they represent the initial idealism of the revolution, they are, as Khvyl'ovyi defined them, 'restless Don Quixote […] still in search of new illusions of the new unknown shores.'[129] At the same time, they are cognizant that their revolution has been betrayed. Khlonia reflects on the future of the revolutionary ideas: 'Years will past, one, two, ten, twenty, and, believe me, the unknown enemy will avenge himself. I can see even now how the thoughts of my teacher [Lenin] are overlaid by a great pile of dirty rubbish and petty distortions. The world's rubble making its way to the Holy of Holies will hide there behind his name and will turn him into a foul instrument of human regress.' His depression is triggered by a realization that he '[would] not see Lenin again.'[130] In despair, he decides to take his own life.

Anarkh is forced into the same impasse. He searches for answers to his despair; he even tries to develop a contact with the outer world. He confesses his alienation in a letter to his sister and begs for help. His sister, however, is one of those exemplary builders of socialism, who cannot understand those 'slobbery symbolists'. Her response is straightforward: 'to live, read newspapers, magazine "*Ogoniok*", enjoy picturesque view from the hill, eat *borshch* and meatballs [...] and not recall his past'.[131] The letter, ironically encapsulating the comforts of the post-revolutionary everydayness, makes *anarkh* thirsty. He tries to quench his thirst, but instead follows Khlonia to 'another side of reality'. These suicides, nonetheless, do not provide a simple answer – were they a sign of them accepting or rejecting the new reality? Had they attempted to leave the sanatorium and join those in 'the real world', or did they simply give up any hope to fit in the society that had already rejected them once?

'So ... in a pile of papers a person got lost'

The transition from war communism to the NEP in 1921 envisaged not only new political and economic strategies but also triggered a change in identity of those who participated in the revolution and the civil war. The new era completely rejected the spontaneous and destructive environment of the previous years. Instead of ending the old order though military violence, it emphasized the social and educational construction of a new society.[132] Ideological fervour and fanatic commitment were replaced by loyalty, moderation and obedience. As stated by the Bolshevik ideologist Nikolai Bukharin in late 1920, while the party still needed 'conscious Communists who have both a fiery heart and a burning revolutionary passion', it was now especially important to develop young Communists 'who have calm heads, who know what they want, who can stop when necessary, retreat when necessary, take a step to the side when necessary, move cautiously weighing and calculating each step.'[133]

Khvyl'ovyi sympathized with those romantic revolutionaries, whom he defined as 'chaste apostles and saintly preachers'.[134] Nevertheless, he could not omit those who managed to fit into the new society. His work derides those 'parasites of the revolution', by making a clear distinction between those who had made the revolution happen and those who were now capitalizing on its outcomes. He defines this latter group as dishonourable opportunists, 'a nasty intellectual (*inteligentishka*), parvenu, scum who impudently bridles up and even more impudently avouches "we" ("we" to define not those who struggled, but those who are now in "power")'.[135]

While his revolutionary romanticists are isolated and excluded from society, their place is taken by myriads of submissive and obsequious 'timeservers', those *mishchany* (philistines), bureaucrats 'serving only one class which is in power'.[136] For them the revolution was a mere change of government reflected in the change of the décor: 'In the room, where once hanged Alexander II, Nikolai II, and some White General on a white horse, – one can now see Lenin, Trotsky, Rakovs'kyi, and a small portrait of Karl Marx.'[137] Among those in power are, for instance, Stefan (*Syliuety*) who managed to easily adapt to the new realities. His life became comfortable, quiet and well-organized: office work, agitation among factory youth, lecturing and reading newspapers. All this he achieved because he learned how 'to understand things profoundly',[138] that was not to dissent but to adjust to the situation. A similar transformation occurred to a former Ukrainian SR Shkits (*Redaktor Kark*). With time, Skits 'began to dress up better, even too much'; he wishes to implement socialist slogans in practice and 'he does not speak about Ukraine, only sometimes, a little.'[139]

However, their comfortable life came at a cost. For Khvyl'ovyi, the price was to become part of a depersonalized and dehumanized social order, where an individual's role was limited to performing a function, becoming an anonymous and invisible part of the bureaucratic state machinery. This loss of one's self is particularly obvious in Khvyl'ovyi's female characters. For instance, the Comrade Zhuchok (*Kit u chobotiakh*, 1922) who eagerly embraced the 'crimson revolution', marched through the field of the civil war in her cap with a pentagonal star on a shaved head – 'not to suit a fashion – but for the march, for convenience'.[140] Later on, she became a secretary for a party cell. And even though she still feels she is introducing a change, she is expendable, only one of many: ' ... Comrade Zhuchok No. 2 ... No. 3 .... No. 4 ... And I don't know how many more ... There is no Comrade Zhuchok No. 1 ... "Puss in Boots" has vanished into hidden entrails of the republic. Comrade Zhuchok has vanished.'[141]

Another example is Tetiana (*Pudel'*, 1923), who eagerly internalized the Bolshevik promises of women's emancipation, equality and justice. Like many other young people, Tetiana was empowered by the revolution and the civil war; she eagerly joined the process of socialist construction. Furthermore, the new Soviet regime provided Tetiana with unparalleled opportunities for education and employment. Yet her new Soviet life does not match her expectations; it is bereft of excitement, it is banal and perhaps not very different from what she had experienced before moving to the big city. Despite anticipation, she finds herself once again a nobody: 'So, in a pile of papers a person got lost. Simply – a person. How do you think, is it a banality? [...] A person got lost amidst a pile of papers, and no one notices her, because they see only a typist.'[142]

Khvyl'ovyi himself had a very pessimistic outlook on the NEP. In 1924, he suddenly resigned from his position at *Golovpolitosvita* and moved back to the factory to, as he explained, 'refresh myself from the suffocating NEP atmosphere'.[143] He doubted his ideological commitment, as seen from his autobiography prepared for the party purge in 1924: 'I am struggling with this question – whether I have the right to carry a party card, am I ballast for the Party? ... In me, there is a romantic, a dreamer – there's always an inner struggle. [...] With more certainty I can call myself a communard rather than a communist.'[144] By calling himself a 'communard', Khvyl'ovyi implied that he was first a revolutionary; making a distinction from being a communist – a party member who necessarily shares its ideology. It is of note that throughout his life, he would often refer to himself and his literary fellows as 'communards'.

Apart from being ideologically confused, Khvyl'ovyi suffered greatly from a personal split with his close friend Ellan-Blakytnyi. This occurred in 1924 when Khvyl'ovyi seceded from the literary group *Hart*, headed by Blakytnyi, owing to unbridgeable differences in their understanding of the future of proletarian art. Lenin's death proved to be another personal blow. In a letter to Mohylians'kyi, dated 23 January 1924, Khvyl'ovyi confessed that the entire epoch had ended with the party chairman's death: 'To me, a romanticist, "Lenin" resonates of long foregone sweet-scented years [19]17, [19]18, [19]19, [19]20. Lenin is a thorny path to the "peaceful lakes of the Commune behind the hills".'[145]

As the Russian context illustrates, concerns about the political centralization and betrayal of revolutionary ideals after 1921 was common among members of the intelligentsia and the civil war veterans across the Soviet Union. Similar themes were introduced in the prose of Pilnyak to whom Khvyl'ovyi was frequently compared.[146] Another common feature with their Russian counterparts was the torrents of criticism that those, once-celebrated, writers received from Soviet critics for their experiments with the revolutionary word. While highly praised for their formal innovations, imagery, instrumentation and subjective expressions in 1923, by mid-1920, those writers found themselves, amidst the ongoing form and content debate, presented as negative examples by politically oriented critics for their creative writing. Khvyl'ovyi's formal experimentations brought against him charges of formalism and departure from the realistic tradition, accusations that the writer tackled during the Literary Discussion analysed later in the book.[147]

Contrary to his Russian fellows, who mostly dealt with literary affairs, Khvyl'ovyi, however, became equally preoccupied with drastic reversals in the national question that were specific to Soviet Ukraine. The more centralized the party became the less discussion was allowed on the question of leadership in Soviet Ukraine. The tolerance for those Ukrainian-minded communists who planned to use the framework of the Bolshevik party for advancing their own political agenda was significantly limited as their presence within the KP(b)U dramatically decreased. Following the purge of the party's membership in 1921, only 118 ex-*Borot'bysty* remained within the KP(b)U ranks.[148] Those 'errant dreamers', who, like Khvyl'ovyi himself, tried to reconcile their adherence to communism with their strong national sentiments became simply redundant once the party was able to secure a faithful replacement. Through one of his fictional characters – a Bolshevik sympathizer journalist called Kark – Khvyl'ovyi expressed his frustration over the fact that it was becoming impossible to be a good Communist and a Ukrainian patriot. Throughout the story, Kark questions himself, 'Am I really superfluous because I love Ukraine madly?'[149] According to Lavrinenko, Redaktor Kark introduced the motive of 'hangover' after highly inspiring civil war years of 1917–22.[150] Although it would still take some years before Khvyl'ovyi would fully develop the autonomist position that would eventually earn him the label of a counter-revolutionary or even a fascist, his frustration with the tightening political controls over Ukrainian culture and politics were slowly taking shape.

Moreover, he was in a creative impasse. Khvyl'ovyi used his fictional writing to reflect and report on recent social developments, on the atmosphere of a growing mismatch between the ideals of the revolution and the post-war normalization. Having gained fame for glorifying the revolution and unmasking everything corrupt in the post-revolutionary society, it was hard to adapt to the new expectations. Rationally, he understood that he needed to re-evaluate his romantic vision of the past and start contributing to the society he himself had brought about. Nonetheless, the adaptation did not come easy. As he confined to Zerov: 'now I'm not writing and, evidently, will not write anymore, because old manner [...] does not satisfy me, and yet I will not produce nothing new – don't have appropriate talent.'[151]

Khvyl'ovyi had also grown greatly dissatisfied with his earlier prose, as seen from a letter to Mohylians'kyi dated from April–May 1924. He wrote,

> I want to share my thoughts about my second book 'Syni Etiudy' [...] I am sure that my 'Syni Etiudy' was "out-voiced" (*perekrychaly*), it was not worth that great (indeed, great) attention. This book includes pieces that I wouldn't have acknowledged now. Honestly, I am ashamed to reread such things as *Baraky, shcho za mistom*, for instance. This is a literary scandal! If I were a critic, I would have taken the book apart so that only bits and pieces remain. But this is not what I'd like to say. I assume, at that time there was a need for those short stories, and there was a need to shout about them. But you see how I feel? Suddenly, I feel such a huge responsibility hanging over me and I feel my little talent will never be able to handle it. [...] In a word: by virtue of fate and due to the generosity of my critics I have become 'the first novelist of Ukraine', and I am confused. My vanity is satisfied. But my mind protests: I don't have the right to be called this way, my literary merit does not live up to those critics' opinion.[152]

As a result, his mental health, already shattered by the experiences of the revolutions and continuous wars, further deteriorated. In another letter to Mohylians'kyi, dated from June 1924, he confessed that his neurasthenia had worsened, his 'fits of hysterics were sometimes so intense that I hit my head against the wall'.[153] He also mentioned hallucinations that were made even worse after copious alcohol intake.[154] In one of these letters, Khvyl'ovyi mentioned that thinking, according to his doctors, had become dangerous for his health.[155] He frequently spoke of suicide. He further confessed to Zerov about his conflicting thoughts on attempting to end his life: 'In a word, it is a Dostoevsky-style pathology, but there is no way I can shoot myself. I went to the field already twice but came back safe and sound both times: evidently I'm a big coward and good for nothing.'[156]

With his first-hand revolutionary experience, Khvyl'ovyi fully represented an early-1920s generation of revolutionary romanticists, united by idealistic belief in the providence promised by the revolution, and complete disillusionment after those expectations were betrayed. By the mid-1920s, Khvyl'ovyi was forced to denounce the very myth he himself had created: that of 'a revolution without buttons', of a 'blue Savoy', of an 'intangible Commune behind the hills'; and to show options on how to deal with the frustration of the NEP years. His revolutionary romanticists were faced with the necessity to decide either to accept the new reality (by compromise or a re-estimation of their values and beliefs) or denounce the world after the earlier prophecies had failed to come true (resorting to resignation or suicide).

In his early prose, Khvyl'ovyi over-romanticized revolution; and this can explain the level of frustration once his dreams and expectations did not come true. The tragedy of Khvyl'ovyi's characters is that they, after having zealously dismantled one social order, found themselves incapable of introducing another. The social construction was, therefore, picked up by pragmatists and opportunists, who succeeded in establishing a new order with only a nominal reference to popular revolutionary slogans. This new society appeared for those revolutionaries as a farcical parody of what they had anticipated. Instead of bringing the system into correspondence with their beliefs and expectations, social norms were re-evaluated. Hence, new ideologemes and mythologies were elaborated upon, stating that the prophecy, promised by the revolution, could happen only through discipline, obedience, loyalty and everyday toil.

In his early prose, Khvyl'ovyi had exposed the potential of the new Soviet Ukrainian literature. Obviously, one could not exploit themes and devices of revolutionary romanticism for very long: the time of post-revolutionary social normalization, economic recovery and political stabilization required new themes and heroes. In 1927, Khvyl'ovyi concluded: 'to my arabesques – *finis*'.[157] This meant the end to his romanticism, his fictional characters full of illusions and his anxious anticipation of a communist future. It took him a few years before he could finally redefine his literary persona. Indeed, his fiction written in the late 1920s hardly resembled his previous manner and style. Nevertheless, several important cultural and social issues were brought to the fore during the civil war period. While none of the existing then – proletarian literary organizations could yet be regarded as instruments of the party's politics, the institutional divide in the Ukrainian letters was slowly becoming clear, with two literary camps being formed – one aspiring to a national form of proletarian culture, and another orienting towards the international proletarian culture under the Russian master.

Khvyl'ovyi and his followers adhered to artistic freedom and literature of distinct artistic merit whereas Russia-led Proletkult and those who shared their vision searched for collective solutions to cultural production. Similarly, Ukrainian writers needed to take a side in the ongoing content and form debate and respond to those critics who assessed their works solely through their use of formal devices. Those literary debates, waged by writers also in other Soviet republics, in the context of Soviet Ukraine, were further complicated by the national question. Already during the civil war, the status of the Ukrainian language and its role in creating what would be an international proletarian culture became an important issue which could not be neglected in the cultural sphere. To answer these questions, broached with the help of imaginative literature and exacerbated during the debates between the representatives of competing literary groups, a different forum was required. The Literary Discussion of 1925–8, analysed in the next section, offered differing sides of the debate a required setting to voice, dispute and negotiate their visions of Soviet Ukrainian literature and culture.

Part Two

Debating Soviet culture in Ukraine

Part Two of the book investigates the debates around the nature of Soviet culture in Ukraine. Here, I utilize the distinction between the two ideological factions or political horizons within the KP(b)U as outlined in the Introduction. The first, originating in the pre-war Ukrainian socialist movements, was developed and executed by the Ukraine-minded faction of the KP(b)U, which pursued a separatist political culture and Ukraine's broad autonomy in political, economic and cultural matters. The second horizon consisted of the KP(b)U members with a clear centripetal orientation towards Moscow, advocating in favour of preserving the historically established relations between centre and periphery, and constructing the all-Soviet political and cultural space. These two political cultures in the KP(b)U endorsed different projects of Soviet culture. On the one end, there was a project of Soviet Ukrainian culture curated from Kharkiv by the cultural wing of the *Borot'bysty* and Ukraine-minded Bolsheviks. Opposing this, the idea of an all-Union Soviet culture, albeit in Ukrainian, was also vigorously promoted.

The process of constructing Soviet culture in Ukraine was introduced side by side with a new Soviet policy of *korenizatsiia*, launched Union-wide in 1923. The two political cultures within the KP(b)U manifested themselves through different understandings of the *korenizatsiia* policies and expectations from its implementation in the context of Soviet Ukraine. The representatives of these two ideological camps coincided in viewing *korenizatsiia* as a long-term strategy to cope with the imperial legacies of Russification. There was a key difference, however. Whereas the Moscow-oriented camp wished to cope with a century-long legacy of distrust of central institutions and redefine the centre-periphery relationship, as well as overcome general illiteracy of the population, the Ukraine-minded faction hoped to free Soviet Ukraine of cultural and economic dependency on Russia and thereby transform it into a national republic.

Different perspectives on the Soviet nationalities policy and its objectives, as presented in Chapters 3 and 4 of this book, resulted in contrasting conceptions of Soviet literature. In line with the central perspective, Soviet literature needed to be mass-oriented, socially useful and party-minded. Most importantly, it needed to be in

Ukrainian to help the popular masses assimilate the Bolshevik values in their native language. Its orientation towards the masses necessarily required the simplification of its content and form. Contrary to Soviet literature in Ukrainian, Soviet Ukrainian literature stood for a national proletarian culture. As envisaged by Khvyl'ovyi, it defended the autonomy of the artistic sphere, targeted educated working-class readers; and envisaged socialist 'high culture'. The shaping of these two conceptions of Soviet literature is the focus of the following chapters.

3

Towards Soviet literature in Ukrainian

Soviet *Korenizatsiia* in the Ukrainian context

The experience of the civil war had proven that to establish a lasting social and political system, the Bolsheviks needed to take the national aspirations of the local elites into account and redefine their view of centre-periphery relations. Already in 1921, the party congress called for a comprehensive national programme, establishing local administration, promoting national languages and cultures and recruiting indigenous elites into the party rank-and-files. Yet it took another two years for these intentions to be incorporated into the Soviet agenda. The new approach in the national question was initiated at the twelfth party congress in April 1923. The rationale behind the new policy was explained by Stalin, then serving as Commissar for Nationalities. According to him, 'Great-Russian chauvinism' had led to an underestimation of specific national features and languages in the party and to an arrogant and disdainful attitude towards such differences. The new nationalities policy would instead reorganize the Soviet Union 'in such a way as to fully reflect not only the common needs and requirements of all the nationalities of the Union, but also the special needs and requirements of each individual nationality'.[1]

The nationalities policy was launched in 1923 and comprised different, but interlinked, national programmes with distinctive goals: *korenizatsiia*, or indigenization, aimed at 'rooting' Soviet rule in the border republics by incorporating ethnic cadres into party work and the state apparatus. This was coupled with a linguistic de-Russification and prompting of the advancement of national languages and cultures. While no discussion of political or economic decentralization was envisaged, the new Soviet policy aggressively promoted symbolic markers of national identity, such as national folklore, museums, dress, food, costumes, opera, poets, progressive historical events and classic literary works.[2] The policy was also modified and adapted to meet the needs of every Soviet republic; *Ukrainizatsiia* was the Ukrainian version of this all-Union policy.

The key aspect of *korenizatsiia* in Ukraine was the language question. Unsurprisingly, the first official document adopted in line with the policy was the KP(b)U decree 'On Measures for Guaranteeing the Equality of Languages and on the Equal Development of the Ukrainian Language' issued on 1 August 1923. According to the decree, the Soviet government assumed the responsibility for ensuring 'a place for the Ukrainian language corresponding to the numerical superiority of the Ukrainian people on the territory of the Ukrainian SSR.'[3] This could be achieved through enrolling and advancing ethnic Ukrainians into the party, promoting the Ukrainian language and encouraging the development of national culture.

The objectives behind embracing national aspirations into the party's political agenda were manifold. Firstly, the Bolsheviks came to accept nationalism as an unavoidable fact. Both Lenin and Stalin insisted that nationality, although an attribute of capitalist societies, would persist even under socialism. Hence, on the way to internationalism, the Bolsheviks needed to foster the development of national cultures so that 'it will exhaust itself completely and thereby create the base for the organisation of an international socialist culture'.[4] National cultures, therefore, were accepted as a transitional phenomenon, a step towards a uniform, common culture that would express the values of the working class and the party.[5] This was as much a taciturn acceptance that the February Revolution had engendered national movements throughout the imperial peripheries. The populaces' newfound national self-awareness, awakened by the revolutions, therefore needed to be channelled in the right direction, or, as one KP(b)U official explained, drawn into 'the orbit of the communist influence'.[6] By embracing a separatist discourse, the Communist Party sought to neutralize the appeal of local nationalism.

To achieve this, the nature of the Bolshevik party in Ukraine needed to change. Throughout the civil war, the Bolsheviks had been seen as a foreign and occupying authority. It was not surprising, since in non-Russian regions, the Bolshevik party consisted predominantly of Russians who had relied almost exclusively on Ukraine's Russified urban areas for support. Indeed, at the end of 1918, only 7 per cent of the KP(b)U's total membership was of Ukrainian origin.[7] Nevertheless, in 1923 this had already risen to 23 per cent, although only 11 per cent of those used Ukrainian in everyday life.[8] *Korenizatsiia*, instead, could draw locals towards the party. As highlighted by Stalin in 1921, in order to make Soviet power 'near and dear to the masses of the border regions of Russia', it was necessary to integrate 'all the best local people' into the Soviet administration, since 'the masses should see that Soviet power and its organs are the products of their own efforts, the embodiment of their aspirations.'[9] During his speech at the VII KP(b)U conference in 1923, the deputy head of the Ukrainian *Radnarkom*, Mikhail Frunze, asserted that the new nationalities policy would create an atmosphere in which Bolshevik power would become understandable to the broad mass of the Ukrainian peasantry.[10]

From the party's perspective, one could suggest that *korenizatsiia* meant, first and foremost, the integration of rural Ukraine into the Soviet order. In 1917, rural Ukrainian speakers constituted the majority of the population, fiercely resisting the establishment of Soviet power throughout the civil war. The future of the Bolshevik project in Ukraine depended heavily on engaging with the countryside and legitimizing their urban-based and nationally alien revolution among the Ukrainian-speaking peasantry.[11] Furthermore, the peasants were themselves considered an integral part of the future workforce, in high demand considering Soviet aims for economic modernization and accelerated industrialization. As Matthew Pauly explained, *Ukrainizatsiia* offered a means to ensure that the Soviet authorities possessed the tools to alter the linguistic environment of the city so that a peasant-centred workforce could more easily acculturate.[12]

Nevertheless, there was a well-justified fear that the arrival en masse of these Ukrainian-speaking peasants, deemed fundamentally alien to the Soviet cause, within the cities could potentially lead to the crystallization of a new anti-Bolshevik opposition and further alienate the party from the industrial proletariat, in whose name it claimed to exercise the dictatorship. Already in 1920, Lenin insisted that the party must ensure its monopoly in the process of peasants' and workers' socialization. Under close party supervision, peasants needed to 'overcome the old habits and re-educate themselves for building communism'. In the end, it was not enough simply to engage the peasantry with the Soviet order, they needed to internalize Soviet values and contribute willingly to the process of socialist construction.[13]

National cultures were to play a key role in internalizing Soviet values. In 1921, the TsK KP(b)U's Department of Agitation and Propaganda underscored the potential benefits in developing a culture of mass mobilization: 'Our task is to exploit the mobilizing power of the arts to its maximum, to make it the most important tool of political and educational work, that is the state propaganda of communism.'[14] Volodymyr Zatons'kyi, a high KP(b)U official and a short-term Commissar for Education, equalled the significance of linguistic Ukrainization to that of industrialization in the process of building socialism. He regarded Ukrainian culture as a 'proletarian tool': by raising the cultural level of Ukrainians, for both peasants and workers, it would provide them with an opportunity to quickly grasp Leninism in their native tongue, and thereby remove any obstacles to the process of socialist construction.[15] The use of the Ukrainian language either for writing newspaper pieces, scholarly outputs or imaginative literature, or creating theatre performances and films, was seen as an instrument to advance political propaganda. Culture was especially valued for the diversity of its means. As Skrypnyk explained in June 1932:

> theatre, artistic performance, cinema are valuable tools of influence. When we read books it only affects our consciousness, but theatre, cinema and music can also impact us emotionally. And we need to temper the communist consciousness in our toilers, we need to subdue all the residues of capitalism, and for this we must use all devices, tools, and means of influence.[16]

The easiest way to promote Soviet values was arguably through the printed word. However, Ukraine's population was still largely illiterate. To overcome this obstacle, in 1919, the Soviet government launched another ambitious campaign – *liknep* (*likbez* in Russian), a set of extraordinary measures to abolish illiteracy among the population. Introduced alongside linguistic Ukrainization, the *liknep* campaign provided the means for all of Ukraine's inhabitants between eight and fifty years old to become literate in their native language. This popular educational campaign achieved incredible results with soaring literacy rates among Ukrainians. According to the 1926 census and the results of surveys on literacy, rates increased by 42 per cent (against 1920) amounting to a national average of 64 per cent (falling to 59 per cent in rural areas).[17]

Nonetheless, literacy was never an aim in itself; it could only provide a means for the success of Soviet propaganda and political education. As admitted back in 1919, Ukrainian was 'a weapon in the communist education of the toiling people'.[18] Lenin highlighted the importance of civic literacy at the Second All-Russian Congress of Political Education Departments: 'An illiterate person stands outside politics; she must first learn her ABC. Without that there can be no politics; without that there are rumours, gossip, fairy-tales and prejudices, but not politics.' The functional role of literacy was highlighted: 'We must not only abolish illiteracy [...] but we must get the people ready to accept our propaganda, our guidance and our pamphlets, so that the result may be an improvement in the national economy.'[19]

Korenizatsiia and massovism

It was widely recognized that in order to complete the political and social revolution, a cultural revolution also had to occur. To achieve this, the Bolsheviks deemed it necessary to promote a new proletarian culture that would replace the bourgeois one of the previous regimes. During the civil war, the project of proletarian culture was endorsed by Proletkult, whose leaders warned that the revolution would not survive without the rapid dissemination of this new culture.[20] The rapid success of this organization, achieved outside of state control, alarmed the Bolshevik leaders; in 1921, official sponsorship for Proletkult was quickly withheld, bringing their endeavours to naught. Having neutralized the Proletkult, the party assumed sole responsibility over the entire range of cultural, didactic and 'enlightenment' initiatives, declaring the cultural sphere a 'third front' in the revolutionary struggle.[21]

Marxist critics got actively involved in debating the nature of the new proletarian literature. One of the fundamental principles of the new literature and art concerned their relationship to reality. In the first post-revolutionary years, different artistic currents emerged. This exuberance resulted in a great variety of formal devices. This diversity was not welcomed by the party ideologists who advocated for a simple literature, useful and clear to the ordinary working-class/peasant reader. The content and form debate eventually became the most important aspect of literary criticism of the 1920s, as abundant contributions on these issues on the pages of the Soviet periodicals indicate.[22] Since the early 1920s, charges of formalism were frequently issued against the futurists, but also against Khvyl'ovyi and his milieu, as well as previous modernist writers. In opposition to those experimentations with the form, politically oriented critics promoted and evaluated literary outputs by Soviet writers based on their adherence to the content – desire for clarity, portrayal of life in a realistic manner, simple and straightforward narrative, emphasis on the plot (*suzhet*) with preserved chronology, a positive hero, moral orientation and positive resolution.[23] Those critics adhered to the cognition theory in defining the function of art as a belief that art recreates, mirrors, life closely, corresponding to actual life and character types. The content and form debate predated the Literary Discussion, discussed in length in the next chapter, but it informed one of its important topics on the issue of literary quality and ideology.[24]

Despite the expectations of the party and the aspiration of the Soviet critics, during the early 1920s, it remained extremely difficult to impose state control over culture due to a lack of communist cadres. Hence, the role of the party was modified. In *Literature and Revolution* (1923), Trotsky explained that 'the sphere of art is not one where the party is called upon to command. It can and must safeguard, assist, and only indirectly – guide.'[25] Until the late 1920s, party intervention in literary matters remained limited. However, it was made clear that the final say in the cultural domain belonged to the party, who still held a monopoly in defining the 'political course' within the cultural sphere overall.[26] To ensure that the party's vision prevailed, the activities of existing artistic groups were controlled by the state officials with power to intervene if the desired alignment of forces was under threat.

To receive state sponsorship, literary organizations needed to comply with the official line on Soviet culture by appealing to and engaging with the general masses. While the 'bourgeois' culture belonged to the upper classes and was created by elites for elites, the new Soviet culture would be proletarian and intended to serve the needs, and satisfy the expectations, of the broad working population. As Lenin explained in 1920, 'Art belongs to the people. It must leave its deepest roots in the very core of the broad toiling masses. It should be understood by the masses and liked by them. It must unite the feelings, thoughts and the will of these masses; it must uplift them. It must reveal artists among the masses and develop them.'[27]

In the foreword to a contemporary study of the literary process in Ukraine – *Desiat' rokiv ukrains'koi literatury* [Ten years of Ukrainian Literature] – contemporary literary critics Oleksandr Leites and Mykola Iashek admitted that Ukrainian literature of the first post-revolutionary decade witnessed a unique phenomenon of 'the chaotic movement from the land, from the workbench to creative writing'.[28] Their creative aspirations were supported by cultural managers and proletarian writers who shared in the conviction that the masses themselves should be the creators of the new proletarian culture. In line with the Bolshevik party agenda, Serhii Pylypenko, the editor of the Kharkiv newspaper *Sil'ski Visti* (Rural News), established in 1922 an All-Ukrainian Peasant Writers' Union, *Pluh* (Plough), to help aspiring writers of peasant origin develop their skills and create literature that would appeal to peasant readers. A year later, Blakytnyi announced the formation of the Association of the Proletarian Writers, *Hart* (Tempering), which devoted itself to nurturing writers of proletarian origin. Nearly all Soviet Ukrainian writers active during the 1920s belonged to one, or even both of these two literary organizations.

Pylypenko embarked on the task of creating mass Soviet literature in Ukrainian that would be both ideologically useful and appealing to the peasants. His organization's aim was to 'unite all dispersed peasant writers who, supporting the idea of a close union of the revolutionary peasantry with the proletariat, will advance with the latter toward the creation of a new socialist culture and will disseminate these ideas among the peasant masses in Ukraine regardless of their nationality.'[29] In order to achieve this aspiration, *Pluh* was even willing to lower the standards of its members' literary work. As a representative of the organization, B. Iakubs'kyi declared: 'The task of our time in the realm of art is to lower it, to bring it down to earth from its pedestal, to make it intelligible and sought-for by all.'[30]

This perspective laid the foundation for *Pluh*'s tactics and ideology, known as massivism (*masovizm*), defined by Pylypenko in *Nashi 'hrikhy'* [Our 'sins'] and published in the group's official organ *Pluzhanyn* in 1926. First, culture should aim at the masses; literature should be accessible, deal with universal topics from the life of the revolutionary peasantry and would be created with 'the greatest simplicity and economy of artistic methods'.[31] Second, literature was a mass movement, and its ranks were open to everyone eager to learn how to write and contribute to the future Soviet culture. For Pylypenko, literature was produced by 'literary forces, from the most ... to the least qualified, the artistic production of *robsil'kory* [worker-peasant correspondents], participants in wall newspapers and hand-written newspapers'.[32] Third, readers were regarded as co-creators of literature; *Pluh*'s activity was based on frequent interaction with audiences to ensure that their authors' literary outputs corresponded to what those readers actually wanted to read.[33] As *Pluh*'s manifesto determined, to gain the readership's interest, the organization expected its members to create literary works with well-developed plots, simple form and ideologically sound content.[34]

On the other hand, Blakytnyi's *Hart* declared itself to be at the forefront of creating proletarian literature in Ukrainian. Blakytnyi outlined his vision of the new literary organization in a document entitled *Bez manifestu* [Without a Manifesto]. Its stated aim was to unite 'the proletarian writers of Ukraine, including the artists active in the field of theatre, art and music, who, using Ukrainian language as the means of artistic expression, aim at creating an international, Communist culture, and who spread Communist ideology and fight against the petit-bourgeois' propertied ideology'.[35] The core of the organization comprised pro-Soviet writers who had previously belonged to the *Borot'bysty* group *Zhovten'* and used to cooperate with the Proletkult. Among its most prominent members were Sosiura, Khvyl'ovyi, Iohansen, Ivan Kulyk, Tychyna, Valer'ian Polishchuk, Ivan Dniprovs'kyi and Koriak.

Hart declared its allegiance to the party's literary policies, claiming that they were an 'organization of communists and communist sympathisers whose aim is to facilitate the work of the Communist Party by gathering all the creative forces and organising the production of art'.[36] Similar to *Pluh*, *Hart* opposed the aesthetic of 'high culture' for its individualism, lack of ideological resoluteness and non-partisan character. Instead, it welcomed 'members of the Communist Party, members of the Komsomol, and workers from the shop floor, regardless of their artistic qualification'.[37] While rejecting artistic talent as a necessary prerequisite for literary work, Blakytnyi believed that proletarian culture in Ukraine could be created through 'practice, as well as specific constructive work'.[38]

These mass literary organizations had full party support and enjoyed financial assistance. They were seen as 'combat units' on the Bolshevik cultural front, tasked with spreading communist ideology and civic literacy by artistic means among the masses of the Ukrainian population. In their everyday activity, they differed little from the institutions of popular education, promoting a functional view of literature. At the same time, they performed a useful role in teaching their members how to read and write in Ukrainian. By using the Ukrainian language to create popular literature dealing with the topics of Soviet everyday life, *Pluh* and *Hart*, as attested by the *Narkomos* 'workers' and peasants" inspection of 1924, 'provide village and city with suitable Ukrainian literature which is also in accord with the party's policy of *Ukrainizatsiia*'. Nevertheless, it recommended that *Pluh* be more aware of how they dealt with the peasantry. To ensure the fulfilment of the party line, 'local branches must be headed by communists, and should also include *robselkory*, Komsomol and Red Army members.'[39]

In addition, party directives demanded the Ukrainization of publishing in Soviet Ukraine, which meant that the number of copies and titles in Ukrainian needed to exceed the number of those in Russian. In 1923, the year when *Ukrainizatsiia* was launched, only 16.3 per cent of titles and 25.3 per cent of books published in Soviet Ukraine were in Ukrainian, against 80.5 per cent and 60.8 per cent in Russian respectively.[40] Achieving *Ukrainizatsiia*'s objectives was not an easy task, especially since there was often nothing to publish. Consequently, *Pluh* and *Hart*'s own writers seized upon this opportunity. Both literary organizations had their own journals and almanacs, while *Hart* also had its own publishing house. In addition, Pylypenko was also head of the State Publishing House of Ukraine (DVU), providing members of mass literary organizations with an opportunity to publish their work.

'For some time now this poet has been kissing the Pope's slipper'

Tychyna was considering moving to the capital of Soviet Ukraine. The reasons for this were not only professional. The available primary sources disclose his deep inner confusion with post-revolutionary Kyiv. One of the main reasons for moving cities was the outflow of artistic forces and the impoverishment of the intellectual milieu. In his diary, the poet confessed how forlorn and lonely he felt on those days: 'There is nobody I can federate with. Semenko – no, Vasyl' [Blakytnyi] – is far away, *hronisty*[41] want to eat me up and benefit from it.'[42] A diary entry of 29 July 1920 suggested the unbearable atmosphere in Kyiv. It read: 'I grow rusty in Kyiv. Yet, the hell with it, even with these stale forces I should continue doing something, while it is still possible.'[43]

In addition, Tychyna found himself in the centre of criticism from all ideological sides. His most acclaimed collection *Soniachni Klarnety* was attacked fiercely by the futurists. Tychyna, who represented a modernist tradition in Ukraine's literature, was seen as '*panych*' (a noble man),[44] a 'bard of the Central Rada' who, thereof, could not represent the new grand-to-be revolutionary literature. In 1922, Futurist Semenko expressed a highly critical opinion towards 'young Ukrainian poetry', represented by Tychyna, Iakiv Savchenko and Dmytro Zahul. He detested Tychyna's poetry which for him represented a continuity of the Ukrainian culture of the nineteenth century: 'Pavlo Tychyna [meanwhile] sat quietly in his little den, content with onanism, translating "beautiful Ukrainian folk songs" into the language of poetry, stylising Ukrainian rugs, restoring ancient *dumy* and other useless things, preparing to become "father's" (or "mother's") little boy and the successor to Voronyi, Lesia Ukrainka, and Oles.'[45] Another futurist poet Geo [Hryhorii] Koliada in his collection *Futur Extra*, later published in Moscow, spoke of Tychyna's forays into revolutionary poetry in the same critical manner:

You,
deeply lyrical,
'genial' Tychynas, Sosiuras et al.
Hands off!
Don't grasp the wheels of the *lokomobili* of history.

Later, Tychyna recalled the criticism he was subjected to during those last years in Kyiv with bitterness: 'Ukrainian nationalist hated me for my *Vidpovid' Zemliakam* (1922). From another side I was pressed by Ukrainian neo-futurists, who labelled me and made the filthiest comparisons. […] From the third side, there were those moderates, preaching for peace and quietness, to whom I replied in *Velykym Brekhunam* [To Big Liars].'[46] In addition, some of Tychyna's admirers took issue with his new poetic style, as presented in *Pluh* and *V Kosmichnomu Orkestri*. In one of his later letters to Lidiia Paparuk, the woman who would become his wife in 1938, the poet referred to those common reproaches: 'They cannot forgive [*zabuty*] me Kharkiv. According to them, I should have stayed in Kyiv and reprinted for the fifth time my first collection [*Soniachni Klarnety*].'[47]

There was yet another reason to consider leaving Kyiv in 1923. The city was not safe for former UNR supporters, as the tragic fates of Murashko and Leontovych had proven. Instead, Kharkiv could offer an easy-to-blend atmosphere. Blakytnyi, who for years supported his childhood friend, could hardly assist his protégé in Kyiv. He suggested Tychyna move to Kharkiv, as his diary entry from 10 November 1921 suggests: 'Every time when Vasyl' [Blakytnyi] comes to Kyiv he advices me to move to Kharkiv. There is a big reason for this. One person is especially threatening me.'[48] There are no records of who this person was. However, according to the recollection of Paparuk, Tychyna at the time had a complicated relationship with the Kyiv Cheka.[49] This assumption was later seconded by Volodymyr P'ianov, an expert on Tychyna and his close friend in the later period. P'ianov pointed out that the poet was blackmailed for his former UNR ties by Vsevolod Balyts'kyi, a Kyiv Cheka vice head at the time.[50] Tychyna, despite his attempts to fashion his persona through ideologically sound poetry, was closely watched by the authorities. One of his poems with a clear anti-Bolshevik message was apprehended by the Cheka during the arrest of his brother Ievhen, a precentor of a Ukrainian autocephaly church, in Chernihiv on 11 April 1923. Tychyna's poem *Do Koho Hovoryt'?* [To Whom to Talk?], written in 1922, was found in his brother's investigation file.[51] The poem reflected the poet's despair and discordance with the state of affairs, with the situation of 'class-less feuds', hypocrisy and mustiness of those in power:

I will show you rare things
In our class-less feuds!
I will show you all the hypocrisy and mustiness
Of those emerged from in-Party struggles!
And fraternal fangs! And friendly lucre!
That wax-like pliable policies!
When were they generals –

We would have known how to act.
And that's a thing, that they are hangmen
From the same class (O.P.)

Given its political sounding, the poem, although it existed in a number of handwritten copies, was never published until 1990.

In the spring of 1923, Tychyna followed Blakytnyi's advice and finally moved to Kharkiv where he was offered a job on the editorial board of *Chervonyi Shliakh*, the first state-sponsored 'thick journal'. Tychyna quickly found his place among the Soviet Ukrainian capital's artistic milieu, joining the writers' association *Hart* and often presenting his work at literary evenings. His first public appearance took place at one such evening, organized by *Pluh*, where his latest poetry was received 'extremely warmly and with much enthusiasm, especially among the youth'.[52]

Already in 1924, Tychyna had published a new poetic collection *Viter z Ukrainy* [Wind from Ukraine], and the poem *Zhyvemo Komunoiu* [We live as a Commune]. *Viter z Ukrainy* included poems that anticipated the bright socialist future (e.g. *Nadhodylo Lito* [Summer is on the Way]), glorified its leaders (*Nenavysti Moiei Syla* [Oh Strength of my Hate]) and slandered its enemies (*Vidpovid' Zemliakam* [A Reply to my Countrymen]). While *Viter z Ukrainy*'s opening titular poem was dedicated to Khvyl'ovyi, the tropes, poetic language and artistic tools of Tychyna's poetry could suggest his accord with the party's functional view on literature. He reflected on the matters of the time and frequently contributed with poems written in the government-endorsed fashion. *Nenavysti Moiei Syla*, for example, was written on the occasion of Lenin's death on 21 January 1921. The poet depicted the dismay of the entire republic that had suddenly lost its leader:

I wouldn't scream so, I wouldn't call out –
But you can't stifle a shout.
For our supreme titan
Has already gone, has already gone

Another verse, composed to commemorate Lenin's death, was often read aloud on literary evenings and public gatherings thanks to its catchy lyrics and mobilizing rhythm:

LENIN!
That sole word, just one,
And we are like a Storm –
Turned on!
[…]
LENIN!
Just five letters in it,
But oh, what power to tear!

This verse was later included in the collection *Chernihiv* (1931).

Viter z Ukrainy received a very mixed response. On the one hand, most critics observed that the collection was Tychyna's highest achievement in mastering a poetic form.⁵³ The collection included pieces written in *vers libre* and hexameter, and there were folk quatrains, blank verses and poetry in prose. Nonetheless, while developing his creative technique, Tychyna simplified the content of his poems, 'democratised his muse', as one critic has put it.⁵⁴ Most reviewers took issue with the ideological elements in Tychyna's poetry. Iefremov, a Kyivan critic and a long-time admirer of Tychyna, commented on his shift towards 'communist other-worldly (*ne od myru tsioho*) romanticism, slander of communist enemies, to some grotesque (*chudnyi*) belief in an "Inter-Republic".'⁵⁵ Writing as a critic, Zerov was more cautious in his appraisals. He reviewed *Viter z Ukrainy* as 'a victorious hymn to the new age, the age of grand social advances'.⁵⁶ As for the new aesthetic, Zerov evasively noted that those 'cold allegories yet needed to be deciphered'.⁵⁷ Zerov was more frank in his private correspondence, however. He admitted that Tychyna's poetic cycle *V Kosmichnomy Orkestri*, initially written in 1921 and included in the 1924 collection, left 'an impression of bastard-ness [*ubliudochnost'*]'. He criticized Tychyna for conflating two different styles – 'on the one hand, "a spirit that had imbued us all," and on the other, "confederations," "aerostats," "socialism".' Zerov accused Tychyna of being dishonest in his poetry, of trying to fit in the expectations of the authorities. Zerov concluded, 'There is too much insincerity floating on the surface and it disturbs – it does not correspond to the inward nature of your thinking.'⁵⁸

Tychyna himself had mixed feelings about *Viter z Ukrainy*, as he confessed to his close friend Mohylians'kyi. In his letter he wrote,

> I am very pleased to hear that my book would definitely leave its mark, but this, my dear Mykhailo Mykhailovych, is not what I was aiming to achieve. My soul is longing for unknown heights, I want to stand like a monolith and my hands are rising upwards. But will I rise? To become a monolith one needs knowledge, strength and health. Unknown heights require universal blossoming and shine. Marks … in order to leave marks on the whole epoch! […] *Viter z Ukrainy* is only a wind, and a storm is yet to come, or it might not.⁵⁹

It is hard to say, what were those 'heights' that Tychyna longed for. With his first poetic collection *Soniachni Klarnety* he reached the heights of symbolism. His experimentations with form suggested his awareness of avant-garde techniques. At the same time, his propaganda rhymes showed his readiness to compromise both form and meaning in favour of ideology and party favour. Literary critic Leites suggested that Tychyna now found himself at a 'historical crossroads'. Although his face was turned towards the revolution, he was still in search of his voice. Tychyna was not simply a *poputchyk* [a fellow traveller], but a *pereputchyk* [the one at the crossroads].⁶⁰ Whilst Iefremov asserted that Tychyna had already made his decision in favour of Soviet literature. He called Tychyna 'a prominent *shkurnyk*' (a profiteer), who switched to the communist camp for material benefits. He explained that the poet used to be 'a sincere Ukrainian', but in the Soviet atmosphere, 'tempted by offices and benefits', he had transformed himself into a Soviet man, breaking his ties with former representatives of the Ukrainian anti-Soviet public. Whereas in Kyiv Tychyna had been a nationalist, in Kharkiv he had swiftly become a Soviet poet.[61]

Tychyna's ideological evolution occurred under close party supervision. Not only was he eager to use his literary skills to produce propaganda poems, he also became a model example of the re-forged nationalist poet who now wholeheartedly accepted the Soviet ideology. From the party's perspective, the Sovietization of Tychyna – the son of a priest educated in a theological seminary and formerly a close associate of the nationalist government – was of great ideological significance. As the party newspaper *Komunist* admitted, winning Tychyna over to the Soviet side was an important victory for the Communist Party, one it was fully ready to exploit.[62] For a long period of time, Tychyna tried to find a place 'above the struggles', as defined by Koriak. Fortunately, for the party, Tychyna 'could not endure this soulless Olimpianism [*bezdushne olimpiistvo*, reference to high-brow literature created by Khvyl'ovyi's circle]' and threw himself 'into the waves of life' (*khvyli zhyttia*).[63]

It was important for the party officials to win over Tychyna. His ideological commitment could testify for the victory of the Bolshevik party over Ukraine's old-line intelligentsia. It was important to declare that Tychyna had eagerly embraced Soviet power – the sign that the Bolshevik ideology was internalized by the former ideological enemies. The ideological value of Tychyna's commitment was highlighted by Leites in the brochure 'The Renaissance of the Ukrainian Literature', published in 1925 in both Russian and Ukrainian. According to the critic,

> the fact that Tychyna, a genuine intellectual [*intelihent z intelihentiv*] and a talented lyrical poet [*liryk z lirykiv*], have become the poet of October proves that the [proletarian] revolution in Ukraine won not only in the material matters (*material'no*), but also spiritually (*dukhovno*) it won over the best part of the old literature and its most conservative domain – its secluded and individualistic lyrical poetry [*lirychna poezia*].[64]

A few years later, Koriak defined Tychyna as a symbol of the self-rejection and self-destruction of Ukrainian nationalism: 'He has been proclaimed a poet of the whole nation; but on its behalf he condemned the "yellow-and-blue" emigration and switched to Soviet literature, reaching its highest ranks.'[65]

After *Viter z Ukrainy*, Tychyna hardly published anything new. In a letter to Mohylians'kyi, he confessed his confusion and how disoriented he was in the current situation when poets composed verses without a calling:

> When I need to think something over, I am always silent. I am silent, because so much is being written and said at the moment. You know, external chaos comes together with an internal confusion. The passion [*horinnia*] is gone but writers insist on writing. [...] I cannot be superficial, I don't want to, because this will be the end of me. This is why I keep silent.[66]

Blakytnyi's premature death in 1925 was another reason for Tychyna's silence. With the passing of his patron, who had guided him during the most turbulent times, Tychyna needed to make his own way within the Soviet establishment.

Figure 7 Soviet Ukrainian writers in Kharkiv, 1925 (Pavlo Tychyna, *in the centre*). © Central State Archive-Museum of Literature and Arts of Ukraine, courtesy of TsDAMLMU.

Red path for Ukrainian literature

In Kharkiv, Tychyna occupied an editorial position in the literary-artistic section of the leading Soviet Ukrainian monthly journal *Chervonyi Shliakh*, launched in 1923.[67] *Chervonyi Shliakh* was a Ukrainian counterpart to the Russian magazine *Krasnaia Nov'*, the first Soviet state-sponsored 'thick journal' launched in 1921.[68] Like with *Krasnaia Nov'*, the intention behind the launch of *Chervonyi Shliakh* was to develop and promote quality Soviet literature and scholarship. It offered a forum to pro-Soviet writers and academics, as well as fellow travellers who had granted their support to the Soviet regime.[69] The journal itself was published under the auspices of the *Narkomos*, with the then Commissar for Education Hryn'ko as its editor-in-chief, later replaced by Shums'kyi in the same capacity. Its editorial board featured prominent literary figures and cultural managers, such as Tychyna, Khvyl'ovyi, Mykhailo Ialovyi and Geo Shkurupii. At the same time, to ensure the 'red path of the Ukrainian cultural construction', the board also included party representatives – the Ukrainian Central Executive Committee's member Andrii Khvylia and the TsK KP(b)U Secretary Zatons'kyi.[70]

Although limited in the scope of their activities, the former *Borot'bysty* Hryn'ko and Shums'kyi turned *Chervonyi Shliakh* into one of the greatest achievements of the *Ukrainizatsiia* decade. Advertised as a journal for cultural, social and political discussion, it provided a unique platform for promoting Soviet Ukrainian literature and culture. The editors saw their task as highlighting grand socio-economic achievements and the republic's cultural developments; publishing and popularizing the best examples of literature, journalism and scholarship in the Ukrainian language; and satisfying the cultural needs and providing Ukrainian readers with an orientation (*orientovka*) in literary and political life, as well as promoting Ukrainian as 'a powerful tool in the cultural development of the labouring masses'.[71] The magazine featured contributions on Ukraine's history, reviews on current political and economic issues, literary outputs by emerging and established Soviet writers, Ukrainian translations of foreign classics, literary criticism, reviews of major cultural events, as well as book reviews and a bibliography section dedicated to new publications.

By sponsoring *Chervonyi Shliakh*, the party wanted to prove its commitment to developing Ukrainian culture.[72] At the same time, the journal sought to promote the Soviet cause abroad and counterbalance the anti-Soviet rhetoric of the nationalist émigré communities. As the foreword to its first issue made clear, *Chervonyi Shliakh* was set up to compete with a journal of a similar type *Nova Ukraina* [New Ukraine], published by the former UNR socialist leaders Shapoval and Vynnychenko in Prague in 1922–8. The editors opposed those 'so-called patriots from abroad' who, 'blinded by class hatred', refused to accept the simple fact that Soviet Ukraine, this 'sovereign member of the Soviet Union and a new factor in international life', was a true embodiment of the revolutionary aims of the Ukrainian population. The second issue of *Chervonyi Shliakh* featured an article by Shums'kyi entitled *Stara Nova Ukraina* [Old and New Ukraine], in which the author accused the nationalist emigration, 'Ukrainian middle-class men' (*panky*) as he called them, of betraying their former socialist beliefs and continuing to oppose the Soviet regime, the only power able to achieve both social and national liberation for Ukraine.[73]

Needless to say, *Chervonyi Shliakh* was received negatively by Ukrainians abroad, many of whom regarded the journal as a 'Trojan Horse' for the Soviet authorities. For the journal's launch, Vynnychenko dedicated an article in *Nova Ukraina*, where he harshly criticized the cultural and nationalities policies of the Communist Party and accused the Soviet government of using Ukrainian writers and scholars to win over the countryside. He outright rejected the idea of a Soviet Ukrainian culture and discarded its platform – *Chervonyi Shliakh*, which he affronted as *Chekists'kyi Shliakh* [Chekist Path] – while blaming those national intellectuals engaged in its publication for betraying the Ukrainian cause.[74] Vynnychenko rejected the commitment of those Ukraine-minded communists and alleged that Ukrainian cultural figures had joined this 'mouthpiece of the RKP' against their free will: 'If only they could decide freely, they would have avoided this journal; [...] with disgust and rage, they would have rejected this offer to cooperate with Chekists and other adventurists.'[75] Vynnychenko was adamant that neither starvation nor threats of persecution or even death should force one to join the ranks of the enemy.[76]

Cultural diplomacy was another method of counterbalancing the negative influence of the anti-Communist emigrants. Throughout the 1920s, writers from Soviet Ukraine often travelled abroad to engage in conversation with those Ukrainians who sympathized with the Soviet regime and were considering whether to return to their

Figure 8 *Hart* writers Valeriian Polishchuk, Pavlo Tychyna and Oleksa Dosvitnii before travelling to Western Europe, 1924. © Central State Archive-Museum of Literature and Arts of Ukraine, courtesy of TsDAMLMU.

homeland. One of these cultural envoys was Tychyna, to whom *Narkomos* granted permission to travel abroad on 21 November 1924. The poet was allowed to travel 'with scholarly purpose and to get acquainted with and learn more about all the constituents of the arts – literature, journalism, theatre, music, art, cinema and publishing'.[77] Thus, in late 1924, Tychyna, together with two other *Hart* writers Oles' Dosvitnii and Polishchuk, embarked on an international tour of Germany, Czechoslovakia and France. According to Iefremov, during their trip the group behaved shamefully, living 'as Moscow merchants of the old times – lavish hotels, best wines, expensive dinners; no mirrors were broken only because in Europe they would have found themselves in prison or a madhouse'. When Tychyna tried to object to his fellows' *bon vivant*, Dosvitnii and Polishchuk retorted that 'they needed to show Europe how the Soviet state was sending its peoples on a mission abroad'.[78]

Their route was designed in a way that allowed the three writers to visit the major centres of Ukrainian emigration. While promoting cultural exchange and introducing European audiences to the latest achievements of Soviet literature and culture, the writers were expected to refute their critics in *Nova Ukraina*, who doubted the commitment of Soviet writers in Ukraine. The *Hart* members were on a mission to prove that Ukrainian writers had willingly come to support the Communist Party, and to rebuff any rumours about the violent and repressive nature of the Soviet regime. Tychyna was perhaps the delegation's most important member. A non-party writer himself, he could vouch for the Soviet government's commitment to developing a non-partisan Soviet Ukrainian culture. He was a speaker on behalf of all those former supporters of the Ukrainian revolution who had rejected their previous affiliation and joined Soviet society in their battle for socialism. More importantly, Tychyna was expected to spread Soviet propaganda among his former fellow-revolutionaries and Ukrainian writers abroad, many of whom he knew personally.

This was not Tychyna's first experience of engaging in heated polemics against nationalist émigrés. His 1922 poem, *Vidpovid' Zemliakam* [The Answer to my Countrymen], which had been included in *Viter z Ukrainy*, had attacked his former fellows for abandoning Ukraine and thus betraying the aims of the national revolution. As an epigraph to the poem, he chose an excerpt from an émigré periodical. It read: "'This poet for several years has been kissing the slipper of the Pope" – From foreign newspapers'. It was a clear reference to his collection *Zamist' sonetiv i oktav*. While the concluding line of his 1921 collection was phrased as a rhetorical question – 'Should I, too, kiss the slipper of the Pope?', the critics from abroad used this line to assert Tychyna's submission to the party.[79] In response to his detractors, Tychyna engaged in excruciating slander of the Ukrainian emigration, dissociating himself from his former close associates. The poem drew a line between Tychyna, by now a Soviet poet, and other Ukrainian writers who chose 'the safety' of exile.

Tychyna places his alter ego in Dante's *Inferno* filled with 'bandits and criminals', 'the fat-guts, the gorged, the mercenaries', 'the trifling, the vengeful, the dim-witted'. Those 'nationalists' are trying to lure him into their camp. Nonetheless, as the concluding line suggests, Tychyna had made his choice: 'I stand firm – like a cliff'. In turn, the émigrés bitterly criticized Tychyna for his ideological choices. For instance, in 1923, *Nova Ukraina* published a review on an excerpt from Tychyna's new poem *Skovoroda*, in which the poet was attacked for his acquiescence to Soviet literary requirements. From the émigré perspective, this poem was yet more proof that 'one of the most talented poets of the new Ukrainian generation slipped towards a slack Little-Russianism [*rozkhliabane malorosiistvo*], diluted with the *kvass* of Moscow internationalism'.[80]

In January 1925, Tychyna arrived in Prague, hoping to meet with his former associates Ievhen Malaniuk and Oles', the most prominent poets of the Ukrainian emigration. Malaniuk eagerly responded to his invitation, having once been a great admirer of Tychyna's talent. Back in 1921, he had described him as 'the voice of the earth for the first time speaking in people's language', as well as, 'one of the most prominent poets in the world literature'.[81] He later responded through his own writing, with same passion, to Tychyna's accord with the party. In November 1924, possibly in response to *Vidpovid' Zemliakam*, Malaniuk published the poem *Na mezhi dvokh epokh* [At the turn of two eras] that heavily alluded to *Soniachni klarnety*, Tychyna's most famous collection. Commenting on his former associate's trajectory from a poet of the national revolution to a Soviet propagandist, Malaniuk mournfully observed that 'from your clarinet only a painted pipe remained; and your bright spring has turned into a bloody October.' Nevertheless, when asked why he still wished to see Tychyna in 1925, Malaniuk explained that his early poetry was still 'like the first love, something that one cannot forget'.[82]

Figure 9 Writer Valeriian Polishchuk. Undated. © Central State Archive-Museum of Literature and Arts of Ukraine, courtesy of TsDAMLMU.

Malaniuk agreed to meet Tychyna alone, without his 'two guardsmen, who prefer their party membership cards to their lyre,' as he referred to Polishchuk and Dosvitnii in a later poem, *Poslanie* [Epistle] (1926). Another Ukrainian émigré in Prague, Mykhailo Mukhin, was present during the meeting and left a detailed account of the encounter in his memoirs.[83] According to Mukhin, Tychyna was frightened, paranoid and insincere. He kept checking the door and looked through the keyhole to make sure that no one was listening. Mukhin concluded that 'it was a shame to talk and see him'.[84] Perhaps, there was a reason for his fear. Later, Dosvitnii and Polishchuk reprimanded Tychyna for having arranged this reunion and threatened to disclose his 'contacts with the political emigration'.[85] Tychyna described his Prague ordeal in a letter to his lover Lidia: 'In Prague, I encountered many troubles and made a few new enemies; during this trip I was with people, who were not necessarily enemies, but only strangers [*chuzhi liudy*].' 'A difficult trip, a confusing trip, an unnecessary trip,' he concluded.[86] Annoyed with 'the two fools' [*durni*], as he characterized his companions in another private letter, Tychyna left them behind and continued his journey to France alone.[87]

Tychyna's hateful exchanges with the Ukrainian émigrés continued. In August 1925, Malaniuk compared Tychyna's ideological evolution to that of his popular Russian contemporary Sergei Yesenin (who subsequently committed suicide in December), noting that the former 'accepted not only the "Soviet style," (*sovietyzm*) but also … kissed his slipper' (yet another reference to Tychyna's earlier poetry).[88] For him, Tychyna was an especially unfortunate example of a Soviet poet. Unlike those who had converted to communists through conviction, such as Khvyl'ovyi or Blakytnyi, Tychyna had not been responsible for his choice. As Malaniuk suggested: 'Had Tychyna switched [to the Soviet side] by himself after becoming, for instance, disillusioned in Ukraine's prospects and turned into an "honest" Moscvophile, it would have been half a trouble. The problem is that Tychyna, using Odesa jargon, "was shifted" *(pereishly)*.'[89] Malaniuk implied that party propagandists used Tychyna in their favour while blaming the poet for not opposing it.

Malaniuk's poem *Poslanie* consequently served as an artistic reprimand of both Tychyna and Ryl's'kyi, the two poets who had stayed in Soviet Ukraine and embraced the new Soviet literature most acutely:

You are a mere son of a
Weak nation, for which
Above the future of Ukraine
a warm routine is more important – […]
And wisdom – 'that this has nothing to do with me' –
is its philosophy (O.P.)

A year later, Malaniuk once more used Tychyna's example to draw attention to the fate of Ukrainian culture: 'What a long journey to national degradation one needed to make in order to end up with the insanity (*marazm*) of Tychyna.'[90] In May 1928, Oles', Tychyna's long-time admirer, wrote perhaps the most painful accusation, while addressing all those national intellectuals who had agreed to serve the Communist Party:

And you too sold out yourself, Tychyna,
And you also went to the *moskal'*
Oh, poor mother, Ukraine,
You are in sorrow
In a bloody sea up to his knees
Stands without a trace of shame in his eyes
The poet, our former Tychyna,
And glorifies deaths and horror.
Publicly bows to the executioners,
He praises hangmen in his songs.
And from down the earth one hears curses
Of the fighters crucified.
Oh Judo, a noble Jew,
He went and hanged himself in solitude.
Pavlo Tychyna … he won't go –
He'd better crucify another (O.P.)

Tychyna did not publish another collection until 1931, although individual poems did appear in various literary journals and periodicals. Otherwise, Tychyna remained mostly occupied with his editorial duties at *Chervonyi Shliakh* and *Skhidnyi Svit* [Oriental World] (later, *Chervonyi Skhid* [Red Orient], 1927–31), a journal published by the All-Ukrainian Scientific Association of Oriental Studies, established under the *Narkomos* in January 1926. He also undertook extensive projects, translating various pieces into the languages of the so-called fraternal people of the Soviet Union, especially Armenian, but also Georgian, Tatar, Bashkir, Yiddish, as well as Russian and Belarusian.

The exchange between Tychyna and the representatives of the Ukrainian emigration exposed how the Soviet policies were understood and interpreted by Ukrainians abroad. For the members of the national emigration, many of whom used to cooperate with the Ukrainian national governments during the civil wars, there could be no excuse for what they saw as collaboration with the Soviet regime. At the same time, those national communists in the Soviet government regarded those émigrés as traitors who, due to lack of commitment or faith could not see the strides Ukraine had made under the Soviet regime. The Ukrainians abroad, in particular, took issue with Tychyna – a poet highly valued for his role in the national revolution. To characterize his transformation a metaphor of 'Little Russian' was used. For those critics, Tychyna came to represent the Moscow perspective on Ukrainianness – he had accepted Ukraine's subordinate status and submitted to 'big' Russia. By the same token, émigré Ukrainians viewed *Ukrainizatsiia* as nothing more than a linguistic and cultural concession utilized by the Soviet authorities to lure Ukraine-minded artists into Soviet work.

4

Defending Soviet Ukrainian literature

Ukrainizatsiia: Ukrainian perspective

In 1923, Moisei Ravich-Cherkasskii, an early historian of the KP(b)U suggested that the party's history was 'a sum of two histories: that of the Ukrainian proletariat and that of the Russian proletariat in Ukraine'.[1] Accordingly, there were two distinct ideological roots in the KP(b)U, one extending from the Russian revolutionary movement and another from the Ukrainian socialist movement. In the early 1920s, 'the Ukrainian root' of the KP(b)U, comprised of the 'old' Bolsheviks with a distinct national orientation, former members of the Ukrainian communist parties, the *Borot'bysty* in particular, and new party members, enrolled in the party from among local activists in the 1920s. The idea of 'two distinct ancestral roots' in Ukraine's Communist Party provides for a more nuanced understanding of the heated debates that surrounded the implementation of the Soviet policies in Ukraine, in our case, the Soviet nationalities policy of *korenizatsiia*.

Ukraine-minded members of the Communist Party welcomed the launch of the Soviet *korenizatsiia*. For them, *korenizatsiia* predominantly meant *Ukrainizatsiia* – the accelerated de-Russification of all spheres of public life, including party and governmental work, combined with an enhanced development of Ukrainian culture and language. While the central party encouraged national diversity as a step towards future unification of the Soviet peoples, its Ukrainian faction hoped that state-endorsed ethnic self-identification would provide the basis for a self-standing Soviet Ukraine with its own Soviet Ukrainian political, economic and cultural elites. From this perspective, the Soviet policy of *Ukrainizatsiia* was seen as a continuation of the initiatives of accelerated nation-building, elaborated and partially introduced by different Ukrainian governments during the civil war, as well as advocated by the members of the Ukrainian communist parties. For both groups – those implementing the Moscow policies and those pursuing the autonomist political path – linguistic Ukrainization, aimed at accelerating de-Russification of the Ukrainian populace, became a necessary yet subordinate objective.

There was a general agreement in the KP(b)U that *korenizatsiia* in the Soviet Ukrainian context was a linguistic and cultural concession devised to integrate the Ukrainian-speaking rural population into the Soviet order. In addition, there was a mutual understanding that more native Ukrainian speakers needed to be engaged in the party ranks and state institutions. Nonetheless, major disparities arose around the question of accelerating the Ukrainization of the republic's urban centres and the working class. Since imperial times, cities were often Russified with Ukrainians being an urban minority.[2] Nonetheless, modernization brought more rural Ukrainians to the cities, where they joined the working class and subsequently the party ranks.[3] By the mid-1920s, Ukraine's working class consisted of three more or less equal groups: Ukrainians, whose national self-identification was the same as their native language; non-Ukrainians (especially those of Russian and Jewish origin); and Russified Ukrainians, who identified themselves as Ukrainians but whose native language was Russian.[4]

Despite a common understanding of how important the working class was for a comprehensive *Ukrainizatsiia*, the party was wary of defining proletarians as its immediate target since it could make the process appear to be non-voluntary and lead to the assimilation of urban Russians under a single Ukrainian identity. In the end, *korenizatsiia* was not just about Ukrainians since the party was also committed to promoting the native languages and cultures of national minorities across the Soviet Union's constituent republics. However, the main challenge concerning Ukraine's Russian-speakers was whether to consider them as Russians or Ukrainians. In the first instance, they were to be exempt from the *Ukrainizatsiia* campaign, in the second, they represented its main targets. The Ukrainization of the Russified portion of the population was especially problematic since many party members and city dwellers considered Ukrainian to be a peasant vernacular and objected to it being forcibly imposed on the territory's urban centres.

These grievances found expression in an article by Dmitrii Lebed', a high-ranking member of the KP(b)U, that appeared in *Kommunist* in March 1923. According to Lebed', in Soviet Ukraine a battle of two cultures was unavoidable: 'In Ukraine, due to historical conditions, the culture of the city was Russian, and the culture of the village was Ukrainian.' He criticized *Ukrainizatsiia* since 'the artificial implantation of the Ukrainian language in the party and the working class, [...] would mean taking the position of the lower culture of the countryside in preference to the higher culture of the city.'[5] The victory of the 'higher' urban culture was inevitable; hence, any attempt to introduce Ukrainian in the city was futile. Although Lebed's 'theory of the struggle of two cultures' was never officially endorsed by the party leadership, it reflected their general attitude to *Ukrainizatsiia*.

The Ukrainian horizon in the KP(b)U, however, held a different perspective on this matter. In response to Lebed', Shums'kyi suggested that the proletariat in the republic was, in fact, of Ukrainian origin since most industrial workers were recruited from the peasantry. On numerous occasions, he highlighted the pivotal importance of broadening *Ukrainizatsiia* to those Russified Ukrainians in order to create the necessary conditions for them to re-internalize their native Ukrainian culture and language. For Shums'kyi, it was obvious that Ukrainian should dominate the urban space, with him arguing in favour of a proper language environment that would gradually help workers identify themselves with Ukrainian culture and language.[6] The strategy was thus 'to re-Ukrainianize the Russified masses' without forced assimilation. In agreement with party doctrine, Shums'kyi asserted that proletarian Ukrainization would infuse the labouring population, legitimize and strengthen the proletarian leadership and alter the direction of Ukrainian culture.[7]

To accelerate *Ukrainizatsiia* among both the proletariat and party apparatus, Ukrainizers needed to reduce prejudice against Ukrainian as a 'backward' tongue.[8] Indeed, the TsK KP(b)U resolution on *Ukrainizatsiia* from 1 August 1923 had already declared the formal equality of the Russian and Ukrainian languages, and measures were taken thereafter to introduce Ukrainian into party work, government bureaucracy, schooling, press and publishing.[9] Nonetheless, to make Ukrainian the language of the urban space, the prestige of the Ukrainian language and culture needed to be increased. During the 1920s, great effort was dedicated to promoting Ukrainian culture with both factions in the party supporting its integration into the cultural sphere.

There was a difference, however. While the official position was to create culture, using Stalin's formula, 'socialist in content, national in form', other factions among the cultural elites sought a national form of proletarian culture in Ukraine. They envisaged this Soviet Ukrainian culture to be modern, urban, national and socialist. At the same time, they were also aware that any further advances towards developing a Soviet Ukrainian culture would be impeded by a lack of social bases. Hence, proletarian Ukrainization was a prerequisite for altering the direction of Ukrainian cultural development. This chapter follows the debates on the nature of proletarian art that was being created in Soviet Ukraine, its audience and the artistic orientation that unfolded on the pages of Soviet press and literary almanacs in 1925–6.

The Literary Discussion of 1925–8

By the mid-1920s, despite generous state support and access to state-owned publishing houses, mass literary organizations had failed to gain a monopoly over Soviet literature. The official party line favoured a compromise between proletarian writers and fellow travellers, as well as tolerated different conflicting views on literature among cultural managers. This party perspective was reiterated by the resolution of the Politburo of the TsK KP(b)U 'Concerning Ukrainian Literary Groupings', issued on 10 April 1925 (a few months prior to a similar all-Union Resolution). According to the resolution, 'no existing literary organisation, including *Hart*, can claim that it alone represents the party in the field of literature, or holds the monopoly in applying the party line in this field.' While defending plurality in literary matters, party preferences fell more on the side of *Hart*:

> Notwithstanding some errors […], the Politburo of the Central Committee recognises that *Hart*, during the entire period of its existence, has accomplished a great deal in uniting around the party and Soviet government the most active and talented representatives of contemporary Ukrainian literature and poetry. To a certain extent *Hart* has unified the Ukrainian front of proletarian writers against the bourgeois nationalist ideology.[10]

The resolution also granted party support to the activities of the organization of peasant writers *Pluh*, providing for the creation of local centres 'where there are party organisations to direct their work'.[11] Similar approaches were implemented at the All-

Union level with the publication of the All-Union resolution 'On Party Policy in the Sphere of Literature' from 1 July 1925. This asserted that 'the hegemony of proletarian writers is, as yet, non-existent, and the Party ought to help those writers to earn for themselves the historical right to such a hegemony.'[12]

Both resolutions were intended to seek a compromise between proletarian writers and fellow travellers and to set limits regarding party intervention in literary matters. At the same time, they created a framework for the literary debates of 1925–6, when two different visions of Soviet literature in Ukraine came into direct opposition. During these debates, the centrally endorsed version of proletarian literature and Soviet culture clashed with the autonomist position of a distinctive Soviet Ukrainian literature, elaborated by Ukrainian cultural managers and writers and supported by the Ukrainian-minded faction of the *Narkomos* and the party leadership, particularly Shums'kyi. The eventual failure of the autonomous vision for a Soviet Ukrainian culture was caused by the political realignment of forces within the KP(b)U after 1926, when new cultural elites centred around Shums'kyi and Khvyl'ovyi lost their strong party support.

The major conflicts among Soviet Ukraine's cultural elites centred on the questions of primacy of form and content, artistic standards and audiences. Already in 1923, three members of *Hart* – Khvyl'ovyi, Dosvitnii and Ialovyi – voiced their objections to Blakytnyi's decision to open up the organization to the broader masses of the

Figure 10 Soviet Ukrainian writers: (on top standing: Tobykovets', Mykola Khvyl'ovyi, Petro Panch; in front sitting: Mykhailo Panchenko, Serhii Pylypenko, Pavlo Tychyna, Volodymyr Sosiura), 1920s. © Central State Archive-Museum of Literature and Arts of Ukraine, courtesy of TsDAMLMU.

population. This group, which became known as the 'Olympians', created a faction with a symbolic name 'Urbino',[13] arguing that art could not be used as a means of general enlightenment and defended the idea that literature should not be diminished to suit middlebrow tastes. Instead, it should set up certain standards to encourage and inspire reading audiences to raise their preferences. Khvyl'ovyi's attempts at drawing writers away from Blakytnyi eventually led to a split between the two. Smolych recorded the bitter exchange during a meeting in Blakytnyi's office, where Khvyl'ovyi accused him of having grown subservient to the party line: 'the apparatchik Vasyl' Blakytnyi has strangled the poet Vasyl' Ellan'. Blakytnyi's response was curt: 'Cain!..'[14] Khvyl'ovyi's Urbino laid the foundation for a new literary association, the Free Academy of Proletarian Literature (VAPLITE), established in 1925. Thereafter, VAPLITE dedicated itself to defending the autonomy of the cultural sphere and advocating for literary quality. The establishment of VAPLITE created a schism in the literary establishment in Soviet Ukraine. The opposition between these two visions of Soviet Ukrainian cultural development was defined as '*prosvita* versus Europe', or mass proletarian/peasant culture versus its more cultivated competitors.

A fairly complete bibliography of the Literary Discussion (around 600 items in total) can be found in the contemporary study of the literary process in Ukraine by Leites and Iashek.[15] Numerous contributions concerned issues of proletarian art, the audience and literature's social role, as well as the artistic orientation of the new proletarian literature being created in Ukraine. Khvyl'ovyi was probably the most established disputant among the participants of the Literary Discussion. His contribution (mostly journalist-style pamphlets and political polemics) was extensive: three cycles of essays (*Kamo Hriadeshy?* [Quo Vadis?] (April–June 1925), *Dumky proty Techii* [Thoughts against the Current] (November–December 1925) and *Apolohety Pysarysmu* [Apologists of Scribbling] (February–March 1926); a censored pamphlet *Ukraina chy Malorosiia?* [Ukraine or Little Russia?] (1926); single polemics published in the party newspapers; and editorials in the almanacs and journals *Vaplite* and *Literaturnyi Iarmarok, Prolitfront*.[16] Khvyl'ovyi's position was supported by his associates and like-minded colleagues, most significantly Zerov, who initiated the public debates within the Ukrainian Academy of Sciences in Kyiv.[17] At the same time, these essays were written in response to his opponents, who mainly represented an official, party-authorized position. The most important among them were Khvylia and Pylypenko. In this chapter, Khvyl'ovyi's four main concepts: *prosvita*, proletarian art, 'Europe' and the Asiatic Renaissance – that would become at the core of Khvyl'ovyi's new cultural strategy – are scrutinized. While some of those concepts resembled the concerns of the larger Soviet debate (form and content debate, the nature of art and its audience), Khvyl'ovyi's position evolved towards a theory of Ukrainian sovereignty and messianism by 1926.

Before analysing Khvyl'ovyi's pamphlets from this period, it is important to note that his ideas can hardly be regarded as a coherent system or a well-elaborated theory. The pamphlets themselves are hermetic, often defined by breaks in logic. They are also rich with free-flowing ideas and highly charged emotional images, which, at times, are hard to comprehend without reference to current literary debates, existing intellectual tradition or Khvyl'ovyi's broader views. Khvyl'ovyi developed his argument while writing these essays and in response to the critics; hence, the definition of his central images was never comprehensive and changed over time. Moreover, the pamphlets contain allusions to Khvyl'ovyi's prose; it seems that the writer was using different means to communicate ideas that had preoccupied him since the early twenties, including questions of language and the nature of the proletarian literature. They, therefore, do not represent a major departure from his literary work, being similar to his use of prose for communicating important political messages (especially the novel *Val'dshnepy* [The Woodcocks], 1927). At times, it seems as if the author was more preoccupied with the style and the language of his essays than the coherence and logic of his arguments. In general, Khvyl'ovyi's pamphlets are of their time and should be read with an awareness of their historical context.[18] Khvyl'ovyi views and polemical tropes can hardly be useful and applicable outside his particular context.

The three cycles of pamphlets, published in mainstream periodicals from 1925 to 1926, received wide recognition and initiated a broad discussion about the prospects of artistic orientation, quality of literature, audiences for the new Soviet culture, cultural and national developments and conflicts underlying Russian–Ukrainian relations. Khvyl'ovyi, with his peculiar manner, sophisticated language and rich references to world cultural heritage, engaged the entire Ukrainian intelligentsia. According to one Kyivan critic, 'The impression, after Khvyl'ovyi's article, was of being in a room so stuffy that breathing was difficult, only for the windows to have suddenly been opened and to have one's lungs filled with fresh air again.'[19] Ultimately, the ideas articulated in Khvyl'ovyi's pamphlets reflected the Ukrainian cultural zeitgeist of the 1920s with its ongoing negotiations about the scope of the *Ukrainizatsiia* campaign and the overall amount of autonomy Ukraine could have within the Soviet Union.

'Prosvita': Proletarian writers and their readers

The Literary Discussion, the most significant intellectual development of the 1920s, began with a squib written by the author Hryts'ko Iakovenko entitled, 'On Critics and Criticism in Literature', published in *Kul'tura i Pobut* [Culture and Daily life], a literary supplement to the governmental newspaper *Visti* on 30 April 1925. Iakovenko, a writer for *Pluh* whose short story had been rejected for a literary competition, accused Khvyl'ovyi and other 'grey-haired Olympians' of barring young writers with 'a proper social origin' from entering the literary field. He used Khvyl'ovyi's short story *Ia (Romantyka)* as an example of literature that could only be read by 'philistines and degenerates, for whom the revolution was an example of acute spiritual sadism'.[20] Instead, he argued, literature should be easily understood by everyone: 'proletarian literature ought to be elementary and simple, but healthy and useful.'[21] Khvyl'ovyi's reply was published in the same issue. This 'First Letter to Literary Youth (On "Satan in a Barrel," Graphomaniacs, Speculators and Other *Prosvita* Types)' initiated a long debate between Khvyl'ovyi, his associates and their opponents, representing the official party-authorized position. The main disagreement between Iakovenko and Khvyl'ovyi concerned the ontological definition of proletarian literature. Through Iakovenko, Khvyl'ovyi attacked the rhetoric of the mass literary organizations, who used literature to spread Soviet propaganda, allowing for the political indoctrination of their members and readers.

The first cycle of pamphlets, *Kamo Hriadeshy?*, published from April to June 1925, was mostly concerned with the orientation of Ukrainian proletarian literature. In this cycle, four main themes were sketched. The first of these was *prosvita*, a name given to various nineteenth-century enlightenment societies, which were used after the revolution for providing basic political education and literacy campaigns. During the 1920s, *prosvity* became centres for propaganda work and nurturing future proletarian writers and readers. Khvyl'ovyi rejected this practice and used the term '*prosvita*' as a psychological category, referring to provincialism, parochial and utilitarian attitude towards literature, exemplified in hackwork and mass culture. He set *prosvity*, with their references to Ukrainian folklore and popular tastes, against high culture and 'academism', 'Olympianism' in Khvyl'ovyi's vocabulary. This opposition also applied to understanding creative writing (a gift or a skill); a writer (a talented individual with his own worldview or a trained one, prepared to reproduce ready-made plots); and a reader (is literature meant to entertain and reflect objective reality or to inspire?). In theory, this dichotomy should not exhaust the options available for readers. During the Soviet 1920, however, literature acquired a two-fold meaning: either as a form of creative activity (hence, autonomous) or a reflection of an underlying political agenda (engaged [*zaanhazhovana*] literature). It was this distinction between social usefulness and party-mindedness that Khvyl'ovyi relied upon in order to judge literary quality.

Undoubtedly, the proliferation of *prosvity* was a by-product of the revolution, which had destroyed established social structures and brought to the fore the lowest, as well as the least educated, social groups. In addition, *korenizatsiia* had exposed a shortage of educated Ukrainian speakers while empowering writers with little or no talent.[22] The *prosvita*-type organizations (such as *Pluh* and *Hart*) embraced this post-revolutionary egalitarianism and encouraged those social activists to learn how to create literature. For Khvyl'ovyi, however, these 'writers' were nothing more than 'pen-pushers',[23] for whom literature was 'a sign outside the State Publishing House, the aphorism on a fence, and the verse on the toilet wall'.[24] Speaking out against the mainstream cultural consensus, Khvyl'ovyi defended the concept of hierarchy, which should be based not on the class, but on the level of education and culture. He detested the orientation towards the countryside, insisting instead on the determinant role of urban proletariat and intelligentsia for Soviet Ukraine's cultural development. For him, proletarian literature was meant to elevate and challenge its readers, rather than appeal to popular mass tastes and appetites.

While Khvyl'ovyi agreed that 'proletarian' literature meant literature that was proletarian in its spirit and written specifically for working-class audiences, his conception of the type of writing that was to be created in Soviet Ukraine was also distinctive. Khvyl'ovyi had a rather idealist vision of the proletariat: highly educated, politically engaged and nationally aware, a rising very much in line with Shums'kyi's interpretation of *Ukrainizatsiia*. Both Khvyl'ovyi and his patron conflated the Ukrainization of the working class with a raising standard of Soviet Ukrainian culture. Instead, as observed by Khvyl'ovyi, the idea of proletarian art was being hijacked and misused by the mass literary organizations. He therefore attempted to redefine the concept and to draft the programme for a new literary organization, tasked not only with promoting revolutionary values, but also with creating an environment for young talented writers to produce literary works of high quality. The members of this new organization were expected to confront numerous pseudo-proletarian writers, dubbed by Khvyl'ovyi as 'red graphomaniacs'.²⁵

This vision for a new literary organization was further elaborated upon in the second cycle of essays, *Dumky proty Techii* (published from November to December 1925). The organization was envisaged to encourage

> the concentration of creative individuals (critics, publicistic critics, creative writers) who would on the one hand satisfy the now rising demands of the worker-peasant masses, and whose distinct and clearly visible ranks would on the other hand be capable of counterpoising the new world-view of a young class to the old ideology of art.²⁶

This vision was realized through VAPLITE, the Free Academy of Proletarian Literature (*Vil'na Akademiia Proletars'koi Literatury*), founded in October 1925.²⁷ The idea of a new literary organization devoted to high-quality literature, however, was originally proposed by Blakytnyi in 1924. In his 'Manifesto of the All-Ukrainian Literary Academy', he had called for the creation of an 'October Ukrainian literature [that] should and does enter the arena of world culture as one of the first proletarian cultures of the world.'²⁸ Blakytnyi's dream did not materialize, owing to his split with Khvyl'ovyi a year later, and his premature death in December 1925, leading to the eventual dissolution of *Hart*.

Figure 11 Ukrainian writers, *in front sitting*: Volodymyr Sosiura, Pavlo Tychyna, and Mykola Khvyl'ovyi. Undated. © Central State Archive-Museum of Literature and Arts of Ukraine, courtesy of TsDAMLMU.

Some of Blakytnyi's concepts were later incorporated into the statute of VAPLITE. Khvyl'ovyi served as the Academy's spiritual leader, the writer Ialovyi (replaced later by the playwright Mykola Kulish) was elected its president, with a writer Arkadii Liubchenko as secretary. Altogether, seventeen writers were present at the first meeting of VAPLITE and throughout its existence, it remained an exclusive and elitist organization.[29] Arkadii Liubchenko later recalled that Khvyl'ovyi had carefully selected its members himself. The 'application process consisted of one-to-one conversations, provocative questions, and, of course, an evaluation of the literary merit of every potential candidate'.[30] This sectarian view on the membership was shared by other VAPLITE members. As Dosvitnii stated:

> an Academy imposes responsibilities. It binds its members as academicians to take a serious attitude towards the creation of proletarian literature, to be cultures writers with definite ideological class principles as opposed to the recently created tradition that a writer should be bound to nothing and literary organisations could spring up like mushrooms after rain, without an obvious need. We have undertaken a great cultural regeneration. We realise that a writer must understand his duties and responsibilities ... We are very young ... therefore let us learn, let us learn.[31]

According to a resolution from the first meeting, the organization aimed 'to unite qualified writers [*kvalifikovani pys'mennyky*] with a [common] ideological basis, while retaining wide autonomy as far as their literary work is concerned'.[32] In general, the new literary organization defended the quality of artistic activity and was open to all members of *Hart* and *Pluh* who shared the same understanding of proletarian literature. According to Khvyl'ovyi, VAPLITE's mission was to revive artistic criteria and promote excellence by replacing the principle 'give me quantity' by 'let's go for quality'.[33] Unlike its rivals, VAPLITE did not intend to teach the proletariat how to produce good literature. The members of the academy shared a similar concern for quality, artistic integrity and originality and developing a 'high culture'.[34] Its mission was to produce worthwhile literature for the proletariat, hoping that its audience would simultaneously cultivate their own level of cultural awareness through which to appreciate it. The Academy published a literary almanac *Vaplite* (1926) and a journal VAPLITE, five issues of which appeared in 1927 and featured poetry and prose, alongside critical studies, book reviews, political and social essays.

'Europe': The question of artistic orientation

In his pamphlets, Khvyl'ovyi audaciously claimed that Soviet Ukrainian culture should orient itself towards Europe and not Moscow. The idea of a Western-orientated Ukrainian culture, however, was not new. By the end of the nineteenth century, an independent cultural tradition had already emerged, based on close ties with Western art that bypassed Russian mediation. Already in the works of Ukrainian modernist and symbolist artists one could find direct reference to predominant European themes and styles. Indeed, the first futurist circles in Ukraine were formed on the eve of the

First World War, while Kyivan Neoclassicists had been inspired by European antiquity. This acquaintance with European tendencies became especially apparent among avant-garde circles.[35] The founders of the Ukrainian avant-garde Vasyl' Iermilov, Alexander Bogomazov, Kazimir Malevich, David Burliuk, Vladimir Tatlin and Aleksandra Ekster – who were connected to Kyiv, as well as Kharkiv, L'viv, and Odesa by birth, education, national tradition or identity, – had been trained and maintained their own studios in different European cities.[36] The most famous Ukrainian theatre director of the 1920s, Kurbas, who had been influenced by the experimentalism he encountered during his studies in Vienna, was responsible for introducing Western traditions into the national theatre. This cultural exchange with European artists was further advanced with the *Narkomos's* support during the 1920s when many artists were able to travel abroad while many former émigrés returned to Soviet Ukraine, inspired by the scope of *Ukrainizatsiia*.

Khvyl'ovyi and his peers had first-hand knowledge of what Europe could offer to the young Soviet Ukrainian republic and its culture. However, their understanding of 'Europe' was not necessarily bound to a political system or limited by geographical borders. In the first cycle of pamphlets, Khvyl'ovyi simply associated 'Europe' with high standards of artistic work and set it against the literary outputs of *'prosvita'* writers with their torrents of low-quality literature, which had inundated the republic's bookstores and libraries during the 1920s. The concept of a 'psychological Europe' was used to counterweight provincialism and epigone art, initiated by the *prosvity*:

> Europe is the experience of many ages. It is not the Europe that Spengler announced "in decline", not the one that is rotting and which we despise. It is the Europe of a grandiose civilisation, the Europe of Goethe, Darwin, Byron, Newton, Marx and so on and so forth.[37]
>
> Einsteins, both great and small, are Europeans, and half-baked professors are prosvita-types.[38]

In *Dumky proty Techii*, Khvyl'ovyi added further definitions to 'Europe':

> You ask: "Which Europe?" Take whichever you like, 'past or present, bourgeois or proletarian, eternal or ever-changing'. Because, to be sure, Hamlets, Don Juans or Tartuffes existed in the past, but they also exist today, they used to be bourgeois, but they are also proletarian, you can consider them 'eternal,' but they will be 'ever-changing'.[39]

As with *'prosvita'*, his 'Europe' was a psychological category. It was defined through certain qualities, which contributed to the creation of a 'grandiose civilisation'. Its development was attributed to civic activism and intellectuality as inherent qualities of a Western civilization. The first component was:

> the *ideal of a civic person*, who over the course of many ages has perfected his biological, or more accurately his psycho-physiological nature, and who *is the property of all classes.*[40]

The second constituent of 'psychological Europe' was intelligence and the value attached to any intellectual activity, as said:

> this is the European intelligent in the best sense of the word. This, if you like, is the sorcerer from Württemberg who revealed a grandiose civilization to us and opened up limitless vistas to our gaze. This is Doctor Faustus, if we conceive of the latter as the inquisitive human spirit.[41]

Obviously, Khvyľovyi's pamphlets were not targeted at laymen. His 'Europe' was clearly an elitist idea, addressed to those well aware of the European intellectual tradition and Western culture. His readers were meant to follow his free flow of thoughts and be comfortable with all the references and allusions. The pamphlets contain abundant references to *Sturm und Drang*, the late eighteenth-century German literary movement, inspired by Johann Gottfried Herder and led by Johann Wolfgang von Goethe. In addition, he alluded to Friedrich Nietzsche and Richard Wagner. The most common point of reference was, however, the German philosopher Oswald Spengler whose vision of 'Europe in decline' served to inform Khvyľovyi's own concept of 'Europe'. The first volume of Spengler's *Der Untergang des Abendlandes* [The Decline of the West], originally published in 1918, was only translated into Russian in 1923.[42]

Khvyľovyi directed his pamphlets towards both young intellectuals and the old-line intelligentsia. His image of 'Europe' became especially associated with the polymathic Zerov, a literary critic, translator of the ancients and an outstanding poet. Such references quickly became an abstract idea by his use of the plural 'Zerovs', meaning those who resembled something akin to an intellectual of the Western type:

> we have to use our Zerovs not only for their technical skills, but also in their psychological dimension. The single, at first glance insignificant (and, in the opinion of some, counter-revolutionary) fact – that they are so resolutely going "against the current" in translating the Romans, gives us the right to view them as real Europeans.[43]

At the same time, Khvyľovyi was well aware of Ukraine's backwardness. He explained it primarily through the lack of a Faustian activist attitude, of that 'inquisitive human spirit' characteristic of Europeans. Century-long Russian domination resulted in a stigma of cultural parochialism, whereby Ukraine became a '*Khokhliandia*', a 'classic country of cultural epigonism' or 'servile psychology',[44] which kept producing 'a sluggish artist'

> capable only of repeating what has already been gone before, of aping. He simply cannot grasp that a nation can express its cultural potential only if it discovers its own particular path of development. He cannot grasp this, because he is afraid *to dare*![45]

In his explosive third cycle of pamphlets *Apolohety Pysarysmu*, Khvyľovyi openly attacked the perceived Russian chauvinism that had negatively impacted on Ukraine's political and cultural development. Khvyľovyi questioned 'by which of the world's literatures should we set our course?' and immediately provided a definite and unconditional answer: 'On no account by the Russian. [...] Ukrainian poetry must flee as quickly as possible from Russian literature and its styles.'⁴⁶ This determination was prompted by a number of factors that, from his perspective, made cultural orientation towards Moscow detrimental to the new Soviet Ukrainian culture. While acknowledging the high literary quality of the Russian canon, Khvyl'ovyi rejected it as an appropriate mediator in the evolution of its Ukrainian counterpart. First, as he believed, young Ukrainian writers had nothing to learn from their Russian opposites. All the great Russian literary works, written during the nineteenth century, had, according to Khvyl'ovyi, no examples of an active citizen, a determinant feature for future cultural development. A 'passive pessimism', claimed to be an inherent feature of the Russian classics, would only produce 'cadres of "superfluous people", or to put it simply parasites, "dreamers", people "without any given responsibility," "whimperers," "grey little people" of the "twentieth rank".'⁴⁷ For him, the golden age of Russian literature had already passed with the 'feeble nobility' and nineteenth-century feudalism. He therefore called upon new writers to seek alternative sources of inspiration and reject any latent proclivity to orientate themselves towards Russia: 'Death to Dostoevskism! Up with the cultural renaissance!'⁴⁸

Second, Russian proletarian literature had nothing to offer with Moscow dismissed as a centre of 'all-Union Philistinism' that 'essentially never saw the October revolution and its heroic struggle'.⁴⁹ For Khvyl'ovyi, the recently ordained capital of the Soviet

Figure 12 Ivan Dniprovs'kyi, Iurii Ianovs'kyi, and Mykola Khvyl'ovyi. Undated. © Central State Archive-Museum of Literature and Arts of Ukraine, courtesy of TsDAMLMU.

Union symbolized only bureaucracy and a perversion of revolutionary slogans. Since it borrowed the new proletarian ethos, Russian literature was unable to kindle any belief in the 'commune behind the hill'. Moreover, he detested the chauvinist attitude of the Russian Proletkult-type writers (the Smithy [*Kuznitsa*] and the Octobrists, and the *Na Postu* circle), for whom Soviet Ukraine was regarded as merely another Russian province.[50] He opposed the dominant Russian (and often Ukrainian) perspective that Ukrainian literature was subservient and hence could not be original. In a word, Khvyl'ovyi was seeking to resist the cultural 'colonization' of Ukraine, in a manner similar to the way Shums'kyi had opposed its political administration.[51]

For this reason, relations between the Ukrainian and Russian writers often acquired political undertones. For example, Khvyl'ovyi took any instances of comparison between Ukrainian writers and their Russian counterparts painfully. He was equally aware of the fact that he himself was often called a 'Ukrainian Pilnyak'; however, he detested this comparison not because of Pilnyak's merit, whose early prose he admired ('where in each line one can see an artist', as the writer had once reviewed[52]), but due to the implied subordinate status it afforded Soviet Ukrainian literature. Pilnyak's visit to Kharkiv in March 1924 was itself indicative of the increasing tensions between the two Soviet republics' literary establishments. During his visit, a literary evening was organized to demonstrate to both Ukraine's 'urban (*mishchans'ka*) intelligentsia, defined as "the patron of the genuine Russian culture," and to Pilnyak himself that Kharkiv was not a Russian (*russkaia*) province, but the capital of the Soviet Ukrainian Republic'.[53] The event ended in scandal, however, with Ukrainian writers expressing open disdain for Pilnyak's new prose. Consequently, Khvyl'ovyi published a scathing review in the literary supplement to *Visti*, calling Pilnyak 'a bard of the moribund noble estate (*umiraiushchee pomestie*)'.[54] In a private letter to Mohylians'kyi, he stated that Kharkiv writers took a militant stand against all 'the brazen fellows Mayakovskis and all the dandies from the Moscow bohemia', who denied the existence of Ukrainian literature.[55]

Khvyl'ovyi believed that the revolution had initiated a distinctive current in Ukrainian literature, which had taken a completely separate path to that of Russia. What was lacking, however, were the civic values offered by European civilization. Such a reorientation towards Western techniques and manners was, nonetheless, conditional. Khvyl'ovyi did not just want to change Soviet Ukrainian literature's 'conductor'; ultimately, his idea was to adopt only those characteristics, which were in short supply among Ukrainians (namely an active citizenry, value of intellect, intellectual activity and civil society) and to enhance them with romantic *vitaism*, the current he and his followers had been perfecting. His idea was as follows:

> When we steer our course toward Western European literature, it is not with the goal of yoking our art to some other wagon bringing up the rear, but with the aim of reviving it after the asphyxiating atmosphere of backwardness. We will travel to Europe to study, but with a secret idea – after several years to burn with an extraordinary flame.[56]

Khvyl'ovyi's pamphlets challenged the intelligent readers and made no concessions to the ignorant ones. Zerov shared in this understanding of culture while trying to deprive Khvyl'ovyi's images of political implications. According to the literary critic, 'Europe' in Khvyl'ovyi's approach was nothing more than a strong cultural tradition. From this point of view, the opposition of 'Europe vs. *Prosvita*' was framed as *kul'tura* vs. *khaltura*, a culture of lasting values versus hackwork.[57] In one of his essays, Zerov observed that:

> In our literary life there is still very little real culture, little knowledge, little education, while our scholarship is at a disadvantage. [...] Khvyl'ovyi is right. A young writer must get rid of his illiteracy in the field in which he wishes to work. [...] Such self-education will be the first step to what Khvyl'ovyi called 'Europe'. We can conquer Europe only when we make their achievement our own.[58]

Nevertheless, this elitist perspective, ran counter to the main social developments and political interests of the time. Khvyl'ovyi denounced the democratization of Soviet culture, which came hand in hand with accommodating middlebrow tastes and orienting towards an unsophisticated, conservative, mass readership. Indeed, the criticism against Khvyl'ovyi exposed the narrow-mindedness of the majority of Ukraine's politicians and literary activists, who did not want to be taught or challenged by another 'grey-haired old man' or 'Olympians'.[59] The public campaign against Khvyl'ovyi and his supporters exposed the unbridgeable differences between the promoters of highbrow and mass conceptions of Soviet culture. The main concern of the debate was the social role of literature: should art be subordinated to political imperatives and be didactic and useful, or should it merely be imagination's plaything, detached from social conditions? A letter from the Kharkiv Institute of Public Education (formerly Kharkiv University) dated from May 1925 and written in response to the literary debate being waged in the republican press, condemned Khvyl'ovyi's 'unpatriotic orientation on literary standards set by Western Europe'. Instead, the Kharkiv Institute's staff called for 'a mass literature accessible to and so badly required by workers'.[60] A similar opinion was voiced by the members of the Ukrainian Academy of Sciences in Kyiv during its hosting of the public discussion 'The Paths for the Development of Contemporary Literature' on 24 May 1925. One of the questions submitted was: 'Which Europe does Khvyl'ovyi want to follow?' The critique was overwhelming: Khvyl'ovyi was accused of advocating a view of Europe that was 'bourgeois, philistine, and hostile to the goals of Communism'. As one participant questioned: 'Should one prefer the Tarzan novel by Edgar Rice Burroughs to the poetry of Mayakovski?'[61] Clearly, Khvyl'ovyi's ideas were not understood and appreciated, instead they were rebutted at face value.

These public attacks came as no surprise. His non-political idea of a 'psychological Europe' was doomed by its ideological connotations, since many critics linked it to a 'capitalist Europe', an orientation that could not find support in a country wishing to achieve communism. His affection to high culture went against the mainstream Soviet cultural establishment. Khvyl'ovyi attempted to rid Ukraine of its provincialism that could be gradually achieved through the creation of art and literature that had little to do with the masses. This, however, could only ever reflect a minority position within the Ukrainian old-line intelligentsia and new cultural elites. Khvyl'ovyi continuously repeated that his concept of proletarian literature was based not on the class origin or ideology of writers, but on their skills and artistic potential. To define his cause, he used an example of Zerov – the old-line literary critic and academician who could hardly be associated with the new proletarian culture. As he explained, 'the Soviet *intelihent* Zerov, who is armed with the higher mathematics of art is – hyperbolically speaking – a million times more useful than a hundred *prosvita*-types, who are about as well versed in this art as a pig in orange-growing'.[62] Nonetheless, these single *intelihenty* could hardly compete with the predominance of the state-encouraged mass literature gaining ground in the second half of the 1920s.

The approach elaborated by the card-carrying communist Khvyl'ovyi in the 1920s was bizarre, to say the least, within the Soviet Union's early ideological framework. He continuously attempted to separate culture from politics: 'one should not confuse our political union with literature'.[63] His primary concern was how to make the new Soviet Ukrainian literature original, self-sufficient and independent from a 'Russian conductor'.[64] Nevertheless, his non-political attitude was, of course, a matter of perspective. With the course on industrialization, adopted in 1925, culture was slowly becoming subordinate to this envisaged grand social and economic transformation. Hence, any debate on cultural autonomism was automatically interpreted through a political lens.

'Asiatic renaissance' or Ukrainian messianism

Another image introduced in *Kamo Hriadeshy?* was that of the 'Asiatic renaissance'. This was the most illogical and emotional concept, to which the Khvyl'ovyi referred to constantly in all his pamphlets. In general terms, Khvyl'ovyi developed the concept of the 'Asiatic renaissance' as a response to Spengler's vision of 'Europe in decline' by enhancing the German theorist's three cycles of cultural development with Marxist principles of causality and historic materialism, and adding a fourth, 'proletarian' cultural-historical type.[65] Khvyl'ovyi seconded Spengler that Europe, which had produced 'feudal' and 'bourgeois' cultural types, had exhausted its powers and thus could not produce this fourth cycle. Khvyl'ovyi therefore agreed that Europe approached its decline, but 'not, however, as a Faustian culture but as the bourgeois type'.[66] The fourth cultural type, according to Khvyl'ovyi, was to be initiated in Asia, where another human energy had started to grow – 'the yellow peril', 'symbolising the real force which will solve the problem of Communist society'.[67]

His interest in the Asian countries was in step with the time. Support for national liberation movements worldwide had entered the Bolshevik doctrine from 1924. Writing in 'The Foundation of Leninism', Stalin had encouraged communists to utilize the 'revolutionary potentialities latent in the revolutionary liberation movement of the oppressed countries […] for transforming the dependent and colonial countries from a reserve of the imperialist bourgeoisie into a reserve of the revolutionary proletariat, into an ally of the latter'.[68] It also became part of the Communist International agenda.[69] Khvyl'ovyi, instead of utilizing the revolutionary potential of the Asiatic countries in overcoming capitalism, wished to exploit the cultural 'Asiatic Renaissance' to hasten the cultural awakening of Europe.

In the long run, he anticipated 'the future unheard-of flowering of art among such nations as China, India, and so forth [...] because Asia, realising that only Communism will liberate it from economic slavery, will utilise art as a factor in the battle'.[70] In the short term, however, an Asiatic renaissance was meant to be triggered by the cultural revival in the Soviet Union. Khvyl'ovyi predicted that the 'mysterious country that will solve the great world problem' already existed within the borders of the Soviet Union, the first and the only country of 'victorious socialism'. It is noteworthy that Khvyl'ovyi assigned an exceptional part in disclosing this great Asiatic potential to Soviet Ukraine. As he further explained:

> In the fact that the spiritual culture of Bolshevism can only express itself clearly in the young Soviet republics and in the first place under the azure skies of the South-Eastern republic of the Communes, which has always been an arena of civil strife and which has raised on its luxuriant steppes the type of the revolutionary conquistador. [...] Inasmuch as Eurasia [*surprisingly often used by the writer as a synonym for Soviet Ukraine*] stands on the boundary of two great territories, of two energies, the avant-garde of the fourth cultural-historical type is constituted by us.[71]
>
> The new art that Europe is awaiting will issue from the South-Eastern republic of the communes, from none other than Soviet Ukraine.[72]

As mentioned above, he was sceptical of Russian revolutionary literature's potential. Instead, he gave priority to Soviet Ukraine. He believed that Russian revolutionary cultural tradition could 'only find the magical balm for its revival beneath the luxuriant, vital tree of the renaissance of young national republics, in the atmosphere of the springtime of once oppressed nations'.[73] His hopes were with Soviet Ukraine, which would be able to champion the fourth proletarian cultural type:

> Romantic *vitaism* [...] is the art of the first period of the Asiatic renaissance. From Ukraine it must flow forth to all parts of the world and play there not a local, limited role but one of the significance for humanity in general.[74]

The messianic role of Ukraine, as predicted by Khvyl'ovyi, suggests at least one main question: why was Russia, the country which possessed the same necessary attributes as Ukraine, unable to spark this great cultural revival in the West? For contemporaries, the reason was irrational – as some critics admitted, Khvyl'ovyi simply did not like Russia,[75] which he once defined as 'the old mother Kaluga'.[76] Khvyl'ovyi's partiality was well known. In one review, Skrypnyk provocatively asked: 'Is he [Khvyl'ovyi] against Russian literary trends and their forms because the latter are bad or because they are Russian?'[77] For many, Khvyl'ovyi's argumentation did not stand up to criticism and rational explanation.

Another question, which suggests itself, however, is whether any prerequisites to claim such predestination existed in the Ukraine of 1926. One must admit that Khvyl'ovyi was fanatically committed to the Ukrainian cause and spared no effort in pursuing its revival. In one private letter to Mohylians'kyi, dated from 17 March 1924, he explained why he could not find the time for a vacation:

> It would be embarrassing now to leave Kharkiv. Our time is so remarkable, so beautiful and Ukraine hasn't experienced anything like this before. It would be a crime now to sit somewhere in a corner and idle away my time. Sometimes I fall into such a melancholy, that, honestly, I can see those lights of the commune behind the hills. I can feel the accelerated rebirth of a young and strong as an oak-Ukraine.[78]

Khvyl'ovyi somewhat optimistically believed that Soviet Ukraine possessed, or was about to acquire, all the necessary components in order to steer the process of world socialist liberation. First, he believed in the potential of the new Soviet Ukrainian intelligentsia. The new cultural and political elites and promoters of a distinct Soviet Ukrainian culture were tasked with spreading the new ethos among Ukraine's workers. He followed Lenin's teaching on the vanguard of the proletariat, who could not create any ideology of their own. As the guidance of the Communist Party was necessary in the political sphere, so no proletarian culture could be created without the help of an intelligentsia. He defended the need for new Soviet Ukrainian elites that would help the proletariat to fulfil their role of fostering Ukraine's cultural revival. Second, Khvyl'ovyi entrusted the task of pursuing a *Geniezeit* (the Age of Genius), a concept developed by the *Sturm und Drang* group,[79] to numerous 'rebellious geniuses' (*m'iatezhni henii*), who went through the revolution and the civil wars and had used their first-hand experience to create world-class literature. The group of talented Ukrainian proletarian writers, the Olympians, had already gathered around Khvyl'ovyi in the VAPLITE, as he explained:

> the powerful Asiatic renaissance in art is approaching and its forerunners are we, the 'Olympians.' Just as Petrarch, Michelangelo, Raphael and others in their time from a tiny corner of Italy set Europe afire with the flame of the Renaissance, in the same way the new artists from the once oppressed Asiatic countries, the new artistic-communards who are travelling with us will climb the peak of Mount Helicon and place there the lamp of renaissance, and, under the distant thunder of fighting on the barricades, it will cast the light of its fiery purple-blue pentangle over the dark European night.[80]

The Vaplitians were to break the centuries-old provincialism of Ukrainian culture and initiate the new civilizational cycle, the 'proletarian' cultural-historical type. Unfortunately, VAPLITE with its scant membership, personally selected by Khvyl'ovyi, could hardly compete with the mass writers' associations for the minds of Ukraine's working class. Apart from *Pluh*, VAPLITE was also forced to contend with the All-Ukrainian Union of Proletarian Writers (*Vseukrains'ka Spilka Proletars'kykh Pys'mennykiv*, VUSPP), established in 1927 and subsequently becoming the main agent for achieving institutional and ideological unification.

As these chapters have shown, there were different understandings of the scope and aims of the *korenizatsiia* policy in the context of Soviet Ukraine. The Soviet central authorities aimed at achieving hegemony in the republic with its predominantly peasant and Ukrainian-speaking population, hence the countryside as the main target of their policies. Whereas Soviet Ukrainian elites aimed at comprehensive *Ukrainizatsiia* that would necessarily include the republic's Russified working class.

Those divisions were also translated into the cultural realm. While Soviet cultural agents targeted rural and newly urbanized peasants with their literary outputs of low artistic value, the promoters of Soviet Ukrainian culture aimed at high quality culture for educated proletariat.

Khvyl'ovyi's concept of a Soviet literature gained shape during the Literary Discussion launched in 1925. His opposition to Soviet culture was, first, institutional – since he opposed cultural dominance and conventional hierarchy with Moscow being the centre of cultural production. Instead, he believed in the potential of Soviet Ukraine and its cultural agents to create a new revolutionary classless culture. While he advocated for reorientation of the proletarian art from Russia to Europe, he permitted their leadership insofar as Soviet Ukrainian artists needed to learn skills and qualities they were bereft off due to the century-long Russian dominance. Second, he opposed the trends in the all-Soviet culture that would turn cultural production into mass culture oriented towards peasants and workers with little or no education. Instead, he aimed at a highbrow proletarian literature. VAPLITE – the literary organization initiated by Khvyl'ovyi – throughout its existence was dedicated to creating high quality proletarian (insomuch as it was created with the universal revolutionary and proletarian values in mind) literature in the Ukrainian language. Although initiated as a mere literary debate, the questions raised during the debate were quickly gaining a political sounding. The public campaign against the separatist cultural (and by extension political) project is the subject of the last part of this book.

Part Three

Fitting in the Soviet canon

Part Three of this book investigates the process of centralization of political and cultural controls in Soviet Ukraine and the reaction of the Soviet Ukrainian cultural agents and political actors towards those homogenizing tendencies of the central government. Two parallel processes are at the centre of the discussion. First, the Literary Discussion, introduced in the previous sections, quickly assumed a political spin, when artists and art officials quickly realized that for their vision of Soviet Ukrainian literature and culture to succeed, they needed to ensure that the respective political elites had power over decision-making and control over economic resources. The political aspect of the Literary Discussion fused with the intensification of the debate about the scope and objectives of *Ukrainizatsiia*, as defined by the Ukrainian faction in the KP(b)U.

Second, by the mid-1920s, many of the objectives of the central party leadership in Soviet Ukraine – party entrenchment, public mobilization and partial linguistic de-Russification – had been mostly achieved. This strengthened the position of the Communist party in the republic whereby the leadership was ready to tighten its control over those separatist developments in the cultural and political spheres. These two tendencies clashed at the 1926 Party Plenum. Chapter 5 scrutinizes the arguments during the Plenum used by both sides to defend their vision of Soviet Ukraine. As will be shown, the reinforced position of the central party leadership allowed them to take more control over the cultural sphere and gain an upper hand in the discussion.

With the party assuming the dominant position in Soviet Ukraine, what happened to those writers promoting the autonomist cultural project? Were they able to redefine their perspective to accommodate the consolidation of the party line? At the same time, how did the position of those writers supporting the Soviet literary canon change after 1926? The following chapters bring the life stories of the two protagonists into a broader discussion of the process of unification of literature in Ukraine and the Soviet Union. The chapters also discuss the redefinition of the *korenizatsiia* policies in the second half of the 1920s and the way those policies were implemented once the centralist perspective gained dominance in the republic.

5

'Ukraine or Little Russia': The battle for cultural autonomy in 1926

'Away from Moscow': The political dimension of the Literary Discussion

The literary debate, engaging literary figures and party officials alike, exposed two different ways for understanding Soviet culture. The first group, represented by the KP(b)U members with a clear centripetal orientation towards Moscow, contributed to the creation of culture that was fully endorsed, sponsored and controlled by the central party leadership and reflected the need for cultural outputs able to engage the public and draw the labouring masses into the Soviet order. The other group, represented by the Ukraine-minded party members and cultural elites, defended autonomous Soviet Ukrainian culture, where cultural managers and artists themselves would have an authority to decide on the questions of its standards, artistic orientation and the audience. These demands, originally voiced by Khvyl'ovyi, soon acquired a political aspect in questioning the cultural and political relationship of Ukraine and Russia. By attacking Ukraine's cultural backwardness, Khvyl'ovyi aligned with Shums'kyi to pinpoint the subordinate status of Soviet Ukraine, whose political and cultural elites had very limited control and deciding power in the republic being subjugated to the political will in Moscow.

Already in the *Apolohety Pysaryzmu* cycle of pamphlets, published from February to March 1926, Khvyl'ovyi ventured to demand political independence for Soviet Ukraine. In the last pamphlet, entitled *Moskovski Zadrypanky* [Moscow's Dusty Backwaters], Khvyl'ovyi edged forward to, in his own words, remove 'the "black mask" of the all-Ukrainian polemical champion Mykola Khvyl'ovyi';[1] that is to expose the true reason for Ukraine's cultural backwardness that could only be resolved politically. He stated that cultural revival in Soviet Ukraine could only be achieved if the new elites shrugged off their dependency on Russia in both the cultural and political realms and changed their orientation solely towards European art. Khvyl'ovyi declared that Soviet Ukraine was independent as much as Russia was, and as such should be treated as a political equal within the Soviet Union:

> In a word, the Union nevertheless remains a Union and Ukraine is an independent entity. […] Under the influence of our economy, we are applying to our

literature not 'the Slavophile theory of originality,' but the theory of Communist independence. [...] Is Russia an independent state? It is! Well, in that case we too are independent.[2]

The politicization of the Literary Discussion reflected a further intensification of the political debates within the KP(b)U. Khvyľovyi seconded Shums'kyi in anticipating a new Soviet Ukrainian elite, who, as defined by Khvyľovyi, would be 'first communards and then Ukrainians'.[3] For him, ideological commitment yet preceded national awareness. This commitment, however, was defined not in the institutional manner. He sought those devoted to the revolution values, and not those of the party, hence 'communards' rather than 'communists'. They placed their hopes on engaging local cadres into the party and state apparatus.

Indeed, party entrenchment had been a key objective of *korenizatsiia* since its launch in 1923. In 1926, thanks to a set of affirmative actions that included the mass enrolment of ethnic Ukrainians and promotion of those Ukrainian-speakers within the party, 47 per cent of party members had registered as Ukrainians, compared to only 23 per cent in 1922.[4] In 1927, this share had risen to 52 per cent. However, only 59 per cent actually claimed Ukrainian as their mother tongue.[5] While some positive tendencies were observed at the lower level, the party's leadership echelon significantly lagged behind. According to some estimates, of the 1,898 top-ranking Bolsheviks in Ukraine in 1926 only 345, or 18 per cent, knew Ukrainian.[6]

At the 1925 TsK KP(b)U Plenum, Shums'kyi argued that the lack of Ukrainian cadres in the party, especially among its leaders, represented *Ukrainizatsiia*'s major weakness. The implementation of the policy had been 'slowed down not because of popular resistance, but due to the opposition at the very top of the party active (*partiinyi aktyv*)'.[7] He feared that this lack of engagement on the side of the party leadership would allow cultural activists, who did not share the Bolshevik values and were 'hostile' to communism all together, to take control of *Ukrainizatsiia*'s implementation.[8]

Shums'kyi also made reference to those cultural and political figures who had been previously affiliated with the Ukrainian nationalist governments and recently returned or were planning to return to Soviet Ukraine. Indeed, the promises of *Ukrainizatsiia* had lured many Ukrainians over the Western border to migrate to Soviet Ukraine in search of employment, especially in the face of the interwar Polish government's assimilationist programme in Western Ukraine.[9] Consequently, the number of Ukrainians crossing the border had increased significantly since 1923. On 16 May 1924, at the VIII All-Ukrainian KP(b)U conference an 'Appeal to the Ukrainian Soviet intelligentsia and to all Soviet society' was read aloud. The appeal was signed by sixty-six famous and authoritative representatives of the Ukrainian cultural and educational elites in Western Ukraine, in which they declared their personal approval of the *Ukrainizatsiia* policy and loyalty to the Soviet government.[10] Although suspicious of these recent arrivals, the Soviet Ukrainian government allowed them entry since they could occupy numerous positions in education and the state apparatus that had been suddenly made available with the launch of *korenizatsiia*.

Hrushevs'kyi, pleased with the strides of Ukraine's cultural development under *Ukrainizatsiia*, urged Galician Ukrainians to come to Soviet Ukraine and join the 'grey army' of ordinary people working towards a better future. In his personal correspondence, he estimated that there were around 50,000 Ukrainians from Polish Eastern Galicia in Soviet Ukraine, all of whom found employment and were generally satisfied with their life.[11] Among those returnees were such authoritative figures as Iurii Tiutiunnyk, a senior UNR officer and a leader of the Anti-Bolshevik campaign during the Polish-Soviet war of 1920-1. In 1926, Stepan Rudnyts'kyi, a famous cartographer, geographer and ethnographer, also emigrated to Soviet Ukraine from Czechoslovakia. There, he founded and headed the Institute of Geography and Cartography, as well as being elected a VUAN academic. Shums'kyi feared that these nationalist leaders would use their status and authority among the broad masses and divert the potential of Soviet Ukrainian culture into the nationalist channel, promoting Ukrainian bourgeois nationalism or *petliurovshchyna*.[12]

Shums'kyi brought his concerns to Stalin's attention during meetings in Moscow in October 1925 and then again in April 1926.[13] He maintained that the Communist Party alone must be in charge of the cultural revival in Soviet Ukraine, yet noted that its political elite could not keep up with developments in the cultural sphere and the rapid growth of the Ukrainian intelligentsia. Instead of championing this process, the predominantly anti-Ukrainian attitude within the KP(b)U could lead the masses towards further alienation from the Soviet regime. For the programme to succeed, he advocated that *Ukrainizatsiia* be carried out both within the ranks of the party and among the proletariat. Crucial changes in the party leadership were therefore necessary, the movement should be championed by those 'who believe in the cause of Ukrainian culture, who know and desire to know this culture'.[14]

According to Shums'kyi, the greatest obstruction was Lazar Kaganovich, a Ukraine-born Jew who had served as first secretary of the KP(b)U since 1925, whom he proposed replacing with Chubar, Skrypnyk or any other Ukrainian who might ensure the proper implementation of *Ukrainizatsiia*.[15] As for the proletariat, Shums'kyi pushed for extending this policy to the entirety of the working class, including those workers who were not ethnically Ukrainian or did not identify themselves as Ukrainians, the so-called Russified Ukrainians (Ukrainians by origin yet Russian speakers).

Stalin indirectly responded to Shums'kyi's criticisms in a letter to Kaganovich on 26 April 1926 in which he voiced his agreement that the implementation of *Ukrainizatsiia* needed to be taken under closer party control, as well as the need to make the party a Ukrainian force.[16] Yet Shums'kyi was reproached for miscalculating the pace at which *korenizatsiia* in Ukraine could safely be implemented. The Commissar for Education, in Stalin's words, had overlooked how weak and insufficient the 'purely Ukrainian Marxist cadres' were. The letter concluded by summarizing Shums'kyi's mistakes: 'by having correct objectives, he does not reckon with the pace. And the pace is the most important now.'[17]

Stalin also addressed Shums'kyi's demands for a comprehensive proletarian Ukrainization. He suggested that the Commissar for Education had misinterpreted the very concept of *korenizatsiia*, confusing the Ukrainization of the party and state apparatus (a declared objective of the policy) with the Ukrainization of the republic's proletariat. Stalin further noted that the Ukrainization of the working class was supposed to be a natural and gradual process whereas Shums'kyi was attempting to impose it 'from above', by forcing the Russian working masses to renounce their Russian language and culture. This, according to the general secretary, 'contradict[ed] the principle of the free development of nationalities [...] and [was] equal to national oppression'. He also predicted that forced Ukrainization from above could provoke 'an outbreak of anti-Ukrainian chauvinism among the non-Ukrainian proletariat' as well as 'a struggle for the alienation of Ukrainian culture from the all-Soviet culture, a struggle against "Moscow", against Russians, against the Russian culture and its greatest achievement, Leninism, altogether.'[18]

Stalin's letter also glossed over the latest trends in Soviet Ukrainian cultural developments, referring to 'a noted Communist' Khvyl'ovyi and his pamphlets – *Kamo Hriadeshy, Dumky proty Techii* and *Apolohety Pysarysmu*. Particular attention was drawn to his 'anti-Russian orientation'. As seen from the letter, Stalin feared that those views of Khvyl'ovyi, a long-standing party member, could spread throughout Soviet Ukraine's political establishment. If even a card-carrying writer like Khvyl'ovyi was promoting a messianic role of the new Ukrainian elites and Soviet Ukrainian exceptionalism, was it not unreasonable to question the overall ideological commitment of writers in Soviet Ukraine?:

> At a time when the proletarians of Western Europe and their Communist Parties are in sympathy with 'Moscow', this citadel of the international revolutionary movement and of Leninism, at a time when the proletarians of Western Europe look with admiration at the flag that flies over Moscow, the Ukrainian Communist Khvilevoy has nothing better to say in favour of 'Moscow' than to call on the Ukrainian leaders to get away from 'Moscow' 'as fast as possible'. And that is called internationalism! What is to be said of other Ukrainian intellectuals, those of the non-communist camp, if Communists begin to talk, and not only to talk but even to write in our Soviet press, in the language of Khvilevoy?[19]

While Khvyl'ovyi was not new to onerous attacks, his critics previously engaged mostly with his views on literary matters – literature's relationship to reality, nature of art, the question of audience[20] – whereas Stalin's intervention initiated a broad political campaign against Khvyl'ovyi for his national, political and cultural views. Together with Khvyl'ovyi, Shums'kyi was also accused of failing to control his protégé and allowing the cultural process in Soviet Ukraine to deviate from its intended path. The campaign against the two reached a climax in June 1926, signalling a new alignment of forces in the KP(b)U and the eventual defeat of the Ukrainian horizon in the party.

June 1926 TsK KP(b)U Plenum

In June 1926, the TsK KP(b)U called a meeting to discuss the results and future prospects of the *korenizatsiia* campaign, as well as to examine problems facing its implementation. During this general party gathering, Kaganovich took the opportunity to consolidate his power as the KP(b)U first secretary and respond to Shums'kyi's attacks. At the Plenum, the Commissar for Education Shums'kyi and his protégé

Khvyl'ovyi became the main targets for criticism. Kaganovich wished to undermine Shums'kyi who, in his capacity as Education Commissar, from the party's perspective, had allowed crude deviations in the cultural sphere to take root. At the same time, Shums'kyi used the party forum to advocate for broadening the scope and increasing the pace of *Ukrainizatsiia*. In his speech, he attacked the top leadership, who were 'living on Russian culture and using Russian in their inner workings', for not engaging with *Ukrainizatsiia*. He reprimanded them for keeping detached from Soviet Ukraine's cultural developments and failing to take the leading role in its cultural revival. Instead, Shums'kyi continued, this process was being supervised by 'a thin membrane (*plivka*) of communists-Ukrainians', who did not have enough power to take the process of cultural development under their direct control and guide it in the right direction.[21] Overall, Shums'kyi attacked the Russified party leadership for not reinforcing the Ukrainian horizon in the party, gathered mostly around his Commissariat, in their battle for Soviet Ukrainian culture.

Kaganovich also addressed issues surrounding the party's lack of control over the implementation of *korenizatsiia* in Ukraine, which had allowed anti-Soviet elements to gain an upper hand in the republic, blaming the NEP for its ideological pluralism and negative effect on the cultural sphere in particular.[22] Many speakers at the Plenum also referred to the NEP that had allowed for 'bourgeois nationalist' elements to gain influence over young party members, including Khvyl'ovyi. Accordingly, his slogan 'Away from Moscow' could 'only be ascribed to the Ukrainian petite intelligentsia, which continues to grow under the NEP. [They] understand the national revival only as a bourgeois restoration, and under "the orientation towards Europe" they, indeed, see the orientation towards a capitalist Europe and therefore [promote] distancing from the fortress of the international revolution, the capital of the USSR, Moscow.'[23] Zatons'kyi's suggested that many young communists had grown ideologically confused due to the permissible atmosphere of the early 1920s. According to the party official, Khvyl'ovyi had failed to discern the tactics of the party, whereby the introduction of the NEP was yet another means of defeating capitalism, causing him to lose faith in the organization. The writer 'does not believe in anything, either that we are building socialism', Zatons'kyi resolved.[24] Using Khvyl'ovyi as an example of ideological ambiguity, he concluded that 'one cannot be born a Bolshevik, instead one becomes a Bolshevik.'[25] To this errant youth, the party should therefore offer a helping hand in assisting them to distinguish right from wrong: 'out of Khvyl'ovyi and Khvyl'ovyis we should tamper true communists [...] who would be useful for the revolution, would not spread the poison of disbelief and liquidationism, but instead would assist the proletariat in its arduous everyday battle.'[26]

For Shums'kyi, however, the ideological pluralism of NEP played only a lesser part. He maintained that NEP had also been implemented in Russia, yet no deviations of Khvyl'ovyi's magnitude had crystallized there. For him, it was the failure of the Communist leaders to resolve the national question once and for all and declare their position on the future of Soviet Ukraine that led such committed Ukrainian communists as Khvyl'ovyi to search for answers elsewhere.[27] Shums'kyi asserted that each and every writer must have clear criteria for evaluating socio-political developments, and when there were none, writers were bound to get confused: 'Only then will a writer have those criteria, when the perspective of social developments, its immediate goal and the ways to achieve them is clear to him. And only the Party, the avant-garde of the advanced social class of the proletariat, can provide such aspirations and define the future path of social development.'[28] Overall, Shums'kyi maintained, hesitations (*khytania*) among those communists were caused by the fact that the party did not take 'an organic active and creative part in the process of social-cultural construction'.[29] He urged the party to finally champion Ukraine's social and cultural development, to master its language and culture. Otherwise, new leaders would emerge among those non-Marxist intellectuals: 'Look at how all those Hrushevs'kyis, Doroshkevychs, Germaises, Iefremovs, Nikovskyis, Zerovs and the likes are now trying to re-establish their social connections in Ukraine in order to prompt the new Soviet social-cultural life.'[30]

While defending the writer, who only 'wished to build socialism',[31] Shums'kyi nevertheless admitted to Khvyl'ovyi's ideological mistakes and scolded his protégé for his extremes. He characterized *Moskovski Zadrypanky* as 'politically harmful'.[32] By charging Khvyl'ovyi, Shums'kyi extrapolated that all those promoting a self-sufficient Soviet Ukrainian culture had failed to develop a cohesive programme:

> If only for a moment I could have imagined that the communist Khvyl'ovyi could promote or agitate the idea of Ukraine as a bourgeois republic and her capitalist and nationalist renaissance, I would have immediately suggested excluding him from the Party.
> But I am truly convinced that these assumptions are false. [...] However, I am also aware that Khvyl'ovyi has no clear perspective as for developing Ukraine's culture and literature. [...] And this might have been the reason for his confusion.[33]

Only during the last session was Khvyl'ovyi granted an opportunity to justify his position. While defending his version for a Soviet Ukraine's cultural development, he did not question his party membership and abided by its discipline. Nonetheless, he admitted possible overstatements and was ready to accept criticism:

> I concede that there could be some exaggerations in the ideas and concepts I have developed [...]. However, overall, I believe there are grains of truth. [...] Nonetheless, if the entire Plenum agrees on my errors, I should acknowledge them and stop. First and foremost, I am a disciplined member of the Party.[34]

Although Khvyl'ovyi admitted to his oversights, official critics were not ready to accept his repentance. Eventually, Khvyl'ovyi's position was linked to all existing political heresies in the Soviet Union. In 1930, the party ideologist Hirchak reminded Khvyl'ovyi of his stance during the Literary Discussion in order to accuse him of the following deviations: orienting Ukrainian literature away from 'Red Moscow' to 'bourgeois Europe'; reviving Lebed's theory of the struggle of two cultures in its Ukrainian variant; promoting the capitalist theory of rebirth of national rebirth; joining forces with 'bourgeois nationalists' (especially Zerov and the *neoklasyky*) and adopting the idea of a united national front; undermining the role of the proletariat in the cultural construction of Ukraine; popularizing Spengler's cycle theory of history and propagating a messianic idea of a Ukrainian-led Asiatic renaissance; adopting Trotsky's views; and, last but not least, 'disseminating the ideas of Ukrainian fascism'.[35] Unsurprisingly, '*khvyl'ovizm*', a catchword encompassing all the above-mentioned heresies, remained one of the most serious ideological accusations for decades to come.

The main resolution adopted at the June TsK KP(b)U Plenum was 'Theses on the results of *Ukrainizatsiia*'. The Plenum scrutinized Shums'kyi's position and outright rejected his demands for a proletarian Ukrainization 'from above'. Instead, it was suggested that 'creating a favourable environment' in the industrial centres of Soviet Ukraine would enable the gradual Ukrainization of the working class. The party's initiatives coupled with the influx of Ukrainian-speaking workers from the countryside would eventually make urban centres more Ukrainian. Otherwise, any attempts to accelerate Ukrainization by 'administrative actions', as Shums'kyi had suggested, would not be tolerated.

Khvyl'ovyi's blueprint for Soviet Ukrainian literature was also scrutinized. On the one hand, the party acknowledged the need to promote art and literature and encourage links between 'Ukrainian socialist culture' and world cultural heritage. On the other, it was certain that this could not be achieved by orienting its culture towards 'bourgeois Europe' and 'contrasting the interests of Ukraine to those of other Soviet Republic', as proposed by Khvyl'ovyi. Instead, the resolution proposed to advance Soviet culture in Ukraine through 'brotherly cooperation between the working class and the toiling masses of all nationalities [aimed] to create the international culture, to which the Ukrainian working class will be able to contribute its share'.[36] In order to achieve those tasks, the TsK Plenum resolved to fight decisively 'the anti-Marxist and anti-Leninist theory of the struggle of the two cultures in its Ukrainian and Russian variants' and promote the creation of Bolshevik cadres 'able to carry on ideological and creative work on the Ukrainian cultural front'.[37] To prevent any further heresy on the literary front, the party also demanded full control over the publication of all literary output in the republic.

Debates concerning *Ukrainizatsiia*, the Literary Discussion and *khvyl'ovizm* continued in the press. This included an article by Chubar, *Pro Vyvykhy* [On the deviations]; Skrypnyk's *Do teorii borot'by dvokh kul'tur* [On the theory of the struggle of two cultures]; and Zatons'kyi's *Natsional'na problema na Ukraini* [The national problem in Ukraine].[38] The position of the above-mentioned articles was summarized by Khvylia in a series of pamphlets published under the title *Iasnoiu Dorohoiu* [On a clear path]. Khvylia maintained:

> The so-called Literary Discussion that have had a great cultural and political resonance, exposed the anti-party, anti-communist nationalistic views on the cultural and national questions developed by one particular small group of party members. And as all of our society already knows, one of its speakers was Khvyl'ovyi who declared the slogans of 'Away from any Moscow', 'the orientation towards psychological (read: bourgeois) Europe', 'Give me the proletariat' (read: accelerate and speed up the Ukrainisation of the proletariat disregarding the historical dominance of the Russified working class).[39]

According to Khvylia, the *Narkomos* chief Shums'kyi had championed a communist group within the KP(b)U that had attempted to gather together all the components of the national Ukrainian front – starting from Khvyl'ovyi up to 'ardent fascists' from the nationalist camp.

Despite harsh criticism, Khvyl'ovyi did not cease in his efforts to agitate the political and cultural climate. In the summer of 1926, he published his most incendiary pamphlet, *Ukraina chy Malorosiia?*, in which he dared to raise the 'most dangerous question of today' – 'Is Ukraine a colony or is it not it?'[40] This included frequent mention of the term *Malorosiia*, or Little Russia, first coined in the eighteenth century to refer to Ukraine and Ukrainians in the Russian Empire, to define the colonial position of Ukraine still being promoted by some politicians. By highlighting Ukraine's culturally and politically colonial status within the Soviet Union, Khvyl'ovyi revived an earlier debate among Ukrainian Marxists who used the colonial/imperial discourse in their writings between 1917 and 1925 to define Ukrainian dependency before and after 1917.[41]

For him, the future of Ukraine was either that of 'Ukraine': an independent and sovereign Soviet republic, or of 'Little Russia': an intrinsic part or colony of Russia with no autonomy or decision-making authority. Khvyl'ovyi opened his pamphlet with two epigraphs, reflecting the crux of his radical argument. The first quote referred to Friedrich Shiller: 'Slavery is shameful, yet slave mentality is disdainful.' Indeed, throughout his literary career, he regarded servitude as the biggest peril for Ukraine's sovereignty. To break with this century-long tradition of following 'the bigger brother', he encouraged the new Soviet Ukrainian elites to start making decisions independently – 'Up with your own good judgement!', as he put it.[42] In another quote, Khvyl'ovyi introduced the famous definition of a nation coined by Stalin in 1913, suggesting that the Ukrainian nation that had already possessed 'a common language, territory, economic life, and psychological make-up manifested in a common culture', had also the right for its own self-sufficient government.[43] Khvyl'ovyi defended cultural and political decolonization of 'Little Russia' and aspired for fully fledged 'Ukraine'.

This pamphlet appeared in response to Iurynets and Khvylia, the official critics of his previous publications. Khvyl'ovyi attacked both cultural officials for abandoning Ukrainian interests in order to serve those of Russia. In *Ukraina chy Malorosiia?*, Khvyl'ovyi once again took the opportunity to promote his theory of Ukraine's autonomous cultural development, refining his concepts of 'proletarian art', 'psychological Europe,' and 'the Asiatic renaissance'. Much hope was placed on the new Soviet Ukrainian intelligentsia that would take the process of Ukrainian national awakening further, towards national independence.[44] And even those 'few morally impotent and materially feeble "khokholian apparatus"'[45] could not stand in the way of Ukraine's awakening, as he remarked in challenge to Khvylia: 'The thing is, comrade Khvylia – you overslept. When you went to bed, there was *Malorosiia*, yet when you woke up – it was already Ukraine.'[46] By employing the dichotomy 'Ukraine and Little Russia', Khvyl'ovyi equally opposed the political and cultural hegemony of Russia over Ukraine, as well as its provincial status and ethnocentric culture before the revolution.

What made *Ukraina chy Malorosiia?* so important for both Khvyl'ovyi's supporters and opponents was its comprehensive critique on existing centre-periphery relations in the Soviet Union, whereby Soviet Ukraine played only a subordinate part. Instead,

Khvyl'ovyi defended the sovereignty of Ukraine and appealed for extending the scope of *Ukrainizatsiia* to include the republic's working class. Being a communist himself, Khvyl'ovyi believed that only the proletariat should enjoy ideological hegemony in Soviet Ukraine. This would be impossible, however, unless workers seized control of Ukrainian culture, involving themselves in the process of its creation and distribution: 'How will the proletariat play first violin, however, when Ukrainian culture is still *terra incognita* for it? [...] Until the proletariat masters Ukrainian culture there can be no certainty that the cultural revolution in Ukraine will give the desired results.'[47] In line with Shums'kyi's position, Khvyl'ovyi concluded:

> We are indeed an independent state whose republican organism is a part of the Soviet Union. And Ukraine is independent not because we, communists, desire this, but because the iron and irresistible will of the laws of history demands it, because only in this way shall we hasten class differentiation in Ukraine. [...] To gloss over independence with a hollow pseudo-Marxism is to fail to understand that Ukraine will continue to be an arena for counter-revolution as long as it does not pass through the natural stage that Western Europe went through during the formation of nation-states.[48]

However, the pamphlet was quickly censored and never reached print. Before 1990, its contents were known only through the excerpt that appeared in official critiques: Khvylia's *Vid ukhylu v prirvu ...* (From Deviation into Abyss ...) and Hirchak's *Na dva fronta v bor'be s natsionalizmom* (On Two Fronts in the Struggle with Nationalism). Despite this censorship, it was widely used thereafter to prove Khvyl'ovyi's anti-Soviet position and expose his incessant deviation from the party line.

'Even to peel a potato one needs to have a skill'

Despite the threat of political censure, Khvyl'ovyi continued to use VAPLITE to advance his view of Soviet Ukrainian literature with much of the organization's creative energy being channelled towards engaging in polemics with party critics.[49] In fact, the months following the 1926 TsK KP(b)U Plenum saw an escalation in the Literary Discussion that would reach its climax in 1927.[50] Right after the June Plenum, VAPLITE released its first publication, *Vaplite: Zoshyt pershyi* [*Vaplite*: First Notebook], followed by *Vaplite: Almanakh* [*Vaplite*: Almanac] and five issues of its house journal *Vaplite*, published from 1926 to 1927. *Vaplite: Zoshyt pershyi* did not feature original literature, focusing instead on programme documents for drafting the organization's statute and summarizing its view on the role of the Literary Academy and its members in the literary process.[51] Articles by Dosvitnii ('On the Development of the Literary Forces'), Slisarenko ('In the struggle for a Proletarian Aesthetics') and Dovzhenko ('On the Problem of Arts') contributed to the ongoing Literary Discussion, touching on issues of artistic orientation, the nature of proletarian literature and the role of ideology in literary practice. The issue also featured reviews on resent publications and debates from European literature.

The content of the *Vaplite* journal that first appeared only two months after the Plenum, came as a surprise to the party ideologists. Kaganovich characterized it as 'a material (*formal'nyi*), ideological, as well as fundamental (*pryntsypovyi*) breach' of the Plenum's Resolutions.[52] Although the editors explained that the magazine's first issue had been ready to go to print before the Plenum, the party leaders were adamant and did not accept these explanations. To exacerbate the situation, the state-sponsored journal *Chervonyi Shliakh* published a positive review of *Vaplite: Zoshyt pershyi*, with the reviewer Pavlo Khrystiuk praising some of the pieces by VAPLITE members.[53] It was Kulish, VAPLITE's president and *Chervonyi Shliakh*'s editor, who approved the review for publication. To make matters worse, Khrystiuk was a former UNR statesman, a historian and a fellow traveller, who, after a short exile in Vienna, returned to Soviet Ukraine in 1924.

It must be noted, however, that following the June Plenum, Shums'kyi was suspended from his duties as *Chervonyi Shliakh*'s editor-in-chief, and the journal for a short time was overseen by Khvyl'ovyi and Ialovyi. Kaganovich quickly turned against these managing editors, who had overlooked a 'disloyal' nature of the review written by an untrustworthy returnee. For Kaganovich, reviews played a major role in 'forming the ideology of our youth' and their significance should not be underestimated, leading him to conclude that only 'our Marxist, Leninist bibliography' could be allowed.[54] A positive review on the officially disavowed VAPLITE appearing on the pages of a state-sponsored magazine added even more fuel to the campaign surrounding Khvyl'ovyi. The TsK KP(b)U Resolution concerning *Chervonyi Shliakh* from 10 September 1926 accused Khvyl'ovyi and Ialovyi, in their capacity as managing editors, of 'not declaring their agreement with the party line on literature as defined by the June [1926] Plenum'.[55] More damning was the fact that they did not reject the line persued by *Vaplite: Zoshyt pershyi*, neither did they take 'a critical stand' towards the journal's content.[56]

This exchange between the journal's editors and the party leadership regarding the ideological purity of *Chervonyi Shliakh* exposed yet another clash of perspectives as to the aims of this important periodical, and by extension of the Soviet culture in Ukraine. While edited by Shums'kyi, the journal played an important role in Soviet Ukraine's cultural development. After the Plenum, *Chervonyi Shliakh* fell into disgrace for disregarding the June 1926 Resolutions. Shortly thereafter, the editorial board of *Chervonyi Shliakh* was reorganized in order 'to improve [its] educational Marxist work'. Ialovyi and Khvyl'ovyi were dismissed and replaced by the party-approved candidates Khvylia, Iurynets, Koriak and Kulyk. The incident also served as grounds for Shums'kyi's official dismissal as editor-in-chief. In November 1926, Shums'kyi was indicted for editing a journal 'in a manner inapt for a Communist', formally relieved of his position and replaced by the party ideologist Zatons'kyi.

During the campaign, Shums'kyi spoke for the final time on the future of Soviet Ukrainian culture and literature at the meeting of party members active (*partiinyi aktyv*) in the *Narkomos* on 25 November 1926. His speech, entitled 'Ideological Struggle in the Ukrainian Cultural Process', glossed over numerous ideological and political errors committed during the Literary Discussion by the artistic elites.[57] This time, Shums'kyi accused Khvyl'ovyi of having revived Lebed's outdated theory in framing the relationship between Ukraine and Russia in terms of cultural struggle. Shums'kyi expressed regret that while searching for the best way to develop Soviet Ukrainian culture, Khvyl'ovyi had 'inadvertently aligned with the Ukrainian nationalistic camp, that adopted his literary formula "Away from Moscow to Europe" as a political slogan'.[58] By persisting with this slogan, Shums'kyi continued, Khvyl'ovyi had abandoned his 'proletarian position' and sided with the bourgeois nationalists.[59] However, he still believed that the writer would come to recognize his errors and, together with the party, would become an active builder of Ukrainian literature and culture, created along the lines approved by the June Plenum.[60]

Shums'kyi's dismissal from the *Narkomos* was linked to his unorthodox view on the implementation of *korenizatsiia* in Soviet Ukraine. In addition, the autonomous project for Soviet Ukrainian culture developed under his tutelage challenged the party's dominant role in the cultural sphere. In the end, there could be only one version of an all-Soviet culture, controlled from Moscow. Created under the slogan of 'unity in diversity', this vision of Soviet culture was meant to unify the republics and bring their peoples closer together.[61] Hence, every attempt was made to prevent the crystallization of any viable cultural opposition, especially in Soviet Ukraine, where Khvyl'ovyi's position had gained wide resonance. The campaign against Shums'kyi and Khvyl'ovyi soon spread to all those associated with VAPLITE, now regarded as promoting an unauthorized version of Soviet Ukrainian culture. The Literary Academy remained under close watch and the party was ready to pre-empt any new forms of 'deviations' among its members.

One of the figures targeted was Tychyna. By the mid-1920s, Tychyna had already earned a reputation as a leading poet in Soviet Ukraine. Acknowledgement of his

Figure 13 Soviet Ukrainian writers (Pavlo Tychyna, Mykola Kulish, Volodymyr Sosiura and others), 1920s. © Central State Archive-Museum of Literature and Arts of Ukraine, courtesy of TsDAMLMU.

artistic commitment to Soviet literature at the highest party level saw him selected to represent Soviet culture during official visits to the other Soviet republics and abroad. And yet his ideological commitment to the Soviet cause remained uncertain. In the end, Tychyna was a member of VAPLITE, contributing to its periodicals and remaining within its ranks until the organization's dissolution. In his capacity as an editor of the poetry section of *Chervonyi Shliakh* he also worked side by side with Shums'kyi. Despite his non-involvement in matters other than literary and editorial ones, he unwittingly found himself amidst the ongoing power struggle between the local and central elites.

In late 1926, Tychyna, following Khvyl'ovyi's requests, offered to submit an untitled fragment from a longer poem to the first issue of the *Vaplite* almanac.[62] The piece became known by its first line – *Chystyla maty kartopliu* [Mother was peeling potatoes]. The published sample comprised three fragments reflecting on the horrors of the civil war in the Ukrainian countryside. The first fragment introduces a peasant family who is split along ideological lines. The mother blames the communists for having caused much of the destruction. Amidst the havoc of the civil war, the old woman is expecting the apocalypse, with Lenin assuming the role of Antichrist warning her son that 'Lenin the antichrist appeared, my son. [...] We must go to battle: the antichrist appeared.' Her son, however, has joined the party and became the harbinger of the new order. He now personifies the enemy and the mother in her hatred turns against him: 'Tell me, what is left to do? Knife me, beat me, and push me into the grave with my little children. Let me be smothered by your knee, same as Ukraine.' The second fragment, entitled *Samosud* [Lynch-law], deals with a group killing of a bandit who came to a village to agitate against the Soviet order; while the third fragment depicts a circle of Stundists – a local religious sectarian group led by Sus Khrystos [a clear reference to Jesus Christ].[63]

The poem quickly became known to the authorities. In January 1927, at the Kharkiv District Party Conference Chubar, by then the Chairman of the Ukrainian Council of the People's Commissars, mentioned this piece without revealing its author. He evasively spoke about 'a non-party' poet who, in a symbolic way, had suggested the involuntary Sovietization of the republic. From the party's perspective, the image of Ukraine as depicted in the poem was 'a subtle reference to a glaring fact', namely the alleged subordinate status of Soviet Ukraine within the Soviet Union. He accused the author of 'national deviationism', of 'insinuating a nationalist opiate under the banner of proletarian literature'.[64] Once the final report of the Kharkiv conference was published on the pages of *Komunist* on 15 January 1927, the attack on Tychyna became public with *Chystyla maty kartopliu* considered an 'artistic' contribution to the political debate being waged by Khvyl'ovyi.[65]

Tychyna denied these allegations in an open letter that also appeared in *Komunist*, claiming that the poem's fragments had been misinterpreted, with the excerpts cited by Chubar having been taken out of context. As explained, the criticized piece only set the scene for a longer poem, on which the author had been working for several years. His intention had been to introduce two opposing social forces in Ukraine during the civil war: 'the old one which is receding and not catching up with life (represented by the mother) and the new, revolutionary and victorious force, which is symbolised by her communist son'. Indeed, he continued, famine, poverty and mistrust of the Bolsheviks were typical in the countryside during the civil war years. Outright rejecting any similarities between his own views and those of the mother, he claimed that his sympathies were with the son, representing the new communist Ukraine.[66]

Tychyna's open letter was immediately accompanied by a short editorial note in which the editor reproached the poet for deliberately misleading readers by presenting them with an uncontextualized sample.[67] Only in 1938 would Tychyna publish the full poem under the title *Shablia Kotovs'koho* [Kotovs'kyi's Sabre].

Tychyna's open letter appeared on page six of *Komunist*. However, the paper deliberately prioritized a contribution to the debate from Zatons'kyi, TsK KP(b)U secretary and the editor-in-chief of *Komunist* at the time. The front page of that same issue featured a column with a meaningful title *Dumky pro te, iak treba chystyty kartopliu* [Thoughts on How to Peel Potatoes]. Zatons'kyi used the opportunity to reiterate the official party position on the literary debate, reinforcing the role of Soviet writers in creating easy-to-understand and ideologically useful Soviet literature. The column attacked 'quasi'-proletarian poets (Tychyna and those in VAPLITE) who continued to ignore the tastes of the working-class audience and instead sided with 'gourmets' of 'psychological Europe' (a reference to their leader Khvyl'ovyi). As Zatons'kyi articulated:

Even to peel a potato one should have a skill. Especially when we speak about our proletarian poets tasked to peel potatoes of truth with the knife of their own talent; they ought to present facts of life not to gourmets, who, because of their bourgeois and Europe-inspired psychologism, at times turn up their noses from native sauerkraut and a salty joke, but for the masses, who require simple but healthy truth.[68]

Tychyna, despite his involvement in nothing but literary affairs, was criticized at the highest levels of government. Although his name was not mentioned in the KP(b)U conference proceedings, this incident signalled an important shift in the way fellow travellers were treated by the authorities who increasingly viewed their non-affiliation with the Communist Party as problematic. Speaking in late 1926, Chubar referred to Tychyna's non-party status as a mitigating factor, implying that certain ideological oversights could be forgiven to poets of non-proletarian and non-party origin. Nonetheless, the exchange between Tychyna and the KP(b)U leaders in the official press proved how close the ideological evolution of Ukrainian authors was followed by a party machine ready to intervene at the earliest suggestion of any deviation in the process of their Sovietization. Moreover, it suggests surveillance of the literary figures.

If we broaden the scope of this incident, however, yet another interpretation comes to mind. It suggests an important difference in relations between culture and politics in Russia and Ukraine. Arguably, the official line towards fellow travellers and their non-political stand had shifted Union-wide, whereby there was less tolerance to their artistic experimentations and ideological inconsistencies. In Soviet Ukraine, however, this distrust was multiplied by the fear of national deviation among those non-aligned cultural agents. This was the reason as to why, while commenting on Tychyna's piece, the party leadership took issue with subordinate status of the republic within the Soviet Union as had been allegedly proposed by the poet.

Tychyna's transition from a poet of the national revolution into a fellow traveller and fully fledged Soviet poet was non-linear. As a member of VAPLITE, he aligned with those writers who defended the autonomous cultural path for Soviet Ukraine. His ideological hesitations in part could be attributed to the implementation and success of *Ukrainizatsiia*, as well as the fluctuations at the top of Soviet Ukraine's political establishment. Nonetheless, he did not publicly take sides in the debate. His personal qualities could potentially explain this political evasiveness. Tychyna represented a now extinct type of intelligentsia ('*intelihent z intelihentiv*', as defined by Leites in 1924), whose creative genius required quiescence and autonomy. He lacked political activism, a feature required for intellectuals of the new Soviet type who eagerly participated in the political and ideological debates. In addition, as Khvyl'ovyi pointed out in 1924, Tychyna also lacked any strong ideological convictions and could be easily swayed. This hesitancy was well known to both sides of the literary debate who wanted to win him over to their camp. There was yet another feature of Tychyna's character. His contemporaries and biographers observed that Tychyna's choices and decisions were often conditioned by fear. For instance, Bilets'kyi aphoristically asserted that Tychyna, above all, feared the Soviet power.[69] This fear could explain why Tychyna always remained aside of the public debates and was ready to return favours to the party if expected. Ironically, it was this fear that would soon guide him all the way up to the summit of the Soviet politics and literature.

Secret services and anti-*Ukrainizatsiia*

After the 1926 TsK PK(b)U Plenum, the status of *korenizatsiia* in Soviet Ukraine was upgraded with the party leaders acknowledging multiple mistakes in its realization. First, a lack of centralized control had led to the rise of national opposition within the party, as the clash between Kaganovich and Shums'kyi had illustrated. Second, the application of *Ukrainizatsiia* created a benign climate in the republic, where the Ukrainian language and culture had started to be aggressively promoted at the local level by the non-party intelligentsia.[70] Since 1923, party directives demanded high results in implementing *korenizatsiia* yet provided little to assist in reaching these set targets. The party simply lacked their own cultural, teaching and executive cadres to staff the *korenizatsiia*-related programmes.

This shortage was not resolved, even after 1927 when Skrypnyk, the new *Narkomos* chef, planned to bring in some 1,500 teachers from Western Ukraine to assist the KP(b)U with its various educational tasks.[71] Skrypnyk further promoted employment opportunities in Soviet Ukraine during his meeting with the L'viv intelligentsia in 1929, stating in his speech that 'Soviet Ukraine requires many intelligent skilled workers necessary for cultural and economic construction. There are plenty of opportunities for Ukrainian forces that would wish to decently and diligently work towards raising Ukraine to a higher position. There are also places for those from the western bank of Zbruch.'[72] Despite the pressing need to resolve its shortage of qualified staff, the party remained wary of those non-party elements with a strong national orientation. While Stalin predicted that *korenizatsiia* would help disarm Ukrainian nationalism,

Kaganovich argued that the policy only 'made them grow bolder rapidly'. According to him, the implementation of *korenizatsiia* led to two parallel processes: 'the process of our growth, the growth of Soviet culture and society; and the growth of hostile forces, which attempt to master this process'.[73] After 1926, the *korenizatsiia* policies, as approved centrally, were pushed forward, whereas the implementation of *Ukrainizatsiia*, in line with the Soviet Ukrainian autonomist perspective, was taken under strict control.

Nevertheless, *korenizatsiia* in Soviet Ukraine was not abandoned; on the contrary, its implementation was reinforced. The 1926 theses on *Ukrainizatsiia*, issued following the June Plenum, prioritized a number of 'practical tasks' that could help the party align this policy with a more general view of the national question. *Rusotiapstvo*, or mindless Russian chauvinism, was declared as the first obstacle. It was recognized that persistent Great-Russian chauvinism 'has weakened the party's grip over the young Ukrainian culture, strengthened nationalist deviations and hindered the process of mastering Lenin's nationalities policy by those party members who have not yet done so'.[74] The second hindrance was the lack of clarity about the policy's scope. To overcome this, party educators were tasked with explaining 'the objectives, nature and the meaning' of *korenizatsiia* in Ukraine to the broad masses, especially the working class.[75]

Thereafter, *korenizatsiia* in Soviet Ukraine was implemented using the mechanisms of hard-line policies: direct leadership, constant control over its implementation through the use of direct pressure or force and restricting disapproving public discussion of the project.[76] Kaganovich assumed full control over the policy, while Shums'kyi was forced to resign his post as Commissar for Education in February 1927. He was eventually transferred to Russia, where he was relegated to minor positions in the Soviet state apparatus.[77] Following the 'Shums'kyi affair', his name in Soviet Ukraine would mainly be used in connection to '*shums'kizm*': a short-hand for 'national deviation' in politics, similar in its negative connotations to '*khvyl'ovizm*' in the cultural sphere.

The dismissal of Shums'kyi and the upgraded status of *korenizatsiia* led to a tightening of party control over the non-party intelligentsia at a local level. The earliest measures to ensure surveillance over Ukrainian intelligentsia were set in motion as early as 1923, when a secret circular 'About the anti-Soviet movement among the intelligentsia' was issued by the Moscow State Political Administration (GPU) on 23 November 1923 and sent to Ukraine.[78] The GPU came to replace the Cheka in 1923, aiming to unite 'all the efforts of the republics in the struggle with political and economic counterrevolution, spying, and banditry'.[79] Within Soviet Ukraine, this unified security apparatus acted under strict control from the Moscow authorities and was the most consistent propagator of the new anti-*Ukrainizatsiia* line.

These anti-*Ukrainizatsiia* actions were extended with the issue of yet another GPU report '*Ob Ukrainskom Separatizme*' (On Ukrainian Separatism) on 4 September 1926. This top-secret report highlighted the danger of those nationalists who took advantage of the benign climate in the republic. According to the GPU's top-secret circular, *Ukrainizatsiia* had been exploited by all those nationalists who, having given up their hopes of overthrowing Soviet power politically, had come to accept its presence as an unavoidable fact. Nevertheless 'the fact that Ukrainian nationalists ceased the open struggle with the Soviet regime and formally acknowledged it, [did] not mean that they [had] definitively reconciled themselves with the present state of affairs and [had] truly given up their hostile plans'.⁸⁰ Instead, they had instrumentalized 'cultural work' as a means of placing 'supporters of the national idea in all important parts of the state organism'.⁸¹

To regain control over the implementation of *korenizatsiia*, the party needed to undermine public faith in this policy and the pre-revolutionary elites.⁸² Unsurprisingly, the report mostly targeted those Ukrainian intelligentsia on the right who had only recently returned to Soviet Ukraine and expressed their support to Shums'kyi's vision of *Ukrainizatsiia*. The directive called for comprehensive surveillance over Ukrainian artists and intellectuals suspected of involvement in the anti-Soviet 'cultural struggle'. Among those first targeted were the members of the Ukrainian Autocephalous Orthodox Church (*UAPTs*), 'a prominent centre of nationalism and a marvellous agitational tool', and the All-Ukrainian Academy of Sciences (VUAN) which 'collected around themselves the dense mass of former eminent figures of the UNR'.⁸³

The secret GPU document encouraged informing and collecting all possible details on Ukrainian intellectuals who have 'changed their tactics but not their ideology'.⁸⁴ The results of their meticulous work can be found, among others, in a collection of weekly top-secret reports (*svodki*), drafted by the GPU Secret Department from 1927 to 1929. These reports focused on individual actions deemed to be of counter-revolutionary or even anti-Soviet character. Among numerous activists, the names Tychyna and Khvyl'ovyi were repeatedly featured. The entries ranged from simple mentions of the writers' disagreement with the Soviet literary politics and the course of proletarian literature in Ukraine up to open accusations of separatism.⁸⁵ Tychyna, for instance, was referred to as a mouthpiece for counter-revolutionary sentiment and calling for an uprising against the Soviet regime.⁸⁶

The evidence compiled by the secret services in Ukraine from 1926 to 1929 suggests that persecution based on political affiliation, often defined by national orientation, had long preceded the class-based discrimination employed during Stalin's 'Great Break'.⁸⁷ In no other Soviet republic were the party divisions on the implementation of the nationalities policies as intense as in Soviet Ukraine. The reason for this was the particularly strong position of the national Soviet elites who were able to shape and partially implement their autonomous political and cultural agendas.⁸⁸ The experience of the central leadership coming to terms with national communist opposition in Soviet Ukraine determined the course of the Soviet nationalities policy in other republics.

The All-Ukrainian Union of proletarian writers

By the end of the 1920s, as was the case elsewhere in the Soviet Union, there was increasingly less official tolerance in Soviet Ukraine towards artists who did not comply with the party line; during this time, they saw the autonomy of their artistic activity being significantly limited. While the centralization of cultural controls was a Union-wide tendency, control over the cultural sphere in Soviet Ukraine was also part of a bigger strategy to prevent the crystallization of national opposition and, as such, also had political and security implications. The extent of the Literary Discussion turned the cultural sphere into a political battlefield, where writers joined in the campaign to expose Russia's dominant status in the Soviet Union and oppose it by non-literary means. In turn, to neutralize this cultural-turned-political opposition in Soviet Ukraine, the central authorities resorted to the secret services.

The new security service initiatives discussed above had serious repercussions in the cultural sphere. Khvyl'ovyi, perhaps the most castigated writer of 1926, had no other choice but to recant his views and actions in the press. Together with Dosvitnii and Ialovyi, he prepared a repentant 'Declaration of the Group of the Communists and VAPLITE Spokesmen' that was published in *Visti* on 4 December 1926. In the declaration, the three writers recognized their errors and admitted in full to the charges issued against Khvyl'ovyi at the June Plenum, namely orientation towards 'psychological Europe', attempts to sever relations with Russian culture and ignore Moscow, as well as deviating from the proletarian line of internationalism. At the same time, they recognized the party's work in the field of cultural reconstruction as 'entirely correct'.[89]

Nevertheless, the campaign against these cultural figures persisted. On 11 December, Koriak denounced those 'Three Musketeers' in a public lecture at the Artem Institute in Kharkiv. The next day, two Kyivan Soviet writers, Kovalenko and Ivan Le, in a talk given at the Institute of People's Education in Kharkiv, openly attacked those affiliated to VAPLITE, especially Tychyna and Khvyl'ovyi.[90] In this malevolent atmosphere, VAPLITE was forced to unanimously expel Khvyl'ovyi, Dosvitnii and Ialovyi from both the Literary Academy and its almanacs' editorial board in order, as explained by the then President Kulish, 'to negate any harmful effect that those members could have on the entire organisation.'[91]

This step was deemed necessary if the Academy wished to continue its work. After Khvyl'ovyi's expulsion, Kulish hastened to assure its members that VAPLITE would continue to exist as an independent literary organization and a harbinger of an autonomous Soviet Ukrainian literature. The organization, he explained, would 'continue the struggle against all literary currents, events, and phenomena that obstruct or falsify the development of Ukrainian proletarian literature'. Kulish further highlighted that the Academy would still abide by the TsK KP(b)U resolutions on literature from July 1925 to June 1926. As for those expelled writers, he underlined that 'we shall not do anything that might stigmatise the expelled comrades or that would express any remorse or voluntary self-flagellation on the part of the organisation'.[92]

In order to defeat the autonomists' project for a Soviet Ukrainian literature, the party needed to offer more than simply discrediting or undermining its main proponents. In addition, a state-controlled literary organization was necessary to proceed with the centralization of cultural controls, a similar process to those in other Soviet republics. Overall, there was a pressing need for a state-sponsored literary organization that could compete with VAPLITE in both the number of prominent members and the quality of their literary output. Indeed, since the dissolution of *Hart* in 1925, Khvyl'ovyi's Literary Academy had hardly any rivals and was able to attract many young writers into its organization virtually unchallenged.[93] So, a new writers' union – the All-Ukrainian Union of Proletarian Writers (*Vseukrains'ka splika proletars'kykh pys'mennykiv*, VUSPP) – was established in late 1926.

The VUSPP's statute was adopted at its well-publicized inaugural congress, held from 25 to 28 January 1927, where the main speakers included Lunacharsky himself.[94]

Representatives from all existing literary organizations that had declared their adherence to creating proletarian literature were invited to the event. In this regard, the VUSPP's position towards VAPLITE was ambiguous. VUSPP ideologists did not want the 'heresy' of VAPLITE to penetrate the organization, yet they needed to invite its members to prove the inclusive nature of their platform. On 27 January, three days into the congress, Mykytenko, who had been appointed as secretary of the VUSPP's organizing committee, sent an ultimatum to VAPLITE demanding they clarify their position by the end of the day. VAPLITE refused the ultimatum and did not attend the congress.[95] The manifesto of the new literary organization was approved on the final day of the congress and signed by fifty-eight writers, including representatives from *Pluh* and *Hart*.[96]

The VUSPP made no secret of its opposition to VAPLITE's members. The latter were defined as 'moderate bourgeois ideologists who only pretend to sympathise with the Soviet system'. The Literary Academy's influence was particularly harmful for those representatives of the Soviet cultural intelligentsia who remained 'weak in its proletarian ideology'. VAPLITE imbued these hesitant writers 'with a nationalist outlook, discouraging it from the creative path of the revolution, and [was inducing] ideological scepticism, and a passive inertness which does not at all harmonise with the volitional and joyous psychology of the victorious class to which the future belongs'.[97] Championed by such trustworthy Soviet critics and writers as Khvylia, Koriak and Mykytenko, the VUSPP declared its readiness to wage class struggle in the process of cultural construction against those writers who wished to create 'a chasm between the proletarian cultures of Soviet Ukraine and Soviet Russia'.[98] It advocated 'the international union of proletarian writers' and sought close ties with the Russian Association of Proletarian Writers (RAPP).[99]

The VUSPP statute resembled, to the letter, the new party resolution on 'Policy of the Party concerning Ukrainian Literature', adopted in May 1927.[100] The resolution encouraged Soviet Ukrainian writers to produce literature that would be proletarian, having been created in a proletarian environment by the new literary talent drawn 'from among the workers', as well as mass-oriented. It defined literature as 'the most important means of strengthening the union of the working class with the peasantry, a weapon of the proletariat in its direction of the entire Ukrainian cultural development'. It also played an important role 'in the cultural advancement of the masses of workers and peasants, in manifesting the building of a new socialist culture'.[101]

Soviet proletarian literature, according to the resolution, was to be created with the mass reader in mind. The authorities encouraged constant interaction with the audience, whereby authors would take inspiration from 'the artistic qualities characteristic of the proletariat' and their literary products would reflect 'a continual mutual influence between the writers and the masses'.[102] Genuine proletarian literature would be deductive, socially useful, ideologically correct and partisan. The resolution stimulated proletarian writers '[to] most clearly define the social significance of their work, [to] definitely rid themselves of all bourgeois influences, and most attentively approach the task set for them by the party – of struggle against the anti-proletarian and counterrevolutionary elements, of combating the ideology of the new bourgeoisie.'[103]

While providing the ideological framework for the future of Soviet literature, the 1927 resolution repeated the message of the 1925 All-Union Resolution on Literature,

Figure 14 Soviet Ukrainian writers near Viis'kove village (Pavlo Tychyna, *in front siting*), 1926. © Central State Archive-Museum of Literature and Arts of Ukraine, courtesy of TsDAMLMU.

reiterating that 'no single literary group existing in Ukraine had a monopoly'.[104] That said, the preference was of the side of the VUSPP, the only state-sponsored literary organization whose statute fully reflected the partisan and ideological nature of Soviet culture as envisaged by the party. Other non-aligned literary groups were singled out. For instance, the Kyivan *neoklasyky* group was defined as a 'bourgeois elements in literature' and condemned for 'anti-proletarian tendencies' in their works.[105] At the same time, the resolution encouraged 'proletarian solidarity' with literary groups in different Soviet republics:

> The association of proletarian writers of Ukraine should enter into friendly relations with similar writers' associations [in other Soviet republics]. This would lead to their union into an All-Union Alliance of Literary Federations of all Peoples of the USSR on the principles of proletarian internationalism, while combating any national opposition or pretensions at hegemony, as well as attempts to belittle the independent cultural creation of each people.[106]

The establishment of the VUSPP also revived the Literary Discussion. Although now taking greater care in moderating his rhetoric, Khvyl'ovyi continued to criticize literary politics in Soviet Ukraine and the VUSPP on the pages of *Vaplite*, the new periodical of the Literary Academy launched in January 1927.¹⁰⁷ In his first squib entitled '"The Sociological Equivalent" of Three Critical Reviews', Khvyl'ovyi attacked the 'critic-enthusiast' and VUSPP leader Koriak, stating that his narrow, vulgar sociological approach to literary criticism prevented him from discerning the aesthetic value of literary work.¹⁰⁸ By this, Khvyl'ovyi implied that a literary work could not be valued solely by its author's class origin. Although the two opponents sprung from the same ideological position, both belonged to the short-lived literary group October opposing the Russian-led Proletkult, Koriak, in Khvyl'ovyi's eyes, had betrayed 'the October' and started promoting 'red trash literary production (*bul'varshchina*)'.¹⁰⁹ Although Koriak remained one of the most celebrated official critics, Khvyl'ovyi accused him of 'ignorance and amateurism' (*bezhramotnist' i dyletanstvo*).¹¹⁰

Khvyl'ovyi's squib solicited a polemical exchange with Koriak immediately responding to his accusations in a letter 'from an ignorant (*temna*) person', published in the first issue of the VUSPP's own official journal *Hart* (Tempering), in which he criticized the nature of art as promoted by Khvyl'ovyi and VAPLITE.¹¹¹ With the squabble between Khvyl'ovyi, the writer, and Koriak, the politically oriented literary critic, the previous form and content debate returned to the press. Khvyl'ovyi was accused of prioritizing form over content (formalism), while Koriak was charged with rigid sociological method of literary criticism. Paraphrasing the party line, Koriak stated that the value of art was not in its cognitive element whereby art only recreates life so that readers can learn about reality, but through its functional ability of spreading class ideology to the masses, strengthening the influence of the dominant class:

> Ideology is something wider than cognition (*piznannia*). Art must unite the thoughts, emotions and wishes of the masses, to elevate them. It must invigorate (*rozburkuvaty*) artists within ordinary people and develop them. Art does not exist to perceive the reality, but to transform it.¹¹²

Only then would Soviet literature create masterpieces in the name of the proletariat, and not 'the art'.¹¹³ In Koriak's view, this was exactly the way to creating Soviet literature that would reach the masses.

The main disagreement between the writer and the critic arose around the question of national culture. Koriak charged Khvyl'ovyi with worshiping national culture as an absolute value in itself while he, and those standing behind him, promoted proletarian culture 'attired in the national form'. With a clear reference to Stalin, Koriak explained that 'proletarian culture does not negate national culture, but provides the content for it; and, on the contrary, national culture does not reject proletarian culture, but provides it with a form'.¹¹⁴

Khvyl'ovyi's response shortly followed.¹¹⁵ In his 'Earnest letter to Volodymyr Koriak', he asserted that the entire VUSPP had no clear perspective of how to defend the interests of Soviet Ukraine in the cultural sphere. Instead, as its inaugural congress had demonstrated, the organization remained under the influence of their Russian mentors, some of whom – namely A. Selivanov'skyi – had spoken during the event. He accepted Koriak's definition of proletarian art in the national form, yet he questioned the VUSPP's ability to create such literary products. For Khvyl'ovyi, the VUSPP was yet another example of the detested '*prosvita*' approach, promoting a 'khokholian enlightenment' instead of proletarian literature.¹¹⁶ Khvyl'ovyi implied that the VUSPP used the Ukrainian (with a pejorative reference to *khokhol*) language in their artwork in order to create digestible literature for the masses. To his mind, Koriak's approach did not differ much from those seeing Soviet Ukraine as a 'Little Russia', countered by Khvyl'ovyi in his earlier pamphlets.

This personal exchange escalated into an institutional debate. The third issue of *Vaplite* featured an extended review of the first issue of the VUSPP journal *Hart*, entitled *Nashe siohodni* [Our Today].¹¹⁷ Although the editorial's author remained anonymous, some scholars attribute it to Khvyl'ovyi.¹¹⁸ According to the reviewers, the outputs included in *Hart* had no creative value and signalled the intellectual poverty of the new literary organization, and, by extension, Soviet literature in Ukrainian. *Nashe siohodni* outlined two paths to developing revolutionary literature in Soviet Ukraine. First, there was a 'revolutionary path', represented by VAPLITE and MARS (*Maisternia revoliutsiinoho slova* – The Workshop of the Revolutionary Word)¹¹⁹, the two literary organizations dedicated to guiding 'talented and seriously minded youth' towards the writing of proletarian literature. Second, there was a 'reactionary' path 'of declarations and manifests', represented by the VUSPP. This literary organization strove to bring Ukrainian literature back to its standing during the civil war years, when writers, having no works of genuine artistic value, receded to the 'weapon of ideological declarations' in fighting against each other. Overall, the VUSPP was a necessary 'excess of the revolution' (*izderzhki revoliutsii*) with no future in Soviet Ukrainian literature.¹²⁰ Instead, VAPLITE had a role of 'guiding our literature out of the populist dumpster of the past and the peasant naiveté of today on to the path of creating proletarian literature, worthy of the great victorious class.'¹²¹ In response, the VUSPP attacked VAPLITE's members for promoting 'anti-communist tendencies', including the loss of faith in the proletariat and the revolution, NEP-inspired disillusionment and unreadiness for future ideological battles.¹²²

'From deviation into abyss'

Once harshly criticized for his political pamphlets, Khvyl'ovyi returned to fiction. His creative writing, however, was now also gaining a political sounding.¹²³ The first instalment of his novel *Val'dshnepy*, written during the summer of 1926, appeared in the fifth issue of the journal *Vaplite* in 1927.¹²⁴ The novel's main protagonist, Dmytrii Karamazov, is a disillusioned communist and former Chekist, as is his wife Hanna. While on vacation, Karamazov meets a young Russian holidaymaker and nationalist called Aglaia with whom he engages in lengthy philosophical and ideological conversations, and eventually he falls in love. The names of Khvyl'ovyi's protagonists are reminiscent of Fyodor Dostoevsky's novels suggesting, as some contemporary critics observed, a similar moral Dostoevskian dilemma of chasing one's ideals and the cost of it.¹²⁵ Karamazov, like many of Dostoyevsky's characters, is a divided self, doomed to self-destruction.¹²⁶ Aglaia, disillusioned in the outcomes of the revolution in Russia, admires the potency of the Ukrainian movement and revolution, leading her to anticipate Ukraine's national rebirth. She came to Ukraine and had even learned the language so as to witness that national reawakening for herself. At first, she took interest in Karamazov, but their conversations made it clear to her that Karamazov would not be the one leading Ukraine forward.

In the words of Aglaia, Karamazov was an embodiment of a Ukrainian revolutionary, who 'jumped out of his grey gymnasium shorts and immediately landed in the era of revolution'; he was that semi-educated oppositionary, who 'has accepted the events through the prism of his romantic view of the world'. Being fascinated by the scope of the social revolution, by social ideals emblazoned on its banner, he committed to die 'in the name of these ideals and he would have been prepared to face a thousand more deaths'.[127] However, when it became obvious that nothing had emerged from that social revolution and that the Communist Party 'very quietly and gradually was being transformed into an ordinary "gatherer of the Russian land" and it had lowered itself, so to speak, on its own initiative to the interest of the cunning philistine bourgeois class', those Karamazovs concluded that there was no way out. It was impossible to break ties with the party because this is not 'only a betrayal of the party, but of those social ideals for which they so romantically went to their deaths; this would be in the end a betrayal of one's own self'. Those revolutionaries had subsequently 'stopped at a kind of idiotic crossroads': being unable to formulate and form new ideologies, they are searching for 'a good shepherd', 'a safety valve' getting committed to yet another idea, this time of the national rebirth.[128]

But was Karamazov a revolutionary romanticist, yet another disillusioned communist like so many characters in Khvyl'ovyi's early prose; or just another philistine, a Woodcock – as the title of the novel suggests – a simpleton, a gullible person, who is easily swayed by any new illusion? Aglaia defines him as a revolutionary who 'lacks that individual initiative and even the proper terms to create the program of their new outlook'.[129] By the time of the novel's publication, there was no tolerance towards irresolute, undecided and melancholic characters, especially in a situation where such traits could easily lead to defeatism, deemed unacceptable in the political struggle. Although Karamazov so neatly aligns with Khvyl'ovyi's other characters, could the author still sympathize with those lost soles in search of answers? One might suggest that by means of the fictional novel, Khvyl'ovyi implied that the failure of an alternative project for Soviet Ukraine was caused not (or not only) by external pressure (the strength of its dominant Russian counterpart), but by internal weakness, specifically the ineffectuality of the Ukrainian nation builders who did not manage to adapt and readjust their tactics to the demands of the day.

In *Val'dshnepy* one can find a 'novelization of the pamphlet', as defined by Peter Sawczak.[130] The novel often adopts the style of a pamphlet with frequent clichés from political propaganda by Ukrainian communists, where the interactions between the characters resemble an exchange of opposing political stances. In this novel, Khvyl'ovyi further and in a more nuanced manner elaborated his criticism to Ukraine's subordinate status in the Union, expressed in the metaphor of 'Little Russia' – provincial and parochial understanding of Ukraine. The main drama of the work, as Sawczak observes, 'enacts "Great Russia's" ongoing hierarchical superiority over "Little Russia," thinly veiled by the plot of an uneven courtship between the headstrong Russian, Aglaia, and the confused Ukrainian revolutionary, Dmytrii'.[131] The relations between the characters in a fictional form exposed the legacy of Russia's imperial dominance over Ukraine. It is presented through references to nineteenth-century literature especially to its most characteristic representatives Taras Shevchenko and Mykola Gogol, presenting opposing ways to engage with the imperial hegemon.[132] Through his characters, Khyl'ovyi denounced the established dynamics between capital and province, as well as a narrow ethnocentric understanding of nationalism, epitomized through the prominent role Shevchenko came to play in the Ukrainian canon.

> [I]t was Shevchenko who castrated our intelligentsia. Wasn't it he who fostered this dim-witted slave-enlightener, whose name is legion? Wasn't it Shevchenko – perhaps not such a bad poet but a weak-willed person amazingly lacking in culture – wasn't it he who taught us to write poems, sentimentalizing in 'Kateryna style,' rebelling in 'Haidamak' style, to look absurdly and aimlessly at the world and its construction through a prism of backwardness sweetened with frightening phrases? Wasn't he, this serf, who taught us to berate the lord behind his back, so to speak, and drink vodka with him and grovel before him when he slaps us familiarly on the shoulder and says: 'You, Matiusha, are a talent, after all.' It was just this image-painting 'Father Taras' who halted the cultural development of our nation and stopped it from forming a state-wide unity at the right time.[133]

While for many, Shevchenko's position in Ukrainian history and literature was that of a prophet, Khvyl'ovyi degrades him to a status of a demigod (*bozhok*), a symbol of provincialism and culture mongering (*kul'turnytstvo*).

The sixth issue of *Vaplite* featuring *Val'dshnepy*'s second instalment was confiscated immediately. The excerpts only became known through Khvylia's extensive critical review *Vid Ukhylu - u Prirvu* [From Deviation into Abyss], published in 1928.[134] Khvylia, the novel's assigned critic, had no doubt that Karamazov was Khvyl'ovyi's alter ego: a disenchanted Marxist who got easily swayed by 'a speaker of the young Ukrainian fascist bourgeoisie' Aglaia.[135] In a similar vein, Skrypnyk commented that the novel reflected the author's psychological identity disorder, when both characters simultaneously can be seen as his alter ego. While criticizing the Communist Karamazov, Khvyl'ovyi, according to Skrypnyk, was moving closer to embracing the 'military Ukrainian fascism' represented by Aglaia.[136] Both critics, however, ignored the fact that Aglaia was herself Russian.

To critics, Khvyl'ovyi's *Val'dshnepy* proved that the writer, despite numerous public recantations, remained unapologetic about his 'nationalist deviation'. He persisted in criticizing the Soviet Union's 'idiotic *Ukrainizatsiia*' that restrained cultural development, and the transformation of revolutionary values when 'the slogans of October became reactionary, and the 1917 banner – a sign of Pharisaism'.[137] Instead, Khvylia continued, the writer dreamt of a national rebirth through which he 'became the apologist of young Ukrainian bourgeoisie', and Ukrainian nationalism.[138] Consequently, *Val'dshnepy* was not an artistic novel but 'a publicistic work dressed up in artistic grab'.[139] Through a fictional form, Khvyl'ovyi wished to replicate the main concepts of his censored brochure *Ukraina chy Malorosiia?*.[140] With this novel, Khvylia summarized, Khvyl'ovyi aimed to show that

Soviet Ukraine is not Soviet, the dictatorship of the proletariat is not real, the nationalities policy is a sham, the Ukrainian people are backward and will-less, the great rebirth is still to come, and finally, the party itself is an organisation of hypocrites.[141]

The party reacted immediately and an attack on VAPLITE's current leaders, unable to break ties with their former leader Khvyl'ovyi, quickly followed.[142] The biggest blow for the organization was an article by F. Taran that linked VAPLITE to anti-Soviet Ukrainian émigré circles, especially the editors of *Nova Ukraina* Vynnychenko and Shapoval. Those public campaigns resulted in the general public viewing the academy as nothing more than a semi-legal political opposition.[143] On 12 January 1928, seventeen VAPLITE members gathered to discuss options for continuing their activities in the face of such an ideologically hostile atmosphere.[144] Slisarenko, implying further divide between high-quality literary outputs and mass literature, highlighted that the Literary Discussion had been exploited by 'certain' writers who 'having failed to gain glory with their poor verses, embark on writing [critical] articles'. While those 'merchants are making profit [...] we, the writers, must neglect our work and reply to their lies and slander.'[145] Worst of all, VAPLITE writers were being denied access to publishing houses, while libraries 'fear to give our publications to the readers'. Slisarenko concluded that 'to maintain our organisation in such conditions means to bring damage to literature. Nonetheless, as bearers of the honourable title of proletarian writers, we feel responsible to the party, to the Soviet citizens, and to the proletariat.'[146] The only way out of this conundrum would be to dissolve the organization, so that each member would become responsible for himself.

Other writers, however, spoke of how their actions would be perceived by the public. None of them wanted their actions to be seen as anti-establishment. Leites, another Vaplitian, for instance, feared that dissolving the academy on such terms would be perceived as a demonstration against the party.[147] Kulish cast further doubt as to the wisdom of such a course of action, sharing his indecisiveness with other members: 'What holds me back as a member of the party is the possibility that our dissolution would hurt the Soviet people. In no way should our actions create an impression that the Academy have been "smothered".'[148]

In an attempt to rescue the Literary Academy from further persecution, Kulish publicly recognized his mistakes as president. In an open letter to *Komunist*, he confessed his oversights in expelling Khvyl'ovyi, Dosvitnii and Ialovyi but failing to restrict their access to the academy's periodicals (referring specifically to the publication of *Val'dshnepy*). He also admitted that Khvyl'ovyi had retained great, albeit negative, influence within VAPLITE: 'The personal influence of Khvyl'ovyi, the literary authority he had at the time, our personal sympathies, the very organisational structure of VAPLITE [...], – all this helped *khvyl'ovizm* to develop and spread out among us.'[149] Unable to withstand the official pressure, on 14 January 1928, the VAPLITE general meeting voted for voluntary liquidation. Its last resolution stated that the atmosphere created in Soviet Ukraine was 'too oppressive, preventing each of us as *members of this organisation* to work productively for the benefit of Ukrainian proletarian literature'.[150] The emphasis on their institutional affiliation as a hindrance to its members' individual artistic development suggested that the conflict in Soviet Ukraine's literary world was first institutional, and only then ideological and/or aesthetic.

Skrypnyk's *Ukrainizatsiia*

On 3 February 1927, the important post of the People's Commissar for Education was assigned to Skrypnyk, an old Communist and a former ally of Lenin. It was believed that Skrypnyk, who had had a long record of occupying high governmental offices in Soviet Ukraine, would respect the limits of *korenizatsiia* set by the party. Skrypnyk himself was devoted to the Ukrainian cause, although he tried to implement it in a more orthodox manner that was adhering to the party line. It was thanks to him that *Ukrainizatsiia* was not abandoned in June 1926 and was even reinforced in official policy.[151] Skrypnyk inherited a lot of power at the Commissariat of Education. *Narkomos* was one of the few republican commissariats that remained independent from Moscow as defined by the bilateral agreements between Soviet Ukraine and the Russian SFSR in June 1919 and December 1920.[152] *Narkomos* was also charged with overseeing all aspects of cultural and educational policies in the republic; apart from education (primary, secondary and higher education) and culture (including theatre, film, music and the arts), a number of separate departments acted under its auspices. These were the highest scientific institution *Golovnauka*, overseeing scholarly and scientific institutions, including the Academy of Sciences; The Central Bureau of Political and Educational Work – *Golovpolitosvita*, managing institutions of political education, including libraries; and a section for literature and publishing, *Golovlit*, that also oversaw the press and the publishing houses, including the DVU and the Book Chamber.

Under Skrypnyk, *Ukrainizatsiia* was revisited along stricter ideological lines whereby its advancement as policy would determine the success of the entire socialist construction. Skrypnyk argued that uneducated workers could not build socialism, just as backward peasants would not achieve high productivity targets.[153] In December 1927, the journal *Radians'ka Osvita* (Soviet Education) published the 'Ten Commandments of the Cultural Construction', outlining the tasks of the *Narkomos* chief. He declared a 'five-year plan of cultural construction' to 'raise the standards of Ukrainian culture and [achieve] Ukrainization of our entire cultural life, while ensuring the cultural and national needs of national minorities on its territory'.[154] Although committed to extending the scope of *Ukrainizatsiia*, Skrypnyk was well aware of its political limitations. During his tenure, he was more authoritative in attacking alleged nationalist deviations both within and outside the party, aiming to prevent any crystallization of an anti-communist opposition or discussion about separating Soviet Ukraine from the Soviet Union.

Skrypnyk's appointment to the Commissariat coincided with the proclamation of the first Five-Year Plan, and his actions in office were conditioned by the atmosphere of anti-nationalism and 'class war' this precipitated.[155] Although committed to constructing a Soviet Ukrainian culture, he needed to approach it with great sensitivity, particularly when addressing the highly contested question of proletarian

Ukrainization that had only recently cost Shums'kyi his post. Unlike his predecessor, Skrypnyk shared Stalin's view that Ukrainization of Ukraine's working class should be a natural and gradual process. His concern, however, was how to convince workers to identify with Ukrainian culture and language.

Skrypnyk believed that this recalibration of working-class identity could be achieved by combining demographic Ukrainization with the necessary promotion of Ukrainian culture. Since compulsion could not be used in respect of workers (the Ukrainian language was obligatory only for government employees), the linguistic Ukrainization of the workers could only be accomplished by creating a totally Ukrainian urban environment: a favourable setting in which the working masses would either convert or became inclined towards the Ukrainian language and new proletarian culture. This was to be achieved by increasing Ukrainian language and culture's socio-political prestige by bringing them directly to the proletariat. This included evening language and country studies courses, public lectures in Ukrainian, distributing books and periodicals and organizing reading circles, concerts, theatre performances and film screenings.

Literature was granted a special role in this process of socialist cultural construction. In an article written shortly after the 1926 Plenum, 'The results of the literary discussion', Skrypnyk declared that the 'literary discussion' had exhausted itself and the party was ready to learn from its mistakes. This public debate had exposed the danger of the 'petty bourgeoisie' and its capacity for fermenting both Russian and Ukrainian chauvinism. While he traced the roots of Russian chauvinism back to Russia's urban *mishchanstvo* (bourgeoisie), Ukrainian chauvinism was described as having originated in the Ukrainian countryside where it was reinforced by the '*spetsy* [the former specialists] and civil servants of a Ukrainian-ised apparatus'.[156] To fight both these forms of national chauvinism, the party now needed to encourage rapprochement and fraternal cooperation between the nations.[157]

This raised the question as to the nature of the relationship between Ukrainian, Russian and Soviet cultures. Skrypnyk, somewhat siding with Khvyl'ovyi's position, defended the right of Soviet Ukraine for independent cultural development. Yet he rejected any claims for a uniform Soviet culture and its hegemony in the Soviet Union. 'On the contrary', he argued that:

> the toiling masses of every nation emancipated by the October Revolution have entered the USSR as equals. The accomplishments of Russian culture, the accomplishments of Ukrainian culture etc. contribute to our collaboration in creating international proletarian culture on the territory of the entire Soviet Union, and no one can claim the hegemony, the formal or informal leadership; and there can be no tutelage or supremacy of one culture over another, no pretence on the unequal relationship between the Soviet peoples, but, on the contrary, there must only be fraternal cooperation under one roof.[158]

Skrypnyk feared that in reaction to Khvyl'ovyi's claims of a European cultural orientation, the response of other writers and arts officials would be to follow and learn from their Russian fellows. He condemned those ideologists who rejected the equal status of two cultures: 'The question should not be about the contemporary Russian literature *helping* the Ukrainian one; on the contrary, while developing independently these two literatures should *help* each other, that is to co-operate and co-assist each other in achieving the same tasks.'[159]

As a *Narkomos* chef, Skrypnyk was regarded as 'an arbiter of literary disputes and referee between fractious literary groupings'.[160] He was also tasked with defining the path of Ukraine's future cultural development, clarifying his literary agenda at a forum held in the Blakytnyi House in Kharkiv from 18 to 21 February 1928. His keynote speech and concluding remarks subsequently appeared in the party journal *Bil'shovyk Ukrainy*, under the title *Nasha Literaturna Diisnist'* [Our Literary Reality], in 1928, and were frequently republished thereafter. In his address, he condemned the sectarian, sociological approach to creative writing and literary criticism taken by the VUSPP that was no less damaging than VAPLITE's 'nationalism'. Skrypnyk also objected to the politicization of fine literature, promoted broad artistic autonomy and was ready to support every writer who remained mindful of their ideological role.[161]

He praised the new generation of Ukrainian writers for creating 'the new proletarian literature, striving to become the writers of the new proletarian state, the new Soviet society'.[162] Nonetheless, he did not approve of the way literary organizations in Soviet Ukraine were formed, being, according to Skrypnyk, based on the 'literary-political' principle, and not around matters of artistic integrity:

> For the most part, our writers create organizations not on the basis of any artistic [or] purely literary principle or movement, but rather based on semi-political platforms which unite various, sometimes even antagonistic artistic currents under a single roof.[163]

Skrypnyk also called the practice of grouping together writers based on ethnicity or language a 'primitive provincial existence', where 'every cat is grey, every writer a Ukrainian, everyone is a representative of proletarian literature'.[164] Instead, he encouraged freedom in defining formal artistic principles that should lay the foundation for literary unions. Using Lenin's famous slogan, Skrypnyk proposed 'to allow writers' self-determination up to separation from their literary organizations, and up to establishing a new literary "country"'.[165]

By the end of the 1920s, the party itself had become averse to the VUSPP's vulgar sociological criticism of the Russian RAPP and Ukrainian VUSPP and took every opportunity to remind its writers of their artistic duty.[166] Literary outputs were still evaluated against the principles of ideological purity but, if applied too strictly, the pursuit of 'communist rigidity' would lead, according to Skrypnyk, to 'Soviet pulp fiction'. Instead, the Commissar encouraged writers to aspire for high aesthetic value:

> We need to evaluate every piece of creative writing from the point of view of its usefulness to the toiling masses of our country; so that they can learn more from it [...] and would gain inspiration to create the new world, the new social relations. Capturing life in artistic forms is yet another way of its cognition

(*piznannia*), and therefore we must demand from every writer and every artist that they give something new, something worthy, able to strengthen the creative potential of the proletariat, [to provide him with] new strength in pursuing his grand creative tasks.¹⁶⁷

In the second half of the 1920s, despite toughened ideological control, literary life remained active. Apart from the state-sponsored VUSPP and the embattled VAPLITE, new organizations appeared. These included the constructivist group *Avanhard* (Avant-Garde) (1926); *Zakhidnia Ukraina* (Western Ukraine) (1927); and *Tekhnomystetska hrupa A* (Techno-artistic group A) (1928), each of which had its own periodical. Nonetheless, the party permitted this institutional diversity insofar as it could help diminish VAPLITE's ideological influence and cultural presence. Among the most frequently published were those writers and literary groups who openly declared their accord with the party's view on literature.¹⁶⁸ If in 1923, *Chervonyi Shliakh* was the only literary-political 'thick' journal, by the end of the decade the state had come to sponsor several regional periodicals: *Zhyttia i Revoliutsiia* [Life and Revolution] in Kyiv, *Zoria* [Teh Star] in Dnipropetrovsk, *Metalevi dni* [Metal Days] in Odessa, *Literaturnyi Donbas* [Literary Donbas] in Artemivs'k (later, Stalino, Donetsk).¹⁶⁹ By 1929, a total of 326 journals were being published in Soviet Ukraine.¹⁷⁰

All of these developments led to important shifts in the Ukrainization of the republic's press and book publishing. In 1928, as a result of state intervention and control over book production, the number of published outputs in the Ukrainian language increased almost eightfold in terms of copies and more than sixfold in terms of titles, when compared to the same numbers in 1923. In 1929, the share of Ukrainian books published in Soviet Ukraine reached 70 per cent in titles and 77 per cent in copies against those in Russian.¹⁷¹ This linguistic transformation of book publishing in Soviet Ukraine contributed greatly to *Ukrainizatsiia*'s ultimate success. Increased book production in Ukrainian also brought changes to book distribution, whereby many more Ukrainian literary products were made available to readers. As a result, urban reading audiences became increasingly habituated towards reading Ukrainian literature, cultivating genuine popular interest in books published in the Ukrainian language.¹⁷² As one worker from Donbas mentioned to a *Visti* reporter: 'Often when we see a Ukrainian book appear in the factory, a mass of these [Russified] workers gravitate to the book and pass it around from hand to hand.'¹⁷³

Skrypnyk also encouraged the development of other artistic spheres. Under his tenure, *Ukrainizatsiia* spread to theatre, film-making and radio-broadcasting. In 1931, for example, Soviet Ukraine boasted sixty-six Ukrainian, twelve Yiddish and nine Russian stationary theatres. The 1920s were also the most productive years for the cinematographic arts, with the All-Ukrainian Photo-Cinema Administration (*Vseukrains'ke Foto-Kino Upravlinnia*, VUFKU), becoming subordinate to the *Narkomos*, which thereafter oversaw the national production of films with four being produced in 1924, sixteen in 1927, thirty-six in 1928 and thirty-one in 1929.¹⁷⁴ Ukrainian radio-broadcasting was launched in 1924–5 while concerts, amateur choirs and literary evenings, all popularizing Ukrainian culture, soon became the norm in industrial areas.

As shown in this chapter, the implementation of *korenizatsiia* in Soviet Ukraine empowered local elites; moreover, the success of the *Ukrainizatsiia* initiatives brought to the fore those cultural agents and political activists who wished to promote and expand the republic's autonomy. This inevitably led to a clash between local and central perspectives on *korenizatsiia* and, by extension, the status of Soviet Ukraine within the Soviet Union. While those promoters of *Ukrainizatsiia* tackled Russia's economic and political dominance, the central authorities reinforced the linguistic and cultural aims of *korenizatsiia*. The republic's working class was placed in the centre of the debate between these two interest groups.

The two horizons in the KP(b)U clashed during the Party Plenum in summer 1926. As seen in this chapter, the centralist perspective gained prominence, whereas the representatives of the autonomist perspective were investigated and castigated. After 1926, *korenizatsiia* was reinforced with the party centrally taking more control over its implementation. Taking control over cultural policies necessarily led to a reaction against those demanding the redefinition of the policy's scope. Unsurprisingly, anti-*Ukrainizatsiia* programmes were set in motion, often requiring the involvement of the secret services. The shift in the policy's status in Soviet Ukraine was marked by reshuffling of the top cultural positions. Against those party expectations, Skrypnyk, who came to replace Shums'kyi as a more reliant executor of the central orders, achieved much of what his predecessor had hoped for. Arguably, under Skrypnyk's tenure, *korenizatsiia* and *Ukrainizatsiia* concurred – the aspirations of the autonomist faction had been realized, although in a more compliant and less obvious way.

The reaction of those Soviet Ukrainian elites to party criticism at the Plenum invites yet another important observation. Despite harsh criticism that often led to professional dismissal, loss of access to professional networks and resources, closure of literary organizations, none of the autonomists repented their loyalty to and compliance with the Soviet state and its cause. It is possible to assume that they did so insincerely, only to avoid possible persecutions. And yet as often seen from the reactions of those frequently accused, they did not regard their actions as anti-Soviet; those punished remained true to their Soviet-selves, as much as to their Ukrainian-selves.

6

State appropriation of literature during the first Five-Year Plan

'The Free Academy of Proletarian Literature is dead – long live State Academy of Literature!'

As the state campaign against VAPLITE unfolded, Khvyl'ovyi resided abroad, having received permission to travel in December 1927. According to A. Liubchenko, this had been obtained through Raisa Azarkh, a patron of Ukrainian writers who worked at the DVU and was an organizer of a literary salon. Khvyl'ovyi often spoke favourably of Azarkh who encouraged the writer to publish his selected works at the DVU, the first volume of which appeared in 1927.[1] Liubchenko, however, remained suspicious of Azarkh, who, as he believed, only 'pretended to be a patron, yet served as Kaganovich's informer'.[2] Khvyl'ovyi went to Europe allegedly to undergo a course of medical treatment for tuberculosis. In numerous private letters prior to his departure, the writer mentioned that his illness had worsened and that he suffered from neurosis.[3] However, considering Khvyl'ovyi's influence in the artistic milieu, his trip may have also represented a form of political exile.[4] For a few months he resided in Vienna and Berlin, from where he could hardly influence or address the flow of criticism against himself, *Val'dshnepy* or VAPLITE.[5] As indicated in a letter to Ialovyi dated from 7 February 1928, Khvyl'ovyi was frustrated with criticism being directed at *Val'dshnepy* and recurrent persecution against him: 'Did we write "a recantation" *(zrechennia)*? We did. What else do they want from us? To lick their butts? If there was no *Val'dshnepy*, they would have found something else to accuse me of.'[6] The reference to the repentance letter published in Visti in December 1926 as 'a recantation' suggests, however, that Khvyl'ovyi might not have been sincere in his penance.

Khvyl'ovyi took rumours about his political dissent even more seriously. In his aggravation, he retorted: 'Not only was I not thinking of giving back my party card, but I will appeal to Stalin himself if anyone should think to take it from me.'[7] This negative reaction towards those who condemned his theories as 'national bourgeois' or even as a form of 'Ukrainian fascism'[8] raises the question of whether Khvyl'ovyi himself believed in crossing the line of what was allowed and expected from a KP(b)U member. His reaction to those speculations could suggest that the writer himself did not regard his position as deviationist as the party leadership was trying to present. In fact, his position was determined by and remained in line with the programmes of the Ukrainian communist parties, who sought an independent Soviet Ukraine, as well as the KP(b)U leaders advocating for Ukraine's autonomy in its broadest sense. In the transitional period of the 1920s, with all its inconsistencies and social experiments, this project of autonomous socialist Ukraine was deemed by many as realistic and feasible.

His attitude towards the KP(b)U remained ambivalent, however. Indeed, he opposed the recent centralizing tendencies, fearing that it would result in limiting Ukraine's cultural autonomy and eventually subjugate the republic to the all-Union control. At the same time, he believed that change could only be introduced from within and even encouraged his fellow writers to join the party: 'We need our lads – [Arkadii] Liubchenko, Ianovs'kyi, Senchenko, Dniprovs'kyi and others, to join the party as a necessity. In this way, they will be given more rights, and we will get to achieve more.'[9] One can say that party membership was not merely a reflection of his ideological preferences, it provided him with the means to shape the course of action in the literary sphere and beyond.

Some biographers mentioned that, abroad, Khvyl'ovyi maintained ties with the Ukrainian political emigration. He was close to Roman Rozdolsky, a co-founder of the Communist Party of Eastern Galicia (later renamed as the Communist Party of Western Ukraine, KPZU), and a doctoral student at the University of Vienna at the time. Rozdolsky represented a faction in the KPZU that sided with Shums'kyi during his conflict with Kaganovich in 1926 over his support of a comprehensive a comprehensive form of *Ukrainizatsiia*.[10] Despite this similar ideological standing, however, Khvyl'ovyi showed little appreciation, or real interest, in diaspora politics. Andrii Zhuk, who had met Khvyl'ovyi in Vienna, recalled that during their encounter he did not stop talking about cultural affairs in Soviet Ukraine without even once enquiring about émigré cultural life or the diaspora's view on developments across the Soviet border.[11]

Following VAPLITE's dissolution, Khvyl'ovyi was obliged to return to Soviet Ukraine to assure his fellow writers that the battle for Soviet Ukrainian literature was not yet lost. Khvyl'ovyi was the leader of his generation. Smolych, a writer only seven years his junior, called him 'a senior [*starshyi*] writer and a recognised literary authority'.[12] Despite his controversial political stance, he remained an important figure in the literary establishment and many writers, especially those not aligned with the VUSPP, looked up at him.

Nevertheless, the dissolution of VAPLITE had placed its former members in an incredibly difficult position. In a situation where literary affairs were highly institutionalized, it became almost impossible for an independent writer (or '*dykyi*' – as they were called) to access the main channels for publishing or disseminating their work.[13] Aware of his status in Soviet Ukraine, Khvyl'ovyi assured his colleagues from abroad that the battle would continue, albeit in a more moderate compliant form. He concluded his letter to Arkadii Liubchenko with an assertive note – 'The Free Academy of Proletarian Literature is dead – long live the State Academy of Literature!'[14]

His return to Soviet Ukraine was conditional, however. Khvyl'ovyi was expected to publicly repent his errors and assure the party of his loyalty. On 22 February 1928, his second letter of recantation appeared in *Komunist*. While glossing over the main points of criticism raised by Khvylia against *Val'dshnepy* and his previous pamphlets, Khvyl'ovyi fully admitted to every error and deviation attributed to him and agreed that *Val'dshnepy* was nothing but another way of promoting ideas earlier expressed in *Ukraina chy Malorosiia?*.[15] He referred to a 'psychological break' experienced during his absence: 'What I've observed abroad made me finally realise that all this time I have been following a wrong path, not the one I should have taken as a communist.'[16]

The letter of recantation was taken ambiguously. Those informers recruited from among Ukraine's literati reported on the reception of Khvyl'ovyi's submission.[17] Some commentators did not regard it as a genuine repentance. One informer maintained that the letter in *Komunist* was not 'a sincere recognition of the counter-revolutionary character of nationalism', but a sign of the writer's 'fear or [change of] tactics'.[18] Another informer's reaction was that Khvyl'ovyi was cunning, or, as one commentator asserted, that he was 'a very clever man [...] an extremely sly and diplomatic person. Khvyl'ovyi is a "tsar and slave of wiles"'.[19] Khvyl'ovyi later allegedly mentioned that his recantation was a 'fictitious letter of a person of changeable disposition influenced by newspaper jabber' and that he would try to recover his reputation in the eyes of the Ukrainian public.[20] However, his close allies took the official recantation as a betrayal. As recorded in the GPU *svodki*, Oleksandr Kopylenko called him a 'hysterical man and a son of a bitch', who had doomed VAPLITE to decline,[21] while another response stated that in recanting his former beliefs Khvyl'ovyi had drew a line under the cultural opposition of 'the young Ukrainians to Russians'.[22]

The years of *Literary Fair*

Despite its ambiguity, Khvyl'ovyi's apparent surrender to the official party line was accepted, and he returned to Kharkiv in March 1929. Shortly thereafter, he gathered the former VAPLITE writers around a new literary almanac – *Literaturnyi Iarmarok* [Literary Fair]. The idea of this 'un-organised organisation of the literary process' belonged to Iohansen, who passed the project on to Khvyl'ovyi. Khvyl'ovyi, however, tried to stay behind the scene, so as not to compromise the almanac through an association with his own political past.[23] The leading position in the editorial house officially belonged to Kulish, with the writer Ivan Senchenko serving as secretary.[24]

Literaturnyi Iarmarok, of which twelve issues appeared between December 1928 and February 1930, was an attempt to preserve some elements of autonomy against the tightening of party control.[25] With its diverse contributions, the almanac also opposed the unification of style as promoted and implemented by the VUSPP. *Literaturnyi Iarmarok* itself marked the high point of an extremely creative literary decade with some of the most ironic, humorous and mystifying texts of the 1920s appearing on its pages while the years after VAPLITE's dissolution were characterized by Smolych as a 'rampant flourishing of a literary Bohemia'.[26] *Literaturnyi Iarmarok* was highly praised by contemporary critics. According to Bilets'kyi, for instance, the almanac 'by virtue of its external appearance which was created by the most prominent artists of the day, by its content, particularly the literary prose, by its refined language and the subtle melding of humour together with a respect for ideas and form, by far surpassed anything that had been done in Ukraine before.'[27]

One of Khvyl'ovyi's most noticeable contributions to *Literaturnyi Iarmarok* was his satire *Ivan Ivanovych*, published in June 1929 in the almanac's *Knyha Sioma* [Book Seven].[28] The story accounts for the everyday life of a party official Ivan Ivanovych, also known under his party nickname Zhan, and his family. The depiction of the family's life is hyper-sincere, to the extent that it becomes sardonic. *Ivan Ivanovych* is a literary example of an excruciating critique of a low-level corruption in the Soviet Union. Khvyl'ovyi uses sarcasm to underline his negative attitude towards the main character and the various opportunists and timeservers, with whom he associates, who used their party membership cards to obtain benefits and privileges.

Unlike ordinary Soviet citizens, Ivan Ivanovych had already witnessed the 'new revolutionary interpretation' of the social order and his family now truly lives under a communist utopia. Symbolically, they reside on Thomas More street with asphalt on the pavements, access to taxis, and flowerbeds in front of each house.[29] Ivan Ivanovych, aware of the housing crisis in the republic, is content with only four rooms and 'had never demanded a separate bedroom for his cook Iavdokha'. He is also cognizant of the economic situation in the country; although earning many times more than an average worker, he considers his financial situation to be rather moderate – a salary of only 250 *karbovanets'*, thus preserving 'the feeling of proletarian equality'.[30] To complete the picture, Ivan Ivanovych also has a model family: his wife Comrade Halakta, who 'loves to read Lenin and Marx, though her hand is stretching involuntarily for a volume of de Maupassant', and two children, a son with the revolutionary name Mai, and a daughter, Violeta, who had been brought up by the family governess Mademoiselle Lucy.

In this 'genuinely' communist atmosphere, Ivan Ivanovych fights ardently for social justice every day. With revolutionary fervour, he tackles reactionary movements and deviations within the party, yet, given the achievements of socialist construction, struggles to comprehend its ideological opponents:

> What do they want from us? Is there a dictatorship of the proletariat? Yes, there is! Is the power in our hands? Yes, it is! Have the factories been nationalised? Yes, they have! Is there a Red Army? Yes, there is? Is there a Comintern? Yes, there is? […] Are we approaching socialism? Yes, we are! […] What else do they want? I simply cannot understand.[31]

Ivan Ivanovych and his wife frequently participate in party cell meetings, held in an artificial, even surreal atmosphere in which party activists, who otherwise live in abundance, gather in shabby clothes, 'well aware of the transitory nature of the period in which they lived'.[32] Party meetings take place in a room, where every corner 'is not just an ordinary corner but above all, a "red corner"',[33] where a 'noble fight for social justice' was taking place. Within the context of the story, the party cell faces a mission of universal importance – to find a culprit accused of sabotaging the process of socialist construction. Khvyl'ovyi's prose ridicules this 'witch-hunt': with no obvious 'wrecker' to put the blame on, activists were choosing between those most dispensable – a cleaning lady or an ordinary party cell member. Unexpectedly, the lot falls on to a Jewish member Comrade Leiter.

The accusation is random and baseless, hence, reversible. At the next cell meeting, the accusations of sabotage are suddenly withdrawn, with Comrade Leiter proclaimed as being 'not a wrecker or bandit, but a devoted Communist',[34] whereas his opponents, Ivan Ivanovych and other members of the presidium, are forced to leave the party. Ivan Ivanovych discovers that he has betrayed the party not through a public process or a hearing, but in a *Visti* article: 'Betrayal of the Revolution. Clear betrayal. Unless the paper is lying? But I always believed in it!'[35] Thus, justice becomes a sham, a whim of those in charge of issuing orders.

The novel received positive reviews, and it was later included in Khvyl'ovyi's selected works.[36] According to a review by the critic Mykhailo Maiorov, the author aptly satirized those individual party members who had taken advantage of the privileges their positions granted them within Soviet society. His Ivan Ivanovych was representative of those 'good people, communists, maybe even fighters during the civil war' who fell under the influence of petty bourgeoisie during the era of the NEP, became corrupted and went against the interests of the party and the working class.[37] Yet was it a story about a single party member who became corrupt? Or the entire party? The literary scholar Alexander Kratochvil maintains that *Ivan Ivanovych* was a deliberate political satire on the social order and a Soviet bureaucracy.[38] The story demonstrates how the party had grown detached from real life and now existed in some parallel reality where, it seemed, communism had already triumphed.

Like his *Povist' pro Sanatoriinu Zonu* (1924), *Ivan Ivanovych* offered yet another example of a confined space. Although its characters were not isolated from the outside world by sanatorium walls, they were likewise detached from the rest of Soviet society apart from rare interactions with their maid or a weekly travesty preceding a party cell meeting. Khvyl'ovyi mocked not only Ivan Ivanovych, but the entire party cell to which he belonged. Hence, through satire, Khvyl'ovyi uncovered the pervasive corruption of the long-anticipated social order, where each and every opportunist suddenly started to consider themselves protected by their membership card, where the absolute truth existed on the pages of a party newspaper, where moral norms were irrelevant or acquired 'new revolutionary interpretation' and where communism had already flourished, but only for the chosen few. As the diaspora literary scholar Iurii Boiko later observed, the author 'found strength to apprehend the Soviet reality as tragicomedy; he depicted the reality, defined by simple formulas, covered with masks, and [represented by] people used as marionettes'.[39]

In their contributions to *Literaturnyi Iarmarok*, those writers formerly affiliated to VAPLITE attempted to ridicule the VUSPP's 'joyous peace of monumental realism' (*mazhorno-monumental'nyi realism*) as defined by Khvyl'ovyi.[40] They deliberately exaggerated the presence of positive heroes, deductive messages and party mindedness in their work to make them seem all the more laughable. Unsurprisingly, their contributions attracted extensive criticism, as numerous defamations sent to the secret services against the 'unnecessary, dangerous squibs' published in the periodical suggest.[41] As these social and political pressures intensified, the almanac's authors were increasingly obliged to temper their criticism and match with the artistic expectations of the time. The changes in their last issues did not go unnoticed. A party critic positively evaluated this tendency stating that 'today we can say with assurance that [...] the majority of [these] "pessimists" will become our own troubadours. They have begun to speak a different language. If you take Issue Number 10 of *Literaturnyi Iarmarok* you will see that it already signals ... a transition to ... an organisation [that is part] of the proletarian front.'[42]

Pondering on the fate of *Literaturnyi Iarmarok*, Smolych explained that it had now become almost impossible to remain 'independent' in the literary process. Indeed, it was not easy to maintain an almanac that did not represent any particular literary organization. The party preferred Soviet authors who belonged to a certain group that expressed a clearly defined ideology. As party intervention intensified, many authors quit creative writing all together, while those who remained were compelled to align with one of four categories: '"our" (*svii*), "allies" (*soiuznyk*), "a fellow traveller" (*poputnyk*) or – God forbid – "an enemy" (*voroh*)'.[43] Only members of the VUSPP and *Molodniak* (The Union of Komsomol Writers)[44] could be regarded as 'ours' while those in *Pluh* were 'allies'; none wanted to be among the 'enemies', yet many 'fellow travellers' started to be treated as such.

Visit to Moscow, 1929

In early 1929, various Soviet Ukrainian writers received an invitation from Russia's Federation of the Unions of Soviet Writers to present their literary achievements in the state capital.[45] The Ukrainian week held in Moscow on 9–15 February was the first official visit of the Ukrainian writers' delegation to Russia. During the tour, writers were granted an opportunity to meet their Russian counterparts, present and discuss their work with Russian audience, negotiate future publication of their translated works in central publishing houses and meet high-ranking Soviet leaders. The Ukrainian week was covered extensively in the Soviet press and came to be regarded as one of the most important events of the 1920s.

As presented by the Soviet Ukrainian press, the visit represented a culmination of Soviet Ukraine's independent literary development, the recognition of the equality between Ukraine and Russia's self-standing Soviet cultures and an acknowledgement of Soviet Ukrainian literature's greatest achievements at the highest Union level. An editorial in *Literaturna hazeta* [Literary Newspaper], for instance, praised the event for bringing two great cultures closer to each other, as well as providing for cultural reconciliation between the republics.[46] The *Visti* literary supplement *Literatura i Mystetstvo* featured a lengthy editorial authored by the *Narkomos* chief Skrypnyk who elaborated on the event's historical and political significance. In Moscow, he explained, 'the new Soviet literature of Russia with its long historic roots and, until the [October] Revolution, dominant position [was] having a fraternal meeting with the new Soviet literature of Ukraine [that had] centuries-long experience of oppression, persecution and neglect (*pryhnichena, hnana ta zanedbana*).'[47] Skrypnyk hoped that this meeting would finally banish old misunderstanding and distrust between the two cultures and lay the foundations for strengthened cooperation in achieving the same goals through different national channels.[48]

The 'misunderstanding' that Skrypnyk and other writers referred to was an incident with a Ukrainian translation of Gorky's famous 1906 novel *Mat'* [Mother]. In 1926, Slisarenko, the editor-in-chief of the editorial house *Knyhospilka*, had written to Gorky seeking his approval for a Ukrainian translation of the novel's abridged version. In his response, Gorky had strongly objected to any changes to the original Russian text, refusing to endorse its translation into what he termed 'a Ukrainian dialect (*narechie*)'.⁴⁹ Justifying this stance, he maintained that the languages would soon merge, with Russian becoming the only one used throughout the Soviet Union. Gorky's claims, unsurprisingly, provoked a negative response from Ukrainian writers. Slisarenko immediately sent a fuming response to Gorky rebuffing his accusations of oppressing the Russian speakers in Soviet Ukraine and accusing him of having a humiliating attitude to 'reviving proletarian Ukraine':

> It is true, the reviving proletarian Ukraine demands from excessively arrogant Russian (*russkii*) officialdom, petty bourgeoisie and intelligentsia to respect its culture and language, but to force a lout (*nakhal*) to respect the master of the country does not yet mean to oppress him. But this presumptuous lout, having lost the ability to spit upon the 'boorish nation' now raves about 'suppression'. Justly there is so much opposition in the press now against a pejorative name of '*khokhol*' that is being so frequently used by Russian intellectuals (*intellihenty*). Ukraine, despite the resentment of the people who used to loot 'Slavic (*slavianskaia*) India', is entering the vast arena of cultural and political development and I hope that the custody (*opeka*) of the big-hearted breaker of its culture and language over her is over. It is wrong, while affirming your language, to speak of eradicating another language in the name of 'universal language'.⁵⁰

The use of the metaphor of 'Slavic India' is most interesting. Slisarenko suggested that Russia had been treating Ukraine as its colony; but that time, he hoped, was over. A similar attitude towards Gorky was expressed by Khvyl'ovyi in his pamphlet *Ukraina chy Malorosiia?*. Khvyl'ovyi recalled the incident and named Gorky 'a great chauvinist, a preacher of Russian messianism and "a gatherer of the Russian lands" for the sake of Russia, and definitely not communism'.⁵¹

Smolych later recalled that when Gorky passed through Kharkiv on his way to Moscow in July 1928, no prominent Ukrainian writers attended a literary evening held in the Blakytnyi House. Those associated with VAPLITE simply ignored the event and that, apart from Pylypenko, Kulyk and Mykytenko, only novice writers were present.⁵²

Many of these Ukrainian writers believed that the attitudes of their Russian counterparts stemmed from limited knowledge and, indeed, interest in contemporary political and cultural developments in Soviet Ukraine. They therefore viewed the trip to Moscow as a means of proving that the development of Ukrainian language and culture was not just a phase that would eventually lead to a merger with 'greater' Russian culture. Literature in Soviet Ukraine developed independently and on a par to that in Russia, or any other Soviet republic, with the Ukrainian language being a powerful tool in literary production.

Almost the entire Soviet Ukraine literary elite, fifty writers and twelve artists, travelled to Moscow in February 1929. Most of these delegates saw themselves as representing Soviet literature and did not mask their support for the Soviet authorities.⁵³ Indeed, the biggest faction within the delegation, nineteen delegates in

Figure 15 Ukrainian artists in Moscow, 1929. © *Literaturna Hazeta*, 1 March 1929 (*standing*: Hnat Iura, Leonid Pervomais'kyi, and Ievhen Pluzhnyk; *in front siting*: Andrii Holovko and Natalia Zabila) (public domain).

total, comprised writers affiliated to the VUSPP and the *Molodniak*. Among them were its leaders Kulyk, Mykytenko and Koriak, as well as other prominent members such as Pavlo Usenko, Natalia Zabila, Zahul, Leonid Pervomais'kyi and Ivan Le. Another group represented the Union of Peasant Writers *Pluh*, headed by Pylypenko and the then editor of *Chervonyi Shliakh*, Ivan Kyrylenko. Among the delegates, there were also the leaders of *Nova Generatsiia*, Semenko and Shkurupii; the modernist group *Avanhard* Valer'ian Polishchuk; and former members of VAPLITE, Khvyl'ovyi,[54] Tychyna, Iurii Ianovs'kyi, Mykola Bazhan, Dosvitnii, Hryhorii Epik, Kulish, Iohansen, A. Liubchenko, Dniprovs'kyi, Iulian Shpol, Slisarenko, Dovzhenko, Sosiura and Ostap Vyshnia. At the same time, no representatives of the Kyivan *neoklasyky* group or VUAN literary scholars were present. Only three non-Soviet writers – Borys Antonenko-Davydovych, Valerian Pidmohyl'nyi and Ievhen Pluzhnyk – joined the delegation.[55]

Participants from both sides of the earlier debate had high hopes and expectations for their meeting in Moscow, the first such gathering to occur in the history of the Soviet Union. One of the delegation's main concerns was Russia's disdainful attitude towards Ukrainian culture, seen as subordinate and provincial.[56] Pylypenko, for instance, hoped that the meeting would generate Russian public's curiosity over developments in other Soviet republics: 'Every Ukrainian, Belarusian, Georgian, Armenian, or Turk besides their mother tongue also knows Russian and is therefore well-equipped to acquire both cultures. At the same time, a Russian citizen is deprived of this opportunity.'[57] The bestselling writer of satirical feuilletons Ostap Vyshnia was instead far more concerned with widespread popular stereotypes of Ukraine as backward and rustic. Revoking the imperial clichés, inspired most probably by the poetry of Taras Shevchenko, he complained that many in Russia still thought of Soviet Ukraine only as a country 'of cherry blossom and sunflowers'.[58] The trip to Moscow would, he hoped, finally 'kill *khokhly*';[59] it will debunk the predominant view of Ukraine's backwardness in comparison to a 'more civilised' Russia. Writers also spoke of a physical and ideological border between the two Soviet republics, tangible even in 1929. Zahul, for example, attested that he, like many of his fellows, had visited Western Europe numerous times, yet had never been to Russia.[60]

Russian writers also commented on the Ukrainians' upcoming Moscow visit.[61] This was mostly articulated as expressions of regret that no such event had ever occurred, encouraging more translations of contemporary Ukrainian literature. Professor Vladimir Friche spoke of Russia's 'huge debt' to Ukrainian literature: 'Neither at universities where we prepare literary scholars, nor in scholarly institutions dealing with literary criticism have we paid enough attention to literary art in Ukraine.'[62] The Russian Soviet writer Aleksandr Serafimovich echoes this sentiment while expressing hope for future interaction between the two cultures that 'should fertilize each other by their experiences, victories and accomplishments'.[63] To achieve this cooperation, more translations were necessary. As one Ukrainian participant recalled, during one such exchange Mayakovski had even promised to translate ten sheets of Ukrainian poetry by the end of the year.[64]

The first engagement of the Ukrainian delegation's week in Moscow was a meeting at the TsK VKP(b) Agitprop. The event's host, and the head of Agitprop Platon Kerzhentsev, underlined the great political and practical significance of the writers' visit to Moscow, describing an urgent need for cultural rapprochement and cooperation between the peoples of the Soviet Union.[65] Ukrainian cultural officials responded by suggesting some practical steps for closing the gap between the Soviet literatures, such as setting up publishing targets for translating the national literatures of the Soviet peoples (Pylypenko), and forming a professional team of reviewers who would prepare reviews of the newest releases in the other Soviet republic for publication in separate sections of the Russian all-Soviet 'thick journals' (Kulyk).[66]

The official opening of the Ukrainian week took place at an evening public event held in the House of the Unions (*Dom Soiuzov*). The opening address was delivered by the Head of the Russian Narkompros Lunacharsky who expressed regret over how little cooperation and exchange there currently was between the two branches of Soviet literature: 'Strange to think! It is much easier for us to get acquainted with English literature than with the Ukrainian one, that is so much closer to us.'[67] Similarly, Mykytenko, serving as speaker for the Ukrainians, pondered as to why it had taken twelve years since the Revolution for such a meeting to occur: 'During this time we have already developed ties with French, German, English and even Turkish writers.'[68] The opening ceremony was followed by a literary evening at the Herzen House, where both Russian and Ukrainian writers presented their work. Pilnyak, Mayakovski, Iurii Olesha and Demian Bedny represented contemporary Russian literature while among the Ukrainian writers, the most popular presentations were from Tychyna, Sosiura and Bazhan, as well as the humourist Ostap Vyshnia.[69]

On 12 February 1929, the Ukrainian writers were invited to Gorky's apartment for a meeting with the Soviet leadership. Here, they were greeted by Kaganovich who had only recently been transferred from Kharkiv back to Moscow. As recalled, Kaganovich addressed the delegation in Ukrainian, despite having hardly ever spoken the language during his tenure in the KP(b)U.[70] Nevertheless, the address demonstrated an awareness of recent literary trends, while Kaganovich already knew many writers personally: 'We felt ourselves as if in Ukraine,' as one participant observed.[71] In his speech, Kaganovich spoke of the Soviet nationalities policy as having promoted equality and supported the cultural developments of every Soviet nationality; he condemned Great-Russian chauvinism, manifesting itself through arrogant insolent attitude of some Russian writers (a reference to Gorky, although without naming him) as for Ukrainian literature and language; and outlined the key tasks of contemporary literature – to fight for class clarity and Marxist criticism.[72]

Kaganovich's speech was interrupted halfway by a sudden appearance from Stalin. What followed was a two-hour-long spontaneous conversation with the Soviet leader based on a series of questions which the Ukrainian delegates had submitted in advance. The entire conversation was preserved in the archive with plans for preparation as part of an eventual selection of works by Stalin, which never materialized.[73] What made this exchange particularly interesting is the fact that it was never officially recorded. Moreover, the Soviet leader's speech was not well edited or subject to the same careful preparation that characterized many of his published addresses. Instead, as the minutes suggest, Stalin was unprepared for constant interruptions, challenges and questions from the writers.

The conversation began with Stalin answering the questions. Among the concerns raised were prospects for developing national cultures, the content and form of national culture in the Soviet Union and the fate of nationalities in the transition period from capitalism to socialism. Stalin used well-known formulas in his answers, assuring the writers that the Soviet Union was dedicated to defending, sponsoring and promoting national cultures. This support aimed to assuage suspicion and establish mutual trust.[74] Ukraine's writers wished to hear about Stalin's view on the future unification of national cultures, which would mean their necessary absorption by the all-Soviet (read: Russian) culture. Stalin tried to allay the Ukrainians by emphasizing that the question of unification could only be raised once the mutual trust between Soviet cultures had been achieved.

Stalin asserted that his approach of 'disunity for the sake of unification (*raz'edinit'sia dlia ob'edineniia*)' was in line with the teachings of Marx and Lenin. 'We sponsor these cultures so that they exhaust themselves completely so that they can then create the basis for a language of the whole world – not Russian, but an international language.'[75] In the meantime, the Soviet authorities would promote national cultures and languages because 'the cultural level of the millions who comprise the popular masses can only be raised on the basis of a native language.'[76]

While his defence of national cultures and languages was not unique and remained consistent with the official party policy since 1920, the application of these features to the case of Soviet Ukraine shocked the writers. While referring to the difference between *natsiia* and *natsional'nost'*, Stalin outright rejected 'the great-power point of view' according to which statehood was a key feature of a nation.[77] For him, instead, language was the key characteristics of a *natsiia*. He used the Ukrainian example to stress that a community that had its clearly defined territory but whose language was 'only now being polished [*shlifovka*]' could only be regarded as a *natsional'nost'*. In Soviet Ukraine, according to Stalin, there was no single language as of yet, with the people using different dialects through which they could barely understand each other: 'Would your people be able to understand people from Kharkiv, [or] Galicians?'[78] At that moment, the conversation got out of hand as the delegates began to intervene and challenge Stalin. As Antonenko-Davydovych recalled, the writers were agape with wonder: 'Until now we believed that we were a *natsiia*, but now it looks like we are only a "*natsional'nost'*"'.[79] One of the attendants joked in response to Stalin's doubt about the Ukrainian language that 'Galicia can be united with Ukraine, Galicia understands us.'[80]

What was considered as a mere joke, it seems, bore greater importance for Stalin who persisted with his queries – Do people in Galicia read literary outputs from Soviet Ukraine? What about scholarly and scientific literature, political journalism [*publitsistika*]? Is there a need to translate and if so who was borrowing from whom?[81] In response to Stalin's questions, Kulyk took the floor. He assured the Soviet leader that 'the centre of literary life in the sense of richness, in the sense of the number of writers, in the sense of the broad variety of themes, was in our country,' in *Velyka Ukraina* – Great Ukraine, as they called it.[82] He also referred to a recent orthographic conference – the first All-Ukrainian Orthography Conference, held in Kharkiv from May to June 1927 – that aimed to codify the Ukrainian language. Apart from the Soviet linguists, the conference had included three delegates from Galicia and one from Transcarpathia, at the time under Czechoslovak control.[83] Stalin was clearly unaware of these developments, further questioning whether Western Ukraine also recognized it.[84] Kulyk maintained that it was the exact same Ukrainian language, albeit with a number of Polonisms: 'We have a remarkable process here: on the one hand – Polonisms, and on the other – Russianisms. Galicia is closer to the Russian language than is our Kievan-Poltavan language.'[85] Stalin's enquiries served a broader purpose, however. If culture and language across the border were the same, could one say that Ukrainians in Galicia and in Soviet Ukraine were the same nation (*natsiia*) and if so, could it be used as a prerequisite for their unification?

Another concern expressed at the meeting was the rights of ethnic Ukrainians in the RSFSR. Polishchuk took the liberty of asking Stalin if those parts of the Voronezh and Kursk *gubernias* which were predominantly populated by Ukrainians could be joined to Soviet Ukraine in the future. Here, Polishchuk followed Stalin's logic to the letter. If the language and ethnic identity of those communities across the border were the same, and according to Stalin's own definition those were the constituent features of a nation (*natsiia*), then why should not those areas be parts of Soviet Ukraine? However, Stalin was clearly not interested in the Russian–Ukrainian side of the border and evasively responded that it had been changed too frequently already and this 'creates a bad impression both within the country and outside the country'.[86]

The writers continued to challenge Stalin, taking issue with the Soviet leader's favourite play *Dni Turbinykh* (The Days of the Turbins) that had been adapted from Nikolai Bulgakov's novel *Belaia Gvardiia* (The White Guard). The delegation had recently seen the play in a Moscow theatre and was outraged with the way it had presented Ukrainians during the revolutionary events of 1917–19, and its interpretation of the civil war al together. All were unanimous in their conclusions: the play was anti-

Ukrainian, chauvinist and, in addition, promoted monarchism. From Stalin's point of view, however, the play, although written by a non-Soviet writer, carried the correct message by teaching proletarian viewers of the Bolsheviks's triumph in the conflict.[87] The writer Oleksa Tesniak retorted: 'When I watched *The Days of the Turbins* the thing that struck me most was that Bolshevism defeats those people not because it is Bolshevism, but because it is creating a unified, great and indivisible Russia. This is the message which strikes everyone who sees the play, and we would be better off without this kind of victory of Bolshevism.'[88] Tesniak summarized the Ukrainian perspective, asserting that the play did indeed justify Great-Russian chauvinism while promoting a pro-monarchist view of Russia that had been persistently rejected by the Soviet leadership. While the party made extensive efforts in seeking to combat chauvinism and nationalism in Soviet Ukraine, the writers complained that nothing comparable had been accomplished in Russia:

> It is our impression and conviction that the formula of the Twelfth Congress to the effect that the fundamental threat is posed by great-power chauvinism and that that threat must be combatted – this formula has been assimilated perfectly well by us in Ukraine, as has the idea that it is necessary to combat local chauvinism at the same time. But this formula has been assimilated poorly in the directing organs, even in Moscow. If we are to speak of great-power chauvinism, we must at the same time raise the question of unmasking that great-power chauvinism in some concrete form. In Ukraine, we had such a concrete form – *Shumskism*, and we fought against in the practice of Moscow [Party] work and the [Party] work in the RSFSR there is nothing like this, even though many instances of chauvinism with regard to Ukraine may be found.[89]

Stalin was caught unprepared and found himself unable to comment on the dangers of Great-Russian chauvinism. He explained that political criteria should not be applied to a play: 'Excuse me, but I cannot demand of a literary author that he must be a Communist and that he must follow the party point of view. For belletristic literature other standards are needed – non-revolutionary and revolutionary, Soviet and non-Soviet, proletarian and non-proletarian. But to demand that literature be Communist – this is impossible.'[90] For the Ukrainian writers, Stalin's justification came as a shock, given that so many of them had observed and even experienced for themselves what this political criterium meant for Soviet Ukrainian literature. By the end of the discussions, it had become obvious that different standards existed for the treatment of anti-Soviet motives in Russian and Ukrainian literatures. The head of the Main Department for Arts of UkrSRS Oleksii Petrenko-Levchenko concluded the debate with a demand that the play must be cancelled.[91]

Overall, hardly any literary or cultural issues were raised during the writers' meeting with Stalin. Instead, many political concerns were discussed. The writers had come prepared to take up their grievances with the leader of the Soviet Union himself and they persisted with politically sensitive questions. Nonetheless, Stalin had other interests to pursue, being more interested in soliciting responses to his own questions regarding Western Ukraine. One might extrapolate that Stalin had started to reflect on the prospect of a unification between Western Ukraine and Belarus long before the Soviet Red Army crossed the Polish–Soviet border in September 1939.

The Ukrainian week in Moscow had resulted in a clash between two competing visions of Soviet culture. The delegation from Soviet Ukraine came to the capital of the RSFSR and the Soviet Union as representatives of a separate Soviet republic, promoters of a separate political identity and producers of a self-standing Soviet literature in the Ukrainian language. They came to promote a Soviet Ukrainian culture that was being constructed at the time by a young nation within the borders of Soviet Ukraine. Apart from the writers, the delegation also included a famous modernist theatre director Les' Kurbas and the film director Dovzhenko. The tour also featured an exhibition of Ukrainian artwork, organized by the Association of Revolutionary Art of Ukraine, known as the Boichukisty group. Paintings by Ivan Padalka, Vasyl' Kasiian, Oleksandr Dovhal', Vasyl' Sedliar and Sofiia Nelepns'ka-Boiuchuk, all of whom had international recognition for their monumental avant-garde art enriched with national motives, were exhibited in Moscow.[92]

Nevertheless, both writers and artists remained frustrated with the treatment they received in Moscow. Indeed, party officials continued to highlight the equality between the Soviet peoples and disdain to great-power chauvinism. In reality, however, the most popular play on stage found it 'perfectly acceptable to twist the Ukrainian language, thereby ridiculing that language' and present Ukrainian military figures as comparable to 'a bandit, quite literally as savage and uncultured'.[93] More importantly, such representation was backed by the Soviet leader himself who rejected that any political innuendoes existed in his favourite play, all while undermining the status of the Ukrainian language by siding with those who dismissed it as a collection of rural dialects. The delegation had come prepared to take a stand against 'Russian chauvinists' who, like Gorky, downgraded Ukrainian to a status of a dialect. They had hoped that the meeting would help solve these 'misunderstandings' as they called them and close the gap between the Soviet literary cultures. Nonetheless, their battle could hardly be won against a camp that was championed by Stalin himself.

The year 1929 was the culmination of a transitional period in Soviet Ukraine, drawing a line under a decade of political and cultural separatism inspired by revolutionary romanticism of 1917 and enabled by the implementation of *Ukrainizatsiia*. Many cultural and political alternatives were developed and tested during the 1920s. Nonetheless, as the writers' climatic meeting with Stalin had proven, there was little appreciation of that variety in the Soviet Union's centre. The Soviet leadership expected compliance and uniformity, albeit framed as national diversity. Yet understanding of national diversity differed significantly between those in Moscow and Kharkiv. While Ukrainian elites, empowered by *Ukrainizatsiia*, sought a separate and fully fledged Soviet Ukraine, the Moscow leadership stripped this national form of its political connotations, allowing it to develop only as an ethnographic category. The 'great break' cut short any attempt to push the permitted boundaries of national cultural development. Those deemed non-compliant would become the targets of political trials and nation-based persecutions.

The process over the Union for the Liberation of Ukraine (SVU)

Conventionally, the 'hard line' campaign against class enemies within the Soviet Union was introduced during the Shakhty trial in 1928, when a large group of mining engineers and technicians from the Donbas area in eastern Ukraine were charged with conspiracy and sabotage. As asserted by Fitzpatrick, the trial marked the beginning of a political confrontation between 'proletarian' communists and the old 'bourgeois' intelligentsia while establishing a pattern for anti-intelligentsia actions in other areas.[94] In Soviet Ukraine, the Shakhty trial was followed by several major national conspiracies and terrorist plots 'unmasked' between 1929 and 1934. The most important trials of the early 1930s concerned conspiratorial 'nationalist' organizations, namely the Union for the Liberation of Ukraine (*Spilka Vyzvolennia Ukrainy, SVU*), the Ukrainian National Centre (*Ukrains'kyi Natsional'nyi Tsentr, UNTs*) and the Ukrainian Military Organization (*Ukrains'ka Viis'kova Orhanizatsiia, UVO*). These show trials were in fact fabricated by the secret police with the aim to break the influence and position of the non-Soviet Ukrainian intelligentsia.[95] As such, they mostly targeted representatives of the suspected Ukrainian 'right': the old-line intelligentsia and *zminovikhivtsi*, recent returnees from abroad, as well as Ukrainian communists and political activists who disagreed with political centralization imposed from above.

As a rule, the processes were swift. In case of the SVU, the first compiled collection of documents dated from 21 May 1929,[96] originally appearing in the Soviet press in November 1929. Already on 1 December 1929, the heads of the DVU's special department Valerii Horoshanin and Borys Kozel's'kyi – both of whom played a key role in fabricating the case[97] – reported that the DVU had disclosed and liquidated a counter-revolutionary organization that aimed 'to overthrow the Soviet power and establish an independent democratic Ukrainian People's Republic'.[98] The trial concluded on April 19 with some 237 volumes comprising hundreds of thousands of pages of material.[99]

Ample evidence suggests that preparation for the SVU trail had been launched long before the case was announced. According to the case material, the organizations existed from June 1926 to July 1929. Unsurprisingly, its start date coincided with the June 1926 KP(b)U plenum that had taken back control over the implementation of *korenizatsiia*, as well as the passing of the GPU top-secret report 'On Ukrainian Separatism' that had initiated anti-*Ukrainizatsiia* measures in the republic. Among those arrested in the SVU case were former prominent members of the UNR, activists of the Ukrainian Autocephalous Church and the VUAN members.[100] 'Despite the fact that many of them had been pardoned by the Soviet authorities', these individuals, according to the DPU head Balyts'kyi, 'did not reject their criminal counterrevolutionary activity and with the help of international bourgeoisie created an organization that aimed to unite Ukrainian anti-Soviet elements using mass agitation, propaganda and sabotage in order to launch an uprising against the Soviet order.'[101]

The 'proletarian' trial of the alleged SVU leaders, held at the Kharkiv Opera House between 9 March and 19 April 1930, became the major political as well as public event of the first Five-Year Plan receiving wide coverage in the Soviet press.[102] Since February 1930, the party newspaper *Visti* regularly published case material under the headline 'The Union for the Liberation of Ukraine (from the SVU accusatory materials)'. Other newspapers also featured contributions from prominent artists, intellectuals and writers incriminating their former fellows and praising the efforts of the secret services in uncovering the organization.

Khvyl'ovyi, although not directly linked to the SVU, became one of these public denunciators. During the trial, two pieces under his name appeared in the newspaper *Kharkivs'kyi Proletar* [Kharkiv Proletariat]: 'Who else sits among the indicted?' (March 16) and 'After Iefremov's diary ... ' (21 and 25 March).[103] While targeting those on trial, Khvyl'ovyi, who at the time was occupied with promoting his *Literaturnyi Iarmarok*, saw it as necessary to reassure the authorities of his political loyalty. On the pages of the republican press, he declared his full support to the party and applauded the GPU's success in uncovering 'the main headquarters of the Ukrainian military counter-revolutionary organization',[104] calling for further actions against yet another 'militant deviation' in the KP(b)U, namely *khvyl'ovizm*.[105] Khvyl'ovyi admitted that parallel with the SVU conspiratorial actions, the creator of *khvyl'ovizm* himself

> was throwing his 'revolutionary' slogans left and right, and hiding behind them or even his party membership card [...] has been storming the party with his counterrevolutionary pamphlets, and finally, got pretty brazen [...] to declare his nationalist programme in the article *Ukraina chy Malorosiia?* and in the novel *Val'dshnepy*. On the bench, next to *iefremovshchyna* [after Iefremov, the alleged SVU leader] must be (and indeed is) *khvyl'ovizm*. Not Khvyl'ovyi or his friends, to whom the party allowed the opportunity to rectify their mistakes and work for the proletarian cause, but *khvyl'ovizm* as a social feature.

Then, as if realizing the limited character of his surrender, Khvyl'ovyi added: 'But of course, one cannot judge a social current without attacking its speakers.'[106] Iurii Shapoval defines these two articles published in 1930 as representing Khvyl'ovyi's third recantation.[107] It is interesting, however, that every new recantation of Khvyl'ovyi coincided with yet another initiative to bring life into the autonomous cultural project.

On 19 April, forty-five Ukrainian intellectuals, writers and theologians, former politicians and activists, and the VUAN's leading members were convicted and sentenced by the Supreme Court of the Ukrainian SSR. Among them were the former UNR leader Iefremov, a former UNR Prime Minister Volodymyr Chekhivs'kyi, the literary scholar and former UNR Foreign Minister Andrii Nikovs'kyi, a former USDRP leader and a professor of the Kyiv Institute of People's Education (former St Vladimir University of Kyiv) Iosyp Hermaize, the writer Liudmyla Cherniakhivs'ka-Staryts'ka and her husband, a professor of the Kyiv Medical Institute, Oleksandr Cherniakhivs'kyi.

Despite the array of prominent names among those condemned, prosecutors were less concerned with incriminating specific individuals. Of far bigger concern was what those under trial represented in the eyes of the authorities, all of whom were categorized under labels such as 'Petliurites', 'nationalists', or 'wreckers'. Through these individuals, the party officials targeted the Ukrainian intelligentsia and Ukrainian culture itself. Such names were behind the highest achievements in culture, scholarship and science, with deep roots in the pre-revolutionary era. The importance of the trial was explained by the public prosecutor Panas Liubchenko in the foreword to its proceedings published in 1931:

In the hands of the toiling masses, the minutes of the SVU proceedings should become a powerful weapon helping to unmask the Cainite methods of plotting, used by the Ukrainian nationalists against the state of soviets. The words of the accused, as recorded in the minutes – of those former leading figures of the *putliurivshchyna* and the UNR, will expose for everyone the aims of the Ukrainian bourgeoisie and Ukrainian nationalists, and show what kind of an 'autonomous' and 'independent' Ukraine they have been fighting for.[108]

One of the main features of the SVU trial was its undisguised anti-Ukrainian character. Across the republic some 30,000 educators and schoolteachers were arrested, allegedly in connection with the SVU.[109] These were non-Soviet elites who had actively engaged in implementing the *Ukrainizatsiia* campaign and filled in the positions necessary to achieve its unrealistic goals. It was precisely due to the success of *Ukrainizatsiia* that the need for punitive actions arose. Whereas the party initially introduced *korenizatsiia* to disarm local nationalism, the lack of resources to implement their policies had allowed the non-Soviet intelligentsia to grow stronger. The SVU trial, as argued by Pauly, was a signal that the *Ukrainizatsiia* policy had been reconsidered and was being taken under direct party control: 'By tarring Ukrainian literature with the slander of nationalism, conflating it with counter-revolutionary reaction, the SVU trial and its reporting also undermined the public's faith in Ukrainisation and the pre-revolutionary cultural elites.'[110]

The persecution of these leading cultural elites had serious repercussions. The SVU trial reversed the lenient attitude towards *zminovikhivtsi* and fellow travellers, signalling the upcoming monopolization of the artistic and cultural life. In addition, it was a sign for those KP(b)U party members, earlier accused of national deviation, that the party kept a record of their activities and was ready to resort to using state power at any point. Addressing the XI KP(b)U Congress in Kharkiv in June 1930, the newly appointed TsK KP(b)U General Secretary Stanislav Kosior admitted that the SVU case was 'a brutal verdict to *shums'kizm*. It has shown that *shums'kizm* was nothing but an offspring of Ukrainian bourgeois nationalism.'[111] In the same manner, shortly after the verdict in the case had been announced, Skrypnyk in a speech to the VXI Congress of the All-Union Communist Party in Moscow maintained that members of the SVU had revived the old theory of a struggle between two cultures, as Khvyl'ovyi had argued during the literary debates of the 1920s.[112]

Nevertheless, Khvyl'ovyi avoided further persecution and was pardoned at the highest party level. In June 1930, Kosior reported that:

In the fight against *shums'kizm* and *khvyl'ovizm* [...] the Party has won. We defeated the deviationists to the last, we inflicted a crushing blow. [...] I reckon that the SVU trial became the most merciless conviction to *shums'kizm* and to the entire Ukrainian chauvinism. Comrade Khvyl'ovyi, who during the process published an article entitled 'Who else sits among the indicted?' raised a pertinent question. Hereby I must admit that the time has come to stop baiting Comrade Khvyl'ovyi for his old sins.[113]

From the party perspective, this act of pardon meant that Khvyl'ovyi could now be used by the authorities for achieving their goals in the cultural sphere. Khvyl'ovyi, however, got a free hand to pursue his activities further, although in a much limited form, as it will be discussed further.

Although the communist Khvyl'ovyi managed to avoid censure, other communists of national orientation were called to account for their alleged deviations. Over the following years, a number of prominent Ukrainian state officials, party members and public activists were charged in connection with the Ukrainian National Centre (*UNTs*) and the Ukrainian Military Organisation (*UVO*). The most prominent convicts of the *UNTs* case were the two Galicia-born Ukrainian academics, and recent returnees to Soviet Ukraine, Hrushevs'kyi and Matvii Iavors'kyi,[114] whereas the *UVO* trial tackled the representatives among the higher political echelons. In 1933, Shums'kyi, demoted in 1927 from the *Narkomos* and reassigned to Moscow, was accused of organizing a fascist coup and consequently sentenced to ten years in a labour camp.[115] The campaign against Skrypnyk, '*skrypnykivshchyna*', led to the *Ukrainizatsiia* policy's curtailment in 1933.[116]

There was yet another long-term impact of the SVU trial. By eliminating the VUAN leadership in 1930, the autonomous status of the institution, first granted in the early 1920s, was abolished. As a consequence, the Academy, the main promoter of academic research, was subjugated to the Communist Party's political agenda with party officials granted control in directing its activities, included the nomination of VUAN candidates. The first by-elections took place in May 1929, well before the SVU trial, with the party already preparing to replace those academics who would soon be arrested. Among those promoted to the soon-to-be-vacated posts was Tychyna, although his candidacy was highly debated with many regarding him as a 'not yet fully developed poet',[117] not to say an academic scholar.

Writing in his diary, Iefremov reflected on a meeting with Tychyna shortly after his candidacy was put forward. Tychyna 'startled as always' had asked the vice-president if his name could be withdrawn from elections to the 'Soviet Academy': 'I was put forward without being asked, – Tychyna explained, – and I don't know what I will do there.' Iefremov commented that: 'Morally he [Tychyna] might be the best among those promoted. At least, he hasn't forgotten how to blush and clearly understands that there's nothing for him to do in the Academy.'[118] Arguably, the party wanted to have a trusted figure at the Academy, one who appeared acceptable to its older members and yet could be easily manipulated. Tychyna further revealed how he himself felt about his position in the Academy. On 13 June 1929, he noted:

I was writing a note to [the poet Ivan] Tsytovych. But then on a postcard I noticed a tiny ant. To blow it off? No-no. To move away with my fingers? No-o-o.

I tore a piece from an American newspaper and scooped the ant from the card. And then: I let her go through the window. Go. Maybe you won't even notice at once where you are and who moved you.

This is how I was carried over to the academy [VUAN].[119]

On 26 June, despite the controversy, Tychyna was elected as a VUAN academic in the sphere of poetry.[120] Iefremov, who had abstained during the vote on Tychyna, commented on the results:

> Nine were elected to the First Department [history and philology]: [Vsevolod] Ihnatovs'kyi, [Mykhailo] Slabchenko, [Dmytro] Iavornyts'kyi, [Matvii] Iavors'kyi, [Filaret] Kolessa, Ianka Kupala, Tychyna, and [Vasyl'] Shchurat. Out of those we have only one 'worker' – Slabchenko. The rest are 'for decoration' only: some are incapable of work, others won't come. The only achievement is that the Department has been expanded.[121]

In less than a year, all those elected to the Academy would become responsible for promoting Soviet scholarship while their predecessors were arrested and sentenced to the camps.

The results of the VUAN by-election appeared on the pages of *Visti*. The same issue also included a new poetic contribution from Tychyna:

> Let Europe quack
> Our mind is set
> On the one and only concern –
> The cutting of traditions
> Collectivization (O.P.)

Antonenko-Davydovych recalled the reaction of Voronyi, who was Tychyna's poetic inspiration during his pre-revolutionary symbolist period. When asked what he thought of the new verse, he replied ironically: 'Well, this is the last poem of the poet and the first work of the academic.'[122]

These political show trials were intended to prevent the crystallization of a possible political opposition in Ukraine, strengthened as a by-product of *Ukrainizatsiia*. The campaigns against Ukrainian politicians and public intellectuals after 1928 signalled the decline of the separatist horizon in the party. At the same time, they marked a watershed in the process of Sovietization of Ukraine. After 1932, it was virtually impossible to find an activist or intellectual in Soviet Ukraine who had not been checked and had not conceded to the party's agenda. Those cleared during the 'class war' of 1928–32 would define the cultural and ideological scene in Soviet Ukraine during High Stalinism.[123] Those Stalin's Ukrainians would contribute to constructing a Soviet type of Ukrainian identity, rewriting the Ukrainian past and creating Soviet culture that complemented but did not undermine Russia's political and cultural dominance.[124]

The Proletarian Literary Front (PROLITFRONT)

The era of the first Five-Year Plan represented possibly the most despondent period in the history of modern Ukrainian literature with literary works produced by authors with little or no talent and evaluated purely in terms of ideology, political intent and social usefulness inundating bookshops. Despite their claims for artistic monopoly, the VUSPP's members produced little of high literary merit. Their periodical *Hart* and the fortnightly *Literaturna Hazeta* [Literary Gazette] were predominantly filled with invectives towards perceived enemies, other literary groups and currents, especially former Vaplitians. Within such an atmosphere, established writers were forced to engage in polemics all while lowering their artistic standards to meet the expectations of the party officials and reach out to the masses. Nevertheless, a few independent literary organizations and personalities did attempt to oppose the VUSPP. These included *Nova Generatsiia* [New Generation], established by the futurist Semenko; Polishchuk's *Avanhard* [Avant-Garde]; and Khvyl'ovyi who, after the almanac *Literaturnyi Iarmarok* was closed down in early 1930 due to its 'opposition to socialist realist style', established a new organization – *Ob'iednannia studii proletars'koho literaturnoho frontu* – PROLITFRONT (The Union of Workshops of proletarian literary front – PROLITFRONT). Other writers, however, unwilling to affiliate with any of these groups, attempted to keep silent or simply withdrew from more ideological debates.[125]

Beginning in September 1929, those writers who comprised Khvyl'ovyi's inner circle had started to consider possibilities for a new literary organization.[126] The debates surrounding it also reflected Khvyl'ovyi's own heightened awareness of the shifting political climate. Kostiuk, who joined Khvyl'ovyi's circle in late 1929, recalled his justifications for founding a new literary organization. According to Khvyl'ovyi, the joyful and independent era of *Literaturnyi Iarmarok* was over. Instead, a new strictly regulated and politically aggravated time was coming. Those proletarian writers who wanted to continue their creative activity would need to either join the VUSPP or establish their own proletarian organizations that could correspond to the political climate of the time. This said, Khvyl'ovyi elucidated that any new literary organization would be proletarian and partisan in its ideology, compliant with the party line on literature and regardful of its perceived enemies. Moreover, it would proactively wage a decisive struggle against both 'primitivism and vulgarism of theorists from the VUSPP and the New Generation', and against 'any manifestations of bourgeois and petty bourgeois worldview, great-state chauvinism and Ukrainian nationalism, including its one peculiar manifestation – *khvyl'ovizm*'.[127] With the reference to *khvyl'ovizm*, a popular buzzword used by the authorities to define Khvyl'ovyi's autonomist worldview, Khvyl'ovyi, probably, wished to assure them that he had recognized and overcome his ideological errors. At the same time, condemning *khvyl'ovizm* in the new literary organization's programme meant that Khvyl'ovyi and its members were well aware of the limits set to their activity.

Khvyl'ovyi's idea for a new literary organization was further advanced by Kulish who spoke of the writers' duty to engage in the process of 'unprecedented social and economic reconstruction of our backward country' and become actively involved in promoting proletarian ideology and the postulates of the Communist Party. Kulish maintained that writers in this time of the 'Great Break' could not remain passive observers:

> A writer does not invent ideas and images in his office but derives them from real life. Therefore, the new operative slogan of our organisation must be: A writer – into the broadest masses of the toiling population! A writer – to the mines,

Figure 16 Ivan Dniprovs'kyi, Mykola Kulish, and Hryhorii Epik. Undated. © Central State Archive-Museum of Literature and Arts of Ukraine, courtesy of TsDAMLMU.

factories, *kolkhozy*, to the masses or workers, peasants and students! This is where our ideas, images and plots are; and most importantly the cadres. This is where our replacement must come from. [...] We will go amidst the toiling masses to jointly create cultural atmosphere and cultural centres, and from there we will recruit gifted individuals. We don't want and cannot stand aside in the shadow of life. We want to be at its forefront.[128]

It is hard to judge the degree to which these words reflected a genuine conviction, and how much can be attributed to the difficult time's in which their speakers lived. It is possible to say that Khvyl'ovyi's own experience had taught him only too well that it was equally dangerous to either be involved in a 'wrong' type of politics or to remain above it. He clarified his position in response to protests from Iohansen and Smolych who rejected the idea of PROLITFRONT as a mass organization. Both would subsequently establish their own organization, *Tekhnomystetska hrupa A* [Techno-artistic group A].[129] Khvyl'ovyi commented that they hoped for a group with 'a-political' orientation that would save them from 'the political blizzard of our days', concluding 'Let them be. Time will tell.'[130] *Tekhnomystetska hrupa A*, however, did not remain independently neutral for long. Already by December 1929, it had joined the All-Ukrainian Federation of Revolutionary Soviet Writers, along with PROLITFRONT and the VUSPP.

In the preface to the last issue of *Literaturnyi Iarmarok*, published in February 1930, Khvyl'ovyi bid farewell to its readers before inviting them to switch to a new literary periodical, *Prolitfront*, the first issue of which appeared in April 1930.[131] Its editorial board consisted of three main editors – Ivan Momot, A. Liubchenko and Khvyl'ovyi, with the latter in charge of the journal's ideological direction.[132] The contributions featured also reflected a clear ideological and partisan position with the first issue of *Prolitfront* including a statute for the new writers' union. Together with other existing proletarian groups, PROLITFRONT assured their position in the vanguard of 'the fight against bourgeois art, against a hostile ideology [...], against nationalist manifestations'.[133] This said, its members articulated this stance by engaging in party-approved activities, reaching out to the masses, and frequently commenting on the current events. Among PROLITFRONT's members were such prominent figures as Tychyna, Khvyl'ovyi, Kulish, Vyshnia, Ianovs'kyi, Dosvitnii, Senchenko, Panch, Epik, Dniprovs'kyi, Ialovyi and others, all of whom were previously affiliated with VAPLITE.

PROLITFRONT gradually embarked on the same path of accommodating the party's vision for literature, as its principle opponent, the VUSPP. In the wake of class war, writers, including those in PROLITFRONT, had no choice but to engage in politics and the state-sanctioned 'witch-hunt' against alleged enemies. In its earlier meetings, PROLITFRONT's soon-to-be affiliated writers were even involuntary involved in the SVU process, being expected to openly declare their position on the matter. Kostiuk, who was also present at the meeting, recalled how hard it was for Ialovyi, who was assigned to speak on the issue, to second the official accusations. The writer half-heartedly admitted that despite previous reservations as to whether such a clandestine counter-revolutionary organization even existed, they had been sufficiently convinced of the defendants' guilt by the trial material and were ready to condemn this 'dangerous organisation of people who have not learned anything from life'.[134] Shortly thereafter, a letter signed by Khvyl'ovyi, Ialovyi, Kulish and Epik was published in the eleventh issue of *Literaturnyi Iarmarok*, praising the GPU for unmasking the 'disgraceful activities of those academic bandits (*akademiko-bandyty*)'.[135]

PROLITFRONT fully embraced the party's literary vision, turning towards Ukraine's industrial workers and peasant communities in search of themes and readers. The organization even adopted the slogan of 'the first Five-Year Plan of art', as defined by the RAPP leader Leopold Averbakh, aiming to bolster mass consciousness and organize the will, mind and enthusiasm of the masses for socialist construction and social reforms.[136] In searching for 'shock-workers' of literature, PROLITEFRONT's members involved themselves in various 'useful' activities including organizing tours to factories and collective farms and travelling to construction sites to collect material and plot ideas for their fictional works. PROLITEFRONT's ranks were also opened to workers who were eager to master the literary craft and participate in 'socialist competition for the best literary results', by establishing literary circles in workplaces, assisted in publishing wall papers and organizing literary evenings at which professional writers presented alongside talented proletarian youth.[137] To provide a platform for these new voices, the idea for a bimonthly *Literaturnyi Tsekh* [Literary Guild], aiming to engage young members of various literary studios opening in Kharkiv's factories, was also posited; however, this never materialized.[138]

PROLITFRONT eventually joined the All-Ukrainian Federation of Revolutionary Soviet Writers, established on 31 December 1929. The Federation, the idea for which had been originally stipulated by the TsK KP(b)U Politburo Resolution from June 1927, aimed to unify proletarian writers. Apart from PROLITFRONT, the statute

Figure 17 Soviet Ukrainian writers in Artemivs'k, 1928. © Central State Archive-Museum of Literature and Arts of Ukraine, courtesy of TsDAMLMU.

of the Federation was signed by the leaders of the VUSPP, *Molodniak* (The Union of Komsomol Writers), the Union of Peasant Writers *Pluh*, the All-Ukrainian Union of the Workers of Communist Culture, *VUSKK*, the Techno-artistic group A, and the Union of Revolutionary Writers *Zakhidnia Ukraina* (Western Ukraine).

Nevertheless, despite their ideological amenability, the mere existence of PROLITFRONT enraged the VUSPP; this organization, while seeking a monopoly over the production of Soviet literature, could not accept any alternative to its claim, no matter how conforming to ideological standards they were. In addition, the VUSPP enjoyed full party support. By contrast, PROLITFRONT was ultimately perceived as a gathering of 'notorious' or politically discredited writers whose formal repentance had never been viewed as sincere. In the end, Khvyl'ovyi always kept 'a nationalist fig in his pocket', as one writer retorted.[139] Beginning in the summer of 1930, reports were sent to the Agitprop's Ukrainian branch accusing the organization of pursuing their own 'dangerous' path. According to these reports, those associated with PROLITFRONT had remained spiritually on the side of the petty bourgeoisie and fellow travellers, with no guarantee that *khvyl'ovizm* – understood as claims for artistic and political autonomy – would not relapse among its members.[140] At the same time, the VUSPP contributed greatly to furthering its negative image in the Soviet press.

Faced with rising political hostility, it soon became increasingly difficult for PROLITFRONT's members to continue in their activities, with the organization being gradually sidelined in Soviet Ukraine's literary affairs. This was exacerbated in November 1930, following its members' rejection of the VUSPP's offer to attend the congress of the International Office of Revolutionary Literature in Kharkiv as a passive observer. As a result, PROLITFRONT was not among the founding members of the International Union of Proletarian and Revolutionary Literature (*Mizhnarodna Orhanizatsiia Proletars'koi ta Revoliutsiinoi Literatury*, MOPRL), which was established at the event. This also meant that financial support for *Prolitfront*'s editorial and printing costs becoming increasingly harder to secure, resulting in the November issue being postponed until January the following year.

Unable to feasibly continue in this largely one-sided struggle, PROLITFRONT self-liquidated in January 1931 with its members passing a resolution declaring the need to consolidate all literary forces in the republic within the VUSPP. The resolution suggested the merger of these groups, since admittedly there were no ideological differences between the two. It was signed by thirty-four writers who wished to also join the VUSPP.[141] Not all of PROLITFRONT's members were accepted, however. For instance, Kulish, Ianovs'kyi and Ostap Vyshnia were initially rejected membership. On 24 February 1931, Khvyl'ovyi addressed a general meeting of the VUSPP's Kharkiv organization where he acknowledged its leading role in shaping Soviet literature in Ukraine while also declaring that there had been no external pressures in PROLITFRONT's self-liquidation. Instead, its members had realized that their views on the future of Ukrainian proletarian literature were futile. In what became his last public recantation, Khvyl'ovyi claimed that PROLITFRONT was unable to formulate

Figure 18 Soviet Writers, members of the VUSPP, 1932. © Central State Archive-Museum of Literature and Arts of Ukraine, courtesy of TsDAMLMU.

a new direction for literary development and had therefore found themselves at an impasse. They now wished to join the VUSPP, the only literary organization that 'did not fail to follow the strategic path of proletarian literature and [did not divert] from the line approved by life'.[142] Well aware of what it would mean to be denied membership, he advocated that all former members of PROLITFRONT be allowed to join the VUSPP.[143] Denying them the opportunity to realistically continue their work went against the interest of proletarian literature to not push away writers who wish to contribute to its strength.[144] The unification of these two groups marked the final stage in the consolidation of all literary forces in Soviet Ukraine.

Although seen by many as a last retreat for 'independent' writers,[145] in reality, PROLITFRONT's activities during the period 1930–1 had only signified the decline of the alternative project of proletarian and Soviet literature in Ukraine, originally launched in 1923 by three 'Olympians' (Khvyl'ovyi, Dosvitnii and Ialovyi) who had envisioned the creation of a literary organization dedicated to promoting more intellectually challenging literature for educated proletarians. This project for establishing a different vision of Soviet Ukrainian literature had reached its zenith in the form of VAPLITE and *Literaturnyi Iarmarok* and exposed its robustness during the Literary Discussion of 1926–8. The ideological compliance of PROLITFRONT did not necessarily symbolize a rejection of these values, however. Its members had simply been forced to accept the changing state of affairs in order to continue working in an environment of toughening control and limited tolerance for artistic pluralism. Their merger with the VUSPP signalled the triumph of the official vision for Soviet literature in Ukraine, created within tight ideological limits and under close party supervision. To exist as writers, that is to write and publish their work, those who had formerly dissented were now obliged to conform and accept their new roles as useful and dedicated 'engineers of human souls', or Soviet cultural workers as later defined by Stalin.[146]

Old writers in a new literary climate

In the climate of class war, Tychyna's position became especially precarious. Given his past, the poet could easily expect to find his name among those being placed on trial for alleged anti-Soviet and counter-revolutionary activity. Indeed, among the SVU defendants one could see Nikovs'kyi, the former editor of *Nova Rada*, where the young poet had worked in 1917 and published his first poems glorifying the achievements of the national revolution. Tychyna also had ties with Iefremov, with whom he had worked closely during his time in Kyiv. Since the mid-1920s, however, Tychyna had gradually moved within the inner circles of Soviet culture, where he had found himself entrusted with important editorial positions and had represented the country abroad. Nonetheless, he remained a non-party member closely linked to Khvyl'ovyi's close circle, with his name featured repeatedly in the SVU trial material. As seen from the investigation files, VUAN member and literary scholar Oleksandr Doroshkevych, for instance, had implicated the poet as a member of a secret organization based at the Kyiv department of the Shevchenko Institute of Literature.[147] Instead of being interrogated, however, Tychyna found himself being elected as a VUAN academic in the summer of

1929, the same year he also became a candidate member to the All-Ukrainian Central Executive Committee (VUTsVK).[148] With these appointments, Tychyna now commenced his career as a state official. This path required different virtues, with party-minded and ideologically correct poetry a necessary attribute for his new role.

In 1931, Tychyna published a new collection of poetry, entitled *Chernihiv*, dedicated to his late friend, the poet Vasyl' Ellan (Blakytnyi), his first original collection since *Viter z Ukrainy* and *Zhyvemo komunoiu* (1924). Prior to this, his poems had only appeared sporadically in periodicals and literary almanacs, excluding republished or new editions of his earlier work.[149] The Soviet scholar Shakhovs'kyi attributes this hiatus to self-censorship.[150] Given his long silence, even more attention was devoted to *Chernihiv* in which many critics expected to find proof of Tychyna's ideological commitment.

The collection was a 'poetic sketch' (*narys v poeziiakh*) consisting of only eight verses that represented separate parts in a conversation between the main character, a nameless worker, and his friend, who had come to see the titular city that had 'regained its youth due through Soviet rule'.[151] While the reader's attention is focused on these protagonists, the author's role is reduced to setting the context for each poem and providing the titles. *Chernihiv* glorified socialist achievements in an ordinary Soviet city, yet its message was projected onto the entirety of Soviet Ukraine. The concluding piece of the collection, tellingly titled *Stara Ukraina Zminytysia Musyt'* [Old Ukraine Must Change], suggested a bright future for the republic. The irreversible transformation from the quiet provincial town of Chernihiv, where Tychyna had spent his childhood and early manhood, into an urbanized and industrialized city symbolized the success of Ukraine's transition into communism.[152]

Despite its socialist content (singing praise to industrialization while referencing Lenin and Stalin's new political course), the collection underwent heavy censorship. Following the first edition, *Chernihiv*'s original eight verses only ever appeared in full once in the 1932 collection of Tychyna's selected poetry. Thereafter, only two verses were ever featured: the first poem *Mii druh robitnyk vodyt' mene po mistu i khvalyt'sia* [My friend, a worker, is showing me around the city and is bragging] and *Lenin* (written in 1924 on the occasion of Lenin's death). Negative reactions to the collection were linked to the contradiction between its 'mature ideology' and 'artificial novel (*novators'ka*) form'.[153] As one Soviet literary critic admitted, Tychyna's 'high' ideological content had been left diminished by his poor choice of poetic form:

> The deep ideas, the great historical meaning of *Chernihiv*, a work constructed out of rich and vital material, were not conveyed by the poet to the reader because the form he chose did not correspond to the content. Here, the poetry loses much as a result of a crying contradiction between content and form. A striking example of this is the poem entitled *A chy ne iest' tse sami nakhvalky abo zapamorochennia vid uspikhiv?* The theme of the poem is the year of the great leap. It is a complex, responsible, historically significant theme. It requires means of artistic treatment that would assure the reader's emotional contact with the ideas embodied in the given image. One should speak in an elevated and solemn voice about the national events which are the basis of this work. The poet, however, chose the form of a *chastushka*.[154]

Nationally oriented critics also disliked the collection. For them, the glorification of socialist achievements in *Chernihiv* signified Tychyna's final submission to the party line. Stus, for example, defined it as being 'Tychyna's way out from the "Solovki situation"', implying that with such an ideologically compliant collection Tychyna bought his way out of the persecutions that could easily befall him otherwise.[155] Ultimately, the driving force behind the collection was fear; with it, Tychyna had attempted to secure his own place in Soviet literature. The motif of fear was further reinforced in the argument 'Tychyna of two personas': one defining him as the 'bard of the revolution' and the Clarinets of the Sun (1918), and the other of a socialist realist poet in the 1930s, with *Chernihiv* symbolizing the commencement of his career as a party official. Other critics, however, used the collection to argue that Tychyna had turned to parodies during the late 1920s in order to 'shield' himself from potential persecution, hence rejecting his commitment to the Soviet canon.[156] Malaniuk, for instance, called *Chernihiv* a 'psychopathic collection of auto-parodies'.[157]

This argument of 'two Tychynas' rejects the poet's gradual evolution towards party-mindedness, ideological and class content (*partiinost'*, *ideinost'*, *klassovost'*), the main components of socialist realism that he would come to represent in the following decades. As the earlier discussion has shown, Tychyna was attempting to attune his poetry to the party line long before 1931. Revisiting *Chernihiv* in the late 1970s, Grabowicz claimed that the collection was not caused by a sudden break in Tychyna's ideology, but represented a detour that was 'in the very mainstream of Tychyna's poetic development; [...] it is, from both a synchronic and a diachronic perspective, a centrepiece of his oeuvre'.[158]

Chernihiv can be interpreted from two different perspectives. On the one hand, it was a sign of Tychyna's search for a *modus vivendi* with the Soviet authorities, similar to his contributions during the early 1920s. Whereas these earlier forays into propagandistic poetry could be vindicated by the obscurity of the civil war period and the concurrent power vacuum, his poetry of the late 1920s onwards should be regarded as an attempt to fit into the restrictive literary ambience of the first Five-Year Plan. On the other hand, *Chernihiv* was only a stage in the poet's non-linear artistic and ideological evolution. One can suggest that since the 1920s, Tychyna had been constantly and gradually simplifying his poetic style and artistic techniques, submitting ideological poetry with an approved social content. *Chernihiv*, therefore, serves as more of a 'missing link' in a complex literary evolution, 'a key to understanding the road [...] from *Sonjachni kljarnety* and *Pluh* to *Partjia vede* and his later poetry'.[159]

Grabowicz convincingly showed that *Chernihiv* was more complex than its critics wished to admit, with many similarities and intertextual references to Tychyna's earlier poetry. Among recurrent motifs were a welcoming of a new urban Ukraine, glorification of youth and youthful energy and a boundless optimism in the power of progress set against a painful realization of its darker side.[160] Moreover, in *Chernihiv*, Tychyna continued experimenting with his poetic form, reaching new heights in fusing meaning, sound and rhythm. Moreover, through this collection, Tychyna perfected the use of language and incorporated allusions to Ukraine's traditional popular culture appropriating the language of newspapers, party slogans, everyday expressions, popular humour and living speech, yet ensuring the dominance of the spoken word. At the same time, he resorted to popular burlesque and vulgar forms, returning to a traditional form of intermedia and shifting readers' attention from propaganda slogans on to the people.[161] Overall, *Chernihiv* 'highlights the various changes that occurred in Tychyna's poetry – of thematic focus, of prosodic and linguistic devices, of the poet's ideology and his stance with respect to the represented world.'[162]

Khvyl'ovyi's work also steadily followed the same path of adaptation to the intolerant mood of the period as reflected in his literary outputs from the early 1930s. Whereas under PROLITFRONT he had not published any original work, as a regular member of the VUSPP he could no longer hide behind senior managerial roles and needed to prove his literary commitment to 'socially useful' understanding of Soviet literature. Consequently, his short stories written during these years featured the most desired objects of the first Five-Year Plan: workers, peasants and exemplary party activists. Among his final contributions were *Ostannii Den'* [The Last Day], *Maibutni Shakhtari* [Future Miners] and *Pro Liubov* [About Love].[163] Excluding a few rare exceptions, devotion to the Soviet duty, loyalty and discipline became the main drivers for his later characters.

One of his most notable later pieces is *Shchaslyvyi Sekretar* [A Happy Secretary], (published in 1930 or early 1931).[164] This short story presents one of the best examples of a positive hero in Soviet literature before socialist realism, depicting a day in the life of a devoted party activist and functionary Comrade Stark, who has been recently transferred to a new, troublesome district. Stark was highly valued by his supervisors due to his excellent managerial skills and compliance with even the most personally inconvenient directives. Having been only recently relocated, he is looking forward to his family reunion. Suddenly, he receives news that his son has had an accident, delivered simultaneously with a telegram demanding his immediate transfer to yet another troublesome region. Forced to choose between social duty and personal attachment, Stark decided to continue with his service to the party and society instead of hastening to his family.

The decision was presented as understandable for such a devoted and loyal communist. Yet Khvyl'ovyi focuses very little on Stark's motivation, his thoughts and feelings remain behind the scene. Fulfilling the duty is the only prominent consideration in the story; the family, it seems, merely represents an obstruction. Nevertheless, the reader feels the artifice of this choice, especially since throughout the story Stark repeatedly confirmed his affection to his family and especially his son. Stark is presented as an ill-willed personality with no agency for individual decision-making, being instead the archetypical model party functionary and executioner of central directives.

It must be admitted that Comrade Stark was not only a fictional character but representative of a real type of committed communists prepared to make the greatest sacrifices in the name of the duty. During the first Five-Year Plan, many shock workers prioritized such duty over families, as seen from the memoirs of the construction team leader, V. Ia. Shidek (1929–31), who had forgotten about his ill son 'under the pressure of work'.[165] Stark, like Shidek, personified the new ideal Soviet citizen, which came to replace the revolutionary romanticists of the early 1920s. Khvyl'ovyi, a creator of the romantic myth of the revolution and civil war, now became the promoter of a new myth, one of an idealized Soviet society where citizens were full of optimism for and devotion to their communist future. The difference between the two modes was obvious. For the characters of Khvyl'ovyi's early prose, the golden age was far gone with pessimism becoming a defining attribute of the time. In contrast, the new builders of communism were to be defined through their optimism; the golden age was only due to arrive, and it was up to each and every community member to pursue it.

Khvyl'ovyi also contributed to Soviet state propaganda, writing journalist style essays on his trips to Soviet Ukraine's provinces. In 1930, for instance, he toured the Kharkiv region and prepared nine sketches that were later published under the title *Po Barvinkivs'komu raioni* [Around the Barvinkove district].[166] Barvinkove was chosen perhaps for its near absolute collectivization, with Khvyl'ovyi being sent there to report on the impact such achievements had had on the lives of the rural populace. The sketches themselves were replete with criticism of religious practices, former kulaks and wreckers and recent violence against the Soviet authorities. At the same time, Khvyl'ovyi praised Soviet accomplishments in the social and cultural sphere including the founding of new hospitals, schools, libraries and reading rooms which had even prompted changes in the moral character of the peasantry. Khvyl'ovyi was astonished to record that he had not seen any drunkards during his trip, instead he highlighted peasants' determination to burn icons 'to heat up their village hall and school'.[167]

Perhaps the most intense episode in Khvyl'ovyi's reportages comes from a description of the collective burning of some 2,000 icons in one of the villages he visited. The villagers gather in the heart of the village to burn the icons accompanied by a brass band performing a traditional Ukrainian dance *hopak*, prompting the men to dance around the bonfire. Khvyl'ovyi welcomes the event, reflecting on 'an old, sad villainous church' in flames that was like 'an old backward and – o glory to you, the new age! – unrepeatable Ukraine'.[168] What the writer did not talk about in his multiple reportages was the famine that would devastate the countryside in a few years' time. Even in his propaganda sketches written at the height of famine in 1932–3, Khvyl'ovyi decided to omit the disaster, talking evasively about the personal misfortunes of individual households forced to give up their last milk cow to the *kolkhoz*, as for instance in *Iz zhyttiepysu popeliastoi korovy* [From the life-story of an ashy-grey cow].[169]

Together with attuning his creative writing, Khvyl'ovyi also tried to rehabilitate his earlier work. In 1932, the first volume of his selected writings was published, consisting of short stories and novels written between 1921 and 1924. Each of these stories was accompanied by a critical commentary in which the author tried to explain his choice of themes and characters. He also prepared a foreword in which he attempted to prove the proletarian nature of his earlier works by attuning them to the demands of the time.[170] Most notably was his referral to a review on a German translation of his novels that stated 'Unsuitable for mature readers, for youth and public libraries, communist!'[171]

This transformation did not go unnoticed among Soviet Ukraine's cultural elites. As one informer reported to the GPU, the cultural milieu was appalled by Khvyl'ovyi's latest works: 'Mykola Khvyl'ovyi was almost an Apostle or a Prophet for the Ukrainian people, best compared to a tragic prophet Jeremiah. However, he was mistaken and needed to recognise his errors; he had been thinking for over half a year and turn[ed] himself into … a buffoon [*blasen*]'.[172] It must be noted that this accommodation with the regime did not come easily. In one of his letters, intercepted by the secret police, he confessed to Kulish that 'logically and in my mind, I have switched over; but emotionally, I have not, and I feel that it will not happen soon. Emotionally I am still the same.'[173]

Khvyl'ovyi: A suicide

In 1930, the Soviet authorities in Moscow intensified the collectivization campaign as more grain and food requisitioning was required to subsidize the country's accelerating industrialization and burgeoning urban growth. A failure to meet these quotas, however, saw a reshuffling in the party leadership. In January 1933, Pavlo Postyshev, well known for his anti-Ukrainian outlook, was sent to Kharkiv to occupy the post of second secretary of the KP(b)U TsK and first secretary of the Kharkiv city and Kharkiv oblast party organizations. In addition, Skrypnyk, accused earlier of national deviation and mismanagement of the *korenizatsiia* campaign, was deposed from the *Narkomos*.[174] Zatons'kyi, who had already occupied this position on three separate occasions between December and April 1924, resumed the role on 23 February 1933, with Khvylia, the former head of Ukraine's Agitprop, as his deputy.[175] With these appointments, a more repressive era in Soviet Ukrainian history began that saw the introduction of highly centralized measures within the cultural sphere.

In the spring of 1933, at the height of the famine, Khvyl'ovyi together with A. Liubchenko, his close friend and a former VAPLITE secretary, were commissioned to further report on conditions in the countryside. They first visited villages in the Poltava region of central Ukraine to assess the extent of the famine. Liubchenko later published his memoirs while in exile abroad, titled *Ioho Taiemnytsia* [His Secret], offering his account of the journey and the last months of Khvyl'ovyi's life. Liubchenko's account details Khvyl'ovyi's desire to travel in areas affected by the famine 'to learn with [his] own eyes what is happening in the villages, where the root of all evil lies, what are the reasons for this catastrophe, this black spring, and finally how all this is likely to end!'[176] During the trip, they stopped in the Lokhvytsia district, where Khvyl'ovyi had good acquaintances among the party officials whom he could trust. Liubchenko recalled a frank conversation between the four of them, speaking about the situation in Soviet Ukraine. By the end of the meeting, Khvyl'ovyi supposedly concluded that the famine was intentionally organized in order 'to provoke resistance and, after having crushed it, to settle once and for all the dangerous Ukrainian problem'.[177]

One of the monologues, recorded by Liubchenko at the time, seems especially important for understanding the motivations leading to Khvyl'ovyi's suicide in May 1933, exposing the writer's views on the role of a public intellectual in Soviet Ukraine at the time. During the trip, Liubchenko fell seriously ill and Khvyl'ovyi feared for his life, admitting that, in their situation, death was not an option:

[Addressing Liubchenko]: What right do you have to die? Who told you can die? Nobody. I'm telling you: you must be prepared to live. To die, my friend, is the easiest way out. Anybody can do it. But to live – that's something worth trying. To live and to struggle – especially now; that's highly praiseworthy. It is true, in certain cases death is a better option, when through death perhaps one can do more for one's fellow men than by living. But such cases are rare[178]

And your death – not of an average man, not of a narrow-minded person – should be well thought-through. [...] We do not belong only to ourselves. If we are sincerely faithful to the idea and our task, we don't even have the right to manage our death. Everything depends on what our duty decides for us. And this is us, and all those who are with us, who should live. To live and to work. In today's circumstances first and foremost of all we should survive physically. This is our main task.[179]

This long monologue, recorded in April 1933, provides a better understanding of the possible motivations for Khvyl'ovyi and his followers; first, to come to terms with the regime and its political agenda, and, subsequently, to take responsibility over their own lives.

Shortly after this conversation, the two travellers returned to Kharkiv. There, Khvyl'ovyi was met with terrible news: his friend Ialovyi, the VAPLITE writer and its first president, had been accused of anti-Soviet activity in connection to an alleged counter-revolutionary *UVO* case and was arrested on 12 May.[180] Both writers initially thought a mistake had been made and considered going to enquire at the GPU.[181] Khvyl'ovyi even proposed calling its deputy head Karl Karlson or the prosecutor of the Supreme Court of the UkrSRS Lev Akhmatov.[182] On 13 May 1933, however, having perhaps realized that Ialovyi's apprehending had not been a mistake but the beginning of a new wave of arrests, Khvyl'ovyi committed suicide. As is known, in his final hours, Khvyl'ovyi invited his friends Kulish and Dosvitnii over to listen to his new novel. With a short presentation ('I was struggling with this novel a lot. However, I learned how a writer in the Stalin age should behave. Maybe I could teach you as well'[183]) the writer withdrew to his study where he shot himself a moment later.

It is believed that Khvyl'ovyi left two death notes, in which he claimed responsibility for having led the generation of the 1920s and provided the instructions regarding his literary heritage.[184] The first note read:

Arrest of Ialovyi – this is the murder of an entire generation ... For what? Because we were the most sincere Communists? I don't understand. Responsibility for the actions of Ialovyi's generation lies with me, Khvyl'ovyi. Today is a beautiful sunny day. I love life – you can't even imagine how much. Today is the 13th. Remember I was in love with this number? Terribly painful. Long live communism. Long live the socialist construction. Long live the Communist Party.

The second note was addressed to his foster daughter Liubov Umantseva:

My precious *Liubystok*! Forgive me, my grey-winged dove, for everything. By the way, yesterday I destroyed my unfinished novel not because I didn't want it to be published, but because I needed to convince myself: if I had courage to destroy the novel – then I have found enough will to do what I am committed to do. Goodbye, my precious *Liubystok*. Your father M. Khvyl'ovyi.[185]

On being informed of the incident, the Party Committee ordered that Khvyl'ovyi's study be sealed while his library, personal documentation and correspondence were confiscated.

State officials, secret police and his fellow writers held differing perspectives on Khvyl'ovyi's suicide. During the funeral itself, party functionaries were already attempting to dissociate the writer's decision from the party line, redefining his public persona as that of a weak, unsteady communist. The main message underlining the official obituary notices and representative's speeches was that Khvyl'ovyi had lacked revolutionary temper in a time although 'every day, every hour of our struggle put us closer to the triumph of Socialism all over the world', as the official obituary read.[186] Thus, his decision was perceived as worthless, tragic and ridiculous, having had nothing to do with his Communist Party membership.[187]

Khvyl'ovyi's death also played into the hands of the secret police whose response proved that the accident had far broader significance than that of mere personal tragedy. As noted, his decision was itself linked to the nationalist orientation and his own anti-government prejudices. In order to stymied the spread of such sentiment, the party 'in cold mind, with all the hatred to capitalism, with all the love to socialism of today and communism of tomorrow [must] fight those prejudices in everyday life, in Khvyl'ovyi, in ourselves.'[188] In less than a year, the name of 'the fascist writer' Khvyl'ovyi appeared in the list of alleged Soviet traitors printed in the official monthly *Chervonyi Shliakh*.[189] Over the subsequent decades, *khvyl'ovizm*, along with *shums'kizm* and *skrypnykivshchyna*, would become synonymous with 'bourgeois nationalism', and used to label any form of national deviation within the party's ranks.[190]

His fellow writers, however, viewed Khvyl'ovyi's suicide as indicative of the tightening centralization of cultural life in the Soviet republic. In the corridors of the *Slovo* apartment building (the building of the writers' union in Kharkiv), it was said that Khvyl'ovyi's suicide was far more significant than that of Mayakovski's; while Khvyl'ovyi reacted to the 'social discontent of [19]33', his Russian fellow committed suicide only 'out of personal discontent in [19]30'.[191] For the writers' guild, their recognized leader's radical course of action signalled that there were no longer any alternatives to compliance with a centralist vision of Soviet literature in Ukraine. The adverse mood was aptly captured by Epik: 'You know, Mykola [Kulish], whatever we write now, we will not be allowed, this is our end.'[192]

Shortly after the suicide, the new image of Khvyl'ovyi as an ambivalent irresolute communist who could not reconcile his ideological standpoints with nationalist sentiments came into prominence and was appropriated by his ideological rivals. From the party's perspective, Khvyl'ovyi's deviations and suicide were linked to his personal ideological irresoluteness, whereby he was unable to decide the degrees to which he identified as a communist and his belief in the Ukrainian national cause. Hence, his dissatisfaction with the regime stemmed not from the limited scope of the Soviet Union's nationalities policies or political centralization, but the mismatch between the practical realities of Soviet rule and Khvyl'ovyi's nationalist outlook on the republic after the revolution.

Conversely, any possible ideological ambivalence surrounding Khvyl'ovyi also played into the hands of those who later created his contemporary persona. It is worth mentioning that Khvyl'ovyi was not rehabilitated in the course of the Soviet liberalization that occurred in the 1950s.[193] By the end of the 1980s, during the so-called era of *glasnost'*, Ukrainian communist intellectuals started to call for 'returning Khvyl'ovyi to his readers'.[194] This was also the time when both his autobiographical notes, whose veracity was discussed in the Introduction, and copies of Khvyl'ovyi's suicide notes, were made public for the first time. Interpretation of these primary sources contributed to a newly emerging narrative centred on Khvyl'ovyi the 'national communist'. The Ukraine-minded political elites of the 1980s–90s 'appropriated' the early Soviet history and used the ambivalence of the epoch to create a historical narrative of inherent anti-communist opposition in the KP(b)U, providing legitimacy for their own attempts to resist the diktats of the central party leadership.

Given these intentions, modern interpreters eagerly picked up and widely promoted an image of Khvyl'ovyi as a romantic, who became ideologically confused in his pursuit of a better social order. The excerpts concerning Khvyl'ovyi attending a congress of soldiers in Romania in October 1917 with two ribbons pinned to his collar, a red and a yellow-and-blue one, as well as his justification ('I wanted to be, so to say, a Ukrainian Bolshevik'[195]) best served this purpose. Overall, the nationalistic approach attempted to rehabilitate and excuse Khvyl'ovyi for being a communist by finding reasons for his decision to join the party and remain a member. In order to cope with the obvious dilemma of him being a talented writer in spite of his membership, an attempt was made to push the concept of Khvyl'ovyi's 'fatal ambivalence', supposedly originating partly from his romantic nature and partly from an idealistic belief in Bolshevik populism. In 1990, the literary scholar Mykola Zhulyns'kyi attributed Khvyl'ovyi's party affiliation and later suicide to his naïve infatuation with revolution: 'The Revolution, which sparked his talent and got him to fall in love with it, while later betraying its chosen one. And he, driven by disappointment and despair, with his own death tried to appeal to the Revolution to have mercy for its fanatic knights.'[196] More recent Ukrainian scholarship has also promoted this interpretation, highlighting Khvyl'ovyi's 'permanent inner ambivalence' towards communism, 'a game that the writer attempted to play with the system and finally with himself.'[197] It must be admitted that in the native historiography there is no attempt to reconcile the two sides of his ideological commitment and accept that he was a Soviet writer as much as he was a Ukrainian one.

Indeed, there are only a few assertions about Khvyl'ovyi that cannot be contested. Firstly, he was a prominent writer, whose creative manner was defined by his revolutionary experience. Moreover, he was a proletarian writer, and it was this artistic identity that Khvyl'ovyi was attempting to preserve, not because of prevailing ideological expectations, but due to his personal convictions and beliefs in the potential of the working class to begin world history anew. Secondly, he was a member of the Communist Party of the Bolsheviks since 1919 and even during the most severe persecutions remained faithful to his membership card. Yet Khvyl'ovyi also adhered to an idea of a nationally defined socialist republic that existed as an equal partner in a loose federation of other socialist republics. In the 1920s, with all its inconsistencies and social experiments, this form of autonomy could be seen as realistic and feasible and Khvyl'ovyi's views were shared by many Ukraine-minded politicians and public intellectuals. This vision of a Soviet Ukraine was also enabled by the very nature of the relationship between the Moscow centre and the border republics at that time.

Khvyl'ovyi came to represent an entire generation of disillusioned intellectuals, who witnessed the discrepancy between the ideals of the revolution and their implementation in Soviet Ukraine. Although a Bolshevik party member, he sympathized with the Ukrainian communists and promoted a separatist vision of a Soviet Ukraine and Soviet Ukrainian culture. Nonetheless, the attempts of the Ukrainian communists and intellectuals to reorganize their territory's power relationships within the wider Soviet Union, along with the cultural flourishing of the 1920s, were crushed by the forcible tendencies aimed at consolidating the Bolshevik party and Stalin's Great Turn of 1928/29.

Tychyna: A poet Laureate

The year 1933 marked a watershed in the history of Soviet Ukraine. With the suicides of both Khvyl'ovyi and Skrypnyk – those promoters of Soviet Ukraine's autonomy – allegations of 'national deviation' in the KP(b)U exhausted themselves. A necessary compromise between Kharkiv and Moscow was reached whereby the KP(b)U's leaders accepted the central leadership authority on all matters of life in the republic. Moreover, the central leadership finally managed to break the passive resistance of the Ukrainian countryside through the enforced collectivization and starvation of the population. The Soviet authorities also overcame their dependence on the 'toiling intelligentsia' (*trudiashcha intelihentsia*), old 'bourgeois' specialists educated from before the revolution. As Stalin asserted, by 1936, 80–90 per cent of the Soviet intelligentsia came from the industrial proletariat, the peasantry or from other strata of the working population.[198] Moreover, through its 1932 decree 'On the Reconstruction of Literary and Artistic Organisations' the party had resolved issues of artistic and ideological competition in Soviet literature by paving the way for the final unification of Soviet writers under a single union, created in 1934.

These accomplishments coincided with the sixteenth anniversary of the October Revolution. The anniversary was chosen as an apt historical moment in which to promote the progress of Soviet Ukraine Union-wide. For the occasion, the Moscow newspaper *Pravda* decided to prepare a special issue dedicated almost entirely to Soviet Ukraine. This held extraordinary importance: *Pravda*, read worldwide, was meant to debunk rumours about the famine in Ukraine, carefully concealed throughout the period. Instead, the plan was to present an optimistic image of the republic and its people, happily enjoying the results of socialist construction achieved under the wise leadership of the Communist Party. To strengthen this massage, the editorial suggested engaging voices from Soviet Ukraine that could corroborate the republic's achievements and cement its people's volition for an all-Soviet unity. Given its purpose, the choice of a speaker could not be accidental. Preferably, it should be a Ukrainian poet, whose easy rhymes, capturing the very essence of crucial social transformations, would reach the widest audience; a poet with an 'uncertain past' whose experiences validated the re-educating and forgiving nature of Soviet power; the one who had yet fully accepted party control; and well known – or even better world known – guaranteeing the sort of publicity befitting such an event.

Unsurprisingly, this burden of responsibility fell to Tychyna. A *Pravda* correspondent, Semen Gershberg, visited the poet to solicit a verse with the necessary tone. Numerous recollections attest to how hesitant Tychyna was towards composing poetry on demand, and even more reluctant to having his verse translated for editorial purposes. According to popular anecdote, Tychyna had recently completed a piece of propagandistic verse intended for a Young Pioneers' newspaper *Na zminu* [To take the turn]. The correspondent, having read through the rhymes with catchy slogan-like rhythm, appropriated it for *Pravda*'s November issue.[199] Tychyna's *Partiia Vede* [The Party Leads] was published in the original version in Ukrainian on page six of the issue, opening and closing with the famous stanza:

> Let them do what they want,
> Let them go mad, let them agonise, –
> We have our task to do:
> All the lords to the same pit,
> Bourgeoisie to bourgeoisie,
> Beat, we will beat!
> Beat, we will beat! (O.P.)

In the context of the famine and the collectivization campaign, the lines about liquidating the 'bourgeois' elements seemed especially ironic. The poem went on to praise 'our glorious five-year plans' (*nashi slavni p'iatyrichky*), the Red Army's protection of the Soviet borders and the young pioneers' securing the future generation of Soviet citizens.

The editorial, written under the same heading 'The Party Leads', praised the 'triumph of the kolkhoz (*kolhospna*) Ukraine, which in the current year had fulfilled the plans for grain deliveries ahead of schedule'.[200] Despite the famine, Ukraine was called 'the country of *kolkhoz* abundance'. *Pravda*'s first page featured a photo with cheerful members of a *kolkhoz* delegation from the Odesa region, expressing their gratitude to the central party leadership, who guided them towards a better communist future. The editorial also mentioned Tychyna, pointing out how this non-partisan poet had managed to successfully grasp the socialist reality and discern the prominent role of the party in approaching communism.[201]

On 21 November 1933, Tychyna, for all his controversial past and questionable political loyalty, had finally received approval from the highest party echelons. The issue's publication date marked his formal admission into the Soviet canon and, as the following years would prove, the very heart of the Union's politics. This recognition had a price, however. From now on Tychyna would serve as a mouthpiece for Soviet politics in Ukraine, a poet laureate who would abuse his muse to report on every development in the republic. This professional entrapment was neatly articulated by an émigré writer Ivan Bahrianyi in one of his caricatures:

> Albeit Kyiv lies in ruins,
> Tychyna is a Narkom,
> Albeit Ukraine is crucified,
> Tychyna has got another Order,
> And Moscow is joyful –
> 'Ukraine is Tychyna'. (O.P.)

Figure 19 Tychyna's poem *Partiia Vede* in *Pravda*. © *Pravda Newspaper*, 21 November 1933 (public domain).

The following year, to mark the occasion of the seventeenth party congress, or 'The Congress of the Victors', as it was dubbed, Tychyna was commissioned to compose a collection of poetry under the same title, *Partiia Vede*. The first edition was notable in that it appeared without mention of an author on the front cover, suggesting the universal, anonymous victory of socialism. Dmytro Nytchenko, who at the time worked at the publishing house *Literatura i Mystetstvo* [Literature and Art] recalled the hassle around the collection's publication. This thin book, consisting of only thirteen pages, was produced at record speed, with a print run of 25,000 copies appearing in only three days. That same year, an expanded version comprising fifty-six pages was published by *Radians'ka Literatura* [Soviet Literature]. In 1934, there were three editions of the collection, and a new enlarged edition appearing each consecutive year.[202]

The poem was rapidly translated into Russian by the poet Nikolai Ushakov as well as the other national languages of the Soviet republics. The public reaction towards Tychyna's new personas and his latest poem were often negative, however, eliciting numerous parodies. Nytchenko recalled that right after the collection's publication, once such parody appeared in the public toilets at Kyiv University:

> Tychyna is the people's poet,
> And he also goes to the toilet,
> But he does not go there on his own –
> The party leads him everywhere. (O.P.)

The NKVD was called to investigate the incident, but the culprit was never found.[203]

The titles of the verses included in the collection corresponded to the edition's respective purpose: *Partiia Vede*, *Pisnia Chervonoi Armii* [Song of the Red Army], *Pisnia Komsomol'tsiv* [Song of Komsomol Members], *Pisnia Traktorystky* [Song of a Tractor Girl], *Pisnia Kuzni* [Song of a Smithy], *Povitrianyi Flot* [Air Fleet], *Lenin, Narody Idut'* [The Peoples are Coming]. Unsurprisingly, the collection received high acclaim among official critics with Kulyk praising Tychyna for embracing 'actual militant themes', testifying to 'a major victory of ours [the party]'.[204]

Following the publication of this poetic collection, Tychyna became highly valued within the party, yet found himself scorned by his former VAPLITE fellows and ridiculed by the general public. Nevertheless, for the poet, who had always feared for his life, *Partiia Vede* held a 'purifying' significance. Later, he mentioned it in his autobiography alongside the editorial in *Pravda* that had 'helped me enormously in my work as well as in all my subsequent life'.[205] In 1935, in a short passage called *Ia Rostu* [I am Growing], written as a preparation for the twentieth anniversary of the October Revolution, the poet reflected on his experience during the early 1930s. The main emphasis, understandably, was placed on the role of the party in his ideological upbringing. This short contribution included an ironic note about the price he had to pay for his future accomplishments: 'Thus, I am approaching the plenum filled and overfilled [*napovnenyi, perepovnenyi*]. Hence, at the plenum I will stand as checked and double-checked [*provirenyi i pereprovirenyi*]. I was taken to pieces and assembled again. By roentgen of self-criticism I was examined not even once. Why should not I be brave now?'[206]

In 1936, Tychyna was appointed as Head of the Institute of Ukrainian Literature, the post which he would occupy throughout the worst years of Stalin's terror. The state's campaign of political repression significantly changed the outlook of Ukrainian literature. As tallied by Lavrinenko, out of 259 men of letters, whose work had been published in 1930, only thirty-six remained active after 1938.[207] Under such circumstances, Tychyna found himself dealing with a constantly changing literary environment. In that atmosphere, the institute was tasked with preparing a new academic edition on the history of Ukrainian literature, omitting the names of those who had perished during the purges.[208] Instead, those who merited reference in the volume were included in a new Soviet literary canon championed by Tychyna, Ryl's'kyi and Bazhan, three prominent poets who had survived the 1930s.[209] Those Ukrainian writers accepted Russia's leading ideological role and conservative aesthetics. Nevertheless, none of them were fully trusted by the party and remained under constant surveillance. In the investigation file on Borys Kovalenko, a Soviet poet arrested in 1936, one document dated from 27 May 1937 included all three names in a list of persons categorized as being 'actively under consideration' [*aktivno razrabatyvaiutsia*] – an interim category

Figure 20 Ivan Mykytenko, Petro Panch, Oleksandr Korniichuk, and Pavlo Tychyna before travelling to the International Congress of Writers for the Defence of Culture in Paris, 1935. © Central State Archive-Museum of Literature and Arts of Ukraine, courtesy of TsDAMLMU.

falling just before 'intended for arrest'.[210] Tychyna's friend, the literary critic Volodymyr P'ianov, recorded in his memoirs how sophisticated such tactics were. According to P'ianov, Tychyna's own personal file even featured a photograph of Vynnychenko, Petliura and Tychyna (with Petliura's hand on Tychyna's shoulder). Before a new award or another trip abroad, this image would occasionally be presented to him with the comment 'And even You, Pavlo Hryhorovych?!'[211]

Nevertheless, Tychyna's rise as a state poet and official continued apace. In June 1938, he was elected as a deputy to the Supreme Soviet of the UkrSSR and, on 31 January 1939, awarded the Order of Lenin for his achievements in developing Soviet literature.[212] Further recognition followed with the publication of a new collection, *Chuttia Iedynoi Rodyny* [Feelings of One Unified Family], in 1938 that glorified the Communist Party for enabling the free development and cultural flourishing of every republic and nation within the Soviet Union. This proved prophetical: in 1939, on the basis of a secret clause in the Molotov-Ribbentrop Pact, the territories of Western Ukraine, western Belorussia and the Baltic States were occupied by the Red Army and subsequently annexed to the Soviet Union. To celebrate this 'unification with the mainland', representatives from Soviet Ukraine, Soviet Belarus and the Baltic States were among the first holders of the highest state honour, the newly established Stalin Prize. Tychyna received the award in recognition of *Chuttia Iedynoi Rodyny*'s celebration of the Slavic peoples' historical unity. On 16 March 1941, the Moscow newspaper *Literaturnaia Gazeta* commented on the prize winners:

> What unites the prose of … the verse of … within the sphere of literature? […]
> All these works deal with the struggle of the peoples of the Soviet Union against

foreigners who would otherwise enslave them ... Works telling of how a forgotten and oppressed nation unfurled its wings for soaring flight, how a sense of family unity was forged among the nationalities of the Soviet Union.[213]

On 16 September 1967, 'one of the founders of Ukrainian Soviet literature, a prominent poet, academic, journalist, translator, state and civil activist, an academic of the Academy of Sciences of the URSR, a corresponding member of the Bulgarian Academy of Sciences, Hero of the Socialist Labour' passed away.[214] This list, compiled by an expert on Tychyna's life and work, was yet incomplete. Throughout his later years, Tychyna had also served as head of the Supreme Council of the UkrSSR for two convocations (1953–9), was a deputy of the Supreme Council for seven (1938–67), a Minister for Education (1943–8), Laureate of the Stalin Prize (1941), Laureate of the Shevchenko Prize (1962), holder of five Orders of Lenin and holder of two Orders of the Red Banner of Labour. However, Tychyna only became a member of the VKP(b) in May 1944.

Despite major differences in the fates of this study's two protagonists, both would later disappear from historical scholarship and public debate. While Khvyl'ovyi fell victim to his own 'ideological ambiguity', being equally condemned as either a communist or a nationalist, any objective accounts on Tychyna were overshadowed by his status as poet laureate. Following his death, Antonenko-Davydovych recalled, in a private letter, the official attitude towards him. In the 1960s, Antonenko-Davydovych had worked as an editor on the journals *Dnipro* and *Ukraina* where, alongside his peers on other publications, any new submission by Tychyna was met with a sense of dread. In the post-Stalin era, allowing Tychyna's work to appear in one's publication was deemed an embarrassment and a compromise of artistic judgement. Yet to reject it could be equally damaging, owing to ramifications from the TsK itself that might have resulted in the dismissal of an entire editorial team. He also recalled an anecdote where one aspiring poet, having been rejected publication in a local newspaper, decided to sign his piece 'Pavlo Tychyna' and submit it to a journal in Kyiv. The poem was quickly published to avoid the feared consequences of rejection. The pretender even claimed an honorarium equal to that which the real Tychyna would have received, which the journal paid in order to avoid further escalation of the situation.[215] These attitudes towards the 'official' Tychyna did not change even after the Soviet Union's collapse. As one critic asserted in 1991: 'Ninety per cent of Ukrainians do not like Tychyna's creative work. No, I think I might be mistaken. Not ninety, but nighty nine. Or maybe even more – ninety-nine-point nine per cent.'[216] The general public disliked the late Tychyna, the one whose ideologically loaded and insincere rhymes were forced on to them at school and in the official press.

Since the late 1980s, however, attempts were made to rehabilitate Tychyna's image as an undeservedly forgotten poet of the early 1920s, who, due to his weak personality and constant fear of terror and violence, had surrendered to the Communist Party. Contemporary literary studies now distinguish him through two personas: the symbolist poet of the early 1920s and the Soviet poet-laureate. Ultimately, however, the majority of Tychyna's poetry was never to stand the test of time. As reflected in the literary canon of independent Ukraine, it is only the work of 'early' Tychyna (up until 1920) and some rare examples of his partisan poetry, written during the Second World War (such as, *Pokhoron Druha* [Funeral of the Friend]) that has endured within the cultural memory.

Epilogue

Although never abandoned officially, *korenizatsiia* in Soviet Ukraine stopped being enforced after 1933. By the end of the 1920s, the party's principal goals had been largely accomplished. *Korenizatsiia*, designed to neutralize the emergence of local nationalism, had succeeded in gathering all national activists under the KP(b)U's umbrella. In the 1930s, their services were no longer required. Throughout the preceding decade, a new generation of Soviet elites educated in the Communist spirit and unquestionably loyal to the party came into existence. The KP(b)U became a centralized organization with vast representation and legitimacy within the republic. Moreover, a mutually beneficial compromise between the Ukrainian and Russian communist movements was established, according to which the KP(b)U could indulge limited autonomy in return for acknowledging Moscow's leadership.[1]

Similarly, *korenizatsiia* was adopted to mobilize the population for the upcoming transformation of the USSR into a great power. In predominantly rural Ukraine, *korenizatsiia* was needed in order to reconcile an urbanized political system with the localized expediencies of the countryside. The peasants were to be encouraged to take part in local administration and, more importantly, to join the ranks of the national proletariat. However, *korenizatsiia* had largely remained a concession, a soft-line policy which was used to prepare the ground on which a more hard-line approach could be elaborated.[2] Unsurprisingly, the curtailment of *korenizatsiia* concurred with the proclamation of forced collectivization in 1929. Instead of coming to terms with the peasantry, their latent resistance was crushed by, first, taking away their strongholds: land and property; and second, their physical extermination during the famine of 1932–3.

While *korenizatsiia*, as centrally envisaged, fulfilled its intended goals, the results of *Ukrainizatsiia* as perceived by the national intelligentsia were far more ambiguous. Comprehensive *Ukrainizatsiia* was always favoured and endorsed by a minority in the party, whose political weight was never substantial enough to defend the Ukrainian cause against the centralist attitudes of the majority. In addition, Ukraine's cultural and political figures were constantly obliged to abide by the government's policy of a 'double bottom' [*podviine dno*]: on the one hand, this policy had provided for vast changes in the republic, on the other, the enthusiastic intentions of local Ukrainizers could challenge the scope of the policy's central endorsement. The political campaigns against Shums'kyi and Khvyl'ovyi, and the nationality-based persecutions initiated in 1926, proved that *korenizatsiia* had always had its limitations and could never be applied to the political sphere in any practical sense. In the end, *Ukrainizatsiia*, paraphrasing the words of one diaspora commentator about the Literary Discussion, 'opened the window for the agents of the occupying power [the Bolshevik party] to see who would be the first to rush to it to catch a breath of fresh air' and 'helped the NKVD to make short work of Ukrainian cultural and public activists either non-Communist or Ukrainian communists'.[3]

Undeniably, *Ukrainizatsiia* resulted in great cultural upheaval, bringing to the fore significant potential for Soviet Ukraine's cultural elites. The enforced usage of the national language and a tolerant attitude towards autonomous artistic currents created the preconditions for a fully fledged cultural flourishing in the republic. Book publishing in Ukrainian along with obligatory language courses created, for the first time in history, a large number of native-language consumers. Yet what was the product of this cultural renaissance? This policy endorsed mass production in Ukrainian to satisfy the demands of the audience, aptly manipulated by the party educators. This promotion of mass publication in Ukrainian went hand in hand with a proletarization of Ukrainian culture and the unification of style, themes and aesthetic devices. Initiated by the great examples of high-quality artistic and literary works, cultural development in the second half of the 1920s slowly pivoted towards the formation of mass culture with a distinct ideological flavour, albeit created in the Ukrainian language. The resultant contributions were Soviet, to warrant its propagandistic and ideologically consistent content, and in Ukrainian, to ensure its outreach up to the remotest village in Western Ukraine. Party-sponsored linguistic and literary Ukrainization, with its orientation towards quantitative objectives, provided for the massification of literature, lowering the standards of creative activity to the most unsophisticated readers, newly proletarized and urbanized peasants, who were being educated in literacy alongside technical skills.

This cultural and linguistic Ukrainization in conjunction with the party's modernization campaigns was intended to change Ukraine's urban identity. Shums'kyi unsuccessfully advocated for the accelerated de-Russification of Ukraine's urban centres. Following his demise, Skrypnyk shifted the emphasis towards more ideological compliance. In his view, endorsed demographic Ukrainization should be accompanied by the creation of a totally Ukrainian urban environment and the increased prestige of the Ukrainian language. Consequently, not only did the proportion of ethnic working-class Ukrainians increase during the 1920s (51.7 per cent in 1926, and 59.2 per cent in 1934[4]), but their identity was shaped during this decade. Liber argues that during the 1920s the urban identity was transformed, 'reflecting the Ukrainian transition from marginality to majority in the urban centres'.[5] However, such statements were premature. The belief in a naturally demographic Ukrainization was naively based on the assumption that those millions of peasants coming to cities would contribute to the de-Russification of the proletariat. As anticipated by Hrushevs'kyi, 'this nationally aware and civilised [*natsional'no svidomyi i vykhovanyi*] class of peasants [...] will not fall victim to Russification but will influence the new environment and will lead to the creation of the Ukrainian working class.'[6]

Instead, extensive migration from the countryside served to 'peasantise' the working class. Peasants, despite the misconceptions of some intellectuals, did not possess a strong national identity and had little sense of connection with the elitist Soviet Ukrainian urban culture of the time. Industrialization had compelled the peasants to move into the cities. *Korenizatsiia* created the façade of a total Ukrainian environment, but it did not necessarily transform peasants into Ukrainians with a modern urban identity.⁷ In fact, *korenizatsiia* did not even make Ukrainian the everyday language of the urban population. Throughout the interwar years, Russian remained the language of Ukraine's economic, industrial, political and academic spheres, whereas Ukrainian was confined to education, propaganda work and (partly) the cultural sphere. Instead of becoming mono-lingual (Ukrainian), urban centres became bilingual, with Russian culture remaining dominant among workers and state functionaries. The Russian language preserved its superior status and urban citizens, as recalled by the contemporaries, were ashamed of speaking Ukrainian, which could easily suggest their social origin.⁸

Nonetheless, *Ukrainizatsiia* was of supreme importance in constructing modern Ukrainian identity while the 1920s witnessed the creation of the modern Ukrainian nation. Firstly, by means of statistics and ethnography, the diverse peoples inhabiting the territory of Ukraine began associating themselves as Ukrainians, contributing to the largest ethnic group in the republic. Secondly, this era witnessed the formal codification of the Ukrainian language. The first comprehensive spelling reform, adopted in 1929, widely known as '*skrypnykivka*' (due to its promotion by Skrypnyk) or 'Kharkiv orthography', was a result of thorough discussion among academics and linguists, representing different areas of Ukraine. Hence, in 1929, based on the previous experiences of language reforms, different vernaculars and dialects, which had long existed on the territory of Ukraine, were codified under the name of the Ukrainian language.⁹ In addition, the 'Kharkiv orthography' was adopted in Western Ukraine, to facilitate the cross-border communication and distribution of publications; a single narrative of Ukraine's history was compiled, uniting ethnically and linguistically different parts of Soviet Ukraine within one discourse;¹⁰ while agreements with neighbouring countries led to the borders of Soviet Ukraine being formally defined in geopolitical terms.¹¹

The process of *Ukrainizatsiia* strengthened the distinctiveness of a separatist horizon in the KP(b)U, whose representatives elaborated on and, with varying measures of success, implemented an alternative vision of Soviet Ukraine and Soviet Ukrainian culture. Ukrainian elites were a proactive force in the process of the formation of the Soviet Union; debates and negotiations between local actors (notably, intellectuals and politicians) and the Moscow party leadership over the status of Ukraine shaped the republic and, at large, accounted for its distinctive status within the Union. This experience of political autonomy provided for ideological pluralism and unprecedented cultural upheaval in the republic. The successes of the *Ukrainizatsiia* campaign also resulted from the activist position of local Ukrainizers, who had used the centrally endorsed initiative to pursue their own nation-building objectives. Amidst these myriad power struggles, a distinct and promising current, Soviet Ukrainian culture, was articulated. Despite the defeat, the separatist vision of a Soviet Ukraine and Soviet Ukrainian culture remained tangible throughout the era of Soviet-rule.¹² The unification of cultural life after 1928, which went hand in hand with a nationality-based persecution, represented a sign of weakness by the Soviet government in Ukraine that had managed to amalgamate Soviet culture mainly through the physical and ideological elimination of other existing cultural alternatives.

As shown, the historical question of Ukraine's cultural Sovietization has no simple answer. Despite being apparently tolerated during the early 1920s, it was clear to the authorities that the construction of Soviet culture could not be spontaneous, and the party could not simply wait until writers and readers alike evolved into the 'ideal' its propagandists had in mind, especially given the challenges that the Soviet cultural model faced in Ukraine. Throughout the decade, the party, despite its declared non-intervention, gradually acquired control over the creation of literature, mainly by manipulating the alignment of the literary forces and underplaying non-conformers. As suggested by Clark, this shift in the continuum of Soviet cultural life had already occurred in the mid-1920s – in 'approximately 1924–6 we can already find the contours of those patterns – institutional, ideological and aesthetic – that in the 1930s were to re-emerge as defining a culture we call "Stalinism".[13]

At the same time, during the 1920s, writers, by trial and error, were searching for their own trajectory for Soviet Ukraine's cultural development, defined as a competition between two opposing visions of Soviet culture: Soviet Ukrainian culture, as emphasized by Khvyl'ovyi, and Soviet culture in Ukrainian, which came to be represented by Tychyna. The two case studies examined in this book exemplified the complexity surrounding cultural Sovietization in Ukraine. Both Khvyl'ovyi and Tychyna underwent the complicated process of adjusting to the expectations of the authorities. While a revolutionary and a communist, Khvyl'ovyi needed to adapt his romanticism inspired by the revolution and the civil wars to a post-revolutionary routine. By contrast, Tychyna, the modernist poet and *intelihent*, sought possibilities for preserving his creative autonomy amidst the homogenizing social and political tendencies of the 1920s.

During this decade, the artistic activity of these two men of letters was heavily mediated by politics and the need to take sides in the ongoing ideological debates about the concept of Soviet culture in Ukraine. The literary outputs of the writer Khvyl'ovyi and the poet Tychyna were respectively used as evidence for the potency of different cultural projects competing for dominance at the time. In spite of different levels of public and political engagement, as well as their political and aesthetic agendas, Tychyna and Khvyl'ovyi both fell victim to the centralization drive carried out from Moscow: in 1933, Khvyl'ovyi took his own life with a gunshot whereas Tychyna 'ascended the Golgotha of Fame'[14] and attuned his poetry to the demands of the party.

This said, Khvyl'ovyi, with his pursuits for autonomous Ukrainian culture and extended power over decision-making, could hardly be regarded as anti-Soviet. On numerous occasions, he had emphasized his loyalty to the state, and conceded to what he regarded as ungrounded accusations in order to continue his literary and cultural activities towards Soviet culture and within the Soviet state, while not always being in agreement with the party ideology. In the end, as he defined himself, Khvyl'ovyi was first a communard and then a communist. By the same token, the Ukrainianness of Tychyna, a Soviet poet bureaucrat, could hardly be disputed. Throughout his career as a government official and a parliamentary member, he, to the best of his abilities, defended the Ukrainian language and Ukrainian culture, although in its Soviet, apolitical compliant form. When the general public rejected Tychyna's poetry, it was not due to his anti-national sounding. The 'official' Tychyna was rejected for his subservient role within the Soviet apparatus when his poetry was forced on the readers, not because of its merit, but because of his status in the republic.

In 1932, the TsK VKP(b) passed a resolution 'On the Restructuring of Literary and Artistic Organisations' putting an end to institutional and ideological pluralism in the world of letters, as well as the potential for any contesting visions of Soviet culture arising in the republics. According to the resolution, existing literary-artistic organizations 'ha[d] become too narrow and [were] slowing the serious sweep of [literary and] artistic creativity'.[15] Nonetheless, by this time, institutional diversity in literature existed only on paper and any ideological or aesthetic differences between literary organizations and groupings had already faded away under the onslaught of the VUSPP (in tandem with the RAPP in Russia). The party wished to take control back from those exclusive proletarian literary organizations and unify writers around common Soviet, rather than narrow proletarian, values. Instead of intolerant proletarian literary associations, the 1932 Resolution provided for a single Union of Soviet Writers, which would embrace the new aesthetic of socialist realism. The creation of the All-Soviet Congress of Soviet Writers in 1934 marked the completion of the organizational and ideological setup of Soviet literature.

After 1932, preparations for the Congress of Soviet Writers were underway in Kharkiv. In total, some 500 applications were submitted to the Organising Committee of the Congress to be considered for membership in the Union of Soviet Writers of Ukraine. The process for approving and inducting members into the Union was highly political. As an organizer of the founding committee of the Writers' Union of Soviet Ukraine and the member of its executive committee, Mykytenko explained that many of the applicants were rejected as the ideological content of their work did 'not answer to the need of Soviet literature'. Many writers active since before 1917, as well as those deemed 'anti-Soviet' (including the futurists and the Kyiv *neoklasyky* group), were regarded 'not yet ready to use their talent for the interest of the party, Soviet power, the interests of the toiling masses and their Soviet motherland'.[16] As a result, of the 500 applications, only 334 were considered by the Organising Committee, while only 120 writers were actually accepted: 73 Ukrainian, 22 Jewish, 19 Russian, 4 Moldavian and 1 Greek. This selection process, according to Luckyj indicated 'the pressure which the Party placed on the writers to make absolute loyalty a prerequisite for joining the Union'.[17] The First All-Ukrainian Congress of Soviet Writers, held on 20 June 1934, approved these new members and elected forty-two delegates to represent Soviet Ukraine at the All-Union Congress to be held on 17 August 1934.

The party ideologists and art officials also needed to provide meaning to the new aesthetic method denominated in 1932 as 'socialist realism'. No unified definition of the term had been achieved before the All-Union Congress, despite the fact that some 400 theoretical and ideological contributions on the matter were published between 1932 and 1934.[18] At the Congress, Andrei Zhdanov, Stalin's spokesman on cultural affairs, defined 'socialist realism' as 'the basic method of Soviet literature and literary criticism [which] demands of a sincere writer a historically concrete representation of reality in its revolutionary development'.[19] This definition was enhanced by outlining the social usefulness of literary outputs created through its methodologies: 'truth and historical completeness of artistic representation must be combined with the task of ideological transformation and education of the working man in the spirit of Socialism'.[20] The official dogma of socialist realism presented a vague and contradictory formula, offering no clear criteria on how to fit this concept. According to the literary critic Marc Slonim, the proposed definition 'confused such different concepts as aesthetic method, artistic intention and point of view, and also confounded such different elements as the requirements of a literary trend and the practical effects of a finished work on the readers'.[21]

Nevertheless, at the 1934 Congress, the Soviet cultural canon was finally established while a unified artistic and institutional method of socialist realism was authorized centrally and endorsed by the creation of the Union of Soviet Writers. The socialist realist method was used to create fine literature that was ideologically correct, aesthetically conservative and content-oriented. The institutional and aesthetic unification of literature also marked the decisive end to the once heated debates over artistic orientation, the nature and purpose of art and the social role of artists and writers in the Soviet state. In other words, in the competition between the two proposed models of Soviet culture, the Soviet culture in Ukrainian, as defined centrally, in both its institutional and artistic forms, emerged victorious over the separatist vision of Soviet Ukrainian culture, ardently promoted by Ukrainian communists and artists since the revolution. With no other practical choices available, Ukrainian writers were obliged to join the Union of Soviet Writers of Ukraine, a section of the All-Soviet Union.

Overall, the unified Soviet canon in Ukraine, cemented in the early 1930s, was an amalgamation of at least two different Soviet cultural projects: Soviet Ukrainian culture and Soviet culture in the Ukrainian language. These projects were conditioned by two different political cultures, developed in parallel to one an other within the institutional framework of the KP(b)U. The distinct project of an autonomous Soviet Ukrainian culture was promoted by Ukraine-minded communists, advocating Ukraine's autonomy in political and cultural matters. The project for an all-Union Soviet culture was based on Moscow's central place within the all-Soviet artistic map and the determinant role of the central leadership in defining cultural policy across the Union. These two cultural projects, often implemented simultaneously by different interest groups, came into direct confrontation with each other. The subsequent triumph of the all-Soviet project was secured by the accelerated processes of economic centralization and Union-wide political consolidation. Nevertheless, the demise of the Soviet Ukrainian cultural project was only partially caused by external force. The inherent contradictions within the KP(b)U (the irreconcilable 'two distinct ancestral roots' in the party), the constant power struggle between the republic's and central elites regarding the extent of the KP(b)U's real political authority and the lack of a single unified vision for what the Soviet Ukrainian cultural project was meant to represent, resulted in weakness and perhaps the inevitable failure of the ambitious project for a Soviet Ukrainian culture.

Nevertheless, the potency of this defeated cultural project can hardly be examined within the conventional 'executed renaissance' paradigm. Firstly, the triumph of Soviet literature was the outcome of a complex and gradual process through which alternative non-Bolshevik and proletarian visions of Ukraine's literature were absorbed and neutralized throughout the 1920s. Literary developments in this period, therefore, cannot be defined by the fates of those highly talented writers who fell as victims of Stalin's Great Terror. At the same time, there is no simple distinction between 'martyrs' and 'perpetrators' of the regime since the ideological and aesthetic evolution of each and every writer was far more complex than the 'either ... or' binary can suggest. In a word, the cultural development of Ukraine did not end with its supposed 'execution' in the 1930s. Rather, it had evolved into a distinct form of Soviet culture in Ukrainian.

Notes

Introduction

1 *Literaturna hazeta*, 1 March 1929, 2.
2 Ibid.
3 Ibid.
4 A similar distinction was suggested by the contemporaries. For instance, Mykola Hlobenko (also known as Ohloblin) in his essay on Khvyl'ovyi maintained that the writer represented 'a group of dreamers (*mriinyky*) who believed that it was possible to build a Ukrainian Soviet State in a union with a power whose existence was based on the national ideology deeply alien to the desire of our people for independence (*samostiinist'*)'. Although they were dreamers, Hlobenko continues, they managed to achieve a lot for Ukraine, that is broad cultural autonomy, national education, scholarship, culture; whereby 'Ukrainian art has overcame its provincialism and literature reached the European level'. See Mykola Ohloblin-Hlobenko, 'Mykola Khvyl'ovyi', in his *Istoryko-literaturni statti* (Zapysky NTSh, vol. CLXVII) (New York; Paris, Munich: NTSh, 1958).
5 Mykola Khvylovy, *Apologists of Scribbling*, in Khvylovy, *The Cultural Renaissance in Ukraine* (Edmonton: CIUS, 1986), 222.
6 *Literaturna hazeta*, 1 March 1929, 2.
7 Based on Terry Martin, *The Affirmative Action Empire: Nations and Nationalism in the Soviet Union, 1923–39* (Ithaca: Cornell University Press, 2001), 12–13.
8 The same approach was used by the Soviet authorities in Western Ukraine in order to integrate those regions into the Soviet system. See Ola Hnatiuk, *Odwaga i Strach* (Wroclaw: Wydawnictwo KEW, 2015); In English: *Courage and Fear* (Boston: Academic Studies Press, 2019). For a similar account on Sovietization see Jan Tomasz Gross, *Revolution from Abroad: The Soviet Conquest of Poland's Western Ukraine and Western Belorussia* (Princeton: Princeton University Press, 1988).
9 On other ethnonational variants of emerging Soviet culture see: Mayhill Fowler, 'Yiddish Theater in Soviet Ukraine: Reevaluating Ukrainian – Jewish Relations in the Arts', *Ab Imperio*, 3 (2011): 167–8; Kate Brown, *A Biography of No Place: Ethnic Borderland to Soviet Heartland* (Cambridge, MA: Harvard University Press, 2004); Jeffrey Veidlinger, *In the Shadow of the Shtetl: Small-Town Jewish Life in Soviet Ukraine* (Bloomington; Indianapolis: Indiana UP, 2013); Yohanan Petrovsky Shtern, *The Anti-Imperial Choice: The Making of the Ukrainian Jew* (New Haven: Yale University Press, 2009); Kenneth Moss, *Jewish Renaissance in the Russian Revolution* (Cambridge: Cambridge University Press, 2009); Brigid O'Keeffe, *New Soviet Gypsies: Nationality, Performance, and Selfhood in the Early Soviet Union* (Toronto: Toronto University Press, 2013). On the omission of this diversity in the scholarship see Mayhill C. Fowler, 'Beyond Ukraine or Little Russia: Going Global with Culture in Ukraine', *Harvard Ukrainian Studies* 34, no. 1/4 (2015–16): 263–5.
10 'Statut Vil'noi Akademii Proletars'koi Literatury VAPLITE', in *Vaplite, Zoshyt Pershyi* (1926), 94–6. Iurii Smolych in his memoirs dedicated a separate chapter

to the patrons of this cultural coterie – 'three musketeers' or 'a holy trinity' as they were called, comprising Borys (Boba) Lifshyts, the editor of the Workers' newspaper *Proletar*, together with Veniamin (Fusia) Furer, the editor of the weeklies *Radians'ke selo* [Soviet Village] and *Proletars'ka Pravda* [Proletarian Truth], and Ivan Postolovs'kyi, the head of the Party TsK Department of Literature and Arts. See Iurii Smolych, *Rozpovid' pro Nespokii* (Kyiv: Radians'kyi Pys'mennyk, 1968), 105–6.

11 Volodymyr Koriak, 'Ukrains'ka Literatura za P'iat' Rokiv Proletars'koi Revoliutsii', in Volodymyr Koriak, *Orhanizatsiia Zhovtnevoi Literatury* (Kharkiv: DVU, 1925), 65.

12 Hnat Mykhailychenko, 'Proletars'ke Mystetstvo (Tezy na Dopovidi Vseukrlitkomu)', in A. Leites and M. Iashek, *Desiat' Rokiv Ukrains'koi Literatury (1917–7)* (Kharkiv: DVU, 1928), vol. II, 25–8.

13 On the methodological issues of researching Ukrainian culture of the period see Fowler, *Beyond Ukraine or Little Russia*.

14 As convincingly shown by Serhy Yekelchyk, the 'dialogue', debates and conversation between the Soviet bureaucracy and intelligentsia did not end in the end of the 1920s. He argues that even during High Stalinism, Ukrainian cultural agents continued to play an active role in developing and revising the official politics. See: Serhy Yekelchyk, 'Diktat and Dialogue in Stalinist Culture: Staging Patriotic Historical Opera in Soviet Ukraine, 1936–1954', *Slavic Review* 3, no. 59 (2000): 597–624; Also his *Stalin's Empire of Memory. Russian-Ukrainian Relations in the Soviet Historical Imagination* (Toronto: Toronto University Press, 2004).

15 The literary developments in the revolutionary period are a well-studied subject, especially among those studying Russia. See, for example: Robert A. Maguire, *Red Virgin Soil: Soviet Literature in the 1920s* (Princeton: Princeton University Press, 1968); Boris Thomson, *The Premature Revolution, Russian Literature and Society, 1917–1946* (London: Weidenfeld and Nicolson, 1972); Lynn Mally, *Culture of the Future. The Proletkult Movement in Revolutionary Russia* (Berkeley: University of California Press, 1990); Evgeny Dobrenko, *Aesthetics of Alienation: Reassessment of Early Soviet Cultural Theories* (Evanston, IL: North-Western University Press, 2005).

16 On the literary developments in Soviet Ukraine see: Myroslav Shkandrij, *Modernists, Marxists and the Nation: The Ukrainian Literary Discussion of the 1920s* (Edmonton: CIUS, 1992); George Luckyj, *Literary Politics in the Soviet Ukraine, 1917–1934* (Durham-London: Duke University Press, [1956] 1990).

17 This book expands on the recent study by Mayhill C. Fowler to examine the process of the construction of culture that was both Soviet and Ukrainian. Mayhill C. Fowler, *Beau Monde on Empire's Edge: State and Stage in Soviet Ukraine* (Toronto: Toronto University Press, 2017).

18 On the history of the KP(b)U and the early debates see: Moisei Ravich-Cherkasskii, *Istoria Kommunisticheskoi Partii (bov) Ukrainy* (Kharkov: Gosizdat Ukrainy, 1923); Mykola Popov, *Narys istorii komunistychnoi parti (bilshovykiv) Ukrainy* (Kharkiv: DVU, 1928); Ivan Maistrenko, *Istoriia komunistychnoi partii Ukrainy* (Munich: Suchasnist', 1972); Vsevolod Holubnychy, 'Outline History of the Communist Party of Ukraine', in *Soviet Regional Economics. Selected Works of Vsevolod Holubnychy*, ed. Iwan S. Koropeckyj (Toronto: CIUS, 1982).

19 Literary scholars Marko Pavlyshyn and Myroslav Shkandrij used post-colonial literary criticism to analyse the relationship between Ukrainian and Russian literatures. See: Marko Pavlyshyn, 'Post-Colonial Features in Contemporary Ukrainian Culture', *Australian Slavonic and East European Studies* 2, no. 6 (1992): 41–55; Myroslav Shkandrij, *Russia and Ukraine. Literature and the Discourse of*

Empire from Napoleonic to Postcolonial Times (Montreal: McGill-Queen's University Press, 2001). Post-colonialism became also widely used by the slavists working in Ukraine. See: Tamara Hundorova and Agnieszka Matusiak (eds.), *Postkolonializm. Heneratsii. Kul'tura* (Kyiv: Laurus, 2015); Ola Hnatiuk, *Pożegnanie z imperium. Ukraińskie dyskusje o tożsamości* (Lublin: Wydawnictwo Uniwersytetu Marii Curie-Skłodowskiej, 2003). In political terms, the imperial/colonial paradigm to defining Ukrainian–Russian relations was examined by Velychenko. See: Stephen Velychenko, *Painting Imperialism and Nationalism Red: The Ukrainian Marxist Critique of Russian Communist Rule in Ukraine, 1918–1925* (Toronto: Toronto University Press, 2015).

20 On the cultural policies in the Soviet Union see: Abbott Gleason, Peter Kenez and Richard Stites (eds.), *Bolshevik Culture: Experiment and Order in the Russian Revolution* (Bloomington: Indiana University Press, 1985); Sheila Fitzpatrick, Alexander Rabinowitch and Richard Stites (eds.), *Russia in the Era of NEP: Explorations in Soviet Society and Culture* (Bloomington: Indiana University Press, 1991); Stefan Plaggenborg, *Revolutionskultur: Menschenbilder und kulturelle Praxis in Sowjetrussland zwischen Oktoberrevolution und Stalinismus* (Köln: Böhlau, 1996); Christopher Read, *Culture and Power in Revolutionary Russia: The Intelligentsia and the Transition from Tsarism to Communism* (New York: St Martin's Press, 1990).

21 Sheila Fitzpatrick, *The Cultural Front. Power and Culture in Revolutionary Russia* (Ithaca; London: Cornell University Press, 1992), 2.

22 Katerina Clark, 'The "Quiet Revolution" in Soviet Intellectual Life', in Fitzpatrick et al., *Russia in the Era of NEP*, 211.

23 Here and thereafter, a clear distinction is made between *Ukrainizatsiia* as a state policy aimed at party entrenchment and promotion of the Ukrainian languages and Ukrainization as a mere de-Russification, which is also reflected in the spelling of these two terms.

24 J. Stalin, 'National Factors in Party and State Affairs: Theses for the Twelfth Congress of the Russian Communist Party (Bolsheviks)', in J. Stalin, *Works* (Moscow: Foreign Languages Publishing House, 1953), vol. 5, 193.

25 For a comprehensive account of *Ukrainizatsiia* see: Martin, *Affirmative Action Empire*; Elena Borisenok, *Fenomen Sovetskoi Ukrainizatsii, 1920–30-e gody* (Moscow: Evropa, 2006); Valerii Smolii et al., *Ukrainizatsiia 1920–30-kh rokiv: Peremodumovy, Zdobutky, Uroky* (Kyiv: NAN Ukrainy, 2003). Scholarships dealing with separate aspects of *Ukrainizatsiia*: J. Mace, *Communism and the Dilemmas of National Liberation: National Communism in Soviet Ukraine, 1918–1933* (Cambridge, MA: Harvard University Press, 1983); Matthew Pauly, *Breaking the Tongue: Language, Education, and Power in Soviet Ukraine, 1923–1934* (Toronto: Toronto University Press, 2014); George Liber, '"Language, Literacy, and Book Publishing in the Ukrainian SSR," 1923–1928', *Slavic Review* 41, no. 4 (1982): 673–85; *Soviet Nationality Policy, Urban Growth, and Identity Change in the Ukrainian SSR 1923–1934* (Cambridge: Cambridge University Press, 2002).

26 In this book, I side with recent research on the Soviet nationality policy that emphasizes the party's intention in 'making nations' and its unique way of managing the multi-ethnic environment inherited from the Russian Empire. See: Yuri Slezkine, 'The USSR as Communal Apartment, or How a Socialist State Promoted Ethnic Particularism', *Slavic Review* 53, no. 2 (1994): 414–52; Ronald Suny, *The Revenge of the Past: Nationalism, Revolution, and the Collapse of the Soviet Union* (Redwood City: Stanford University Press, 1993); Martin, *Affirmative Action Empire*; Francine Hirsch, *Empire of Nations: Ethnographic Knowledge and the Making of the Soviet*

Union (Ithaca: Cornell University Press, 2005); Peter Blitstein, 'Cultural Diversity and the Interwar Conjuncture: Soviet Nationality Policy in Its Comparative Context', *Slavic Review* 2, no. 65 (2006): 273–93; Adrienne Edgar, *Tribal Nation: The Making of Soviet Turkmenistan* (Princeton: Princeton University Press, 2006). At the same time, this study highlights the role of Ukraine-minded communists in defining and implementing this policy in the republic. The role of the local agents in promoting *Ukrainizatsiia* has been discussed by: Mykola Doroshko, *Nomenklatura: Kerivna verkhivka radians'koi Ukrainy (1917–1938 rr.)* (Kyiv: Nika-Tsentr, 2008), 288–300; Borisenok, *Fenomen Sovetskoi Ukrainizatsii*.

27 In her rethinking of Ukrainization, Halyna Hryn refers to the documents of the surveillance of the members of Ukrainian intelligentsia in the mid-1920s compiled by the secret services to underscore how precarious and conditional the nature of the policy of *korenizatsiia* was, whereby various cultural policies were contradictory and often worked at cross purposes with each other. See: Hryn, *Executed Renaissance*, 71. Based on the analysis of documents from the secret services, the Ukrainian historian Vasyl' Danylenko confirmed that while initiating *korenizatsiia*, the party centrally already had an intention of clandestine counter-Ukrainization aimed to eliminate alleged counter-revolutionaries and nationalists. See: Danylenko, *Intelihentsia i Vlada*, 21. A similar approach is introduced in Myroslav Shkandrij and Olga Bertelsen, 'The Soviet Regime's National Operations in Ukraine, 1929–1934', *Canadian Slavonic Papers/Revue Canadienne des Slavistes* 55, no. 3–4 (2013): 417–48.

28 See Liber, *Soviet Nationality Policy*.

29 On Kharkiv see: Iurii Sherekh, 'Chetvertyi Kharkiv', in Sherekh, *Porohy i Zaporizhzhia* (Kharkiv: Folio, 1998), vol. 1, 478–92; Vladimir Kravchenko, *Kharkov/Kharkiv: Stolitsa Pohranich'ia* (Vilnus: EGU, 2010); Titus D. Hewryk, 'Planning of the Capital in Kharkiv', *Harvard Ukrainian Studies* XVI, no. 3/4 (1992): 325–60; Markian Dobczansky, *From Soviet Heartland to Ukrainian Borderland: Searching for Identity in Kharkiv, 1943–2004*, PhD thesis, Stanford University, 2016.

30 On the readers' appetites see: Myroslav Shkandrij, 'The Ukrainian Reading Public in the 1920s: Real, Implied and Ideal', *Canadian Slavonic Papers/Revue Canadienne Des Slavistes* 2, no. 5 (2016): 160–83; Olena Palko, 'Reading in Ukrainian: The Working Class and Mass Literature in Early Soviet Ukraine', *Social History* 44, no. 3 (2019): 343–68.

31 The revisionist approach to study Stalinist culture emerged in the 1970s. Those scholars started questioning the orthodox view on Stalinism according to which Soviet society was the passive object of an all-powerful state. See: Vera S. Dunham, *In Stalin's Time: Middleclass Values in Soviet Fiction* (New York; London: Cambridge University Press, 1976); Sheila Fitzpatrick, 'Culture and Politics under Stalin: A Reappraisal', *Slavic Review* 2, no. 35 (1976): 211–31, a revised version reprinted as 'Cultural Orthodoxies under Stalin' in her *The Cultural Front*, 238–56; Katerina Clark, *The Soviet Novel: History as Ritual* (Chicago; London: Chicago University Press, 1981); Boris Groys, *The Total Art of Stalinism: Avant-garde, Aesthetic Dictatorship, and Beyond* (Princeton: Princeton University Press, 1992); Katerina Clark, *Petersburg, Crucible of Cultural Revolution* (Cambridge, MA; London: Harvard University Press, 1995); Peter Kenez, *Cinema and Soviet Society, 1917–1953* (Cambridge: Cambridge University Press, 1992); Régine Robin, *Socialist Realism: An Impossible Aesthetic*, trans. Catherine Porter (Stanford: Stanford University Press, 1992); Richard Stites, *Russian Popular Culture: Entertainment and Society since 1900* (Cambridge: Cambridge University Press, 1992); Jeffrey Brooks, *Thank You, Comrade*

Stalin! Soviet Public Culture from the Revolution to Cold War (Princeton: Princeton University Press, 2000); Yekelchyk, *Diktat and Dialogue in Stalinist Culture*; also his, *Stalin's Empire of Memory*; Evgeny Dobrenko, 'The Disaster of Middlebrow Taste, or, Who "Invented," in Socialist Realism', in *Socialist Realism without Shores*, ed. Thomas Lahusen and Evgeny Dobrenko (London: Durham, NC, 1997); Jonathan Waterlow, *It's Only a Joke, Comrade! Humour, Trust and Everyday Life under Stalin* (Oxford: CreateSpace Independent Publishing Platform, 2018).

32   Katerin Clark suggested that the shift in the continuum of Soviet cultural life towards centralization had already occurred in the mid-1920s. See: Clark, *Petersburg*.

33   The paradigm was introduced by the survivors of the Stalin purges who ended up in the emigration after the Second World War. See: Iu. Lavrinenko, *Rozstriliane Vidrodzhennia. Antolohiia 1917–1933* (Kyiv: Smoloskyp, 2007); Halyna Hryn, 'The "Executed Renaissance" Paradigm Revisited', *Harvard Ukrainian Studies* 27 (2004–5): 67–96.

34   Mayhill Fowler, 'Mikhail Bulgakov, Mykola Kulish, and Soviet Theater: How Internal Transnationalism Remade Center and Periphery', *Kritika: Explorations in Russian and Eurasian History* 16, no. 2 (2015): 263–90; also her *Beyond Ukraine or Little Russia*.

35   Fowler, *Mikhail Bulgakov, Mykola Kulish, and Soviet Theater*; *Beyond Ukraine or Little Russia*. Fowler builds upon new methodological approaches to studying Soviet Union, such as: Georgiy Kasianov and Philipp Ther, *Ukraine: A Laboratory of Transnational History* (Budapest and New York: CEU Press, 2009); Michael David-Fox, 'The Implications of Transnationalism', *Kritika: Explorations in Russian and Eurasian History* 4, no. 12 (2001): 885–94.

36   Yekelchyk, *Stalin's Empire of Memory*, 9.

37   The rehabilitation of patriotism, national pride and historical heroes in the mid-1930s was not only a Ukrainian phenomenon. On the revival of the Russian patriotism see: D. L. Brandenberger and A. M. Dubrovsky, '"The People Need a Tsar": The Emergence of National Bolshevism as Stalinist Ideology, 1931–1941', *Europe-Asia Studies* 5, no. 50 (1998): 873–92; David Brandenberger, *National Bolshevism: Stalinist Mass Culture and the Formation of Modern Russian National Identity, 1931–1956* (Cambridge MA: Harvard University Press, 2002); David Brandenberger and Kevin Platt (eds.), *Epic Revisionism. Russian History and Literature as Stalinist Propaganda* (Madison, WI: Wisconsin University Press, 2006).

38   Yekelchyk, *Stalin's Empire of Memory*, 11.

39   Ibid; Fowler, *Beyond Ukraine or Little Russia*, 265.

40   The Soviet literary canon and socialist realism is a well-studied subject. See, for instance: Régine, *Socialist Realism*; Clark, *The Soviet Novel*; Lahusen, Dobrenko, *Socialist Realism without Shores*; Hans Guenther and Evgeny Dobrenko (eds.) *Sotsrealisticheskii Kanon* (Sankt-Peterburg: Akademicheskii Proekt, 2000); Yekelchyk, *Stalin's Empire of Memory*; Kathleen Parthé, 'What Was Soviet Literature?' *The Slavic and East European Journal* 2, no. 38 (1994): 290–301; Valentyna Kharkhun, *Sotsrealistychnyi Kanon v Ukrains'kii Literaturi: Henesa, Rozvytok, Modyfikatsii* (Nizhyn: Hidromaks, 2009).

41   Pierre Bourdieu, 'L`Illusion Biographique', *Actes de la Recherche en Science Sociales* 62 (1986): 69–72; In Russian: Pier Burbie, 'Biograficheskaia Illiusiia', *Inter* 1 (2002): 75–83.

42   Private collections of Mykola Zerov and Mykola Mohylians'kyi at the Institute of Manuscripts (*Instytut Rukopysu*) of the Vernads'kyi National Library of Ukraine. Many were published in Tychyna Pavlo, *Tvory u Dvanadtsiaty Tomakh* (Kyiv:

Naukova Dumka, 1983–90); Mykola Khvyl'ovyi, *Tvory u P'iat'okh Tomakh* (New York-Baltimore-Toronto: Smoloskyp, 1978–86); *Tvory u Dvokh Tomakh* (Kyiv: Dnipro, 1990–1).

43 Based on the works of Jochen Hellbeck, *Revolution on My Mind: Writing a Diary under Stalin* (Cambridge, MA: Harvard University Press, 2006); Igal Halfin, *Terror in My Soul. Communist Autobiographies on Trial* (Cambridge, MA: Harvard University Press, 2003).

44 *Tsentral'nyi Derzhavnyi Arkhiv Hromads'kykh Ob'iednan' Ukrainy* (TsDAHOU), F.1, op.20, spr.1852, ark.73–80; Mykola Khvyl'ovyi, 'Uryvok z avtobiohrafii', *Vitchyzna* 12 (1987): 106–8; 'Kratkaia Biografiia Chlena KP(b)U Nikolaia Grigor'ievicha Fitileva', in Khvyl'ovyi, *Tvory u Dvokh Tomakh*, vol. 2, 830–7.

45 Mykola Zhulyn'skyi (ed.), *Z Arkhivu P. Tychyny* (Kyiv: Naukova Dumka, 1990).

46 Eric Naiman, 'On Soviet Subjects and the Scholars Who Make Them', *Russian Review* 60, no. 3 (2001): 307–15.

47 Vasyl' Danylenko (ed.), *Ukrains'ka Intelihentsia i Vlada: Zvedennia Sekretnoho Viddilu DPU USRR 1927–1929 rr.* (Kyiv: Tempora, 2012); Iurii Shapoval and Volodymyr Panchenko (eds.), *Poliuvannia na 'Val'dshnepa'. Rozsekrechenyi Mykola Khvyl'ovyi* (Kyiv: Tempora, 2010).

48 A. Graziosi, 'The New Soviet Archival Sources. Hypotheses for a Critical Assessment', *Cahiers du Monde Russe* 40 (1999): 56.

49 István Rév, *Retroactive Justice: Prehistory of Post-Communism* (Redwood City: Stanford University Press, 2005): 1–3.

50 E.g. V. Depkat, 'The "Cultural Turn" in German and American Historiography', *Amerikastudien/American Studies* 54, no. 3 (2009): 425–50; Naiman, *On Soviet Subjects*.

51 The term is borrowed from Grabowicz. See: George Grabowicz, 'Symbolic Autobiography in the Prose of Mykola Khvyl'ovyi (Some Preliminary Observations)', *Harvard Ukrainian Studies* 22 (1998): 165–80.

52 Oleksander Doroshkevych, *Pidruchnyk Istorii Ukrains'koi Literatury* (Kyiv: Knyhospilka, 1927), 304.

53 Olena Palko, 'Between Two Powers: A Soviet Ukrainian Writer Mykola Khvyl'ovyi', *Jahrbücher für Geschichte Osteuropas* 4 (2016): 575–98.

54 *Bol'shaia Sovetskaia Entsyklopediia*, vol. 59 (Moscow: Sovetskaia Entsyklopediia, 1935), 488.

55 *Soviet Ukraine* (Kiev: Editorial office of the Ukrainian Soviet Encyclopedia, Academy of Sciences of the Ukrainian S.S.R, 1969), 469.

56 Ohloblin, *Mykola Khvyl'ovyi*, 60.

57 One of those most notable voices in defence of Khvyl'ovyi came from the famous Soviet Ukrainian poet and a KP(b)U member and the future leader of the *Narodnyi Rukh Ukrainy* Ivan Drach. See: Ivan Drach, Vystup na plenumi pravlinnya Spilky Pys'mennykiv Ukraiiny pro neobpidnist' povernennшa chytacham tvoriv M. Khvyl'ovogo, *Literaturna Ukraina*, 9 July 1987; Also Serhii Grechaniuk, 'Den' povernennia Mykoly Khvyl'ovogo', *Ukrains'ka mova i literatura u shkoli* 2 (1987): 17–26.

58 Oleksandr Bilets'kyi, *Dvadtsiat' Rokiv Novoi Ukrains'koi Liryky* (Kharkiv: DVU 1924); Volodymyr Koriak, *Ukrains'ka Literatura*; 'Pershe Desiatyrichchia', Volodymyr Koriak, *V Boiakh: Statti in Vystupy*, 1925–1930 (Kharkiv: Literatura i Mystetstvo, 1933), 250–8; Volodymyr Iurynets', *Pavlo Tychyna. Sproba Krytychnoi Analisy* (Kharkiv: Knyhospilka, 1928).

59 Leonid Novychenko, *Poeziia i Revoliutsiia. Tvorchist' P.Tychyny v Pershi Pisliazhovtnevi Roky* (Kyiv: Dnipro, 1968); Semen Shakhovs'kyi, *Pavlo Tychyna* (Kyiv: Dnipro, 1968); Stanislav Tel'niuk, *Pavlo Tychyna. Bibliohrafichna Povist'* (Kyiv: Molod', 1979).
60 Vasyl' Stus, *Fenomen Doby (Skhodzhennia na Holhofu Slavy)* (Kyiv: Znannia Ukrainy, 1993), 91.
61 Roman Rahmannyi, *Dmytro Dontsov i Mykola Khvyl'ovyi, 1923-1933* (London: Ukrains'ka Vydavnycha Spilka, 1984), 23.
62 Introduction to Dmytro Dontsov, *Mykola Khvyl'ovyi*, ([s.l.], 1947) II.
63 E.g. Ivan Koshelivets', *Suchasna Literatura v URSR* (New York: Proloh, 1964); Vasyl' Barka, *Khliborobs'kyi Orfei, abo Kliarnetyzm* (Munich: Suchasnist', 1961).
64 E.g. Iurii Lavrinenko, *Pavlo Tychyna i Ioho Poema 'Skovoroda' na Tli Epokhy* (Munich: Suchasnist', 1980).
65 For the intellectual development within the Ukrainian immigration in the interwar period see: Alexander J. Motyl, *The Turn to the Right: The Ideological Origins and Development of Ukrainian Nationalism, 1919-1929* (Boulder; New York: Columbia University Press, 1980).
66 E.g. Vasyl' Pliushch, *Pravda pro Khvyl'ovizm* (Munich: Spilka Vyzvolennia Ukrainy: 1954); Roman Zadesnians'kyi, *Shcho nam dav Mykola Khvyl'ovyi*, ([s.l.]: 1979); M. Liaskovets' [L. Mosendz], *Mykola Khvyl'ovyi: lehenda i diisnist'* (Salsburg-Innsbruck: Zveno, 1948).
67 Hryn, *Executed Renaissance*, 68.
68 For instance, Ievhen Malaniuk, 'M.Ryl's'kyi v P'iatdesiatylittia', Ievhen Malaniuk, *Knyha Sposterezhen'* (Toronto: Homin Ukrainy, 1962), vol. 1, 298–322.
69 On the dangers of national narrative in history writing see: G. Kasianov and O. Tolochko, 'Natsional'ni Istorii ta Suchasna Istoriohrafiia: Vyklyky i Nebezpeky pry Napysani Novoi Istorii Ukrainy', *Ukrains'kyi Istorychnyi Zhurnal* 6 (2012): 4–21; Andreas Kappeler, Guido Hausmann, Olena Petrenko and Frank Golczewski, 'Diskussion: Wie soll man ukrainische Geschichte betreiben?', *Jahrbücher für Geschichte Osteuropas* 4 (2016): 626–45.
70 Mark von Hagen, 'Does Ukraine Have a History?' *Slavic Review* 54, no. 3 (1995): 658–73.
71 Christopher Gilley, *The 'Change of Signposts' in the Ukrainian Emigration. A Contribution to the History of Sovietophilism in the 1920s* (Stuttgard: ibidem-Verlag, 2009), 23.
72 Iurii Shapoval, 'Fatal'na Ambivalentnist' (Mykola Khvyl'ovyi u Svitli Dokumentiv GPU)', in *Poliuvannia na 'Val'dshnepa'*, 12–45; Volodymyr Panchenko, 'Khvyl'ovyi: Istoriia Iliuzii i Prozrin'', in *Poliuvannia na 'Val'dshnepa'*, 46–81; Their analysis in Mayhill C. Fowler, Review of 'Poliuvannia na "Val'dshnepa". Rozsekrechenyi Mykola Khvyl'ovyi', *Kritika: Explorations in Russian and Eurasian History* 13, no. 2 (2012): 491–500.
73 E.g. Stanislav Tel'niuk, 'Mistyfikatsiia Poeta v Totalitarnomu Pekli', *Dnipro* 1 (1991): 181–97; O. Iarovyi, 'Poet na Perehresti Pohliadiv: Krytyka Riznykh Rokiv pro Tychynu', *Ukranis'ka Mova ta Literatura* 18 (1997): 1–3; O. Tarnavs'kyi, 'T. S. Eliot i Pavlo Tychyna', *Vsesvit* 6 (1990): 130–6; Leonid Novychenko, 'Tychyna i Ioho Chas: Nezaivi Dopovnennia', Leonid Novychenko, *Dvadtsiati Roky: Literaturni Dyskusii, Polemiky. Literaturno-Krytychni Statti.* (Kyiv: Dnipro, 1991), 314–66.
74 The exception is George Grabowicz, 'Tyčyna's "Černihiv"', *Harvard Ukrainian Studies* I, no. 1 (1977): 79–114; Also his paper 'Modernism in Ukrainian Poetry: The

Paradigm of Pavlo Tychyna', presented at the international conference 'Ukrainian Modernism in Context, 1910–1930', Harvard University, Center for Government and International Studies (CGIS), 14–15 April 2007; Kharkhun, *Sotsrealistychnyi Kanon*; '"Mytets' v Kanoni", Sotsrealistychna Poeziia Pavla Tychyny 1930–60-kh Rokiv', *Slovo i Chas* 10 (2006): 38–51.

75   Some recent studies are trying to close this gap by highlighting the value of Soviet Ukrainian culture. The most notable example is the recent book of Mayhil Fowler; see: Mayhill Fowler, *Beau Monde on Empire's Edge: State and Stage in Soviet Ukraine* (Toronto, Toronto University Press, 2017). The approach that regarded socialist realism as a continuation and pinnacle of modernism, especially of the avant-garde, were developed by Groys, *The Total Art of Stalinism*; Petre Petrov, *Automatic for the Masses: Authorship and Agency in Early Soviet Culture* (Toronto University Press, Scholarly Publishing Division, 2015).

Chapter 1

1   On Great Reforms in Russia see: Ben Eklof, John Bushnell and Larissa Zakharova (eds.), *Russia's Great Reforms, 1855–1881* (Bloomington, IN: Indiana University Press, 1994); Bruce W. Lincoln, *The Great Reforms: Autocracy, Bureaucracy, and the Politics of Change in Imperial Russia* (DeKalb, IL: Northern Illinois University Press, 1990); Terence Emmons and Wayne S. Vucinich (eds.), *The Zemstvo in Russia: An Experiment in Local Self-Government* (Cambridge: Cambridge University Press, 1982); Volodymyr Doroshenko, *Z istorii zemstva na Ukraini* (Lviv: NTSh, 1910).

2   On Chernihiv Zemstvo see: Oleksandr Rakhno, *Chernihivs'ki zemtsi (istoryko-biohrafichni narysy)* (Chernihiv: Chernihivs'ki oberehy, 2009), as well as his multiple publications on Ukrainian history journals.

3   On the Ukrainian national movement in the late imperial Russia see: Johannes Remy, *Brothers or Enemies: The Ukrainian National Movement and Russia from the 1840s to the 1870s* (Toronto: Toronto University Press, 2016); Andreas Kappeler, 'Die Formierung einer ukrainischen nationalen Elite im Russischen Reich 1860–1914', Andreas Kappeler, *Der Schwierige Weg zur Nation. Beiträge zur neueren Geschichte der Ukraine* (Wien: Böhlau, 2003), 99–122

4   Pavlo Tychyna, *Iz Shchodennykovykh Zapysiv* (Kyiv: Radians'kyi Pys'mennyk, 1981), 238.

5   Pavlo Tychyna, '[Avtobiohrafiia], Tychyna', *Tvory* 8, no. 1: 9; Tychyna, *Iz Shchodennykovykh Zapysiv*, 43.

6   Tychyna, *Avtobiohrafiia*, in *Tvory*, vol. 8.1, 9.

7   Correspondence between Pieshkov [Gorky], Tychyna and Kotsiubyns'kyi in Pavlo Tychyna, *Z mynuloho – v Maibutnie* (Kyiv: Dnipro, 1973), 21–3.

8   Tychyna, *Iz Shchodennykovykh Zapysiv*, 238–9.

9   Since Russian was the only official language on the empire's territory, Pavlo was registered as Тychynin (Тычининъ), the surname he would use for official purposes up until 1917.

10 This name was used for his application to the Kyiv Commercial Institute, the student of which he became in 1913. *Derzhavnyi Arkhiv mista Kyieva* (DAK), f. 153, op.5, spr.8080, ark.17.

11 During the second half of the nineteenth century, the Russian Empire was combating thr possible rise of Ukrainian nationalism by banning the usage of

the Ukrainian language. The Valuev circular of 1863 placed limits on Ukrainian-language publications, stating 'no separate Little Russian language ever existed, doesn't exist, and couldn't exist'. The circular banned the publication of all literature directed at the common people limiting its usage primarily to belles-lettres. In 1876, the circular was included in the Ems decree further restricting Ukrainian publishing. The Ems decree remained in force until the first Russian Revolution of 1905. See: Johannes Remy, 'The Valuev Circular and Censorship of Ukrainian Publications in the Russian Empire (1863–1876): Intention and Practice', *Canadian Slavonic Papers/Revue Canadienne des Slavistes* 49, no. 1–2 (2007): 87–110; Alexei Miller, *The Ukrainian Question. The Russian Empire and Nationalism in the 19th Century*, (Budapest: CEU Press, 2003); David Saunders, 'Russia and Ukraine under Alexander II: The Valuev Edict of 1863', *The International History Review* 17, no. 1 (1995): 23–50.

12 More on Chykalenko in Inna Starovoitenko, *Ievhen Chykalenko: liudyna na tli epokhy* (Kyiv: Tempora, 2009).
13 Dmytro Doroshenko, *Istoriia Ukrainy 1917–1923 rr.*, 2 vols. (1930; repr., Kiev: Tempora, 2002), 1: 29.
14 Pavlo Tychyna, 'Autobiografia', in *Sovetskie Pisateli. Avtobiohrafii v dvukh tomakh* (Moscow: Gosudarstvennoe Izdatel'stvo Khudozhestvennoi Literatury), vol. II, 505.
15 Tychyna, *Tvory*, vol. 12, Part 1, 8–10.
16 Tychyna *Avtobiografia*, in *Tvory*, vol. 8.1, 9.
17 For summaries of the historiography of the Ukrainian revolution see: John-Paul Himka, 'The National and the Social in the Ukrainian Revolution: The Historiographical Agenda', *Archiv Für Sozialgeschichte* 34 (1994): 95–110; Christopher Gilley, 'Untangling the Ukrainian Revolution', *Studies in Ethnicity and Nationalism* 17, no. 3 (2017): 326–38. For the most complete studies of the period in English see: John Reshetar, *The Ukrainian Revolution, 1917–1920: A Study in Nationalism* (Princeton: Princeton University Press, 1952) and Taras H. Hunczak (ed.), *The Ukraine, 1917–1921: A Study in Revolution* (Cambridge, MA: Harvard Ukrainian Research Institute, 1977); for contemporary historical accounts see: Pavlo Khrystiuk, *Zamitky i materiialy do istorii ukrains'koi revoliutsii*, 4 vols. (Vienna: Institut sociologique ukrainien, 1921–1922); Dmytro Doroshenko, *Istoriia Ukrainy 1917–1923 rr.*, 2 vols. (1930; repr., Kiev: Tempora, 2002); Volodymyr Vynnychenko, *Vidrodzhennia Natsii*, 3 vols. (Kyiv: Dzvin, 1991, [1920]). For a historical overview in Ukrainian see: V. Soldatenko, *Ukraina v revoliutsiinu dobu: istorychni ese-khroniky*, 4 vols. (Kyiv: Svitohliad, 2008–10); V. Smolii et al., *Narysy istorii ukrains'koi revoliutsii 1917–1921 rokiv*, 2 vols. (Kyiv: Naukova dumka, 2011–12).
18 *Kievlianin*, 3 March 1917.
19 *Kievlianin*, 5 March 1917.
20 Mykola Borovs'kyi, 'Natsionalno-sotsialni perehrupuvannia liudnosti Kyeva u porevoliuciinykh chasakh', in *Kyiv Ta Yoho Okolycia v Istorii ta Pamiatkah* (Kiev: DVU, 1926), 433–9; On Ukrainians in Russian Kiev see: Michael F. Hamm, *Kiev. A Portrait, 1800–1917* (Princeton: Princeton University Press, 1993).
21 V. Verstiuk, 'Sklad i struktura Ukrains'koi Tsentral'noi Rady', *Problemy vyvchennia istorii Ukrains'koi revoliutsii 1917–1921 rokiv*, 4 (2009): 27; V. Koroliv-Staryi, 'Tsentral'na Rada (zhadka)', *Tryzub*, 16 (1927), 21.
22 Ievhen Chykalenko, *Spohady (1861–1907)* (Kyiv: Tempora, 2011), 238.
23 Doroshenko, *Istoriia Ukrainy*, 1:52

24 *Kievskaia Mysl'*, 5 March 1917. Also in: V. Verstiuk (ed.), *Ukrains'kyi natsional'no-vyzvol'nyi rukh. Berezen'-lystopad 1917 roku: Dokumenty i materialy* (Kyiv: Vydavnytstvo Oleny Telihy, 2003), 37–8.
25 'Do Ukrains'koho narodu', *Nova Rada*, 1917, 25 bereznia. Also in: V. Verstiuk et al. (eds.), *Ukrains'ka Tsentral'na Rada. Dokumenty i materialy* (Kyiv: Naukova Dumka, 1996), 1, 38–9.
26 O. Stanimir, *Moia uchast' u vyzvol'nykh zmahanniakh 1917–1920 rr.* (Toronto, 1966), 16.
27 *Kievskaia Mysl'*, 16 March 1917.
28 *Kievskaia Mysl'*, 18 March 1917; Verstiuk, *Ukrains'ka Tsentral'na Rada*, 1: 48–9.
29 *Kevskaia Mysl'*, 19 March 1917; 21 March 1917.
30 Mykhailo Hrushevs'kyi, 'Spomyny', *Kyiv*, 8 (1989), 143.
31 Ibid.
32 Quote from Shkandrij, *Modernists, Marxists*, 20.
33 Tychyna, *Tvory*, vol. 12, Part 1, 10–11.
34 *Kievskaia Mysl'*, 7 April 1917.
35 *Visti z Ukrains'koi Tsentral'noi Rady*, 3 April (1917); Verstiuk, *Ukrains'ka Tsentral'na Rada*, 1: 54.
36 On the All-Ukrainian Military Congress see: Volodymyr Vynnychenko, *Vidrodzhennia Natsii* (Kyiv: Dzvin, [1920]), 139–45; *Visti z Ukrains'koi Tsentral'noi Rady*, 7 May 1917.
37 'Povidomlennia tsentral'noi Rady pro khid perehovoriv z Tymchasovym Uriadom Rosii', Verstiuk, *Ukrains'ka Tsentral'na Rada*, 1: 92–3.
38 *Kievskaia Mysl'*, 3 June 1917.
39 'Pershyi Universal Ukrains'koi Tsentral'noi Rady', in Verstiuk, *Ukrains'ka Tsentral'na Rada*, 1: 101–5; Excerpts in English in Hunczak, *Ukraine, 1917–1921*, 382.
40 'Universal', *Kievskaia Mysl'*, 13 June 1917; 'Eshche ob Universale', *Kievskaia Mysl'*, 15 June 1917; 'Universal i ispolnitel'nyi komitet', *Kievskaia Mysl'*, 17 June 1917; 'Uzurpatory vlasti', *Kievskaia Mysl'*, 18 June 1917; 'O heneral'nom sekretariate tsentral'noi rady', *Kievskaia Mysl'*, 22 June 1917.
41 See: Vynnychenko, *Vidrodzhennia*, 275–8.
42 'Druhyi Universal Ukrains'koi Tsentral'noi Rady', in Verstiuk, *Ukrains'ka Tsentral'na Rada*, 1: 164–8; Hunczak, *Ukraine*, 382.
43 *Visti z Ukrains'koi Tsentral'noi Rady*, 10 June 1917; Verstiuk, *Ukrains'ka Tsentral'na Rada*, 1: 163–4; Kievskaia Mysli, 9 July 1917. On the negotiations between the Rada leadership and the Provisional Government in the summer of 1917 see: Reshetar, *The Ukrainian Revolution*, 55–77.
44 'Vidozva Kraiovoho komitetu okhorony revoliutsii v Ukraini vid 27.10.1917', in Verstiuk, *Ukrains'ka Tsentral'na Rada*, 1: 364–5.
45 'Vidozva Heneral'noho Sekretariatu do hromadia, uriadovykh i hromads'kykh ustanov', in Verstiuk, *Ukrains'ka Tsentral'na Rada*, 1: 390–1.
46 'Tretii Universal Ukrains'koi Tsentral'noi Rady' in Verstiuk, *Ukrains'ka Tsentral'na Rada*, 1: 398–401; Hunczak, *Ukraine*, 382.
47 For the law on national-personal autonomy see: Verstiuk, *Ukrains'ka Tsentral'na Rada*, 2:99–101. The Rada's executive body, a General Secretariat, included a separate General Secretary for Inter-Nationality Affairs (*Heneral'nyi sekretar mizhnational'nykh sprav*), headed by Iefremov and later Oleksandr Shul'hyn. On Rada's approach to Ukraine's national minorities see: Matityahu Mintz, 'The Secretariat of Internationality Affairs (*Sekretariiat Mizhnatsional'nykh Sprav*) of

the Ukrainian General Secretariat (1917–1918)', *Harvard Ukrainian Studies* 6, no. 1 (1982): 25–42; R. Simonenko, 'National'no-kul'turnaia avtonomiia na Ukraine v 1917–1918 godakh', *Voprosy istorii* 1 (1997): 50–63.
48 'Postanova Ukrains'koi Tsentral'noi Rady shchodo zatverdzhennia zakonu pro vybory do Ukrains'kykh ustanovchykh Zboriv, 11 ta 16 lystopada 1917', in Verstiuk, *Ukrains'ka Tsentral'na Rada*, 1: 412.
49 *Kievskaia Mysl'*, 10 November 1917.
50 Mykyta Shapoval, *Velyka Revoliutsiia* (Prague: Vil'na Spilka, 1928), 35.
51 Valerii Soldatenko, *Ukraina v Revoliutsiinu Dobu* (Kyiv: Svitohliad, 2010), vol. 1, 151–2. On the soviets in Ukraine and their diverse political allegiance in 1917 see: Iurii Hamrets'kyi, *Rady robitnychykh deputativ Ukrainy v 1917 rotsi (period dvovladdia)* (Kyiv, Naukova Dumka, 1966); Iurii Hamretsky, 'Bilshovyky ta ikhni politychni protivnyky na Ukraini v 1917 r.', *Ukrainsky istorychnyi zhurnal*, 11 (1987): 64–79; Iurii Hamrets'kyi et al., *Rady Ukraiany v 1917 r. Lypen'-hruden' 1917 r.* (Kyiv, Naukova Dumka, 1974).
52 *Shestoi s'ezd RSDRP (bol'shevikov) avgust 1917 goda. Protokoly* (Moscow: Gospolitizdat, 1958), 205.
53 *Kievlianin*, 25 July 1917.
54 Borovs'kyi, *Natsionalno-sotsialni perehrupuvannia liudnosti*, 433–9.
55 For more on the social and ethnic composition of Kyiv before 1917 see Serhiy Bilenky, *Imperial Urbanism in the Borderlands: Kyiv, 1800–1905* (Toronto: University of Toronto Press, 2018), 239–75.
56 Steven L. Guthier, 'The Popular Base of Ukrainian Nationalism in 1917', *Slavic Review* 38, no. 1 (1979): 37.
57 Table 2.1. Votes for the Constituent Assembly, November 1917 (totals by region) in Jeremy Smith, *Red Nations. The Nationalities Experience in and after the USSR* (Cambridge, Cambridge University Press, 2013), 23–4.
58 *Kievlianin*, 25 July 1917. Nonetheless, it must be admitted that the Central Rada's legitimacy beyond Kyiv was precarious at best. It had little control over rural regions and little contact with the local authorities there. See: Doroshenko, *Istoriia Ukrainy*, 1: 115–16. The electoral success of the UPSR in November 1917 can be attributed to their agrarian programme. Overall, as the most recent studies of Ukraine's peasantry in the revolutionary period suggest, the majority of peasants remained indifferent to nationalist slogans, and prioritized their economic needs, at the same time identifying themselves mostly with their village community rather than with any nation or class. See: Mark R. Baker, *Peasants, Power, and Place: Revolution in the Villages of Kharkiv Province, 1914–1921* (Cambridge, MA: Harvard University Press, 2016), esp. 77–89; and Guthier, *The Popular Base*.
59 'Manifest k ukrainskomu narody', *Dekrety Sovetskoi Vlasti*, vol. 1, (Moscow: Moscow, Institut marksizma-leninizma pri TsK KPSS, 1957), 178–9.
60 'Materialy i dokumenty z'iizdu robitnychykh, selians'kykh i soldats'kykh deputativ Ukrainy, 4–6 grudnia 1917', in Verstiuk, *Ukrains'ka Tsentral'na Rada*, 1: 502–12; The rejection of the Ultimatum: 'Vidpovid' Heneral'noho Sekretariatu na manifest radnarkomu. 5 grudnia 1917', ibid., 512–14.
61 'The Fourth Universal', in Hunczak, *Ukraine*, 382–3.
62 Valerii Smolii, *Istoriia Ukrainy* (Kyiv: Al'ternatyvy, 1997), 230; Serhy Yekelchyk, *Ukraine: Birth of a Modern Nation* (New York: Oxford University Press, 2007), 73.
63 'Pokhoron studentiv-sichovykiv', *Nova Rada*, 7 (20) March 1918, 2.

64 Tychyna, 'On the Anniversary of Kruty (In Memory of the Thirty) (Deep in the Mound of Askold)', *Zhinochyi Svit=Woman's World* 25.1, no. 289 (1974): 17.
65 For more on the German interests and alliances in Ukraine see: Frank Golczewski, *Deutsche und Ukrainer 1914-1939* (Paderborn: Schöningh, 2010).
66 More on the history of the Hetmanate: Reshetar, *The Ukrainian Revolution*, 149-51; Taras Hunczak, 'The Ukraine under Hetman Pavlo Skoropadsky', in Hunczak, *Ukraine*, 61-81; Mark von Hagen. '"I Love Russia, and/but I Want Ukraine," or How a Russian General Became Hetman of the Ukrainian State, 1917-1918', *Journal of Ukrainian Studies* 29, no. 1-2 (2004): 115-48. For the first-hand account of the events see: Pavlo Skoropads'kyi, *Spohady (kinets' 1917-hruden' 1918)*, ed. Iaroslav Pelens'kyi (Kiev; Philadelphia: Instytut ukrains'koi arkheohrafii ta dzhereloznavstva im. M.S. Hrushevs'koho NAN Ukrainy et al., 1995).
67 Paul Robert Magocsi, *A History of Ukraine: The Land and Its Peoples* (Toronto: Toronto University Press, 2010), 519.
68 Tel'niuk, *Pavlo Tychyna*, 87-8.
69 Luckyj, *Literary Politics*, 27.
70 Shkandrij, *Modernists, Marxists*, 21.
71 *Muzahet: Misiachnyk Literatury i Mystetstva*, 1-3 (1919).
72 On *neoklasyky* see: Viktor Domontovych, 'Bolotiana Lukroza. Spomyny', Viktor Domontovych, *Divchynka z Vedmedykom* (Kyiv: Krytyka, 1999), 261-300.
73 Oleh Ilnytzky, 'The Modernist Ideology and Mykola Khvyl'ovyi', *Harvard Ukrainian Studies* 15, no. 3/4 (1991): 257-62; Shkandrij, *Modernists, Marxists*, 20.
74 Iurii Lavrinenko, 'Literatura Vitaizmu, 1917-1933', in Lavrinenko, *Rozstriliane Vidrodzhennia*, 941.
75 Luckyj, *Literary Politics*, 121.
76 Serhii Iefremov, *Istoriia Ukrains'koho Pys'menstva* (Kyiv: Femina, 1995), 483.
77 Oleksander Leites, *Renesans Ukrains'koi Literatury* (Kharkiv: DVU, 1925), 15.
78 Iurii Sherekh, 'Trends in Ukrainian Literature under the Soviets', *The Ukrainian Quarterly* 2 (1948): 152.
79 Ibid., 102.
80 Biletskyi, *Dvadtsiat' Rokiv*, 25.
81 M. Halahan, *Z moikh spomyniv (1880-ti-1920 r.)* (Kyiv: Tempora, 2005), 337.
82 'Deklaratsiia Fraktsi Nesalezhnykh', in *Chervonyi Prapor* (Kyiv), 22 January 1919.
83 Mykhailo Tkachenko, *Borot'ba* (Vienna), 7-8 April 1920.
84 On the Ukrainian Marxists' critique of Lenin's Bolshevism as a form of imperialism see: Velychenko, *Painting Imperialism and Nationalism Red*.
85 'Iedyne Natsional'ne Vyzvolennia', *Borot'ba* (Kyiv), 20 February 1919.
86 'Do Nashoi Taktyky', *Borot'ba* (Kyiv), 13 August 1919.
87 Iurii Shapoval, *Oleksandr Shums'kyi. Zhyttia, dolia, nevidomi dokumenty: doslidzhennia, arkhivni materialy* (Kyiv; Lviv: Ukraina moderna; Ukrains'ki propilei, 2017), 85.
88 H. Donets (ed.), *Spivets' Novoho Svitu: Spohady pro Pavla Tychynu* (Kyiv: Dnipro, 1971), 54.
89 Semen Shakhovs'kyi, *V Maisterni poetychnoho slova* (Kyiv: Derzhlitvydav, 1958), 46-50; Iurii Smolych, *Moi suchasnyky* (Kyiv: Radians'kyi Pys'mennyk, 1978), 327.
90 The name of the Soviet Republic in Ukraine changed from Ukrainian People's Republic of Soviets (adopted by the First All-Ukrainian Congress of Soviets in December 1917), Ukrainian Soviet Republic, proclaimed on 19 March 1918 and Ukrainian Socialist Soviet Republic, declared on 10 March 1919.

91   It was similar to *L'Internationale* in Arkadii Kots' translation that was used as a defacto anthem of Soviet Russia. See: Tel'niuk, *Pavlo Tychyna*, 108-9.
92   Tel'niuk, *Pavlo Tychyna*, 109-110.
93   Tychyna, *Iz Shchodennykovykh Zapysiv*, 260.
94   It is believed that Tychyna's wife, Lidiia Paparuk (1900-75) was in charge of the way Tychyna was presented in the press and scholarship. She carefully went through all volumes of memoirs and published primary sources to make sure that the legacy of Tychyna would not be challenged or questioned.
95   Tychyna, *Tvory*, vol. 11, 13.
96   Quote from Oleh S. Ilnytzkyj's *Ukrainian Futurism, 1914-1930. A Historical and Critical Study* (Cambridge MA: Harvard University Press, 1998), 32.
97   Novychenko, *Poeziia i Revoliutsiia*, 14.
98   Ievhen Sverstiuk, 'Proshchannia z Madonnoiu', Ievhen Sverstiuk, *Bludni Syny Ukrainy* (Kyiv: Znannia, 1993).
99   Lavrinenko, *Literatura Vitaizmu*, 950.
100 Vasyl' Ellan-Blakytnyi, 'Pavlo Tychyna (Shkitz)', in Ellan-Blakytnyi, *Tvory* (Kyiv: Derzhlitvydav, 1958), vol. 2, 77.
101 *Zhovten'. Zbirnyk Prysviachenyi Rokovynam Proletars'koi Revoliutsii* (Kharkiv: Vseukrlitkom, 1921), cover page.
102 Tychyna, *Tvory*, vol. 11, 33.
103 Myron Stepniak, 'Do Problem Poetyky Pavla Tychyny', *Chervonyi Shliakh* 11-12 (1930): 107.
104 Shakhovs'kyi, *V maisterni*, 1958, 55.
105 Bilets'kyi, *Dvadtsiat' Rokiv*, 27-8.
106 Pavlo Tychyna, *V kosmichnomu orkestri* (1923).
107 Volodymyr Iurynets', 'Zhovtneva literatura v marksysts'komu osvitlenniu', *Bil'shovyk Ukrainy* 4-5 (1926): 148.
108 Iefremov, *Istoriia Pys'menstva*, 483.
109 Tychyna, *Tvory*, vol. 11, 15.
110 Stanislav Tel'niuk, '*Molodyi ia, molodyi*'. *Poetychnyi Svit Pavla Tychyna. 1906-1925* (Kyiv: Dnipro, 1990), 397. For an overview of the events see: Orlando Figes, *A People's Tragedy: The Russian Revolution 1891-1924* (London: Jonathan Cape, 1996), 698.
111 Lynne Viola, *Peasant Rebels under Stalin: Collectivization and the Culture of Peasant Resistance* (New York: Oxford University Press, 1999), 48.
112 The Sovnarkom Decree on 'Suppression of Hostile Newspapers', *Izvestiia*, 27 October 1917, no. 209, 1917, 2. Also in Robert V Daniels (ed.), *A Documentary History of Communism* (Burlington: University of Vermont Press, 1993), 65.
113 See: Olena Koliastruk, *Intelligentsia USRR v 1920-ti Roky: Povsiakdenne Zhyttia* (Kharkiv: Rarytety Ukrainy, 2010); Chapter 3, 'Realii zhyttia intelihentsii USRR 1920-kh rr.: vid normatyvnoi do ekstremal'noi povsiakdennosti'.
114 Vladimir Vernadskii, *Dnevniki. 1917-1921* (Kyiv: Naukova Dumka, 1994), 178; 180.
115 *Tsentral'nyi Derzhavnyi Arkhiv-Muzei Literatury i Mystetstva Ukrainy* (TsDAMLMU), f.542, op.1, spr.45, ark.228.
116 Domontovych, *Bolotiana Lukroza*.
117 Tychyna, *Iz Shchodennykovykh Zapysiv*, 23.
118 Ibid., 27.
119 On the Bolshevik attitude towards the old intelligentsia during the civil war period see, for example: Read, *Culture and Power*; Ihor Kazanin, *Zabytoe budushchee: Sovetskaia vlast'*

i rossiiskaia inteligentsiia v pervoe posleoktiabr'skoe desiatiletie (Volgograd: Volgogradskii Gosudarstvennyi universitet, 2001); Koliastruk, *Intelligentsia USRR v 1920-ti Roky.*
120 Iu. Kondufor (ed.), *Kul'turne Budivnytstvo v Ukrains'kii RSR. 1917–27: Zbirnyk documentiv i materialiv* (Kyiv: Naukova Dumka, 1979), 157–8.
121 Read, *Culture and Power*, 65.
122 O. Koliastruk, 'Diial'nist' Vseukrains'koho komitetu spryiannia vchenym u 20-ti roky XX st'., *Intelihentsiia i Vlada* 13 (2008): 105.
123 For the memoirs on intellectual life in Kyiv in the early 1920s see, e.g. Iurii Klen, *Spohady pro neoklasykiv* (Munchen: Ukrains'ka vydavnycha spilka, 1947); Vira Aheeva (ed.), *Kyivs'ki neoklasyky. Ukrains'ki memuary* (Kyiv: Fakt, 2003); Viktor Domontovych, *Bolotiana Lukroza*.
124 Pavlo Tychyna, *Podorozh iz Kapeloiu Stetsenka. Shchodennyk* (Kyiv: Radians'kyi Pys'mennyk, 1982).
125 *Visti*, 18 February 1921.
126 Tychyna, *Tvory*, vol. 12, Part 2, 369.
127 Sheila Fitzpatrick, 'The Civil War as a Formative Experience', in *Bolshevik Culture: Experiment and Order in the Russian Revolution*, ed., Abbott Gleason et al. (Bloomington: Indiana University Press, 1985), 66–7.
128 Tychyna, *Tvory*, vol. 11, 19.
129 Tychyna, *Tvory*, vol. 11, 38.
130 Tychyna, *Tvory*, vol. 11, 39.
131 E.g. Tel'niuk, *Mistyfikatsiia Poeta*; Iarovyi, *Poet na Perehresti Pohliadiv*; Tarnavs'kyi, *T. S. Eliot i Pavlo Tychyna*; Novychenko, *Tychyna i Ioho Chas*.
132 O. Sharvarok, 'Dvi Doli – Odna Tragediia. Pavlo Tychyna – Ievhen Malaniuk: Dialoh bez Vidstani, Rozmova Cherez Tlumachiv', *Kyiv* 11 (1993): 127–30.
133 Koshelivets', *Suchasna Literatura*, 85.
134 Mykola Khyl'ovyi, Lysty do Zerova in Khyl'ovyi, *Tvory u dvokh tomakh*, vol. 2, 843 (italics mine).

Chapter 2

1 Khyl'ovyi, *Lysty do Zerova*, 840.
2 Khvyl'ovyi, *Kratkaia Biografiia*, 830.
3 Ibid., 830.
4 Khvyl'ovyi, *Lysty do Zerova*, 852.
5 Khvyl'ovyi, *Kratkaia Biografiia*, 832.
6 Ibid., 833; Hryhorii Kostiuk, 'Mykola Khvyl'ovyi: Zhyttia, Doba, Tvorchist'', in Khvyl'ovyi, *Tvory u p'iat'okh tomakh*, vol. 1, 30.
7 O. Gan [Pavlo Petrenko], *Trahediia Mykoly Khvyl'ovoho* ([s.l.], 1947), 19.
8 Khvyl'ovyi, *Uryvok z avtobiografii*, 106–8.
9 *Shestoi s"ezd* RSDRP, 207.
10 On the separate peace negotiations see: Oleh S. Fedyshyn, *Germany's Drive to the East and the Ukrainian Revolution, 1917–1918* (New Brunswick, NJ: Rutgers University Press, 1971), 60–86; Borislav Chernev, *Twilight of Empire: The Brest-Litovsk Conference and the Remaking of East-Central Europe, 1917–1918* (Toronto: University of Toronto Press, 2017), 126–38.
11 Magocsi, *A History of Ukraine*, 515–16.

12 'The Resolution of the First KP(b)U Meeting', in Ravich-Cherkasskii, *Istoria Kommunisticheskoi Partii*, 203.
13 The name was changed to the Ukrainian Soviet Socialist Republic in 1937. Holubnychy, *Outline History*, 70.
14 M. Donii, *Bol'shevitskie organizatsii Ukrainy v period podgotovki i provedeniia Velikoi Oktiabr'skoi sotsialisticheskoi revoliutsii: mart-noiabr' 1917 g.: sbornik dokumentov i materialov* (Kiev, Gospolitisdat, 1957), 82–3.
15 Valerii Soldatenko, *Ukraina v Revoliutsiinu Dobu*, vol. 2, 132.
16 Khvyl'ovyi, *Kratkaia Biografiia*, 834.
17 Ibid.
18 Ibid.
19 Quote from Velychenko, *Painting Imperialism and Nationalism Red*, 124.
20 'The Resolution of the First KP(b)U Meeting', in Ravich-Cherkasskii, *Istoria Kommunisticheskoi Partii*, 220–1.
21 V. Lenin, 'Telehrama Kh. Rakovs'komu', in Lenin, *Povne zibrannia tvoriv*, vol. 50 (Kyiv: Politvydav, 1975), 282, 283.
22 'The draft of the Constitution of Soviet Ukraine', in *III Vseukrains'kyi z"izd Rad (6–10 bereznia 1919). Stenohrafichnyi zvit* (Kharkiv: Vydannia tsentral'noho arkhivnoho upravlinnia URSR, 1932).
23 'Rezoliutsiia TsK RKP(b) o Sovetskoi Vlasti na Ukraine', in Lenin, *Polnoie Sobraniie sochinenii* (Moskva: Izdatelstvo Politicheskoi Literatury, 1970), vol. 39, 334–7; Ravich-Cherkasskii, *Istoria Kommunisticheskoi Partii*, 226–2.
24 Khvyl'ovyi, *Kratkaia Biographia*, 832.
25 Ibid, 833.
26 Ibid, 832.
27 Kostiuk, *Mykola Khvyl'ovyi*, 32.
28 Petro Shyhymaga, 'Fakty do Biohrafii Mykoly Khvyl'ovogo', in Khvyl'ovyi, *Tvory u p'iat'okh tomakh*, vol.5, 117.
29 Khyl'ovyi, *Lysty do Zerova*, 840–1
30 Khvyl'ovyi, *Kratkaia Biografiia*, 836.
31 On the 'war scare' in the second half of the 1920s see: John P. Sontag, 'The Soviet War Scare of 1926–27', *The Russian Review* 34, no. 1 (1975): 66–77; Lennart Samuelson, *Plans for Stalin's War Machine: Tukhachevskii and Military Economic Planning, 1925-1941* (Basingstoke; London: Macmillan Press, 2000); Timothy Snyder, *Sketches from a Secret War: A Polish Artist's Mission to Liberate Soviet Ukraine* (New Haven: Yale University Press, 2005); Peter Whitewood, 'The International Situation: Fear of Invasion and Growing Authoritarianism', in *The Fate of the Bolshevik Revolution. Illiberal Liberation, 1917–1941*, ed. Lara Douds, James R. Harris and Peter Whitewood. 173–186. (London: Bloomsbury, 2020).
32 M. Dolenho, 'Kyiv ta Kharkiv – Literaturni Vzaiemovidnoshennia', *Chervonyi Shliakh* 6 (1923), 151.
33 Results of the elections in 1917: http://www.electoralgeography.com/ru/countries/r/russia/1917-uchreditelnoe-sobranie-russia.html (accessed 12 April 2019).
34 Dolenho, *Kyiv ta Kharkiv*, 151–7.
35 Dolenho, *Kyiv ta Kharkiv*, 151.
36 Maik Iohansen, 'Knyha pro Misto Industrial'nykh Veletniv', *Literaturna hazeta*, 12 June 1936, 2; Iaryna Tsymbal, '"Kharkivs'kyi Tekst" 1920-kh: Obirvana Sproba', *Ukrains'ka Literature XX Stolittia. Literaturoznavchi Obrii* 18 (2010): 54–61.
37 Shkandrij, *Modernists, Marxists*, 25.

38 Khyl'ovyi, *Lysty do Zerova*, 844.
39 Lenin, *Collected Works*, vol. 30 (Moscow: Progress Publishers, 1965), 291–7.
40 Ibid.
41 'Memorandum Ukrains'koi Komunistychnoi partii (borot'bystiv) Vykonavchomu Komitetovi II-ho Komunistychnogo Internatsionaly (serpen' 1919 r.)', in Taras Hunchak and Roman Sol'chanyk (eds.), *Ukrains'ka Suspil'no-Politychna Dumka v 20 Stolitti* (Munich: Suchasnist', 1983), vol. 1, 427–37.
42 Quote from Ivan Majstrenko, *Borot'bism: A Chapter in the History of Ukrainian Communism* (New York: Research Program on the U.S.S.R., 1954), 184–518.
43 Minutes of the Second Congress of the Communist International: https://www.marxists.org/history/international/comintern/2nd-congress/ch10a.htm (accessed 12 April 2019).
44 Quote from *Arkhiv Rozstrilianoho Vidrodzhennia: Materialy Arkhivno-Slidchykh Sprav Ukrains'kykh Pys'mennykiv 1920–1930-h Rokiv*, ed. L. Ushkalov, O. Ushkalov (Kyiv: Smoloskyp, 2010), 23.
45 Quote from Shapoval, *Oleksandr Shums'kyi*, 83.
46 Vladimir Lenin, 'Proekt rezoliutsii ob ukrainskoi partii Borot'bistov', in Lenin, *Polnoie Sobraniie*, vol. 40, 122.
47 Ibid.
48 Maistrenko, *Istoriia Komunistychnoi Partii*, 74; Popov, *Narys Istorii Komunistychnoii Partii*, 219.
49 *Chetverta konferentsiia Komunistychnoi partii (bil'shovykiv) Ukrainy. 17–23 bereznia 1920 r. Stenohrama* (Kyiv: Al'ternatyvy, 2003), 441–2.
50 The official daily of the TsK KP(b)U *Kommunist* appeared in Russian until 15 June 1926. Afterwards, it started to be published in Ukrainian with the name changed to *Komunist*.
51 In October 1922–March 1924, the *Narkomos* was headed by the Bolshevik Volodymyr Zatons'kyi.
52 Khvyl'ovyi, *Kratkaia Biographia*, 835.
53 Koriak, *Ukrains'ka Literatura*, 62.
54 Mally, *Culture of the Future*, 61–2.
55 For more on the role of the Proletkult in literature see: Lynn Mally, *Blueprint of a New Culture: A Social History of the Proletkult, 1917–1921* (Berkley: University of California Press, 1990); Dobrenko, *Aesthetics of Alienation*; Mark Slonim, *Soviet Russian Literature. Writers and Problems* (New York: Oxford University Press, 1964), 32–40.
56 'Kyivs'kyi Proletkul't', *Mystetstvo*, 1 (1919), 33–4; Iaroslav Hordyns'kyi, *Literaturna Krytyka Pidsoviets'koi Ukrainy* (Munchen: Otto Sagner Verlag, 1985 [1939]), 36.
57 Luckyj, *Literary Politics*, 36–7; Hordyns'kyi, *Literaturna Krytyka*, 36.
58 'Vseukrains'kyi Proletkul't', *Shliakhy Mystetstva*, 1 (1921), 62.
59 Quote from Ilnytzkyj, *Ukrainian Futurism*, 39.
60 Hnat Mykhailychenko, 'Proletars'ke Mystetstvo (Tezy na Dopovidi Vseukrlitkomu)', Leites, Iashek, *Desiat' rokiv*, vol. II, 27–8.
61 'Nash Universal', *Zhovten'*, 1 (1921), 1–2.
62 'Dekliaratsiia Vseukrains'koi Federatsii Proletars'kyh Pys'mennykiv i Myttsiv', *Arena*. 1 (1922): 3–4.
63 *Arena*, 1 (1922).
64 Khvyl'ovyi stems from 'khvylia', a wave in Ukrainian.
65 Quote from Leites, Iashek, *Desiat' rokiv*, vol. 1, 526.

66 Doroshkevych, *Pidruchnyk*, 304.
67 Mykola Khvyl'ovyi, 'Vstupna novela', in Khvyl'ovyi, *Tvory u p'iat'okh tomakh*, vol. 1, 112-13.
68 Ibid., 112-13.
69 Khvylovy, 'Quo Vadis?', in Khvylovy, *Cultural Renaissance*, 70 (here and thereafter all the citations are from Khvylovy, *Cultural Renaissance*, if not stated otherwise).
70 Due to those changes, Khvyl'ovyi's manner is sometimes compared with the endeavour of the Russian OPOJAZ group (Society for the Study of Poetic Language (*Obshchestvo izuchenija POeticheskogo JAZyka*) which was a prominent group of linguists and literary critics (included Viktor Shklovsky, Boris Eikhenbaum, Osip Brik and Yury Tynianov) active in St. Petersburg between 1916 and the early 1930s, and especially with Boris Pilnyak (see Alexander Kratochvil, *Mykola Chvyl'ovyi: Eine Studie zu Leben und Werk* (Munchen: Verlag Otto Sagner, 1999), 154-67). Kostiuk argues that this manner of Khvylovy was not an adoption from Russian colleagues but his own search for the new forms, since the same attempts to crack traditional narration were also made by French writer André Gide in his novel *Les Faux-monnayeurs (The Counterfeiters)* written in 1925. See: Kostiuk, *Mykola Khvyl'ovyi*, 51-2.
71 Grabowicz, *Symbolic Autobiography*, 165-80.
72 Dolly M. Ferguson, 'Lyricism and the Internal Landscape, in the Early Creative Prose of Mykola Khvyl'ovyi', *Canadian Slavonic Papers/Revue Canadienne des Slavistes* 18, no. 4 (1976), 429.
73 Here and hereafter the year of the first publication is indicated.
74 Thanks to this feature, the fictional plots of Khvyl'ovyi's stories were repeatedly used to fill in the gaps in his biography and hence compensate for the paucity of primary sources. See, for example: Zadesnians'kyi, *Shcho nam dav*, 30-1; Ihor Bondar-Tereshchenko, *U Zadzerkalli 1910-1930-h Rokiv* (Kyiv: Tempora, 2009), 287.
75 On youth after the revolution see: Matthias Neumann, '"Youth, It's Your Turn!": Generations and the Fate of the Russian Revolution (1917-1932)', *Journal of Social History* 46, no. 2 (2012): 273-304; Anne E. Gorsuch, *Youth in Revolutionary Russia: Enthusiasts, Bohemians, Delinquents* (Bloomingtonand Indianapolis: Indiana University Press, 2000); also idem. 'Soviet Youth and the Politics of Popular Culture during tbe NEP', *Social History* 17, no. 2 (1992): 189-201; 'NEP be Damned! Young Militants in the 1920s and the Culture of Civil War', *Russian Review* 56, no. 4 (1997): 564-80; Also: Diane Koenker, 'Urban Families, Working-Class Youth Groups, and the 1917 Revolution in Moscow', in *The Family in Imperial Russia: New Lines of Historical Research*, ed. David L. Ransel (Urbana: University of Illinois Press, 1978), 280-304; also numerous contributions in the edited volume by Corinna Kuhr-Korolev et al., *Sowjet Jugend 1917-1941: Generationzwischen Revolution und Resignation* (Essen, Klartext Verlag, 2001); Matthias Neumann, *The Communist Youth League and the Transformation of the Soviet Union, 1917-1932* (London; New York: Routledge, 2011).
76 With his early writings, Khvyl'ovyi was often placed on par with his Russian contemporary Boris Pilnyak (1884-1938), the author of the unorthodox chronicles of the Bolshevik Revolution *Golyi God* [Naked Year, 1922]. To define a revolution, Pilnyak used a metaphor of a blizzard, an unplanned, uncontrollable element valued for its purgative function. Later on, Pilnyak resented the bureaucratization and centralization of the party, and sympathized with those left aside during the post-revolutionary transformation as is presented in his later prose *Povest' o*

nepogashenoi lune [Tale of the Unextinguished Moon] (1926) and Krasnoie derevo [*Mahogany*] (1927). On Pilnyak see: Evelyn Bristol, 'Boris Pil'nyak', *The Slavonic and East European Review* 41, no. 97 (1963): 494–512; Philip Maloney, 'Anarchism and Bolshevism in the Works of Boris Pilnyak', *Russian Review* 32, no. 1 (1973), 43–53; Vera T. Reck, *Boris Pil'niak: A Soviet Writer in Conflict with the State* (Montreal: McGill-Queen's University Press, 1975). The myth of the revolution and the civil war in Russian literature was developed by a 'leftist' group of writers that included, Aleksandr Fadeev, Aleksandr Serafimovich, Nikolai Tikhonov, Konstantin Trenev, Mikhail Svetlov and others. The revolution features prominently in the works of Aleksandr Block, Isaak Babel, Boris Pasternak and Mikhail Sholokhov.

77 Khvylovy, 'Puss in Boots', in *Stories from the Ukraine*, ed. G. Luckyj (New York: Philosophical Library, 1960), 16.
78 Khvyl'ovyi, 'Synii Lystopad', in Khvyl'ovyi, *Tvory u p'iat'okh tomakh*, vol. 1, 230–1 (here and thereafter all the citations are from Khvyl'ovyi, *Tvory u p'iat'okh tomakh*, if not stated otherwise).
79 Khvyl'ovyi, *Chumakivska Komuna*, vol. 1, 250.
80 Khvyl'ovyi, *Syliuety*, vol. 1, 212.
82 Khvyl'ovyi, *Zhyttia*, vol. 1, 118.
81 Khvyl'ovyi, *Shliahetne Hnizdo*, vol. 1, 216–17.
83 Khvyl'ovyi, *Liliuli*, vol. 1, 373–4.
84 Quote from Leites, Iashek, *Desiat' Rokiv*, vol. 1, 527.
85 Khvyl'ovyi, *Lehenda*, vol. 1, 319.
86 Khvyl'ovyi, *Zhyttia*, 119.
87 Khvyl'ovyi, *Liluli*, 372.
88 Khvyl'ovyi, *Sentymental'na Istoriia*, vol. 2, 214.
89 Neumann, *Youth, It's Your Turn!*, 281–2.
90 Khvylovy, Sentimental Tale, in *Stories from Ukraine*, 77.
91 Khvylovy, 'My self (Romantica)', in *Stories from Ukraine*, 34.
92 Ibid., 33.
93 Ibid., 31.
94 Ibid., 33.
95 Ibid., 38.
96 Ibid., 31.
97 Ibid., 45.
98 Ibid., 35.
99 Ibid., 54.
100 Ibid., 52.
101 *Literatura. Mystetstvo. Nauka.* 10 (1923), 4.
102 See: V. Pliushch, *Pravda pro Khvyl'ovizm* (Munich: Spilka Vysvolennia Ukrainy, 1954); Zadesnians'kyi, *Shcho Nam Dav Mykola Khvyl'ovyi*.
103 This short story, first published in the collection 'R. XV. Rik Zhovtnevoi Revolutsii XV' (1932), has not been included in any of Khvyl'ovyi's Selected Works. It was republished for the first time in Kharkiv Almanac *Ukrains'kyi Zasiv* 1, no. 13 (1994): 47–74.
104 *Spadshchyna. Literaturne Dzhereloznavstvo*, vol. VII, 206–7.
105 *Puss in boots*, 18–19; *Kit u chobotia*, 155.
106 William G. Rosenberg, 'Introduction', in *Russia in the Era of NEP*, 3.
107 From Lenin's letter to Sokolov, May 16, 1921. Available online: https://www.marxists.org/archive/lenin/works/1921/may/16mfs.htm (accessed 12 February 2020)

108 Khvyl'ovyi, *Zaulok*, vol. 1, 328.
109 Preliminary Draft Resolution of the Tenth Congress of the R.C.P.On Party Unity; https://www.marxists.org/archive/lenin/works/1921/10thcong/ch04.htm (accessed 12 February 2020).
110 Stanislav Kul'chyts'kyi, *Komunism v Ukraini; Pershe Desiatylittia (1919-1928)* (Kyiv: Osnovy, 1996), 248.
111 Khvyl'ovyi, *Kolonii, Vily*, vol. 1, 125.
112 Khvyl'ovyi, *Shliahetne Hnizdo*, vol. 1, 218.
113 Mykola Khvylovy, 'Woodcocks', in *Before the Storm: Soviet Ukrainian Fiction of the 1920s*, ed. G. Luckyj (Ann Arbor: Ardis, 1986), 19.
114 Khvyl'ovyi, *Na Hlukhim Shliakhu*, vol. 1, 183.
115 Khvyl'ovyi, *Yurko*, 1 vol. 1, 70.
116 Ibid., 177.
117 Khvyl'ovyi, *Sentymental'na Istoriia*, vol. 2, 192.
118 Khvyl'ovyi, *Synii Lystopad*, vol. 1, 223-4.
119 About suicides in the Soviet Union in the 1920s see, e.g.: Kenneth M. Pinnow, *Lost to the Collective: Suicide and the Promise of Soviet Socialism, 1921-1929* (Ithaca; London: Cornell University Press, 2010); 'Violence against the Collective Self: Suicide and the Problem of Social Integration in Early Bolshevik Russia', in *Histories of Suicide: International Perspectives on Self-Destruction in the Modern World*, ed. John Weaver and David Wright (Toronto: Toronto University Press, 2009), 201-30; Gabor T. Rittersporn, 'Between Revolution and Daily Routine in the Soviet Union in the Interwar Period', in *Sowjet Jugend 1917-1941*, 63-82.
120 Khvyl'ovyi, *Povist' pro Sanatoriinu Zonu*, vol. 2, 92.
121 Khvyl'ovyi, *Zaulok*, 324.
122 Sheila Fitzpatrick, 'The Legacy of the Civil War', in *Party, State, and Society in the Russian Civil War* ed. Diane P. Koenker et al. (Bloomington: Indiana University Press, 1989), 393. Also: Mark von Hagen, 'Soldiers in the Proletarian Dictatorship: From Defending the Revolution to Building Socialism', in *Russia in the Era of NEP*, 156-73.
123 Mattias Neumann, 'Revolutionizing Mind and Soul? Soviet Youth and Cultural Campaigns during the New Economic Policy (1921-8)', *Social History* 33, no. 3 (2008): 262-3.
124 Anatoli Rybakow, *Roman der Erinnerung: Memoiren* (Berlin: Aufbau Verlag, 2001), 16; Quote from Neumann, *Youth, It's Your Turn!*, 282.
125 Vira Aheeva, 'Zaivi liudy' u prozi M.Khvyl'ovoho', *Slovo i Chas* 10 (1990): 3-9.
126 Luckyj, *Literary Politics*, 114.
127 Khvyl'ovyi, *Povist' pro Sanatoriinu Zonu*, 158.
128 Ibid., 163.
129 Khvyl'ovyi, *Na Ozera*, vol. 1, 259.
130 Khvyl'ovyi, *Povist' pro Sanatoriinu Zonu*, 92.
131 Ibid., 146.
132 Gorsuch, *NEP Be Damned!*, 565.
133 Quote from Gorsuch, *NEP Be Damned!*, 564.
134 Khvyl'ovyi, *Povist' pro Sanatoriinu Zonu*, 113.
135 Ibid., 113.
136 Ibid., 133; Similar characters can be found in the prose of A. Liubchenko, *Obraza* [Grudge], 1927; H. Epik, *Nepiia* [NEP-ya], 1930; *Bez Hruntu* [Without Ground], 1931; O. Kopylenko, *Vyzvolennia* [Liberation], 1930.
137 Khvyl'ovyi, *Zaulok*, 322.
138 Khvyl'ovyi, *Syliuety*, 201.

139 Khvyl'ovyi, *Redaktor Kark*, 146.
140 Khvyl'ovyi, *Kit u chobotia*, 155.
141 Khvyl'ovyi, *Kit u chobotia*, 167.
142 Khvyl'ovyi, *Pudel*, vol. 1, 361.
143 Khvyl'ovyi, *Kratkaia Biografiia*, 835.
144 Ibid., 836-7.
145 *Instytut Rukopysu* (IR) F.131, no. 183, ark.1.
146 Leites, *Renesans*, 22; Kratochvil, *Mykola Chvyl'ovyi*, 154-67.
147 Literary critics initially favoured Khvyl'ovyi's devices and regarded them as revolutionary. See: O. Bilets'kyi, 'V shukanniakh novoi povistiars'koi formy', Shliakhy Mystetstva 5 (1923): 62-3; Iu. Mezhenko, 'Tvorchist' M. Khvyl'ovoho,' *Shliakhy mystetstva* 5 (1923): 57-8; O. Doroshkevych, *Istoriia ukrains'koi literatury*, 2nd edn. (Kharkiv: Knyhospilka, 1926) cited in Khvyl'ovyi, *Tvory u p'iatiokh tomakh*, vol. 5, 397, 396; Mykola Chyrkov, 'Mykola Khvyl'ovyi u ioho prozi,' Zhyttia i revoliutsiia 9 (1925): 38. The criticism increased, however. See: F. Iakubovs'kyi, 'Do kryzy v ukrains'kii khudozhnii prozi,' Zhyttia i revoliutsiia 1 (1926): 43; S. Shchupak 'Pro sprobu stvoryty nove literaturne ob'iednannia,' Proletars'ka pravda, 25 October 1925, cited in Khvyl'ovyi, *Tvory u p'iatiokh tomakh*, vol. 5, 189; V. Iurynets', 'M. Khvyl'ovyi iak prozaik,' Chervonyi shliakh 1 (1927): 257-8, 267-8; P. Khrystiuk, 'Sotsial'ni motyvy v tvorchosti M. Khvyl'ovoho,' Chervonyi shliakh 4-5 (1924): 256. Similar criticism was made about Pilnyak. See: Mihaychuk, *The Role of the 1920s Form and Content Debate*, f58; Peter A. Jensen, *Nature as Code. The Achievements of Boris Pilnjak, 1915-1924* (Copenhagen: Rosenkilde & Bagger, 1979) 98-106.
148 *XII s'iezd RKP(b). 17-25 aprelia 1923 g. Stenohraficheskii otchet* (Moscow: Politizdat, 1968), 572.
149 Khvyl'ovyi, *Redaktor Kark*, vol. 1, 149.
150 Iurii Lavrinenko, 'Dukh Nespokoiu,' in Lavrinenko, *Zrub i Parosty*, (Munich: Suchasnist', 1971), 53.
151 Khyl'ovyi, *Lysty do Zerova*, 853.
152 IR, F.131, nos 183-95; *Spadshchyna. Literaturne Dzhereloznavstvo*, VIII (2013), 252-3.
153 IR, F. 131, nos 183-95; *Spadshchyna. Literaturne Dzhereloznavstvo*, VIII (2013), 255.
154 Arkadii Liubchenko, 'Spohady pro Khvyl'ovoho: Iz Zapysnoi Knyzhky', in *Vaplitians'kyi Zbirnyk*, ed. Iu. Luts'kyi (Oakwill: Mosaika, 1977), 37.
155 IR, F.131, nos 183-195; *Spadshchyna. Literaturne Dzhereloznavstvo*, VIII (2013), 255.
156 Khyl'ovyi, *Lysty do Zerova*, 835.
157 Khvyl'ovyi, *Arabesky*, vol. 1, 414 (italics in the original).

Chapter 3

1 Stalin, *National Factors*, 193.
2 Martin, *Affirmative Action Empire*, 13.
3 'Postanova VUTsVK i RNK USRR pro zakhody zabezpechennia rivnopravnosti mov i dopomohu rozvytkovi ukrains'koi movy', in *Natsional'ni Vidnosyny v Ukraini v XX st.: Zbirnyk Dokumentiv i Materialiv*, ed. Mai Panchuk et al. (Kyiv: Naukova Dumka, 1994), 107.
4 Quote from Martin, *Affirmative Action Empire*, 5.

5   Hélène Carrère d'Encausse, *The Great Challenge: Nationalities and the Bolshevik State, 1917-1930* (New York: Holmes & Meier, 1992), 194.
6   Mykola Stsibors'kyi, *Ukraina i natsional'na polityka Sovietiv* (New York: [s.l.], 1938), 37.
7   M. Frolov, *Kompartiino-Radians'ka Elita v USRR (1917-1922 rr): Stanovlennia i Funktsionuvannia* (Zaporizhzhia: Prem'ier, 2003), 30.
8   Valerii Smolii et al. *Ukrainizatsiia 1920-30-kh rokiv: Peremodumovy, Zdobutky, Uroky* (Kyiv: NAN Ukrainy, 2003), 62.
9   'Politika partii po natsional'nomu voprosu', *Pravda*, 10 October 1920; J. Stalin, *Sochineniia* (Moscow: OGIZ, 1947), vol. 4, 358.
10 *Visti VUTSVK*, 14 April 1923.
11 George Liber, *Soviet Nationality Policy, Urban Growth, and Identity Change in the Ukrainian SSR 1923-1934* (Cambridge University Press, 2002), 7; *Total Wars and the Making of Modern Ukraine, 1914-1954* (Toronto: Toronto University Press, 2016).
12 Pauly, *Breaking the Tongue*, 5.
13 Vladimir Lenin, 'Rech' na Vserossiiskom soveshchanii Politprosvetov gubernskikh i uezdnykh otdelov narodnogo obrazovaniia 3 noiabria 1920', in Lenin, *Polnoie Sobranie*, vol. 21, 402.
14 O. Kruchek, *Stanovlennia derzhavnoi polityky URSR u galuzi natsional'noi kul'tury (1920-23)* (Kyiv: NAN Ukrainy, 1996), 11.
15 Volodymyr Zatons'kyi, *Natsional'na problema v Ukraini* (Kharkiv: DVU, 1927).
16 Mykola Skrypnyk, 'Druha kul'turna p'iatyrichka ta zavdannia osvity', Mykola Skrypnyk *Vybrani tvory* (Kyiv: Ukraina, 1991), 524.
17 Bohdan Krawchenko, *Social Change and National Consciousness in Twentieth-Century Ukraine* (Basingstoke: Macmillan, 1986), 23.
18 'Rezoliutsiia TsK RKP(b) o Sovetskoi Vlasti na Ukraine', 334-7.
19 Lenin's speech on the Second All-Russia Congress of Political Education Departments, in Lenin, *Polnoie Sobraniie*, vol. 44, 174-5.
20 On the links to the Vperedist platform in the formulation of Proletkul't's mission see: Mally, *Culture of the Future*.
21 Fitzpatrick, *The Cultural Front*, 2.
22 Selected publication on the issue: A. Chuchmar'ov, 'Sotsiolohichnyi metod v istorii i teorii literatury', *Chervonyi shliakh* 7-8 (1926): 208-32; A. Shamrai, 'Formal'nyi metod v literaturi', *Chervonyi shliakh* 7-8 (1926): 233-66; V. Boiko, 'Formalizm i marksyzm', *Chervonyi shliakh* 11-12 (1926): 141-65; Oleksii Poltorats'kyi, *Literaturni zasoby. Sproba sotsiolohichnoi analizy* (Kharkiv: DVU, 1929); also his 'Kriz' formal'nu metodu', *Nova heneratsiia* 2 (1927): 38-43; V. Koriak, 'Forma i zmist', *Shliakhy mystetstva* 2-4 (1922): 40-7; Iurii Mezhenko, 'Na shliakhakh do novoi teorii', *Chervonyi shliakh* 2 (1923): 199-210; V. Hadzins'kyi, 'Shche kil'ka sliv do pytannia "formy i zmistu"', *Chervonyi shliakh* 4-5 (1923): 173-9; B.Iakubs'kyi, *Sotsiolohichnyi metod u pys'menstvi* (Kyiv: Slovo, 1923); Samiilo Shchupak, 'Osnovni problemy mystetstva v pohliadakh radians'kykh marksystiv', *Zhyttia i revoliutsiia* 6 (1926): 53-61; 7 (1926): 58-70; Bilets'kyi, *V shukanniakh novoi povistiars'koi formy*, 56-63. George Mihaychuk. 'The Role of the 1920s Form and Content Debate in Ukraine', *Canadian Slavonic Papers/Revue Canadienne des Slavistes* 37, no. 1/2 (1995): 107-26; Maguire, *Red Virgin Soil*; Terry Eagleton, *Marxism and Literary Criticism* (Berkeley: University of California Press, 1976).
23 Maguire, *Red Virgin Soil*, 281-2; Mihaychuk, *The Role of the 1920s Form and Content Debate*, 118.
24 Mihaychuk, *The Role of the 1920s Form and Content Debate*, 107-8.

25 Katerina Clark and Evgeny Dobrenko (eds.), *Soviet Culture and Power: A History in Documents, 1917-1953* (New Haven: Yale University Press, 2007), 33.
26 Ibid.
27 Quote from Luckyj, *Literary Politics*, 50.
28 Leites, Iashek, *Desiat' rokiv*, vol. I, 8.
29 Leites, Iashek, *Desiat' rokiv*, vol. II, 75.
30 B. Iakubs'kyi, 'Zhyttia molode: Sproba literaturnoi kharakterystyky 'kyivs'kykh pluzhan', *Chervonyi Shliakh* 9 (1925), 159.
31 *Pluh*, Almanakh, 1 (1924), 215; 'Platforma Ideolohichna i Khudozhnia Spilky Selians'kykh Pys'mennykiv "Pluh"', in Leites, Iashek, *Desiat' Rokiv*, vol. II, 76.
32 Serhii Pylypenko, 'Nashi "hrikhy"', *Pluzhanyn*, 4–5 (1926), 1–2.
33 James Mace, *Communism and the Dilemmas of National Liberation* (Cambridge, MA: Harvard UP, 1983), 126–9.
34 *Pluh*, Almanakh, 1 (1924), 211–12.
35 Leites, Iashek, *Desiat' rokiv*, vol. II, 374.
36 Blakytnyi, 'Bez manifestu', in Leites, Iashek, *Desiat' rokiv*, vol. II, 84–5.
37 Vasyl Ellan-Blakytnyi, *Tvory* (Kyiv: Derzhlitvydav, 1958), vol. 2, 143; Shkandrij, *Modernists, Marxists*, 37.
38 Blakytnyi, *Bez manifestu*, 95.
39 Literaturnyi dodatok do Visti VUTsVK, 36 (1926), quote from Luckyj, *Literary Politics*, 51.
40 George Liber, 'Language, Literacy, and Book Publishing in the Ukrainian SSR', 1923-1928, *Slavic Review* 41, no. 4 (1982): 680–1.
41 *Hrono* – literary group in Kyiv formed in 1920 and headed by Valerian Polishchuk.
42 Tychyna, *Iz Shchodennykovykh*, 36.
43 Tychyna, *Tvory*, vol. 11, 12–13.
44 Tychyna, *Iz Shchodennykovykh*, 43.
45 Quote from Ilnytzkyj, *Ukrainian Futurism*, 33.
46 Tychyna, *Iz Shchodennykovykh*, 290–1.
47 Tychyna, *Tvory*, vol.11, 28.
48 Tychyna, *Iz Shchodennykovykh*, 37.
49 Tel'niuk, *Molodyi ia, Molodyi*, 372.
50 See Tetiana Sosnovs'ka, '"Iak ia Zheniu – Svoho Brata –Riatuvav u Cheka". Malovidome z Zhyttia Poeta Pavla Tychyna', *Z arkhiviv VUCHK, GPU, NKVD, KGB*, 1 (1994), 166.
51 See Sosnovs'ka, *Iak ia Zheniu*, 163–7.
52 *Chervonyi Shliakh*, 2 (1923), 258.
53 Luckyj, *Literary Politics*, 121.
54 Stus, *Fenomen doby*, 71.
55 Iefremov, *Istoriia Pys'menstva*, 482.
56 Mykola Zerov, 'Viter z Ukrainy' (Tretia Knyzhka Tychyny)', in Zerov, *Tvory* (Kyiv: Dnipro, 1990), vol. 2, 494.
57 Ibid, 499.
58 Quote from R. Kharchuk, 'Zmina oblychchia: PavloTychyna', *Dyvoslovo* 2 (2011): 58–62.
59 Pavlo Tychyna, 'Lysty do M. K. Zerova, M. M. Mohylians'koho', *Radians'ke Literaturoznavstvo*, 11 (1971): 75–6.
60 Leites, *Renesans*, 17.

61 *Haluzevyi derzhavnyi arkhiv Sluzhby Bezpeky Ukrainy* (HDA SBU), F.13, spr.370, t.13, ark.310; Nadiia Myronets', 'Ukrains'ka Revoliutsiia v Doli i Tvorchosti Pavla Tychyny', in Nadiia Myronets', *Dzherela Istorychnoi Pam'iati* (Kyiv: NAN Ukrainy, 2008), 129–31.
62 *Komunist*, 21 February 1924, also quoted in Novychenko, *Poeziia i Revoliutsiia*, 124.
63 Koriak, *Ukrains'ka Literatura*, 60.
64 Leites, *Renesans*, 17.
65 Volodymyr Koriak, 'Pershe Desiatyrichchia', in Koriak, *V Boiah*, 250.
66 Tychyna, *Lysty*, 76.
67 Mykhailo Dolenho, *Krytychni Etiudy* (Kharkiv: DVU, 1925), 18.
68 On *Krasnaia Nov'* see: Maguire, *Red Virgin Soil*.
69 Clark, *Quiet Revolution*, 217.
70 The political significance of *Chervonyi Shliakh* was emphasized in the letter of Iu. Ozers'kii (Secretary of the Journal) to O. Dosvitniia, IR, F.255, od.zb. 3; the letter from Hryn'ko to P. Ladan, *Tsentral'nyi Derzhavnyi Arkhiv Vyshchykh Orhaniv Vlady ta Upravlinnia* (TsDAVOU), F.487, op.1, apr.12, ark.53.
71 'Vid redaktsii', in *Chervonyi Shliakh* 1 (1923), v–vi.
72 Mace, *Communism and Dilemmas*, 91.
73 Oleksandr Shums'kyi, 'Stara i Nova Ukraina', *Chervonyi shliakh* 2 (1923): 91–110.
74 See: Volodymyr Vynnychenko, 'Znamenna Podiia', *Nova Ukraina* 6 (1923): 14.
75 Vynnychenko, *Znamenna Podiia*, 9.
76 Nevertheless, in the second half of the 1920s, Vynnychenko himself considered returning to Soviet Ukraine and joining the Soviet government. See: Chris Gilley, 'Volodymyr Vynnychenko's Mission to Moscow and Kharkov', *The Slavonic and East European Review* 84, no. 3 (2006): 508–37.
77 Materialy do biohraphii, in *Z arkhivu Tychyny*, 40–1.
78 Serhii Iefremov, *Shchodennyky*, 1923–1929 (Kyiv: Biblioteka hazety Rada, 1997), 201.
79 For instance, Malaniuk, *Ryl's'kyi v P'iatdesiatylittia*.
80 'Pavlo Tychyna, Skovoroda. Review by S. Rasnyts'kyi', *Nova Ukraina* 10 (1923): 178–9; *Literatura, Nauka, Mystetstvo* 10, no. 278 (1923): 4.
81 Ievhen Malaniuk, 'Naprovesni [Vyimky z bloknota literatura]', *Ukrains'kyi Holos*, 8 January 1922, 1–2; *Literaturna Ukraina*, 6 February 1997.
82 O. Sharvarok, 'Dvi Doli – Odna Tragediia. Pavlo Tychyna – Ievhen Malaniuk: Dialoh bez Vidstani, Rozmova Cherez Tlumachiv', *Kyiv* 11 (1993): 127–30.
83 Hryden', (Mukhin, Mykhailo) 'Z mynulykh Lit', *Suchasnist'*, 8 (1968), 40–1.
84 Ibid.
85 Iefremov, *Shchodennyky*, 201.
86 Letters to Paparuk, in Tychyna, *Tvory*, V.12, Part 1, 43; 44.
87 Lyst do A. Liubchenka, ibid, 46.
88 Ievhen Malaniuk, 'Kinets' rosiis'koi literatury', Ievhen Malaniuk, *Knyha Sposterezhen'* (Toronto: Homin Ukrainy, 1962), vol. 1, 354–5.
89 Ievhen Malaniuk, 'Buriane polittia (1917–27)', in *Knyha sposterezhen'*, vol. 1, 22.
90 Malaniuk, *Buriane polittia*, 16.

Chapter 4

1 Ravich-Cherkasskii, *Istoria Kommunisticheskoi Partii*, 5.
2 Borovs'kyi, *Kyiv Ta Yoho Okolycia*; Hamm, *Kiev. A Portrait*.

3   Krawchenko, *Social Change*, 101.
4   On social and ethnic composition of Ukraine's urban areas see: Liber, *Soviet Nationality Policy*; Krawchenko, *Social Change*.
5   Dmitrii Lebed', 'Nekotoryie voprosy partiinoho s'ezda', *Kommunist*, 27 March 1923.
6   Pauly, *Breaking the Tongue*, 139.
7   Ibid., 140.
8   I follow Pauly's understanding of the category of 'Ukrainizer' to reference individuals employed as instructors in Ukrainian-studies courses, public advocates of the expansion and deepening of Ukrainian-language use (who sometimes published in the pedagogical press), inspectors, *Narkomos* section heads and leaders who were tasked with the promotion of Ukrainian-language use, party and Komsomol activists and their patrons in the KP(b)U leadership. See: Pauly, *Breaking the Tongue*, f3, 360.
9   *Natsional'ni Vidnosyny*, 106–9.
10 'Postanova Politbiuro TsK KP(b)U "Pro Ukrainis'ki Khudozhni Ugrupuvania"', in *Kul'turne Budivnytstvo v Ukrains'kii RSR*, 387–9; 'Resolution of the Politbureau of the Central Committee of the CP(b)U on Ukrainian Literary Groupings, 1925', Appendix C in Luckyj, *Literary politics*, 277–8.
11 Ibid.
12 'On Party Policy in the Sphere of Literature', in *Soviet Culture and Power*, 40–4.
13 A reference to the Italian city Urbino which became the predecessor of the Renaissance culture.
14 Smolych, *Rozpovid' pro Nespokii*, 37.
15 Leites, Iashek, *Desiat' Rokiv*, vol. II, 323–56.
16 These pamphlets appeared in Khvyl'ovyi, *Tvory u P'iat'okh Tomakh*, vol. 4; For English translations see: Khvylovy, *The Cultural Renaissance in Ukraine*; Mykola Khvyl'ovyi, 'Ukraina chy Malorosiia?' TsDAHOU, F.1, op.20, spr. 2257; The first publication of the pamphlet was in *Vitchyzna*, 1 (1990): 181–8; 2 (1990): 168–78; and *Slovo i Chas*, 1 (1990): 7–31. 'Ukraina chy Malorosiia?' in Khvyl'ovyi, *Tvory u dvokh tomakh*, vol. 2, 576–621; Excerpts in English: Khvylovy, 'Ukraine or Little Russia', in Khvylovy, *Cultural Renaissance*, 225–32.
17 *Shliakhy Rozvytku Suchasnoi Literatury: Dysput 24 Travnia 1925 r.* (Kyiv, 1925); In the course of the debate, Zerov published three essays: 'Ievropa – prosvita – osvita – liknep', 'Evraziis'kyi Renesans i Poshekhons'ki Sosny' and 'Zmishchena Pozytsiia' in Mykola Zerov, *Do Dzherel* (Krakiv; Lviv: Ukrains'ke Vydavnytstvo, 1943).
18 Iurii Shevel'ov, 'Lit Ikara (Pamflety Mykoly Khvyl'ovoho)', in Iurii Shevel'ov, *Vybrani Pratsi: Literaturoznavstvo* (Kyiv: Kyievo-Mohylians'ka Akademiia, 2009), Kn.II, 289.
19 *Shliakhy Rozvytku*, 43.
20 H. Iakovenko, 'Pro Krytykiv i Krytyku v Literaturi', *Kul'tura i Pobut* 17 (1925): 25 April 1925.
21 Ibid.
22 One of such writers was a charater Stepan Radchenko aptly presented by Valerian Pidmohyl'nyi in his novel *Misto* (1928).
23 Khvylovy, *Quo Vadis*, 53.
24 Mykola Khvylovy, 'Thoughts against the Current'. in Khvylovy, *Cultural Renaissance*, 109.
25 This concept was developed in his pamphlet 'On "Satan in a Barrel," Graphomaniacs, Speculators and Other *Prosvita* Types', the first pamphlet in his polemic cycle *Kamo hriadeshy*, 69–84; for an English translation see: *Quo Vadis?*, 43–54.
26 Khvylovy, *Thoughts against the Current*, 138.

27 'Protokol Narady Pys'mennykiv m. Kharkova', in *Dzherela do Istorii Vaplite*, ed. Iu. Luts'kyi (Munchen: Ukrains'ka Literaturna Hazeta, 1956), 3–4.
28 Luckyj, *Literary politics*, 275–6.
29 *Dzherela do Istorii Vaplite*, 3.
30 See: Liubchenko, *Spohady pro Khvyl'ovoho*, 44.
31 O. Dosvitnii, 'Do rozvytku pys'mennyts'kykh syl', *Vaplite, Zoshyt Pershyi* (1926): 9, quote from Iurii Luc'kyi, *Vaplitians'kyi Zbirnyk* (Edmonton: CIUS; Mosaika, 1977), 10–11.
32 Ibid., 4.
33 Khvylovy, *Thoughts against the Current*, 139.
34 *Vaplitians'kyi Zbirnyk*, 10.
35 On Ukrainian Futurism see: Ilnytzkyj's *Ukrainian Futurism*; Myroslava Mudrak, *The New Generation and Artistic Modernism in the Ukraine* (Ann Arbor: UMI Research Press, 1986).
36 Hryn, *Executed Renaissance*, 73.
38 Ibid., 130.
37 Khvyl'ovyi, *Dumky proty Techii*, 110.
39 Khvylovy, *Thoughts against the Current*, 120.
40 Ibid., 120 (italics in original).
41 Ibid.
42 Oswald Spengler, *Der Untergang des Abendlandes. Umrisse einer Morphologie der Weltgeschichte*, B.1 (Wien: Braumüller, 1918). The first Russian translation: Osvald Shpengler, *Zakat Evropy. Ocherki Morfologii Mirovoi Istorii*, t.1 (Moscow-Petersburg: Izdatel'stvo L. D. Frenkelia, 1923).
43 Khvylovy, *Quo Vadis*, 91–2.
44 Khvylovy, *Thoughts against the Current*, 124.
45 Ibid., 124 (italics in original).
46 Khvylovy, *Apologists of Scribbling*, 222.
47 Khvylovy, *Ukraine or Little Russia*, 229.
48 Khvylovy, *Apologists of Scribbling*, 223–4.
49 Khvylovy, *Ukraine or Little Russia*, 228–9.
50 Khvyl'ovyi attacked the Russian Proletkult and those lliterary groupings affiliated with it in his third letter to the literary youth, entitled 'On Waters of Demagogy or the Real Address of Ukrainian Voronsyism, Free Competition, VUAN, etc.', in *Quo Vadis?*, 77–93.
51 On Khvyl'ovyi's approach to 'cultural decolonisation' see: Hryn, *Executed Renaissance*.
52 IR, F.131, nos 183–195; *Spadshchyna. Literaturne Dzhereloznavstvo*, VIII (2013), 251.
53 Ibid.
54 Mykola Khvyl'ovyi, 'Pil'niak, "Slovobludie" i "Niekii" Retsensent', *Kul'tura i Pobut*, 11 (1924), 3.
55 IR, F.131, nos 183–195; *Spadshchyna. Literaturne Dzhereloznavstvo*, VIII (2013), 251.
56 Khvylovy, *Apologists of Scribbling*, 223–4.
57 Mace, *Communism and Dilemmas*, 141.
58 Zerov, *Do Dzherel*, 256.
59 *Kul'tura i Pobut*, 30 April 1925.
60 Quote from Shkandrij, *Modernists, Marxists*, 54.
61 *Shliakhy Rozvytku*, 7.
62 Khvylovy, *Quo Vadis?*, 45–6.
63 Khvylovy, *Thoughts against the Current*, 124.
64 Khvylovy, *Apologists of Scribbling*, 222.

65 See, footnote 1 in Shevel'ov *Lit Ikara*, 309–310; V. Holubenko, 'Khvyl'ovyi i Shpenhler', *Suchasnist'* 5 (1963): 53–70.
66 Khvylovy, *Ukraine or Little Russia*, 231.
67 Ibid., 231.
68 Stalin, *The Foundation of Leninism* (1924), in *Essential Texts on Marxism-Leninism*, ed. J. F. Pointon (Springfield, MO: Pravda-Media, 2017), vol. 1, 307.
69 E.g. the position of M. N. Roy, who advocated that capitalism could be shaken only by the support of the national-liberation movements in the colonies. See: Demetrio Boersner, *The Bolsheviks and the National and Colonial Question (1917–1928)* (Geneva: Libraire E. Droz, 1957).
70 Khvylovy, *Quo Vadis*, 67.
72 Ibid., 85.
71 Khvylovy, *Ukraine or Little Russia*, 232.
73 Ibid., 229.
74 Khvylovy, *Quo Vadis*, 70.
75 Shevel'ov, *Lit Ikara*, 309.
76 Khvylovy, *Quo Vadis*, 70.
77 Mykola Skrypnyk, *Do Teorii Borot'by Dvokh Kul'tur* (Kharkiv: DVU, 1926), 25–6.
78 IR, F.131, spr. 183, ark.2
79 Hryn, *Executed Renaissance*, 78–9.
80 Khvylovy, *Quo Vadis*, 65–6.

Chapter 5

1 Khvylovy, *Apologists of Scribbling*, 224.
2 Ibid., 222.
3 Mykola Khvyl'ovyi, *Ukraina chy Malorosiia?* (Kyiv: Ukrains'ka Pres-Hrupa, 2012), 30.
4 'Tezy chervnevoho plenumu TsK KP(b)U 1926 roku "Pro pidsumky Ukrainizatsii", *Komunist*, 15 June 1926; *Stenograficheskii Otchet Plenuma TsK KP(b)U*, TsDAHOU, F.1, op.1, spr.208, reprinted in *Budivnytstvo radians'koi Ukrainy*, Vyp. 1 (Kharkiv: DVU, 1929), 58–65; Leites, Iashek, *Desiat' rokiv*, vol. II, 293–303.
5 See Tables 5.5–5.88 in Liber, *Soviet Nationality Policy*, 93–6.
6 M. Frolov, *Kompartiino-Radians'ka Elita v Ukraini (1923–1928 Rr): Osoblyvosti Isnuvannia ta Funktsionuvannia* (Zaporizhzhia: Prem'ier, 2004), 588–9.
7 TSDAHO, F.1, op 20, spr.2631, ark.115.
8 Shapoval, *Oleksandr Shums'kyi*, 123.
9 O. Rubliov and Iu. Cherchenko, 'Stalinshchyna i dolia zakhidnoukrains'koi intellihentsii', *Ukrains'kyi Istorychnyi Zhurnal* 1 (1991): 8–9.
10 'Vidozva do ukrains'koi radians'koi intelihentsii ta vsioho radians'koho suspil'stva, zachytana razom z pryvitanniam na Vseukrains'kii partkonferentsii KP(b)U', *Visti VUTsVK*, 18 May 1924.
11 Rubliov, Cherchenko, *Stalinshchyna i dolia*, 9–10.
12 While many Ukrainians did indeed move to Soviet Ukraine from Poland encouraged by *Ukrainizatsiia*, they were unaware of being under constant surveillance of the GPU. See: Olga Bertelsen and Myroslav Shkandrij, 'The Secret Police and the Campaign against Galicians in Soviet Ukraine, 1929–34', *Nationalities Papers: The Journal of Nationalism and Ethnicity* 42, no. 1 (2014): 37–62.

13 Shapoval, *Oleksandr Shums'kyi*, 127-9.
14 Luckyj, *Literary politics*, 88.
15 'Doklad o Predvaritel'nykh Itogah Ukrainizatsii v Sviazi s Zaiavleniem Tovarishcha Shumskoho, Zaslushanyie na Zasedanii Politbiuro TsK KP(b)U ot 12-20 Maia, 1926 goda', TsDAHOU, F.1, op.6, spr.88, ark.110-38.
16 TsDAHOU, F.1, op.20, Spr.2248; On Khvyl'ovyi and Shums'kyi, ark.1-7; Fist publication of the letter was in Stalin, *Sochineniia* (Moscow: OGIZ, 1948), vol. VIII, 149-54; Also in Khvyl'ovyi, *Tvory u p'iat'okh tomakh*, vol. 5, 485-89; For an English translation see: Luckyj, *Literary Politics*, 66-8.
17 Luckyj, *Literary politics*, 68.
18 Ibid., 67.
19 Ibid, 67-8.
20 The bibliography of the polemics during the Literary Discussion see: Leites, Iashek, *Desiat' rokiv*, vol. II, 323-39; Khvyl'ovyi, *Tvory u p'iat'okh tomakh*, vol. 5, 231-360.
21 O. Shums'kyi, 'Promova na chervnevomu plenumi TsK KP(b)U', *Budivnytstvo radians'koi Ukrainy*, 28.
22 L. Kaganovich, 'Promova na chervnevomu plenumi TsK KP(b)U', *Budivnytstvo radians'koi Ukrainy*, 40-54.
23 'Pro pidsumky ukrainizatsii', *Budivnytstvo radians'koi Ukrainy*, 64.
24 O. Zatons'kyi, 'Pro pidsumky ukrainizatsii. Z dopovidi na chervnevomu plenumi TsK KP(b)U 1926 roku', *Budivnytstvo radians'koi Ukrainy*, 22.
25 Zatons'kyi, *Pro pidsumky ukrainizatsii*, 24; *Stenograficheskii Otchet Plenuma*, ark.45.
26 Ibid.
27 Shums'kyi, *Promova na chervnevomu plenumi*, 25-31.
28 Ibid., 27.
29 Ibid., 29.
30 Ibid., 29.
31 Ibid., 30.
32 Ibid., 30.
33 Ibid., 30.
34 *Stenograficheskii Otchet Plenuma*, ark.79-zv.-80-zv.
35 Ie. Hirchak, *Na Dva Fronty v Boro'tbi proty Natsionalizmu* (Kharkiv: Proletar, 1932), 50. It must be admitted, however, that already in 1928 Khvyl'ovyi himself labelled 'khvyl'ovism' as 'as a theory of struggle against the KP(b)U, formulated under the ideological pressure of militant Ukrainian fascism and of that urbanised Ukrainian bourgeoisie, who dreams of making Ukraine a great imperialist state.' See: Khvyl'ovyi, 'V iakomu vidnoshenni do "khvyl'ovizmu" vsi ti...', in Khvyl'ovyi, *Tvory u p'iat'okh tomakh*, vol. 4, 579-94.
36 'Pro pidsumky ukrainizatsii', in *Budivnytstvo radians'koi Ukrainy*, 64.
37 'Pro pidsumky ukrainizatsii', in *Budivnytstvo radians'koi Ukrainy*, Vyp. 1, 58-65; Leites, Iashek, *Desiat' rokiv*, vol. II, 293-303.
38 Vlas Chubar, 'Pro vyvykhy', *Komunist*, 30 May 1926; Also in *Shliakhy rozvytku ukrains'koi proletars'koi literatury* (Kharkiv: Ukrains'kyi robitnyk, 1928), 209-12; Skrypnyk, *Do terorii borot'by*; Zatons'kyi, *Natsional'na problema*.
39 Andrii Khvylia, 'Orhanizator hromads'koi dumky sotsialistychnoi Ukrianiny', in Khvylia, *Iasnoiu dorohoiu (Rik na literaturnomu fronti)* (Kharkiv, 1927), 199-200.
40 *Ukraine or Little Russia*, 227.
41 For the documents illustrating Ukrainian communist position see *Dokumenty Ukrains'koho Komunizmu*, ed. I. Maistrenko (New York: Proloh, 1962 [1928]); For

the English translation see Appendices in Velychenko, *Painting Imperialism and Nationalism Red*.
42 Khvylovy, *Apologists of Scribbling*, 223.
43 This definition was coined by Stalin in his 'Marxism and the National Question', first published in *Prosveshcheniye*, nos 3-5, March-May 1913.
44 *Ukraine and Little Russia*, 228.
45 Ibid., 228.
46 *Ukraina chy Malorosiia*, 31.
47 Khvylovy, *Apologists of Scribbling*, 211.
48 *Ukraine or Little Russia*, 227.
49 Danylenko, *Intelihentsiia i Vlada*, 119.
50 Luckyi, *Literary Politics*, 92-112.
51 Statut Vil'noi Akademii Proletars'koi Literatury VAPLITE, in *Vaplite, Zoshyt Pershyi* (1926), 94-6; Quote from *Vaplitians'kyi zbirnyk*, 255.
52 'Promova L. Kaganovycha na Politbiuro TsK KP(b)U, 20. IX. 1926 r.', *Budivnytstvo radians'koi Ukrainy*, 110.
53 Pavlo Khrystiuk, 'Rets.: Vaplite. Zoshyt pershyi. Kh., 1926', *Chervonyi Shliakh*, 9 (1926): 264-5.
54 *Promova L. Kaganovycha na Politbiuro TsK KP(b)U*, 110.
55 'Resoliutsiia politbiura pro zhurnal Chervonyi Shliakh', in *Budivnytstvo radians'koi Ukrainy*, 114-15.
56 Ibid., 115.
57 Oleksandr Shums'kyi, 'Ideolohichna borot'ba v ukrains'komu kul'turnomu protsesi', *Bil'shovyk Ukrainy*, 2 (1927): 11-25; *Natsional'ni Protsesy v Ukraini*, 2, 86.
58 Ibid., 88.
59 Ibid., 91-2.
60 Ibid., 99-100.
61 In defining the long-term objectives of the Soviet nationality policy, I side with Francine Hirsch and her concept of 'double assimilation'. See: Hirsch, *Empire of Nations*.
62 Tel'niuk, *Pavlo Tychyna*, 173.
63 *Al'manakh VAPLITE*, 1 (1926), 7-11.
64 'XI Kharkivs'ka Okruzhna Konferentsiia KP(b)U. Robota TsKKP(b)U ta Cherhovi Zavdannia Partii. Dopovid' Tov. V. Ia. Chubaria', *Komunist*, 15 January 1927, 2-3.
65 Tel'niuk, *Pavlo Tychyna*, 174.
66 Pavlo Tychyna, 'Lyst do Redaktsii', *Komunist*, 3 February 1927, 6.
67 Ibid.
68 *Komunist*, 3 February 1927.
69 Quote from Volodymyr Panchenko, 'Dyptykh pro Vtrachenu Svobodu', *Naukovi Zapysky NaUKMA. Filolohichni Nauky*, 150 (2013): 59.
70 Pauly, *Breaking the Tongue*, 153, 165.
71 As mentioned by Panas Liubchenko in his speech to the joint TsK and TsKK KP(b) U Plenum in November 1933, *Chervonyi Shliakh*, 10 (1933), 198-99. Also in Ivan Koshelivets', *Mykola Skrupnyk* (Munchen: Suchasnist', 1972), 188-9.
72 The river Zbruch was used as a border between Soviet Ukraine and Western Ukraine that remained under Poland. Quote from Rubliov, Cherchenko, *Stalinshchyna*, 10.
73 Quote from Martin, *Affirmative Action Empire*, 225.
74 'Pro pidsumky ukrainizatsii', in *Budivnytstvo radians'koi Ukrainy*, 64-5.
75 Ibid.

76 Martin, *Affirmative Action Empire*, 87.
77 Until recently, little was known about Shums'kyi life and career after 1927. The recent documentary collection on Shums'kyi fills this gap in the scholarship. See: Shapoval, *Oleksandr Shums'kyi*.
78 Danylenko, *Intelihentsiia i Vlada*, 21.
79 Iurii Shapoval, '"On Ukrainian Separatism" a GPU Circular of 1926', *Harvard Ukrainian Studies* XVIII, no. 3/4 (1994): 209–12.
80 Shapoval, *On Ukrainian separatism*, 292–3.
81 Ibid.
82 Pauly, *Breaking the Tongue*, 249.
83 Shapoval, *On Ukrainian Separatism*, 293.
84 Ibid., 293.
85 Danylenko, *Intelihentsiia i Vlada*, 119; 179.
86 Ibid., 164.
87 On the national component in the repressions of the mid-1920s see: Shkandrij and Bertelsen, *The Soviet Regime's National Operations in Ukraine*.
88 Olena Palko, 'Debating the Early Soviet Nationalities Policy: The Case of Soviet Ukraine, in Lara Douds, James R. Harris and Peter Whitewood (eds.), *The Fate of the Bolshevik Revolution. Illiberal Liberation, 1917–1941*. 157–172. (London: Bloomsbury, 2020).
89 Leites, Iashek *Desiat' Rokiv*, vol. II, 205–6.
90 Ardadii Liubchenko's Literaturnyi Shchodennyk ('A Literary Diary') in *Vaplitians'kyi Zbirnyk*, 251.
91 'Postanova Zagal'nykh Zboriv VAPLITE vid 25. I. 27 r.' in Luts'kyi, *Dzherela do istorii*, 4–5; Lyst do Redaktsii, *Komunist*, 18 March 1927.
92 See: *Vaplitians'kyi Zbirnyk*, 238.
93 Of course, there were other literary organizations active at the time in Soviet Ukraine. Among them were the futurists, united in the organization *Aspanfut* (later renamed *Komunkul't*) and since 1927 – *Nova Heneratsiia*; Lanka in Kyiv; all-Ukrainian union *Pluh*, *Zakhidna Ukraina*, *Avanhard*, *Maisternia revoliutsiinoho slova* and others.
94 Leites, Iashek *Desiat' Rokiv*, vol. II, 230–2.
95 *Vaplitians'kyi zbirnyk*, 238.
96 'Manifest Vseukrains'koho Z'izdu Proletars'kykh Pys'mennykiv', in Leites, Iashek *Desiat' Rokiv*, vol. II, 233–6.
97 Quote from Luckyj, *Literary politics*, 76.
98 'Manifest Vseukrains'koho Z'izdu', in Leites, Iashek, *Desiat' rokiv*, vol. II, 233.
99 On RAPP see Harriet Borland, *Soviet Literary Theory and Practice during the First Five-Year Plan, 1928–32* (New York: Greenwood Press, 1969); E. Brown, *The Proletarian Episode in Russian Literature, 1928–1932* (New York: Octagon Books, 1971).
100 *Budivnytstvo radians'koi Ukrainy*, 115–18; English translation in Luckyj, *Literary politics*, 279–83.
101 'Polityka Partii v spravi Ukrains'koi Khudozhnioi Literatury', *Komunist*, 15 June 1927; Leites, Iashek, *Desiat' rokiv*, vol. II, 306–10; Quote from the English translation in Luckyj, *Literary politics*, 280.
102 Luckyj, *Literary politics*, 280.
103 Ibid., 279.
104 Ibid.
105 Ibid., 281.

106 Ibid., 282.
107 For Khvyl'ovyi's pamphlets from 1927 see: Khvyl'ovyi, *Tvory u p'iat'okh tomakh*, vol. 4, 347–413.
108 Khvyl'ovy, '"Sotsiologichnyi ekvivalent" triokh krytychnykh ohliadiv', Vaplite, 1 (1927), 80–101; Khvyl'ovyi, *Tvory u p'iat'okh tomakh*, vol. 4, 347–75.
109 Ibid., 374.
110 'Nashe siohodni', in Khvyl'ovyi, *Tvory u p'iat'okh tomakh*, vol. 4, 381.
111 Volodymyr Koriak, 'Khvyl'ovistychnyi sotsiolohichnyi ekvivalent', Hart 1 (1927): 74–103.
112 Ibid., 77–8.
113 Ibid., 90.
114 Ibid., 82.
115 Khvyl'ovyi, 'Odvertyi lyst do Volodymyra Koriaka', Vaplite 5 (1927): 158–73; Khvyl'ovyi, *Tvory u p'iat'okh tomakh*, vol. 4, 391–411.
116 Ibid., Khvyl'ovyi, *Tvory u p'iat'okh tomakh*, vol. 4, 393.
117 The review on Hart, 1 (1927): 'Nashe siohodni', Vaplite 3 (1927): 131–40; Khvyl'ovyi, *Tvory u p'iat'okh tomakh*, vol. 4, 377–90.
118 Khvyl'ovyi, *Tvory u p'iat'okh tomakh*, vol. 4, 389, f 1.
119 *Maisternia Revoliutsiinoho Slova* – a literary organization formed in Kyiv in 1927 uniting the writers previously belonging to *Lanka*, among them Antonenko-Davydovych, Ievhen Pluzhnyk, Valetian Pidmohyl'nyi, Hryhorii Kosynka, Todos' Os'machka, Ivan Bahrianyi and others.
120 *Nashe siohodni*, 379.
121 Ibid., 378.
122 Shkandrij, *Modernists, Marxists*, 105.
123 The political sounding of this novel was obvious to its readers. See the evaluation by M.Ohloblin, for example: Ohloblin, *Mykola Khvyl'ovyi*, 65–6. On this also see: P. Sawczak, 'The novelazation of the pamphlet. Aesthetic compromise as argument: Mykola Khvyl'ovyj's Woodcocks', *Journal of Ukrainian Studies* 1–2 (Summer–Winter) (1995): 53–60.
124 Liubchenko, *Spohady pro Khvyl'ovoho*, 35.
125 Mace, *Communism and Dilemmas*, 152; The choice of the protagonists' names is a clear reference to Dostoevsky and his Aglaia Epanchyna (*Idiot*) and Dmitrii Karamazov (*Bratiia Karamazovy*). See: Danylo H. Struk, 'Tupyk or Blind-Alley: "Val'dshnepy" of M. Khvyl'ovyi', *Canadian-American Slavic Studies*, II, 2 (1968), 244.
126 Luckyj, introduction to *Before the Storm*, 10–11.
127 Khvylovy, *Woodcocks*, 63–4.
128 Ibid., 63–4.
129 Ibid., 64.
130 Sawczak, *The Novelazation of the Pamphlet*.
131 Ibid., 55.
132 On those modes see: Myroslav Shkandrij, *Russia and Ukraine. Literature and the Discourse of Empire from Napoleonic to Postcolonial Times* (Montreal: McGill-Queen's University Press, 2001).
133 Khvylovy, *Woodcocks*, 29–30.
134 Andrii Khvylia, *Vid Ukhylu u Prirvu* (Kharkiv: DVU, 1928).
135 Khvylia, *Vid Ukhylu u Prirvu*, 17.
136 Mykola Skrypnyk, *Nasha liteaturna diisnist'* (Kharkiv: DVU, 1928), 18.
137 Khvylia, *Vid ukhvylu*, 12, 13.

138 Ibid., 25, 26.
139 Quote from Shkandrij, *Modernists, Marxists*, 106.
140 Khvylia, *Vid ukhvylu*, 40–1.
141 Ibid., 3.
142 Andrii Khvylia, 'Do Stanu na Literaturnomu Vidtinkovi', TsDAHOU, F.1, op.20, spr.2257, ark.94–7.
143 Shkandrij, *Modernists, Marxists*, 107.
144 'Protokol zahal'nykh zboriv VAPLITe vid 12 sichnia 1928', in *Vaplitians'kyi Zbirnyk*, 238–45.
145 *Vaplitians'kyi Zbirnyk*, 240–1.
146 Ibid., 241.
147 Ibid.
148 Ibid., 242–3.
149 M. Kulish, 'Lyst do redaktsii', *Komunist*, 10 January, 1926. TsDAHOU, F.1, op.20, spr.6218, arl149-157; ark.151.
150 'Rezoliutsia Zagal'nykh Zboriv Vil'noi Akademii Proletars'koi Literatury "VAPLITE" vid 14 sichnia 1928 roku', in Luts'kyi, *Vaplitians'kyi Zbirnyk*, 245–6 (*Highlight* in the original).
151 Borisenok, *Fenomen Sovetskoi Ukrainizatsii*, 187.
152 A decree 'On the Unification of the Soviet Republics of Russia, Ukraine, Latvia, Lithuania, and Belarus for the Struggle against War Imperialism', in *Dekrety Sovetskoi Vlasti*, vol. V: 259–61; A separate agreement between Russia and Ukraine, signed on 28 December 1920 in *Natsional'ni Vidnosyny*, 97–8.
153 Volodymyr Soldatenko, *Nezlamnyi. Zhyttia i smert' Mykoly Skrypnyka* (Kyiv: Knyha Pamiati Ukrainy, 2002), 149–50.
154 Mykola Skrypnyk, 'Desiat' zapovidei kul'turnoho budivnytstva', *Radians'ka Osvita* 12 (1927): 1–2.
155 Shkandrij, *Ukrainian Reading Public*, 163–4.
156 Mykola Skrypnyk, 'Pidsumly "Literaturnoi Dyskusii"', *Bil'shovyk Ukrainy* 1 (1926): 18–36; Here quote from Mykola Skrypnyk, *Statti i Promovy z Natsional'noho Pytannia* (Munich: Suchasnist', 1974 [1930]), 59.
157 Ibid., 60–1.
158 Ibid., 68.
159 Ibid., 69 (italics in the original).
160 Shkandrij, *Modernists, Marxists*, 112.
161 Skrypnyk, *Nasha liteaturna diisnist'*; Mykola Skrypnyk, *Statti i promovy* (Kharkiv: DVU, 1930), vol. 5: Literatura i mystetstvo, 7–29.
162 Skrypnyk, *Nasha literaturna diisnist'*, 9.
163 Ibid., 9.
164 Ibid., 10.
165 Ibid.
166 Ilnytzkyj, *Ukrainian Futurism*, 108. Similarly, the party became impationt with its Russian counterpart RAPP. See: Borland, *Soviet Literary Theory and Practice*; Brown, *The Proletarian Episode*.
167 Skrypnyk, *Nasha literaturna diisnist'*, 16.
168 On publishing and readers' appetites in the 1920s see: Palko, *Reading in Ukrainian*.
169 Iurii Shevel'ov, *Ukrains'ka Mova v Pershii Polovyni Dvadtsiatoho Stolittia (1900–1941). Stan i status* (Munchen: Suschasnist', 1987), 143–4.
170 Ibid.

171 Mykola Skrypnyk, 'Novi Linii u Natsional'no-Kul'turnomu Budivnytstvi', in Skrypnyk, *Statti i Promovy z Natsional'noho Pytannia*, 212.
172 Palko, *Reading in Ukrainian.*
173 Quote from Krawchenko, *Social Change,* 82.
174 Volodymyr Kubijovyč (ed.), *Ukraine: a Concise Encyclopaedia*, vol. 1 (Toronto: Toronto University Press, 1971), 661.

Chapter 6

1 Khvyl'ovyi, *Vstupna novella*, written in 1927 as a foreword to his first volume of *Tvory*, published under Azarkh encouragement. Khvyl'ovyi, *Tvory u p'iat'okh tomakh*, vol. 1, 112.
2 Liubchenko, *Spohady pro Khvyl'ovoho*, 43.
3 Mykola Khvyl'ovyi, 'Lysty', *Spadshchyna. Literaturne Dzhereloznavstvo* VIII (2013): 255.
4 Kratochvil, *Mykola Chvyl'ovyi,* 35.
5 Some insight into his stay there in the letter to Liubchenko, *Vaplitians'kyi Zbirnyk*, 208–10.
6 HDA SBU, Sprava-Formuliar S-183, ark.17–20: Excerpts from the censored letter of Khvyl'ovyi to Ialovyi, dated from 7 February 1928, ark.19.
7 Ibid., ark.19.
8 Based on the resolution of the June 1926 Plenum, Khvyl'ovyi was accused of 'disseminating the ideas of Ukrainian fascism'. See: TsDAHOU fond 1, op. 20, sprava 6218, ark.151.
9 Liubchenko, *Spohady pro Khvyl'ovoho*, 40.
10 Janusz Radziejowski, *The Communist Party of Western Ukraine, 1919–29* (Edmonton: The Canadian Library in Ukrainian Studies, 1983).
11 The letter from Andrii Zhuk to Rrof. Iurii Lutskyi from 11 September 1961, in Khvyl'ovyi, *Tvory u p'iat'okh tomakh*, vol. 5, 85–6.
12 Smolych, *Rozpovid' pro nespokii*, 34.
13 As recalled by the writer and DVU staff member Nytchenko, Ostap Vyshnia once characterized the role and significance of the DVU through a word game. Derzhvydav 'held and pressed' Ukrainian writers (the famous satirist split the word 'Derzhvydav' into two Ukrainian words for to hold (*derzhaty*) and press (*davyty*). See: Dmytro Nytchenko, *Vid Zin'kova do Mel'borna. Iz khroniky moho zhyttia* (Melbourne: Bayda Books, 1990 (*c*. 1944), 89.
14 The letter to Liubchenko, dated from 2 March 1928, *Vaplitians'kyi Zbirnyk*, 210.
15 TsDAMLMU, F.1208, op.1, spr.5: Mykola Khvyl'ovyi, 'Lyst do gazety Komunist'. Also in Khvyl'ovyi, *Tvory u p'iat'okh tomakh*, vol. 4, 571.
16 Ibid., 573.
17 Information gathered from local informers on Khvyl'ovyi and his milieu can be found in the State Political Administration (GPU)'s file on Khvyl'ovyi that has been kept in the archives since the 1930s. The file can be found in *Haluzevyi Derzhavnyi Arkhiv Sluzhby Bezpeky Ukrainy* (HDA SBU) (State Archives Department of the Security Service of Ukraine), Sprave S-183. Those documents were identified and published by the historian Iurii Shapoval and literary scholar Volodymyr Panchenko in 2010. See: Shapoval and Panchenko, *Poliuvannia na 'Val'dshnepa'*. Another collection of similar documents is: Danylenko *Ukrains'ka Intelihentsia i Vlada*.

18 HDA SBU, Spr. S-183, ark.35.
19 Ibid., ark.51.
20 HDA SBU, Spr. S-183, ark.137.
21 Danylenko, *Intelihentsiia i Vlada*, 305.
22 Ibid., 306.
23 Smolych, *Rozpovid' pro Nespokii*, 136.
24 Nonetheless, Khvyl'ovyi authored forewords to Vaplite separate books (as the issues of the periodical were called). Khvyl'ovyi, *Tvory u p'iat'okh tomakh*, vol. 4, 431–7.
25 Halyna Hryn, *Literaturnyi Iarmarok: Ukranian Modernism's Defining Moment*, PhD Thesis University of Toronto, 2005.
26 Smolych, *Rozpovid' pro Nespokii*, 135.
27 Quote from Hordyns'kyi, *Literaturna Krytyka*, 45.
28 *Literaturnyi Iarmarok*, 7 (137) (1929), 5–56.
29 Khvylovy, 'Ivan Ivanovich', in *Stories from Ukraine*, 161–2.
30 Ibid., 172.
31 Ibid., 168–9.
32 Ibid., 184.
33 Ibid., 187.
34 Ibid., 213.
35 Ibid., 208.
36 Its second publication was in Khvyl'ovyi, *Tvory*, vol. 3, Kharkiv, 1930; Third publication, in the German translation of his works, published in Kharkiv, 1931.
37 M. Maiorov, 'Kil'ka sliv pro Ivaniv Ivanovychiv', *Literaturnyi Iarmarok* 7 (1929): 56–9.
38 Kratochvil, *Mykola Chvyl'ovyi*, 214–15.
39 Iurii Boiko (-Blochyn) *Vybrani Pratsi* (Kyiv: Medykom, 1992), 276.
40 Khvylovy, *Ivan Ivanovich*, 167.
41 HDA SBU, S-183, ark.16.
42 Quote from Ilnytzkyj, *Ukrainian Futurism*, 157.
43 Smolych, *Rozpovid' pro Nespokii*, 141.
44 The organization of Komsomol writers *Molodniak* was founded in 1926 with several branches throughout Soviet Ukraine. Among its members were such Soviet writers as Pavlo Usenko, Leonid Pervomais'kyi, Oleksandr Korniichuk, Anatolii Shyian and others. The organization edited the journal of the same name. It existed until 1932 and was disbanded in line with the 1932 resolution 'On the Restructuring of Literary and Artistic Organisations'.
45 *Literatura i Mystetstvo*, no. 6, 9 February 1929.
46 *Literaturna hazeta*, no. 5, 1 March 1929.
47 *Literatura i Mystetstvo*, no. 6, 9 February 1929.
48 Ibid.
49 The letter from Gorky to Slisarenko, in *Natsional'ni vidnosyny*, 149.
50 Quote from Iana Prymachenko, 'Ukrains'ka literaturna dyskusiia 1920-x rr.: vid pytannia profesiinykh standartiv do problemy nacional'noi identychnosti', *Problemy istorii Ukrainy: fakty, sudzhennia, poshuky*, Vyp. 23 (2015), 239.
51 Khvyl'ovyi, *Ukraina chy Malorosiia*, 44.
52 Hryhorii Kostiuk, *Zustrichi i Proshchannia. Spohady* (Edmonton: CIUS, 1987), vol. 1, 282–3; The coverage of the literary evening is in *Komunist*, 12 July 1928.
53 Borys Antonenko-Davydovych, 'Spohad pro pryiom Stalinom ukrains'koi delehatsii 1929 roku', *Suchasnist'* 7–8 (1984): 4.

54 Liubchenko states that it was the first and only time when Khvyl'ovyi went to Moscow: 'Moscow he hated so much that he never agreed to go there, although he had been invited and sent to different meetings and conferences', Liubchenko, *Spohady pro Khvyl'ovoho*, 36.
55 'Ukrainski pys'mennyky pro podorozh u Moskvu', *Literatura i Mystetstvo*, no. 6, 9 February 1929, 1.
56 Those quotes are from 'Ukrainski pys'mennyky pro podorozh u Moskvu', *Literatura i Mystetstvo*, no. 6, 9 February 1929: 1. Andrii Paniv, 'Podorozh do Moskvy', *Pluh* 2 (1929): 53–63; Antonenko-Davydovych, *Spohad pro pryiom*, 4–12.
57 *Literatura i Mystetstvo*, no. 6, 9 February 1929, 1.
58 Ibid.
59 Khokhol – a pejorative exonym to denominate Ukrainians, which dates back to the seventeenth century.
60 *Literatura i Mystetstvo*, no. 6, 9 February 1929, 1.
61 'Rus'ki pys'mennyky, poety i krytyky pro ukrains'kyi tyzhden' u Moskvi', *Literatura i Mystetstvo*, no. 7, 17 February 1929, 1.
62 Ibid.
63 Ibid.
64 Paniv, *Podorozh do Moskvy*, 55.
65 *Komunist*, 9 February 1929.
66 Ibid.
67 'Ukrains'kyi tyzhden u Moskvi', *Literaturna hazeta*, 1 March 1929, 2.
68 Ibid.
69 Paniv, *Podorozh do Moskvy*, 57.
70 Antonenko-Davydovych, *Spohad pro pryiom*, 8.
71 'Ukrains-kyi tyzhden u Moskvi', *Literaturna hazeta*, 1 March 1929, 2.
72 Paniv, *Podorozh do Moskvy*, 59.
73 Leonid Maximenko, 'Stalin's meeting with a delegation of Ukrainian writers on 12 February 1929', *Harvard Ukrainian Studies* XVI, nos 3/4 (1992): 361–431.
74 Ibid., 401.
75 Ibid., 402.
76 Ibid., 403.
77 Ibid., 399.
78 Ibid., 411.
79 Antonenko-Davydovych, *Spohad pro pryiom*, 9.
80 Maximenko, *Stalin's meeting*, 411.
81 Ibid., 413.
82 Ibid., 415.
83 On this, see: Ivan Ohiienko, *Narysy z istorii ukriins'koi movy. Systema ukrains'koho pravopysu* (Winnipeg: Volyn', 1990), 301–2; Olena Palko, Roman Horbyk, 'Righting the Writing: The Power Dynamic of Soviet Ukraine Language Policies and Reforms in the 1920s–1930s', *Studi Slavistici* XIV (2017): 77–9.
84 Maximenko, *Stalin's meeting*, 416.
85 Ibid., 417.
86 Ibid., 409.
87 The play was based on the novel *The White Guard* and written by Bulgakov in 1925. Subsequently, there were three editions of the play with some changes.
88 Maximenko, *Stalin's meeting*, 419.
89 Ibid., 424–5.

90 Ibid., 405-6.
91 Ibid., 421. In April 1929, the play was cancelled due to severe criticism in the Soviet press. It returned in 1932.
92 Paniv, *Podorozh do Moskvy*, 56.
93 Ibid., 419.
94 Sheila Fitzpatrick, 'Cultural Revolution of the First Five Year Plan', in *Cultural Revolution in Russia, 1928-1931*, ed. Sheila Fitzpatrick (Bloomington: Indiana University Press, 1978), 6.
95 Iurii Shapoval, *Ukraina 20-50-h Rokiv (Storinky Nenapysanoi Istorii)* (Kyiv: Naukova Dumka, 1993); *ChK-GPU-NKVD v Ukraini: Osoby, Fakty, Dokumenty*, ed. Iu. Shapoval, et al. (Kyiv: Abrys, 1997).
96 V. Prystaiko, Iu. Shapoval, *Sprava 'Spilky Vyzvolennia Ukrainy'. Nevidomi dokumenty i fakty* (Kyiv: Intel, 1995), 102.
97 Ibid., 52-3.
98 Ibid., 202.
99 Ibid., 414.
100 Ibid., 131.
101 Quote from ibid., 13-14.
102 A writer Dmytro Nytchenko remembered in his memoirs that all staff members of the DVU were given free entry tickets to view the SVU process. See: Nytchenko, *Vid Zin'kova*, 85.
103 Mykola Khvyl'ovyi, 'A Khto Shche Sydyt na Lavi Pidsudnyh? (do Procesu "Spilky Vyzvolennia Ukrainy"),' *Kharkivs'kyi Proletar*, 16 March 1930; 'Za Shchodennykom S.O. Iefremova – Vozhdia, Akademika, "Sovisti Zemli Ukrains'koi", shcho Palahkotyt' 'Velykym Polum'iam", *Kharkivs'kyi Proletar*, 21 March 1930; *Kharkivs'kyi Proletar*, 25 March, 1930.
104 *Kharkivs'kyi Proletar*, 16 March 1930.
105 Ibid.
106 Ibid.
107 Iurii Shapoval, *Fatal'na Ambivalentnist'*, 23.
108 *Spilka Vyzvolennia Ukrainy. Stenohrafichnyi zvit sudovoho protsesu*, vol. 1 (Kharkiv: DVU, 1931), 1. Prystaiko and Shapoval, *Sprava 'Spilky Vyzvolennia Ukrainy'*, 44-5.
109 *ChK-GPU-NKVD v Ukraini*, 135.
110 Pauly, *Breaking the Tongue*, 249.
111 *XI Z'izd KP(b)U. 5-15 chervnia 1930 r.: Stenoh. Zvit.* (Kharkiv: DVU, 1930), 285.
112 Prystaiko and Shapoval, *Sprava 'Spilky Vyzvolennia Ukrainy'*, 89.
113 *XI Zizd KP(b)U. 5-15 chervnia 1930 r.*, 285.
114 On Hrushevs'kyi see: Plokhy, *Unmaking Imperial Russia*; V. Prystaiko, Iu. Shapoval, *Mykhailo Hrushevs'kyi: Sprava 'UNTs' i Ostanni Roky* (Kyiv: Krytyka, 1999).
115 Shapoval, *Oleksandr Shums'kyi*, 162-5.
116 Soldatenko, *Nezlamnyi*, 229-35.
117 Danylenko, *Intelihentsiia i Vlada*, 545.
118 Iefremov, *Shchodennyky*, 769.
119 Tychyna, *Iz shchodennykovykh zapysiv*, 57.
120 Tel'niuk, *Pavlo Tychyna*, 188.
121 Iefremov, *Shchodennyky*, 776.
122 Mykhailyna Kotsiubyns'ka (ed.) *Z Liubov'iu i Bolem: Spohady pro Pavla Tychynu* (Kyiv: Milenium, 2005), 19.

123 My understanding of 'class war' during the first Five-Year Plan is similar to that of Sheila Fitzpatrick. See: Fitzpatrick, *Cultural Revolution*.
124 On redefining Ukrainian history and culture in late Stalinism see: Yekelchyk, *Stalin's Empire of Memory*.
125 Smolych, *Rozpovid' pro nespokii*, 135–41; Nytchenko, *Vid Zin'kova*, 76–7.
126 Kostiuk, *Mykola Khvyl'ovyi*, 80.
127 Kostiuk, *Zustrichi ta proshchannia*, vol. 1, 259–60.
128 Ibid., 260.
129 More in Smolych, *Rozpovid' pro Nespokii*, 141–53.
130 Kostiuk, *Zustrichi ta proshchannia*, vol. 1, 261.
131 Mykola Khvyl'ovyi, 'Proloh do Knyhy Sto Sorok Druhoi', Khvyl'ovyi, *Tvory u p'iat'okh tomakh* 4: 447; 'Deklaratyvna peredmova do pershoho chysla misiachnyka "Prolitfront"' 1 (1930): 5–10. Also: 'Do chytacha', in Khvyl'ovyi, *Tvory u p'iat'okh tomakh*, vol. 4, 595–9.
132 Kostiuk, *Zustrichi ta proshchannia*, vol. 1, 268.
133 'Do Chytacha', in Khvyl'ovyi, *Tvory u p'iat'okh tomakh*, 595–9.
134 Kostiuk, *Zustrichi ta proshchannia*, vol. 1, 268–9.
135 'Pliamuemo hanebnu robotu zradnykiv', *Literaturnyi Iarmarok*, kn. 11, 149 (1929): 309–11.
136 Borland, *Soviet Literary Theory and Practice*, 23.
137 Luckyj, *Literary politics*, 158.
138 Kostiuk, *Zustrichi ta proshchannia*, vol. 1, 271.
139 Smolych, *Rozpovid' pro Nespokii*, 142.
140 Kostiuk, *Zustrichi ta proshchannia*, vol. 1, 271–2.
141 'Rezoliutsiia zahal'nykh zboriv PROLITFRONTu (19 sichnia 1931 r.)', Khvyl'ovyi, *Tvory u p'iat'okh tomakh*, vol. 4, 607.
142 'Promova M.Khvyl'ovoho na zahal'nykh zborakh karkivs'koi orhanizatsii VUSPP, 24.II.1931', in Khvyl'ovyi, *Tvory u p'iat'okh tomakh*, vol. 4, 614–15.
143 Kostiuk, *Mykola Khvyl'ovyi*, 87.
144 *Promova M.Khvyl'ovoho na zahal'nykh zborakh*, 615.
145 Kostiuk, *Zustrichi i Proshchannia*, 251–88; Luckyj, *Literary politics*, 156.
146 Usually this phrase is attributed to Stalin who used it on 26 October 1932 during his meeting with Soviet writers at Gorky's apartment in Moscow. This phrase was first coined by the Soviet writer Iurii Olesha and was frequently used by Stalin afterwards.
147 TsDAHOU, F. 263. Op. 1. № 57013 FP/kor. 1388, ark. 167–8; Quote from Serhii Bilokin', 'Dosie shevchenkoznavtsia [Mykhaila Novyts'koho]', *Literaturna Ukraina*, 4 October 2007, 1, 8; 11 October 2007, 7–8.
148 Tychyna, *Tvory*, vol. 12, Part 2, 372.
149 The fourth edition of Pluh appeared in 1927; *Nadkhodyt' lito. Vtybrani poezii* (1929) *Poezii* (1929); *Na maidani. Vybrani poezii* (1930).
150 Shakhovs'kyi, *V maisterni*, 100.
151 Quote from Grabowicz, *Černihiv*, 92.
152 Kharkhun, *Mytets' v Kanoni*, 42.
153 Shakhovs'kyi, *V maisterni*, 100.
154 Arsen Ishchuk, *Pavlo Tychyna* (Kyiv: Derzhlitvydav, 1954), 85. Also quote from Grabowicz, *Černihiv*, 90.
155 Stus, *Fenomen doby*, 81.
156 Lavrinenko, *Pavlo Tychyna*. Volodymyr Dibrova differentiates a number of personae of Tychyna: 'an author of "arfamy-arfamy" (reference to the collection *Soniachni*

klarnety)', 'a poet of school profanation', 'order-holder and an academic' and 'a collaborator who sold out and wasted his talent'; see: Volodymyr Dibrova, 'Chernihiv P.Tychyny (Sproba prochytannia)', Suchasnist' 11 (1995): 87–104.
157 Malaniuk, Ryl's'kyi v P'iatdesiatylittia, 302.
158 Grabowicz, Černihiv, 90.
159 Ibid., 90–1. Similar approach in Kharkhun, Mytets' v Kanoni.
160 Ibid., 96–8.
161 Ibid., 94.
162 Ibid., 90–1.
163 Khvyl'ovyi, Tvory v dvokh tomakh, vol. 3.
164 Mykola Khvyl'ovyi, 'Shchaslyvyi Sekretar', Tvory u p'iat'okh tomakh. 3: 387–97.
165 Edward Acton and Tom Stableford (eds.), The Soviet Union. A Document History. vol. 1, 1917–40 (Exeter: Exeter University Press, 2005), 311–4.
166 Mykola Khvyl'ovyi, Po barvinkivs'komu raioni, Z bl'oknotu korespondenta (Kharkiv, 1930); Khvyl'ovyi, Tvory u p'iat'okh tomakh, vol. 3, 463–93.
167 Ibid., 477, 481.
168 Ibid., 483.
169 Mykola Khvyl'ovyi, 'Iz zhyttiepysu popeliastoi korovy', in Khvyl'ovyi, Tvory v dvokh tomakh, vol. 2, 347–53.
170 'Peredmova i Vstupni Slova M.Khvyl'ovoho do Pershoho Tomu Ioho "Vybranyh Tvoriv" 1932 r.', Khvyl'ovyi, Tvory u p'iat'okh tomakh, vol. 4, 618–19.
171 Ibid.
172 Full manuscript of the article: 'Nove amplua Mykoly Khcyl'ovoho', GDA SBU, Spr. S-183, ark.50–66; Quote from ark.64.
173 GDA SBU, spr.S-183, ark.115.
174 Panas Liubchenko, 'Pro deiaki pomylky na teoretychnomu fronti', Visti VUTsVK, 6 July 1933; Soldatenko, Nezlamnyi, 239–41.
175 Soldatenko, Nazlamnyi, 208–9.
176 Arkadii Liubchenko, 'His Secret', in Stories from Ukraine, 218.
177 Liubchenko, His Secret, 231. The partiality of the memoirs, however, is worth noting. Following the Second World War, Liubchenko, one of many, ended up in exile and became an architect of the glorification narrative of the Ukrainian 1920s in the diaspora historiography, later shaped within the 'executed renaissance' paradigm. The memoirs, first published in 1943, could also be used to adjust Khvyl'ovyi's persona to the demands of the new ideological narrative.
178 Liubchenko, His Secret, 232–4.
179 Liubchenko, 'Iogo Taiemnytsia', in Liubchenko, Vybrani Tvory (Kyiv: Smoloskyp, 1999), 438–9.
180 On Ialovyi's case see: Ushkalov, Arkhiv Rozstrilianoho VidrodzhenniaI, 13–144.
181 Kostiuk, Mykola Khvyl'ovyi, 94.
182 HDU SBU, S-183, ark.98–9.
183 Quote from the documentary 'Tzar i Rab Khytroshchiv' (scriptwriters Iryna Shatokhina, Iurii Shapoval, 2009).
184 The controversy of the suicide notes is discussed in Palko, Between Two Powers, 591–3.
185 Copies of the death notes were accessed in TsDAMLMU, F.1208, op.1, Spr.5, ark.1; Spr.6, ark.1.
186 Speech of comrade Kyrylenko in Khvyl'ovyi, Tvory u p'iat'okh tomakh, vol. 5, 142.
187 Ibid., 138.

188 Speech of Bezymens'kyi in Khvyl'ovyi, *Tvory u p'iat'okh tomakh*, vol. 5, 145.
189 Quote from Luckyj, *Literary politics*, 221.
190 Khvylevoi Mykola in *Bol'shaia Sovetskaia Entsyklopediia*, vol. 59 (Moscow: Sovetskaia Entsyklopediia, 1935), 488.
191 Shapoval and Panchenko, *Poliuvannia na 'Val'dshnepa'*, 190.
192 Kulish A., 'Smert' i Pokhoron Khvyl'ovoho', in Khvylovy, *Tvory u p'iat'okh tomakh*, vol. 5, 172.
193 Khvyl'ovyi was rehabilitated in September 1989. See: TsDAHOU, F.39, op.1, spr.819, ark.46-9; TsDAHOU, F.1, op.11, spr.2224, ark.60.
194 See, e.g., Mykola Zhulyns'kyi, 'Talant nezvychainyi i superechlyvyi', *Vitchyzna* 12 (1987): 144–9.
195 Khvyl'ovyi, *Uryvok z avtobiohrafii*, 107.
196 Mykola Zhulyns'kyi, *Iz Zabuttia-v Bezsmertia (Storinky Pryzabutoi Spadshchyny)* (Kyiv: Dnipro, 1990), 266.
197 Shapoval, *Fatal'na Ambivalentnist'*, 12.
198 I. V. Stalin, 'O proekte Konstitutsii Soiusa SSR. Doklad na Cherezvychainom VIII Vsesoiuznom S'ezde Sovetov, 25 Noiabria 1936 goda'. Available online: https://www.marxists.org/russkij/stalin/t14/t14_40.htm (accessed 12 February 2020). On Soviet Ukraine see: L. Tkachova, *Intelihentsiia radians'koi Ukrainy v period pobudovy osnov sotsialismu* (Kyiv: Naukova dumka, 1991); Hryhorii Kasianov, *Ukrains'ka intelligentsia 1920-30-h rokiv: sotsial'nyi portret ta istorychna dolia* (Kyiv: Hlobus; Vik; Edmonton: Canadian Institute of Ukrainian Studies, 1992).
199 Tel'niuk, *Pavlo Tychyna*, 189–201.
200 *Pravda*, 21 November 1933.
201 'Patiia vedet', *Pravda*, 21 November 1933.
202 Nytchenko, *Vid Zin'kova*, 137.
203 Ibid., 137–8.
204 I. Kulyk, 'Ukrains'ka Literatura do Z'iizdu', *Za Markso-Lenins'ku Krytyku* 5 (1934): 11.
205 Tychyna, 'Avtobiohrafiia', in Tychyna, *Z Mynuloho v Maibutnie*, 24.
206 Tychyna, 'Ia Rostu', in Tychyna, *Tvory*, vol. 8, Part 1, 57–8.
207 Lavrinenko, *Rozstriliane Vidrodzhennia*, 12–13; G. S. N. Luckyj, *Keeping a Record: Literary Purges in Soviet Ukraine (1930s): A Bio-Bibliography* (Edmonton: CIUS, 1988).
208 Stus, *Fenomen doby*, 88.
209 On Ryl's'kyi see: 'Sprava no 272 (Z Arkhivu KDB)', *Kyiv* 2 (1991): 79–101; Vira Aheeva, *Mystetstvo Rivnovahy: Maksym Ryl's'kyi na Tli Epohy* (Kyiv: Knyha, 2012).
210 *Literaturna Ukraina*, 2 April 1992.
211 Volodymyr P"ianov, 'Pravdyvym Bud', ale…', in P"ianov, *Vyznachni, Vidomi i 'ta Inshi…' Spohady, Essei, Narysy*, (Kyiv: Ukrains'kyi Pys'mennyk, 2002), 48.
212 Tychyna, *Tvory*, vol. 12, Part 2, 376.
213 Quote from Alla Latyning, 'The Stalin Prize for Literature as the Quintessence of Socialist Realism', in *In The Party Spirit. Socialist Realism and Literary Practice in the Soviet Union, East Germany and China* (Critical Studies 6), Hilary Chung (ed.) (Amsterdam; Atlanta, Rodopi Editions, 1996), 106–28.
214 Tychyna, *Tvory*, vol. 1, 5.
215 Kotsiubyns'ka, *Z liubov'iu*, 23–4.
216 Tel'niuk, *Mistyfikatsiia Poeta*, 182–3.

Epilogue

1. Robert Sullivant, *Soviet Politics and the Ukraine 1917–1957* (New York-London: Columbia University Press, 1962), 139.
2. Sheila Fitzpatrick introduced the distinction between the soft liberal line (pre-1928) and the hard line of 'class war' in cultural policies. See: Sheila Fitzpatrick, 'The "Soft" Line on Culture and Its Enemies: Soviet Cultural Policy, 1922–1927', *Slavic Review* 33, no. 2 (1974): 267–872. Terry Martin redefined this distinction to separate hard-line policies (e.g. core Bolshevik tasks such as unmasking enemies, promoting vigilance, receiving denunciations and arresting and deporting enemies) and soft-line policies (those of secondary consideration designed to make hard-line policies palatable to the larger population). In the context of *korenizatsiia*, Martin maintains that education and 'cultural building' belonged to the soft-line policies, in comparison to hard-line policies in economic and political institutions. See: Martin, *Affirmative Action Empire*, 21–2; 76. Matthew Pauly challenged Martin's assertion on 'soft-line' Ukrainization highlighting the importance of education. See: Pauly, *Breaking the Tongue*, 17.
3. Zadesnians'kyi, *Shcho nam dav*, 159–60.
4. Liber, *Soviet Nationality Policy*, 77.
5. Ibid., 120.
6. Quote from Kostiuk, *Zustrichi i Proshchannia*, vol. 1, 192.
7. Here I disagree with Liber and his argument on transformed national and social identity. See: Liber, *Soviet Nationality Policy*, 119–20.
8. Shevel'ov, *Ukrains'ka Mova*, 15; 153.
9. Palko, Horbyk, *Righting the Writing*.
10. Ukraine's historical identity was cemented during the 1920s by the historians members of the VUAN Historical-philological division. Among its main representatives were academics Hrushevs'kyi, Bahalii and Matvii Iavors'kyi. On the process of creating a separate historical narrative see: Plokhy, *Unmaking Imperial Russia*. On the role of history in shaping collective memory and the sense of Ukrainianness during late Stalinism see: Yekelchyk, *Stalin's Empire of Memory*.
11. Francine Hirsch, 'Towards an Empire of Nations: Border-Making and the Formation of Soviet National Identities', *The Russian Review* 59 (2000): 201–62; Borisenok, *Fenomen Sovetskoi Ukrainizatsii*, 99–106.
12. Olena Palko, 'Ukrainian National Communism: Challenging History', *Journal of Contemporary Central and Eastern Europe* 22, no. 1 (2014): 27–48; Also her *Debating the early Soviet Nationalities Policy*.
13. Clark, *Petersburg*, 184.
14. Reference to Stus, *Fenomen doby*.
15. Resolution of the TsK VKP(b) 'On Restructuring Literary and Arts Organizations', in *Soviet Culture and Power*, 151–2.
16. Ivan Mykytenko, 'Put'' k soiuzu', *Literaturnaia gazeta*, 14 June 1934. On the formation of the Writers' Union of Ukraine see: Luckyj, *Literary Politics*, 227–30.
17. Luckyj, *Literary Politics*, 228.
18. Robin, *Socialist Realism*, 43.
19. Quote from Slonim, *Soviet Russian Literature*, 160–1.
20. Ibid., 161.
21. Ibid.

Bibliography

Primary Sources

Archives

Derzhavnyi Arkhiv Mista Kyieva (DAK) (State Archive of Kyiv).
Haluzevyi Derzhavnyi Arkhiv Sluzhby Bezpeky Ukrainy (HDA SBU) (State Archives Department of the Security Service of Ukraine).
Tsentral'nyi Derzhavnyi Arkhiv Hromads'kykh Ob'iednan' Ukrainy (TsDAHOU) (Central State Archives of Public Organisations of Ukraine).
Tsentral'nyi Derzhavnyi Arkhiv-Muzei Literatury i Mystetstva Ukrainy (TsDAMLMU) (Central State Archive of Literature and Arts of Ukraine).
Tsentral'nyi Derzhavnyi Arkhiv Vyshchykh Orhaniv Vlady ta Upravlinnia Ukrainy (TsDAVOU) (Central State Archive of Supreme Bodies of Power and Government of Ukraine).

Creative Writing

Arena. 1 (1922).
Dolenho, Mykhailo. *Krytychni Etiudy*. Kharkiv: DVU, 1925.
Ellan-Blakytnyi, Vasyl'. *Tvory u Dvokh Tomakh*. Kyiv: Derzhlitvydav, 1958.
Khvyl'ovyi, Mykola. *Po barvinkivs'komu raioni, Z bl'oknotu korespondenta*. Kharkiv: DVU, 1930.
Khvyl'ovyi, Mykola. 'Iz zhyttiepysu popeliastoi korovy'. In Khvyl'ovyi, *Tvory v dvokh tomakh* 2: 347–53.
Khvyl'ovyi, Mykola. 'Odvertyi lyst do Volodymyra Koriaka', *Vaplite*, 5 (1927): 158–73.
Khvylovy, Mykola. 'Woodcocks'. In *Before the Storm: Soviet Ukrainian Fiction of the 1920s*, edited by George Luckyj, 15–69. Ann Arbor: Ardis, 1986.
Khvylovy, 3 Mykola. *Stories from the Ukraine*. New York: Philosophical Library, 1960.
Khvylovy, Mykola. *The Cultural Renaissance in Ukraine*. Edmonton: CIUS, 1986.
Khvyl'ovyi, Mykola. *Ukraina chy Malorosiia?* Kyiv: Ukrains'ka Pres-Hrupa, 2012.
Khvyl'ovyi, Mykola. *Tvory u Dvokh Tomakh*. Kyiv: Dnipro, 1990–1.
Khvyl'ovyi, Mykola. *Tvory u P'iat'okh Tomakh*. New York-Baltimore-Toronto: Smoloskyp, 1978–86.
Liubchenko, Arkadii. *Vybrani Tvory*. Kyiv: Smoloskyp, 1999.
Luts'kyi, Iurii (ed.). *Vaplitians'kyi Zbirnyk*. Oakwill: Mosaika, 1977.
Muzahet: Misiachnyk Literatury i Mystetstva. 1–3 (1919).
Shliakhy Mystetstva. 1 (1921).
Shliakhy Rozvytku Suchasnoi Literatury: Dysput 24 Travnia 1925 r. Kyiv, 1925.

Tychyna, Pavlo. 'On the Anniversary of Kruty (In Memory of the Thirty) (Deep in the Mound of Askold)'. *Zhinochyi Svit=Woman's World* 25.1, no. 289 (1974): 17.
Tychyna, Pavlo. *The Complete Early Poetry Collections of Pavlo Tychyna*. Lviv: Litopys, 2002; London: Glagoslav Publications, 2017.
Tychyna, Pavlo. *Tvory u 12 Tomakh*. Kyiv: Naukova Dumka, 1983–90. mo
Zerov, Mykola. *Tvory*. 2 vols. Kyiv: Dnipro, 1990.
Zhovten'. Zbirnyk Prysviachenyi Rokovynam Proletars'koi Revoliutsii. Kharkiv: Vseukrlitkom, 1921.

Sources Published During the Period of Study

Antonenko-Davydovych, Borys. 'Spohad pro pryiom Stalinom ukrains'koi delegatsii 1929 roku'. *Suchasnist'* 7–8 (1984): 4–12.
Barka, Vasyl'. *Khliborobs'kyi Orfei, abo Kliarnetyzm*. Munich: Suchasnist', 1961.
Bilets'kyi, Oleksandr. 'V shukanniakh novoi povistiars'koi formy'. *Shliakhy Mystetstva* 5 (1923): 59–63.
Bilets'kyi, Oleksandr. *Dvadtsiat' Rokiv Novoi Ukrains'koi Liryky*. Kharkiv: DVU, 1924.
Boiko, V. 'Formalizm i marksyzm'. *Chervonyi shliakh* 11–12 (1926): 141–65.
Borovs'kyi, Mykola. *Kyiv Ta Yoho Okolycia v Istorii ta Pamiatkah*. Kyiv: DVU, 1926.
Chubar, Vlas. 'Pro vyvykhy'. In *Shliakhy rozvytki ukrains'koi proletars'koi literatury*. Kharkiv: Ukrains'kyi robitnyk, 1928.
Chuchmar'ov, A. 'Sotsiolohichnyi metod v istorii i teorii literatury'. *Chervonyi shliakh* 7–8 (1926): 208–32.
Chyrkov, Mykola. 'Mykola Khvyl'ovyi u ioho prozi'. *Zhyttia i revoliutsiia* 9 (1925): 38–44.
Dolenho, Mykhailo. 'Kyiv ta Kharkiv – Literaturni Vzaiemovidnoshennia'. *Chervonyi Shliakh* 6 (1923): 151–7.
Donets', Roman. 'Suchasne Mystetstvo Ukrainy'. *Nova Ukraina* 10–11 (1922): 29–35.
Dontsov, Dmytro. *Mykola Khvyl'ovyi*. [s.l.], 1947.
Dontsov, Dmytro. *Dvi Literatury Nashoi Doby*. Toronto: Homin Ukrainy, 1958.
Doroshenko, Dmytro. *Istoriia Ukrainy, 1917–1923 rr*. New York: Bulava, 1954 [1930–2].
Doroshenko, Volodymyr. *Z istorii zemstva na Ukraini*. Lviv: NTSh, 1910.
Doroshkevych, Oleksandr. *Istoriia ukrains'koi literatury*, 2nd edn. Kharkiv: Knyhospilka, 1926.
Doroshkevych, Oleksandr. *Pidruchnyk Istorii Ukrains'koi Literatury*. Kyiv: Knyhospilka, 1927.
Dosvitnii, O. 'Do rozvytku pys'mennyts'kykh syl'. *Vaplite, Zoshyt Pershyi* (1926): 9.
Hadzins'kyi, V. 'Shche kil'ka sliv do pytannia "formy i zmistu"'. *Chervonyi shliakh* 4–5 (1923): 173–9.
Hirchak, Ievhen. *Na Dva Fronty v Boro'tbi proty Natsionalizmu*. Kharkiv: Proletar, 1932.
Hordyns'kyi, Iaroslav. *Literaturna Krytyka Pidsoviets'koi Ukrainy*. Munich: Otto Sagner Verlag, 1985 [1939].
Iakovenko, H. 'Pro Krytykiv i Krytyku v Literaturi'. *Kul'tura i Pobut* 17 (1925), 25 April 1925.
Iakubovs'kyi, F. 'Do kryzy v ukrains'kii khudozhnii prozi'. *Zhyttia i revoliutsiia* 1 (1926): 41–8.
Iakubs'kyi, B. 'Zhyttia molode: Sproba literaturnoi kharakterystyky "kyivs'kykh pluzhan"'. *Chervonyi shliakh* 9 (1925): 159–71.
Iakubs'kyi, B. *Sotsiolohichnyi metod u pys'menstvi*. Kyiv: Slovo, 1923.

Iefremov, Serhii. *Istoriia Ukrains'koho Pys'menstva*. Kyiv: Femina, 1995 [1911; 1917].
Iurynets', Volodymyr. 'Zhovtneva literatura v marksysts'komu osvitlenniu'. *Bil'shovyk Ukrainy* 4–5 (1926): 132–54.
Iurynets', Volodymyr. 'M. Khvyl'ovyi iak prozaik'. *Chervonyi shliakh* 1 (1927): 253–68.
Iurynets', Volodymyr. *Pavlo Tychyna. Sproba Krytychnoi Analizy*. Kharkiv: Knyhospilka, 1928.
Khrystiuk, Pavlo. 'Sotsial'ni motyvy v tvorchosti M. Khvyl'ovoho' *Chervonyi shliakh* 4–5 (1924): 256–63.
Khrystiuk, Pavlo. 'Rets.: Vaplite. Zoshyt pershyi. Kh., 1926'. *Chervonyi Shliakh* 9 (1926): 264–5.
Khvylia, Andrii. *Natsional'nyi Vopros na Ukraine*. Kharkiv: DVU, 1926.
Khvylia, Andrii. *Iasnoiu dorohoiu (Rik na literaturnomu fronti)*. Kharkiv: DVU, 1927.
Khvylia, Andrii. *Vid Ukhylu u Prirvu*. Kharkiv: DVU, 1928.
Khvylia, Andrii. *KP(b)U v Borot'bi za Lenins'ku Nacional'nu Polityku*. Kharkiv: DVU, 1933.
Koriak, Volodymyr. 'Etapy'. *Zhovten'* (1921): 83–97.
Koriak, Volodymyr. 'Forma i zmist'. *Shliakhy mystetstva* 2–4 (1922): 40–7.
Koriak, Volodymyr. 'Ukrains'ka Literatura za P'iat' Rokiv Proletars'koi Revoliutsii'. Volodymyr Koriak, *Orhanizatsiia Zhovtnevoi Literatury*, 56–70. Kharkiv: DVU, 1925.
Koriak, Volodymyr. *Orhanizatsiia Zhovtnevoi Literatury*. Kharkiv: DVU, 1925.
Koriak, Volodymyr. 'Khvyl'ovistychnyi sotsiolohichnyi ekvivalent'. *Hart* 1 (1927): 74–103.
Koriak, Volodymyr. *Shliakhy Rozvytku Ukrainskoi Proletarskoi Literatury: Lit. Diskusiia (1925–8)*. Kharkiv: DVU, 1928.
Koriak, Volodymyr. *V Boiakh: Statti i Vystupy, 1925–1930*. Kharkiv: Literatura i Mystetstvo, 1933.
Koroliv-Staryi, V. 'Tsentral'na Rada (zhadka)'. *Tryzub* 16 (1927).
Kostel'nyk, Havryil. *Lomannia Dush*. Lviv: Dobra Knyzhka, 1923.
Kostiuk, Hryhorii. 'Mykola Khvyl'ovyi: Zhyttia, Doba, Tvorchist". In Khvyl'ovyi, *Tvory u P'iat'okh Tomakh*, vol. 1, 15–106. New York-Baltimore-Toronto: Smoloskyp, 1978–86.
Kulyk, Ivan. *Dopovid' na Pershomu Vseukrains'komu Z"izdi Radians'kykh Pys'mennykiv*. Kharkiv: Radians'ka Literatura, 1934.
Kulyk, Ivan. 'Ukrains'ka Literatura do Z'izdu'. *Za Markso-Lenins'ku Krytyku* 5 (1934): 5–12.
Lavrinenko, Iurii. *Pavlo Tychyna i Ioho Poema 'Skovoroda' na Tli Epokhy*. Munich: Suchasnist', 1980.
Lavrinenko, Iurii. *Zrub i Parosty*. Munich: Suchasnist', 1971.
Leites, O. and Iashek, M. *Desiat' Rokiv Ukrains'koi Literatury (1917–1927)*, in 2 vols. Kharkiv: DVU, 1928.
Leites, Oleksandr. *Renesans Ukrains'koi Literatury*. Kharkiv: DVU, 1925.
Liaskovets' M. [Mosendz L.], *Mykola Khvyl'ovyi: lehenda i diisnist'*. Salsburg-Innsbruck: Zveno, 1948.
Maiorov, M. 'Kil'ka sliv pro Ivaniv Ivanovychiv'. *Literaturnyi Iarmarok* 7 (1929): 56–9.
Malaniuk, Ievhen. 'Naprovesni [Vyimky z bloknota literatura]'. *Ukrains'kyi Holos*. 8 January 1922, 1–2.
Malaniuk, Ievhen. *Knyha Sposterezhen'*. Toronto: Homin Ukrainy, 1962.
Mazepa, Ivan. 'Ukrainians under Bolshevist Rule'. *The Slavonic and East European Review* 12, no. 35 (1934): 323–46.
Mazlakh, Serhii and Shakhrai, Vasyl. *Do Khvyli: Shcho Diiet'sia na Ukraini i z Ukrainoiu?* New York: Proloh, 1954.

Mazlakh, Serhii and Shakhrai, Vasyl. *The Current Situation in the Ukraine*. Michigan: Michigan University Press, 1970.
Mezhenko, Iurii. 'Na shliakhakh do novoi teorii'. *Chervonyi shliakh* 2 (1923): 199–210.
Mezhenko, Iurii. 'Tvorchist' M. Khvyl'ovoho'. *Shliakhy mystetstva* 5 (1923): 55–9.
Nikovs'kyi, Andrii. *Vita Nova. Krytychni Narysy*. Kyiv: [s.l.], 1919.
Ohloblin-Hlobenko, Mykola. 'Mykola Khvyl'ovyi'. In his *Istoryko-literaturni statti*. (Zapysky NTSh, vol. CLXVII), 60–9. New York; Paris; Munich: NTSh, 1958.
Poltorats'kyi, Oleksii. 'Kriz' formal'nu metodu'. *Nova heneratsiia* 2 (1927): 38–43.
Poltorats'kyi, Oleksii. *Literaturni zasoby. Sproba sotsiolohichnoi analizy* (Kharkiv: DVU, 1929).
Popov, Mykola. *Narys Istorii Komunistychnoi Partii (Bil'shovykiv) Ukrainy*. Kharkiv: DVU, 1928.
Pylypenko, Serhii. 'Nashi "Hrikhy"'. *Pluzhanyn* 4–5 (1926): 1–2.
Radek, Karl. *Intellihentsiia i Sovetskaia Vlast'*. Moscow: Sovetskii Mir, 1919.
Rasnyts'kyi, S. 'Vidhuk na "Skovorodu" Pavla Tychyny'. *Nova Ukraina* 10 (1923): 178–9.
Ravich-Cherkasski, Moisei. *Istoria Komunisticheskoi Partii (bov) Ukrainy*. Kharkiv: Gosizdat Ukrainy, 1923.
Shamrai, A. 'Formal'nyi metod v literaturi'. *Chervonyi shliakh* 7–8 (1926): 233–66.
Shapoval, Mykyta. *Bol'shevyzm i Ukraina*. Prague: Vil'na Spilka, 1926.
Shapoval, Mykyta. *Velyka Revoliutsiia*. Prague: Vil'na Spilka, 1928.
Shchupak, Samiilo. 'Osnovni problemy mystetstva v pohliadakh radians'kykh marksystiv' *Zhyttia i revoliutsiia* 6 (1926): 53–61; 7 (1926): 58–70.
Shchupak, Samiilo. 'Podolaty Vidstavannia Krytyky'. *Za Markso-Lenins'ku Krytyku* 6 (1934): 3–8.
Shliakhy Rozvytku Suchasnoi Literatury: Dysput 24 Travnia 1925 r. Kyiv, 1925.
Shums'kyi, Oleksandr 'Ideolohichna borot'ba v ukrains'komu kul'turnomu protsesi'. *Bil'shovyk Ukrainy* 2 (1927): 11–25.
Shums'kyi, Oleksandr. 'Stara i Nova Ukraina'. *Chervonyi shliakh* 2 (1923): 91–110.
Siropolko, Stepan. *Istoriia Osvity v Ukraini*. Lviv: Afisha, 2001 [1937].
Skorovstans'kyi [Mazlakh], V. *Revoliutsiia na Ukraine*. Saratov: [s.l.], 1919.
Skrypnyk, Mykola. 'Desiat' zapovidei kul'turnoho budivnytstva'. *Radians'ka Osvita* 12 (1927): 1–2.
Skrypnyk, Mykola. *Do Teorii Borot'by Dvokh Kul'tur*. Kharkiv: DVU, 1926.
Skrypnyk, Mykola. 'Pidsumky 'Literaturnoi Dyskusii'', *Bil'shovyk Ukrainy* 1 (1926): 18–36.
Skrypnyk, Mykola. 'Khvyl'ovizm chy Shums'kizm?' *Bilshovyk Ukrainy* 2 (1927): 26–39.
Skrypnyk, Mykola. *Nasha liteaturna diisnist'* (Kharkiv: DVU, 1928).
Skrypnyk, Mykola. 'Zavdannia kul'turnoho budivnytstva na Ukraini (Dopovid' na X z"izdi KP(b)U)', *Radians'ka Osvita* 1 (1928): 1–11; 2 (1928): 14–32.
Skrypnyk, Mykola. *Statti i Promovy z Natsional'noho Pytannia*. Munich: Suchasnist', 1974 [1930].
Skrypnyk, Mykola. *Statti i promovy*. vol. 5: Literatura i mystetstvo. Kharkiv: DVU, 1930.
Skrypnyk, Mykola. *Vybrani tvory*. Kyiv: Ukraina, 1991.
Stepniak, Myron. 'Do Problem Poetyky Pavla Tychyny'. *Chervonyi Shliakh* 5–6 (1930): 129–46; 11–12 (1930): 99–118.
Stsibors'kyi, Mykola. *Ukraina i natsional'na polityka Sovietiv*. New York: [s.l.], 1938.
Vedmits'kyi, Ol. *Literaturna Dyskusiia 1925–1928*. Kharkiv: Pluzhanyn, 1932.
Vynnychenko, Volodomyr. *Vidrodzhennia Natsii*, 3 vols. Kyiv: Dzvin, 1991, [1920].
Vynnychenko, Volodymyr. *Ukrains'ka Komunistychna Partiia (UKP) i Komunistychna Partiia (Bol'shevikiv) Ukrainy (KP(b)U)*. Vienna: Biblioteka 'Novoi Doby', 1921.

Vynnychenko, Volodymyr. 'Znamenna Podia'. *Nova Ukraina* 6 (1923): 8-27.
Vynnychenko, Volodymyr. 'Z Neopublikovanykh Zapysok "Dumky pro Sebe na Tim Sviti": [pro Samohubstvo M. Khvyl'ovoho i M. Skrypnyka]'. *Suchasnist* 9 (1971): 7-18.
Vynnychenko, Volodymyr. *Zapovit Bortsiam za Vyzvolennia*. Kyiv: Krynytsia, 1991.
Zatons'kyi, Volodymyr. *Natsional'na Problema na Ukraini*. Kharkiv: DVU, 1927.
Zerov, Mykola. *Do Dzherel*. Krakiv; Lviv: Ukrains'ke Vydavnytstvo, 1943.

Published Collections of Primary Sources

Acton, Edward and Stableford, Tom (eds.). *The Soviet Union. A Documentary History*. Vol. 1. 1917-1940. Exeter: Exeter University Press, 2005.
Budivnytstvo Radians'koi Ukrainy, Vyp. 1. Kharkiv: DVU, 1929.
Chetverta Konferentsiia Komunistychnoi Partii (Bil'shovykiv) Ukrainy 17-23 bereznia 1920 r. Kyiv: Vydavnychyi Dim Al'ternatyvy, 2003.
Clark, Katerina and Dobrenko, Evgeny. *Soviet Culture and Power: A History in Documents 1917-1953*. New Haven: Yale University Press, 2007.
Daniels, Robert V. (ed.). *A Documentary History of Communism*. Burlington: University of Vermont Press, 1993.
Dekrety Sovetskoi Vlasti. Moscow: Institut marksizma-leninizma pryi TsK KPSS; Institut istorii AN SSSR, 1957-2009.
'Do Istorii Mizhnatsional'nykh Protsesiv na Ukraini'. *Ukrains'kyi Istorychnyi Zhurnal* 6-11 (1990); 1-2 (1991).
Donii M. *Bol'shevitskie organizatsii Ukrainy v period podgotovki i provedeniia Velikoi Oktiabr'skoi sotsialisticheskoi revoliutsii: mart-noiabr' 1917 g.: sbornik dokumentov i materialov*. Kiev: Gospolitisdat, 1957.
Dotsenko, O. *Litopys Ukrains'koi Revoliutsii. Materaly i Dokumenty do Istorii Ukrains'koi Revoliutsii*, 2 vols. Philadelphia: Doslidnyts'kyi Instytut Modernoi Istorii, 1988 [Lviv 1923/4].
Hunchak, Taras and Sol'chanyk, Roman. *Ukrains'ka Suspil'no-Politiyhna Dumka v 20 Stolitti*, 3 vols. Munich: Suchasnist', 1983.
Ievseev, O. (ed.), *Kul'turne Budivnytstvo v Ukrains'kii RSR. Vazhlyvishi rishennia Komunistychnoi partii i Radians'koho uriadu 1917-1959 rr. Zbirnyk dokumentiv*, vol. 1. Kyiv: DVU, 1959.
II Konferentsia KP(b)U. 9-14 kvitnia 1929: Stenoh. Zvit. Kharkiv: DVU, 1929.
III Vseukrains'kyi z"izd Rad (6-10 bereznia 1919). Stenohrafichnyi zvit. Kharkiv: Vydannia tsentral'noho arkhivnoho upravlinnia URSR, 1932.
Iurchuk, Valentyn et al. (eds.). *Komunistychna Partiia Ukrainy v Rezoliutsiiakh i Rishenniakh Z'izdiv, Konferentsii i Plenumiv TsK*. Kyiv: Politvydav, 1976, vol. 1: 1918-41.
Khrystiuk, Pavlo. *Zamitky i Materiialy do Istorii Ukrains'koi Revoliutsii 1917-1920*, 4 vols. New York: Vydavnytsvo Chartoryis'kykh, 1969.
Khvyl'ovyi, Mykola. 'Lysty'. *Spadshchyna. Literaturne Dzhereloznavstvo*, vol. VIII (2013): 228-732.
Kondufor, Iu. (ed.). *Kul'turne Budivnytstvo v Ukrains'kii RSR. 1917-27: Zbirnyk documentiv i materialiv*. Kyiv: Naukova Dumka, 1979.
Leites, O. and Iashek, M. *Desiat' Rokiv Ukrains'koi Literatury (1917-1927)*, 2 Vols. Kharkiv: DVU, 1928.

Lenin, Vladimir. *Collected Works*. 45 volumes. Moscow: Progress Publishers, 1960–70.
Lenin, Vladimir. *Polnoie Sobraniie Sochinenii*, in 55 vols. Moscow: Izdatelstvo Politicheskoi Literatury, 1967–1975.
Lozyts'kyi, V. (ed.) *Ukrains'ka Politychna Emihratsiia 1919–1945: Dokumenty i Materialy*. Kyiv: Parlaments'ke Vydavnytstvo, 2008.
Luc'kyi, Iurii (ed.). *Vaplitians'kyi Zbirnyk*. Edmonton: CIUS; Mosaika, 1977.
Luts'kyi, Iurii (ed.). *Dzherela do Istorii VAPLITE*. Munich: Ukrains'ka Literaturna Hazeta, 1956.
Maistrenko, Ivan (ed.). *Dokumenty Ukrains'koho Komunismu*. New York: Proloh, 1962.
Maximenko, Leonid. 'Stalin's Meeting with a Delegation of Ukrainian Writers on 12 February 1929'. *Harvard Ukrainian Studies* XVI, nos 3/4 (1992): 361–431.
Natsional'nyi Perepys Robitnykiv ta Sluzhbovtsiv Ukrainy (zhovten'-lystopad 1929). Kharkiv: DVU, 1930.
Panchuk, Mai et al. (ed.) *Natsional'ni Vidnosyny v Ukraini v XX st.: Zbirnyk Dokumentiv i Materialiv*. Kyiv: Naukova Dumka, 1994.
Panibud'laska, Volodymyr (ed.). *Natsional'ni Protsesy v Ukraini. Istoriia ta suchasnist'. Dokumenty i Materialy*. Part 2. Kyiv: Vyshcha Shkola, 1997.
Prystaiko V. and Shapoval Iu. *Sprava 'Spilky Vyzvolennia Ukrainy'. Nevidomi dokumenty i fakty*. Kyiv: Intel, 1995.
Prystaiko V. and Shapoval, Iu. *Mykhailo Hrushevs'kyi: Sprava 'UNTs' i Ostanni Roky*. Kyiv: Krytyka, 1999.
Radians'ke budivnytstvo na Ukraini v roky hromadians'koi viiny (lystopad 1918-serpen' 1919). Zbirnyk dokumentiv i materialiv. Kyiv: Vydavnytstvo AN URSR, 1962.
Rezoliutsii Vseukrains'kykh Z'izdiv Rad. Kharkiv: Proletar, 1932.
Shapoval, Iurii. '"On Ukrainian Separatism" A GPU Circular of 1926'. *Harvard Ukrainian Studies* XVIII, no. 3/4 (1994): 275–302.
Shapoval, Iurii. *Oleksandr Shums'kyi. Zhyttia, dolia, nevidomi dokumenty: doslidzhennia, arkhivni materialy*. Kyiv; Lviv: Ukraina moderna; Ukrains'ki propilei, 2017.
Shapoval, Iurii et al. (eds.). *ChK-GPU-NKVD v Ukraini: Osoby, Fakty, Dokumenty*. Kyiv: Abrys, 1997.
Shapoval, Iurii and Panchenko, Volodymyr (eds.). *Poliuvannia na "Val'dshnepa". Rozsekrechenyi Mykola Khvyl'ovyi*. Kyiv: Tempora, 2010.
Shapoval, Iurii, Prystaiko, Volodymyr and Zolotar'ov, Vadym. *ChK-GPU-NKVD v Ukraini: Osoby, Fakty, Dokumenty*. Kyiv: Abrys, 1997.
Shestoi s"ezd RSDRP (bol'shevikov) avgust 1917 goda. Protokoly. Moscow: Gospolitizdat, 1958.
Spilka Vyzvolennia Ukrainy. Stenohrafichnyi zvit sudovoho protsesu, vol. 1. Kharkiv: DVU, 1931.
'Sprava no. 272 (Z arkhivu KDB)'. *Kyiv* 2 (1991): 79–101.
Stalin, J. V. *Works*, 13 vols. Moscow: Foreign Languages Publishing House, 1953–4.
Trud i Profsoiuzy na Ukraine. Statisticheskii Spravochnik 1921–28 gg. Kharkiv: DVU, 1928.
Tychyna, Pavlo. 'Lysty do M. K. Zerova, M. M. Mohylians'koho'. *Radians'ke Literaturoznavstvo* 11 (1971): 75–6.
Tychyna, Pavlo. *Z Mynuloho – v Maibutnie*. Kyiv: Dnipro, 1973.
Tychyna, Pavlo. *Iz Shchodennykovykh Zapysiv*. Kyiv: Radians'kyi Pys'mennyk, 1981.
Ushkalov, L. and Ushkalov, O. (eds.) *Arkhiv Rozstrilianoho Vidrodzhennia: Materialy Arkhivno-Slidchykh Sprav Ukrains'kykh Pys'mennykiv 1920–1930-h Rokiv*. Kyiv: Smoloskyp, 2010.
Verstiuk V. (ed.). *Ukrains'kyi Natsional'no-Vyzvol'nyi Rukh. Berezen'-Lystopad 1917 Roku: Dokumenty i Materialy*. Kyiv: Vydavnytstvo Oleny Telihy, 2003.

Verstiuk, V. et al. (eds.). *Ukrains'ka Tsentral'na Rada. Dokumenty i Materialy*. Kyiv: Naukova Dumka, 1996.
XI Z"izd KP(b)U. 5-15 chervnia 1930 r.: Stenoh. Zvit. Kharkiv: DVU, 1930.
XII s'iezd RKP(b). 17-25 aprelia 1923 g. Stenohraficheskii otchet. Moscow: Politizdat, 1968.
Zbirnyk Uzakonen' ta Rozporiadzhen' Robitnycho-Selians'koho Uriadu Ukrainy. Kharkiv: DVU, 1924-5.
Zhulyn'skyi, Mykola (ed.). *Z Arkhivu P. Tychyny*. Kyiv: Naukova Dumka, 1990.

Memoirs and Diaries of Contemporaries

Antonenko-Davydovych, Borys. *Zemleiu Ukrains'koiu*. Philadelphia: Kyiv, 1955.
Antonenko-Davydovych, Borys. 'Spohad pro pryiom Stalinom ukrains'koi delehatsii 1929 roku'. *Suchasnist'* 7-8 (1984): 4-12.
Butsenko, A. 'O Raskole USDRP (1917-1918)'. *Letopis' Revoliutsii* 4 (1923): 121-2.
Chykalenko, Ievhen. *Spohady (1861-1907)*. Kyiv: Tempora, 2011.
Domontovych, Viktor. 'Bolotiana Lukroza. Spomyny'. Viktor Domontovych, *Divchynka z Vedmedykom*. 261-300. Kyiv: Krytyka, 1999.
Donets', H. (ed.). *Spivets' Novoho Svitu: Spohady pro Pavla Tychynu*. Kyiv: Dnipro, 1971.
Halahan, M. *Z moikh spomyniv (1880-ti-1920 r.)*. Kyiv: Tempora, 2005.
Hrushevs'kyi, Mykhailo. 'Spomyny'. *Kyiv* 9 (1988)-3 (1992).
Hryden', (Mukhin), Mykhailo. 'Z mynulykh lit'. *Suchasnist'* 8 (1968): 40-1.
Ialovyi, Mykhailo. 'Pershi khorobri'. *Chervonyi Shliakh* 9 (1923): 111-19.
Iefremov, Serhii. *Shchodennyky, 1923-1929*. Kyiv: Biblioteka Hazety Rada, 1997.
Khvyl'ovyi, Mykola. 'Uryvok z Avtobiohrafii'. *Vitchyzna* 12 (1987): 106-8.
Klen, Iurii. *Spohady pro Neoklasykiv*. Munich: Ukrains'ka Vydavnycha Spilka, 1947.
Kostiuk, Hryhorii. *Zustrichi i Proshchannia, Spohady*, 2 vols. Toronto: CIUS, 1987.
Kotsiubyns'ka, Mykhailyna (ed.). *Z Liubov'iu i Bolem: Spohady pro Pavla Tychynu*. Kyiv: Milenium, 2005.
Kravchenko, Victor. *I Chose Freedom*. London: Robert Hale Limited, 1947.
Liubchenko, Arkadii. 'His Secret'. In *Stories from the Ukraine*, 215-34. New York: Philosophical Library, 1960.
Liubchenko, Arkadii. 'Spohady pro Khvyl'ovoho: Iz Zapysnoi Knyzhky'. In *Vaplitians'kyi Zbirnyk*, edited by Iu. Luts'kyi. Oakwill: Mosaika, 1977.
Nytchenko, Dmytro. *Vid Zin'kova do Mel'borna. Iz Khroniky Moho Zhyttia*. Melbourne: Bayda Books, 1990 [1944].
Ovcharenko, Fedir. *Spohady*. Kyiv: Oriiany, 2000.
Paniv, Andrii. 'Podorozh do Moskvy'. *Pluh* 2 (1929): 53-63.
Petliura, Symon. *Articles. Correspondence. Documents*. Vol. II. New York: UVAN, 1979.
P'ianov, Volodymyr. 'Pravdyvym Bud', ale … '. P'ianov Volodymyr, *Vyznachni, Vidomi i 'ta Inshi … ' Spohady, Essei, Narysy*, 32-64. Kyiv: Ukrains'kyi Pys'mennyk, 2002.
Polons'ka-Vasylenko, Natalia. 'Kyiv Chasiv M. Zerova ta P. Fylypovycha'. In *Kyivs'ki Neoklassyky*, edited by. V. Aheeva. Kyiv, Fakt, 2003.
Polons'ka-Vasylenko, Natalia. *Spohady*. Kyiv: Kyievo-Mohylians'ka Akademiia, 2011.
Sharvarok, O. 'Dvi Doli - Odna Tragediia. Pavlo Tychyna - Ievhen Malaniuk: Dialoh bez Vidstani, Rozmova Cherez Tlumachiv'. *Kyiv* 11 (1993): 127-30.
Sherekh, Iurii. 'Chetvertyi Kharkiv'. Iurii Sherekh, *Porohy i Zaporizhzhia*, vol. 1, 478-92. Kharkiv: Folio, 1998.
Shyhymaga, Petro. 'Fakty do Biohrafii Mykoly Khvyl'ovogo'. In Mykola Khvyl'ovyi, *Tvory u P'iat'okh Tomakh*, vol. 5, 113-17. New York-Baltimore/Toronto: Smoloskyp, 1978-86.

Skoropads'kyi, Pavlo. *Spohady (kinets' 1917–hruden' 1918)*. Edited by Iaroslav Pelens'kyi (Kiev; Philadelphia: Instytut ukrains'koi arkheohrafii ta dzhereloznavstva im. M. S. Hrushevs'koho NAN Ukrainy [et al.], 1995).
Smolych, Iurii. *Rozpovid' pro Nespokii*. Kyiv: Radians'kyi Pys'mennyk, 1968.
Smolych, Iurii. *Rozpovid' pro Nespokii Tryvaie*. Kyiv: Radians'skyi Pys'mennyk, 1969.
Smolych, Iurii. *Rozpovid' pro Nespokii Nemae Kintsia*. Kyiv: Radians'kyi Pys'mennyk, 1970.
Smolych, Iurii. *Moi Suchasnyky*. Kyiv: Radians'kyi Pys'mennyk, 1978.
Stanimir, O. *Moia uchast' u vyzvol'nykh zmahanniakh 1917–1920 rr*. Toronto: [s.l.], 1966.
Tychyna, Pavlo. *Iz Shchodennykovykh Zapysiv*. Kyiv: Radians'kyi Pys'mennyk, 1981.
Tychyna, Pavlo. *Podorozh iz Kapeloiu Stetsenka. Shchodennyk*. Kyiv: Radians'kyi Pys'mennyk, 1982.
Vernadskii, Vladimir. *Dnevniki. 1917–1921*. Kyiv: Naukova Dumka, 1994.

Selected Secondary Sources

Adams, Arthur E. *The Bolsheviks in the Ukraine: The Second Campaign, 1918–1919*. New Haven: Yale University Press, 1963.
Aheeva, Vira. 'Zaivi liudy' u prozi M.Khvyl'ovoho'. *Slovo i Chas* 10 (1990): 3–9.
Aheeva, Vira (ed.). *Kyivs'ki Neoklasyky. Ukrains'ki Memuary*. Kyiv: Fakt, 2003.
Aheeva, Vira. *Mystetstvo Rivnovahy: Maksym Ryl's'kyi na Tli Epohy*. Kyiv: Knyha, 2012.
Armstrong, John. A. *Ukrainian Nationalism*. Littleton: Ukrainian Academic Press, 1980.
Bertelsen, Olga and Shkandrij, Myroslav. 'The Secret Police and the Campaign against Galicians in Soviet Ukraine, 1929–34'. *Nationalities Papers: The Journal of Nationalism and Ethnicity* 42, no. 1 (2014): 37–62.
Bilenky, Serhiy. *Imperial Urbanism in the Borderlands: Kyiv, 1800–1905*. Toronto: University of Toronto Press, 2018.
Blitstein, Peter. 'Cultural Diversity and the Interwar Conjuncture: Soviet Nationality Policy in Its Comparative Context'. *Slavic Review* 2, no. 65 (2006): 273–93.
Blitstein, Peter. 'Nation and Empire in Soviet History, 1917–1953'. *Ab Imperio*, no. 1 (2006): 197–219.
Bl'um, A. *Za Kulisami 'Ministerstva Pravdy'. Tainaia Istorii Sovetskoi Tsensury, 1917–29*. Sankt-Peterburg: Akademicheskii Proekt, 1994.
Bociurkiw, Bohdan R. 'Soviet Nationalities Policy and Dissent in the Ukraine'. *The World Today* 30, no. 5 (1974): 214–26.
Boersner, Demetrio. *The Bolsheviks and the National and Colonial Question (1917–1928)*. Westport, CT: Hyperion Press, 1981.
Boiko (-Blochyn), Iurii. *Vybrani Pratsi*. Kyiv: Medykom, 1992.
Bojcun, Marko. 'Approaches to the Study of the Ukrainian Revolution'. *Journal of Ukrainian Studies* 24, no. 1 (1999): 21–38.
Bojko-Blochyn, G. 'Mykola Chvyl'ovyj'. In G. Bojko-Blochyn, *Gegen den Strom: Angewählte Beiträge zur Geschichte der slavishen Literaturen*, 327–45. Heidelberg: Winter, Univ.-Verlag, 1979.
Bondar-Tereshchenko, Ihor. *U Zadzerkalli 1910-1930-h Rokiv*. Kyiv: Tempora, 2009.
Borisenok, Elena. *Fenomen Sovetskoi Ukrainizatsii, 1920-30-e Gody*. Moscow: Evropa, 2006.
Borland, Harriet. *Soviet Literary Theory and Practice during the First Five-Year Plan, 1928–32*. New York: Greenwood Press, 1969.

Borowsky, Peter. 'Germany's Ukrainian Policy during World War I and the Revolution of 1918-19'. In *German-Ukrainian Relations in Historical Perspective*, edited by Hans-Joachim Torke and John-Paul Himka, 84-94. Edmonton and Toronto: CIUS, 1994.

Borysenko M. *Unifikatsiia Literaturnoho Zhyttia Ukrainy v 1920-1930h Roka*. Kyiv: UNISERV, 2001.

Bourdieu, Pierre. 'L`Illusion Biographique'. *Actes de la Recherche en Science Sociales* 62/62 (1986): 69-72;

Brandenberger, David. *National Bolshevism: Stalinist Mass Culture and the Formation of Modern Russian National Identity, 1931-1956*. Cambridge, MA: Harvard University Press, 2002.

Brandenberger, D. L. and Dubrovsky, A. M. '"The People Need a Tsar": The Emergence of National Bolshevism as Stalinist Ideology, 1931-1941,' *Europe-Asia Studies* 5, no. 50 (1998): 873-92.

Brandenberger, David and Platt, Kevin M. F. (eds.). *Epic Revisionism. Russian History and Literature as Stalinist Propaganda*. Madison, WI: University of Wisconsin Press, 2006.

Bristol, Evelyn 'Boris Pil'nyak'. *The Slavonic and East European Review* 41, no. 97 (1963): 494-512.

Brooks, Jeffrey. 'Public and Private Values in the Soviet Press, 1921-1928'. *Slavic Review* 48, no. 1 (1989): 16-35.

Brooks, Jeffrey. *Thank You, Comrade Stalin! Soviet Public Culture from the Revolution to Cold War*. Princeton: Princeton University Press, 2000.

Brown, E. J. *The Proletarian Episode in Russian Literature, 1928-1932*. New York: Octagon Books, 1971.

Brown, Kate. *A Biography of No Place: Ethnic Borderland to Soviet Heartland*. Cambridge, MA: Harvard University Press, 2004.

Burbank, Jane. *Intelligentsia and Revolution: Russian Views of Bolshevism, 1917-1922*. New York: Oxford University Press, 1986.

Burd'iu, Pier. 'Biograficheskaia Illiusiia'. *Inter* 1 (2002): 75-83.

Chaplenko, V. P*ropashchi Syly: Ukrains'ke Pys'menstvo pid Komunistychnym Rezhymom (1920-1933)*. Winnipeg: UVAN, 1960.

Chernev, Borislav. *Twilight of Empire: The Brest-Litovsk Conference and the Remaking of East-Central Europe, 1917-1918*. Toronto: University of Toronto Press, 2017.

Clark, Katerina. *The Soviet Novel: History as Ritual*. *Chicago*; London: Chicago University Press, 1981.

Clark, Katerina. 'The "Quiet Revolution" in Soviet Intellectual Life'. In *Russia in the Era of NEP*, edited by Sheila Fitzpatrick, Alexander Rabinowitch and Richard Stites, 210-30. Bloomington: Indiana University Press, 1991.

Clark, Katerina. *Petersburg, Crucible of Cultural Revolution*. Cambridge, MA; London: Harvard University Press, 1995.

Clark, Katerina. *Moscow the Fourth Rome: Stalinism, Cosmopolitanism, and the Evolution of Soviet Culture, 1931-1941*. Cambridge, MA: Harvard University Press, 2011.

Danylenko, Vasyl' (ed.). *Ukrains'ka Intelihentsia i Vlada: Zvedennia Sekretnoho Viddilu DPU USRR 1927-1929 rr*. Kyiv: Tempora, 2012.

Danylenko, Vasyl, and Kasyanov, Georgii. *Stalinizm i Ukrainska Intelihentsiia (20-30-ti roky)*. Kyiv: Naukova Dumka, 1991.

David-Fox, Michael. 'What Is Cultural Revolution?' *Russian Review* 58, no. 2 (1999): 181-201.

David-Fox, Michael. 'The Implication of Transnationalism'. *Kritika: Exploration in Russian and Eurasian History* 12, no. 4 (2011): 885-904.

d'Encausse, Hélène Carrère. *The Great Challenge: Nationalities and the Bolshevik State, 1917–1930*. New York: Holmes & Meier, 1992.

Dibrova, Volodymyr. 'Chernihiv P.Tychyny (Sproba prochytannia)'. *Suchasnist'* 11 (1995): 87–104.

Dobczansky, Markian. *From Soviet Heartland to Ukrainian Borderland: Searching for Identity in Kharkiv, 1943–2004*, PhD thesis, Stanford University, 2016.

Dobrenko, Evgeny. 'The Disaster of Middlebrow Taste, or, Who "Invented" Socialist Realism?' In *Socialist Realism without Shores*, edited by Thomas Lahusen and Evgeny Dobrenko, 135–64. London; Durham, NC: Duke University Press, 1997.

Dobrenko, Evgeny. *The Making of the State Reader. Social and Aesthetic Contexts of the Exception of Soviet Literature*. Redwood City: Stanford Univesity Press, 1997.

Dobrenko, Evgeny. *Aesthetics of Alienation: Reassessment of Early Soviet Cultural Theories*. Evanston, IL: North-Western University Press, 2005.

Dormik, Wolfram et al. (eds.). *Die Ukraine zwischen Selbstbestimmung und Fremdherrschaft, 1917–1922*. Graz: Leykam, 2011.

Doroshenko, Dmytro. *Istoriia Ukrainy 1917–1923 rr.*, 2 vols. 1930; repr., Kiev: Tempora, 2002.

Doroshko, Mykola. *Nomenklatura: Kerivna Verkhivka Radians'koi Ukrainy (1917–1938 rr.)* Kyiv: Nika-Tsentr, 2008.

Douds, Lara, Harris, James R. and Whitewood, Peter (eds.). *The Fate of the Bolshevik Revolution. Illiberal Liberation, 1917–1941*. London: Bloomsbury, 2020.

Dunham, Vera. *In Stalin's Time: Middleclass Values in Soviet Fiction*. New York; London: Cambridge University Press, 1976.

Dziuba, Ivan. *Mykola Khvyl'ovyi: "Aziatskii Renesans" i "Psykholohichna Ievropa"*. Kyiv: Kyievo-Mohylians'ka Akademiia, 2005.

Eagleton, Terry. *Marxism and Literary Criticism*. Berkeley: University of California Press, 1976.

Edgar, Adrienne. *Tribal Nation: The Making of Soviet Turkmenistan*. Princeton: Princeton University Press, 2006.

Eklof, Ben, Bushnell, John and Zakharova, Larissa (eds.). *Russia's Great Reforms, 1855–1881*. Bloomington, IN: Indiana UP, 1994.

Fedyshyn, Oleh. *Germany's Drive to the East and the Ukrainian Revolution, 1917–1918*. New Brunswick, NJ: Rutgers University Press, 1971.

Ferguson, Dolly. 'Lyricism and the Internal Landscape, in the Early Creative Prose of Mykola Khvyl'ovyi'. *Canadian Slavonic Papers/Revue Canadienne des Slavistes* 18, no. 4 (1976): 427–41.

Figes, Orlando. *A People's Tragedy: The Russian Revolution 1891–1924*. London: Jonathan Cape, 1996.

Fitzpatrick, Sheila. *The Commissariat of Enlightenment. Soviet Organization of Education and the Arts under Lunacharsky, October 1917–1921*. Cambridge: Cambridge University Press, 1970.

Fitzpatrick, Sheila 'The "Soft" Line on Culture and Its Enemies: Soviet Cultural Policy, 1922–1927'. *Slavic Review* 33, no. 2 (1974): 267–87.

Fitzpatrick, Sheila. 'Culture and Politics under Stalin: A Reappraisal'. *Slavic Review* 2, no. 35 (1976): 211–31.

Fitzpatrick, Sheila. 'Cultural Revolution as Class War'. In *Cultural Revolution in Russia, 1928–1931*, edited by Sheila Fitzpatrick, 8–40. Bloomington: Indiana University Press, 1978.

Fitzpatrick, Sheila. 'The Civil War as a Formative Experience'. In *Bolshevik Culture: Experiment and Order in the Russian Revolution*, edited by Abbott Gleason, Peter Kenez and Richard Stites, 57–77. Bloomington: Indiana University Press, 1985.

Fitzpatrick, Sheila. 'The Bolsheviks' Dilemma: Class, Culture, and Politics in the Early Soviet Years'. *Slavic Review* 47, no. 4 (1988): 599–613.

Fitzpatrick, Sheila. 'The Legacy of the Civil War'. In *Party, State, and Society in the Russian Civil War*, edited by Diane P. Koenker, William G. Rosenberg and Ronald Grigor Suny, 385–98. Bloomington: Indiana University Press, 1989.

Fitzpatrick, Sheila. *The Cultural Front. Power and Culture in Revolutionary Russia*. Ithaca; London: Cornell University Press, 1992.

Fitzpatrick, Sheila. *Everyday Stalinism: Ordinary Life in Extraordinary Times; Soviet Russia in the 1930s*. New York, NY: Oxford University Press, 1999.

Ford, Chris. 'Reconsidering the Ukrainian Revolution 1917–1921: The Dialectics of National Liberation and Social Emancipation'. *Journal of Contemporary Central and Eastern Europe* 15, no. 3 (2007): 279–306.

Ford, Christopher. 'Outline History of the Ukrainian Communist Party (Independentists): An Emancipatory Communism 1918–1925'. *Journal of Contemporary Central and Eastern Europe* 17, no. 2 (2009): 193–246.

Fournier, Anna. 'Mapping Identities: Russian Resistance to Linguistic Ukrainisation in Central and Eastern Ukraine'. *Europe-Asia Studies* 54, no. 3 (2002): 415–33.

Fowler, Mayhill C. 'Yiddish Theater in Soviet Ukraine: Reevaluating Ukrainian–Jewish Relations in the Arts'. *Ab Imperio* 3 (2011): 167–88.

Fowler, Mayhill C. 'Review on Poliuvannia na "Val'dshnepa". Rozsekrechenyi Mykola Khvyl'ovy'. *Kritika: Explorations in Russian and Eurasian History* 13, no. 2 (2012): 491–500.

Fowler, Mayhill C. 'Beyond Ukraine or Little Russia: Going Global with Culture in Ukraine', *Harvard Ukrainian Studies*, 34, no. 1/4, THE FUTURE OF THE, PAST: NEW PERSPECTIVES ON UKRAINIAN HISTORY (2015–2016): 259–84.

Fowler, Mayhill C. 'Mikhail Bulgakov, Mykola Kulish, and Soviet Theater: How Internal Transnationalism Remade Center and Periphery'. *Kritika: Explorations in Russian and Eurasian History*, 16 2 (2015): 263–90.

Fowler, Mayhill C. *Beau Monde on Empire's Edge: State and Stage in Soviet Ukraine*. Toronto: Toronto University Press, 2017.

Frolov, M. *Kompartiino-Radians'ka Elita v USRR (1917–1922 rr.): Stanovlennia i Funktsionuvannia*. Zaporizhzhia: Prem'ier, 2003.

Frolov, M. *Kompartiino-Radians'ka Elita v Ukraini (1923-1928 rr): Osoblyvosti Isnuvannia ta Funktsionuvannia*. Zaporizhzhia: Prem'ier, 2004.

Gan, O. *Trahediia Mykoly Khvyl'ovoho*. [s.l.], 1947.

Geldern, von James and Stites, Richard (eds.). *Mass Culture in Soviet Russia: Tales, Poems, Songs, Movies, Plays, and Folklore, 1917–1953*. Bloomington: Indiana UP, 1995.

Gilley, Christopher. 'Volodymyr Vynnychenko's Mission to Moscow and Kharkov'. *The Slavonic and East European Review* 84, no. 3 (2006): 508–37.

Gilley, Christopher. *The 'Change of Signposts' in the Ukrainian Emigration. A Contribution to the History of Sovietophilism in the 1920s*. Stuttgard: ibidem-Verlag, 2009.

Gilley, Christopher. 'Untangling the Ukrainian Revolution,' *Studies in Ethnicity and Nationalism* 17, no. 3 (2017): 326–38.

Golczewski, Frank. *Deutsche und Ukrainer 1914–1939*. Paderborn: Schöningh, 2010.

Golubkov, M. *Utrachennyie Al'ternativy. Formirovanie Monisticheskoi Kontseptsii Sovetskoi Literatury, 20-30 Gody*. Moscow: Nasledie, 1992.

Gorsuch, Anne E. 'Soviet Youth and the Politics of Popular Culture during tbe NEP'. *Social History* 17, no. 2 (1992): 189–201.
Gorsuch, Anne E. '"NEP be Damned!' Young Militants in the 1920s and the Culture of Civil War'. *Russian Review* 56, no. 4 (1997): 564–80.
Gorsuch, Anne E. *Youth in Revolutionary Russia: Enthusiasts, Bohemians, Delinquents*. Bloomingtonand Indianapolis: Indiana University Press, 2000.
Grabowicz, George. 'Tyčyna's "Černihiv"'. *Harvard Ukrainian Studies* I, no. 1 (1977): 79–114.
Grabowicz, George. 'Commentary: Exorcising Ukrainian Modernism'. *Harvard Ukrainian Studies* 15, 3/4 (1991): 273–83.
Grabowicz, George. 'Symbolic Autobiography in the Prose of Mykola Khvyl'ovyi (Some Preliminary Observations)'. *Harvard Ukrainian Studies* 22 (1998): 165–80.
Graziosi, Andrea. 'The New Soviet Archival Sources. Hypotheses for a Critical Assessment'. *Cahiers du Monde Russe* 40, no. 1/2 (1999): 13–63.
Gross, Jan Tomasz. *Revolution from Abroad: The Soviet Conquest of Poland's Western Ukraine and Western Belorussia*. Princeton: Princeton University Press, 1988.
Groys, Boris. *The Total Art of Stalinism: Avant-Garde, Aesthetic Dictatorship, and Beyond*. Princeton, NJ; Oxford: Princeton University Press, 1992.
Guenther, Hans and Evgeny Dobrenko (eds.). *Sotsrealisticheskii Kanon*. Sankt-Peterburg: Akademicheskii Proekt, 2000.
Gundorova, Tamara. 'Mykola Khvyl'ovyi i Ruinuvannia Romantychnoi Metafizyky'. *Slovo i Chas*, 11 (1993): 22–9.
Guthier, Steven L., 'The Popular Base of Ukrainian Nationalism in 1917'. *Slavic Review* 38, no 1 (1979): 30–47.
Hagen, Mark von. 'Soldiers in the Proletarian Dictatorship: From Defending the Revolution to Building Socialism'. In *Russia in the Era of NEP*, edited by Sheila Fitzpatrick, Alexander Rabinowitch and Richard Stites, 156–73. Bloomington: Indiana University Press, 1991.
Hagen, Mark von. 'Does Ukraine Have a history?' *Slavic Review* 54, no. 3 (1995): 658–73.
Hagen, Mark von. '"I Love Russia, and/but I Want Ukraine," or How a Russian General Became Hetman of the Ukrainian State, 1917–1918'. *Journal of Ukrainian Studies* 29, no. 1–2 (2004): 115–48.
Halfin, Igal. *Terror in My Soul. Communist Autobiographies on Trial*. Cambridge, MA: Harvard University Press, 2003.
Halfin, Igar. *Red Autobiographies: Initiating the Bolshevik Self*. Washington, Washington University Press, 2011.
Hamm, Michael. *Kiev: A Portrait, 1800–1917*. Princeton: Princeton University Press, 1993.
Hamrets'kyi, Iurii et al. *Rady Ukraiany v 1917 r. Lypen'-Hruden' 1917 r*. Kyiv, Naukova Dumka, 1974.
Hamrets'kyi, Iurii. *Rady Robitnychykh Deputativ Ukrainy v 1917 rotsi (period dvovladdia)*. Kyiv, Naukova Dumka, 1966.
Hamrets'kyi, Iurii. 'Bilshovyky ta ikhni politychni protivnyky na Ukraini v 1917 r'. *Ukrainsky Istorychnyi Zhurnal* no. 11 (1987): 64–79.
Haugen, Arne. *The Establishment of National Republics in Soviet Central Asia*. New York: Palgrave, 2003.
Hellbeck, Jochen. *Revolution on My Mind: Writing a Diary under Stalin*. Cambridge, MA: Harvard University Press, 2006.
Hewryk, Titus D. 'Planning of the Capital in Kharkiv'. *Harvard Ukrainian Studies* XVI, no. 3/4 (1992): 325–60.

Himka, John-Paul. 'The National and Social in the Ukrainian Revolution of 1917-20: The Historiographical Agenda'. *Archiv für Sozialgeschichte* 34 (1994): 95-110.

Hirik, Serhii. '"The Permanent Revolution" and "the Asian Renaissance": Parallels between the Political Conceptions of Leon Trotsky and Mykola Khvylovy'. *Journal of Contemporary Central and Eastern Europe* 17, no. 2 (2009): 181-91.

Hirsch, Francine. 'Toward an Empire of Nations: Border-Making and the Formation of Soviet National Identities'. *The Russian Review* 59, no. 2 (2000): 201-26.

Hirsch, Francine. *Empire of Nations: Ethnographic Knowledge and the Making of the Soviet Union*. Ithaca: Cornell University Press, 2005.

Hlobenko, Mykola. 'Thirty-Five Years of Ukrainian Literature in the U.S.S.R.' *The Slavonic and East European Review* 33, no. 80 (1954): 1-16.

Hnatiuk, Ola. *Pożegnanie z Imperium. Ukraińskie Dyskusje o Tożsamości*. Lublin: Wydawnictwo Uniwersytetu Marii Curie-Skłodowskiej, 2003.

Hnatiuk, Ola. *Odwaga i Strach*. Wroclaw: Wydawnictwo KEW, 2015.

Hnatiuk, Ola. *Courage and Fear*. Boston: Academic Studies Press, 2019.

Holubenko, Petro. *VAPLITE*. [s.l.]: Orlyk, 1948.

Holubenko V. 'Khvyl'ovyi i Shpenhler'. *Suchasnist'* 5 (1963): 53-70.

Holubnychy, Vsevolod. 'Outline History of the Communist Party of Ukraine'. In *Soviet Regional Economics. Selected Works of Vsevolod Holubnychy*, edited by Iwan S. Koropeckyj, 66-140. Edmonton: CIUS, 1982.

Horbyk, Roman and Palko, Olena. 'Righting the Writing: The Power Dynamic of Soviet Ukraine Language Policies and Reforms in the 1920s-1930s'. *Studi Slavistici* XIV (2017): 77-9.

Hornykiewicz, Theophil (ed.). *Ereignisse in der Ukraine, 1914-1922*, 4 vols. Philadelphia: W.K. Lypynsky East European Research Institute, 1966-9.

Hryn, Halyna. 'The "Executed Renaissance" Paradigm Revisited'. *Harvard Ukrainian Studies* 27 (2004-5): 67-96.

Hryn, Halyna. *Literaturnyi Iarmarok: Ukranian Modernism's Defining Moment*. PhD thesis, University of Toronto, 2005.

Hunczak, Taras (ed.). *The Ukraine, 1917-1921: A Study in Revolution*. Cambridge, MA: HURI, 1977.

Hunczak, Taras. 'The Ukraine under Hetman Pavlo Skoropadsky'. In *The Ukraine, 1917-1921: A Study in Revolution*, edited by Hunczak Taras. Cambridge, MA: HURI, 1977, 61-81.

Hundorova, Tamara and *Matusiak*, Agnieszka (eds.). *Postkolonializm. Heneratsii. Kul'tura*. Kyiv: Laurus, 2015.

Iarovyi, O. 'Poet na Perehresti Pohliadiv: Krytyka Riznykh Rokiv pro Tychynu'. *Ukrains'ka Mova ta Literature* 18 (1997): 1-3.

Il'nyts'kyi, M. 'Polemika Futurystiv z Khvyl'ovym u Period Politfrontu'. *Zapysky NTSH (Lviv)* 221 (1990): 136-56.

Ilnytzky, Oleh. 'The Modernist Ideology and Mykola Khvyl'ovyi'. *Harvard Ukrainian Studies* 15, no. 3/4 (1991): 257-62.

Ilnytzkyj, Oleh S. *Ukrainian Futurism, 1914-1930. A Historical and Critical Study*. Cambridge, MA: Harvard University Press, 1998.

Ishchuk, Arsen. *Pavlo Tychyna*. Kyiv: Derzhlitvydav, 1954.

Jensen, Peter A. *Nature as Code. The Achievements of Boris Pilnjak, 1915-1924C*. Copenhagen: Rosenkilde & Bagger, 1979.

Joravsky, David. 'Cultural Revolution and the Fortress Mentality in Bolshevik Culture'. In *Bolshevik Culture: Experiment and Order in the Russian Revolution*, edited by Abbott Gleason, Peter Kenez and Richard Stites, 93-113. Bloomington: Indiana UP, 1985.

Kagarlitsky, Boris. *The Thinking Reed: Intellectuals and the Soviet State 1917 to the Present*. London: Verso, 1988.

Kappeler, Andreas, Hausmann, Guido, Petrenko, Olena and Golczewski, Frank. 'Diskussion: Wie soll man ukrainische Geschichte betreiben?' *Jahrbücher für Geschichte Osteuropas* 4 (2016), 626-45.

Kappeler, Andreas. *The Russian Empire: A Multiethnic History*. Harlow: Pearson Education Limited, 2001.

Kappeler, Andreas. *Der Schwierige Weg zur Nation. Beitrage zur neueren Geschichte der Ukraine*. Wien: Bohlau, 2003.

Kasianov, G. and Tolochko, O. 'Natsional'ni Istorii ta Suchasna Istoriohrafiia: Vyklyky i Nebezpeky pry Napysanni Novoi Istorii Ukrainy,' *Ukrains'kyi Istorychnyi Zhurnal* 6 (2012): 4-21.

Kazanin, Ihor. *Zabytoe Budushchee: Sovetskaia Vlast' i Rossiiskaia Inteligentsiia v Pervoe Posleoktiabr'skoe Desiatiletie*. Volgograd: Volgogradskii Gosudarstvennyi universitet, 2001.

Kemp-Welch, A. *Stalin and the Literary Intelligentsia, 1928-1939*. London: Palgrave Macmillan, 1991.

Kenez, Peter. *The Birth of the Propaganda State. Soviet Methods of Mass Mobilization, 1917-1929*. Cambridge: Cambridge University Press, 1985.

Kharchuk, R. 'Zmina oblychchia: PavloTychyna'. *Dyvoslovo* 2 (2011): 58-62.

Kharkhun, Valentyna. '"Mytets' v Kanoni", Sotsrealistychna Poesiia Pavla Tychyny 1930-60-kh Rokiv'. *Slovo i Chas* 10 (2006): 38-51.

Kharkhun, Valentyna. *Sotsrealistychnyi Kanon v Ukrains'kii Literaturi: Genesa, Rozvytok, Modyfikatsii*. Nizhyn: Hidromaks, 2009.

Khvyl'ovyi - Zbroia KGB. New York: Prezydiia Svitovoi Rady SVU, 1983.

Kochetkova, Inna. *The Myth of the Russian Intelligentsia: Old Intellectuals in the New Russia*. London, New York: Routledge, 2010.

Koliastruk, O. 'Diial'nist' Vseukrains'koho komitetu spryiannia vchenym u 20-ti roky XX st.'. *Intelihentsiia i Vlada* 13 (2008): 97-111.

Koliastruk, O. *Intelligentsia USRR v 1920-ti Roky: Povsiakdenne Zhyttia*. Kharkiv: Rarytety Ukrainy, 2010.

Komarenko, T. and Shypovych, M. *Vlada i Literaturno-Mystets'ka Intelihentsiia Radians'koi Ukrainy: 20-ti rr. XX st*. Kyiv: NAN Ukrainy, 1999.

Koshelivets', Ivan. *Suchasna Literatura v URSR*. New York: Proloh, 1964.

Koshelivets', Ivan. *Mykola Skrypnyk*. Munich: Suchasnist', 1972.

Kostiuk, Hryhorii. *Stalinizm v Ukraini (Geneza i Naslidky). Doslidzhennia i Sposterezhennia Suchasnyka*. Kyiv: Smoloskyp, 1995.

Kotkin, Stephen. '1991 and the Russian Revolution: Sources, Conceptual Categories, Analytical Frameworks'. *The Journal of Modern History* 70, no. 2 (1998): 384-425.

Kovaliv, Iurii. *Literaturna Dyskusiia 1925-1928 rr*. Kyiv: Znannia, 1990.

Kratochvil, Alexander. *Mykola Chvyl'ovyi: Eine Studie zu Leben und Werk*. Munchen: Verlag Otto Sagner, 1999.

Kravchenko, Vladimir. *Kharkov/Kharkiv: Stolitsa Pohranichiia*. Vilnus: EGU, 2010.

Krawchenko, Bohdan. 'The Impact of Industrialization on the Social Structure of Ukraine'. *Canadian Slavonic Papers/Revue Canadienne des Slavistes* 22, no. 3 (1980): 338-57.

Krawchenko, Bohdan. *Social Change and National Consciousness in Twentieth-Century Ukraine*. Basingstoke: Macmillan, 1986.
Kruchek, O. *Stanovlennia Derzhavnoi Polityky URSR u Haluzi Natsional'noi Kul'tury (1920–23)*. Kyiv: NAN Ukrainy, 1996.
Krupa, Pawel. *"Na Zachód" i "Z dala od Moskwy"? Publicystyka Mykoły Chwylowego lat 1925–1926. Historia–idee—konteksty*. Krakow: Universitas, 2018.
Kuhr-Korolev, Corinna et al. (eds.). *Sowjet Jugend 1917–1941: Generation zwischen Revolution und Resignation*. Essen, Klartext Verlag, 2001.
Kulchytsky, Stanislav. 'The Phenomenon of Soviet Statehood'. In *Culture, Nation, And Identity: The Ukrainian-Russian Encounter, 1600–1945*, edited by Andreas Kappeler, Zenon E. Kohut, Frank E. Sysyn and Mark von Hagen, 344–59. Edmonton: CIUS, 2003.
Kul'chyts'kyi, Stanislav. *Komunism v Ukraini; Pershe Desiatylittia (1919–1928)*. Kyiv: Osnovy, 1996.
Latynina Alla, 'The Stalin Prize for Literature as the Quintessence of Socialist Realism'. In *In the Party Spirit. Socialist Realism and Literary Practice in the Soviet Union, East Germany and China*, edited by Hilary Chung, 106–28. Amsterdam; Atlanta, Rodopi Editions, 1996.
Lavrinenko, Iurii. *Na Shliakhakh Syntezy Kliarnetyzmu*. New York: Suchasnist', 1977.
Lavrinenko, Iurii. *Pavlo Tychyna i Ioho Poema 'Skovoroda' na Tli Epokhy*. Munich: Suchasnist', 1980.
Lavrinenko, Iurii. *Rozstriliane Vidrodzhennia. Antolohiia 1917–1933*. Kyiv: Smoloskyp, 2007 [1959].
Liber, George. 'Language, Literacy, and Book Publishing in the Ukrainian SSR, 1923–1928'. *Slavic Review* 41, no. 4 (1982): 673–85.
Liber, George. 'Urban Growth and Ethnic Change in the Ukrainian SSR, 1923–1933'. *Soviet Studies* 41, no. 4 (1989): 574–91.
Liber, George. *Soviet Nationality Policy, Urban Growth, and Identity Change in the Ukrainian SSR 1923–1934*. Cambridge: Cambridge University Press, 2002.
Liber, George. *Total Wars and the Making of Modern Ukraine, 1914–1954*. Toronto: Toronto University Press, 2016.
Lincoln, Bruce W. *The Great Reforms: Autocracy, Bureaucracy, and the Politics of Change in Imperial Russia*. DeKalb: Northern Illinois UP, 1990.
Luckyj, George S. N. *Literary Politics in the Soviet Ukraine, 1917–1934*. Durham-London: Duke University Press, 1990.
Luckyj, George. S. N. *Keeping a Record: Literary Purges in Soviet Ukraine (1930s): a Bio-Bibliography*. Edmonton: CIUS, 1988.
Mace, James. *Communism and the Dilemmas of National Liberation: National Communism in Soviet Ukraine, 1918–1933*. Cambridge, MA: Harvard University Press, 1983.
Magocsi, Paul Robert. *A History of Ukraine: The Land and Its Peoples*. Toronto: Toronto University Press, 2010.
Maguire, Robert A. *Red Virgin Soil: Soviet Literature in the 1920s*. Princeton: Princeton University Press, 1968.
Majstrenko, Ivan. *Borot'bism: A Chapter in the History of Ukrainian Communism*. New York: Research Program on the U. S. S. R., 1954.
Maistrenko, Ivan. *Istoriia Komunistychnoi Partii Ukrainy*. Munich: Suchasnist', 1979.
Makarov, V. and Khristoforov, V. (eds.). *Vysylka Vmesto Rastrela. Deportatsiia Intelligentsyi v Dokumentah VCHK-GPU. 1921–23*. Moscow: Russkii Put', 2005.

Mally, Lynn. *Blueprint of a New Culture: A Social History of the Proletkult, 1917–1921.* Berkeley: University of California Press, 1990.
Mally, Lynn. *Culture of the Future. The Proletkult Movement in Revolutionary Russia.* Berkeley: University of California Press, 1990.
Maloney, Philip. 'Anarchism and Bolshevism in the Works of Boris Pilnyak'. *Russian Review* 32, no. 1 (1973): 43–53.
Martin, Terry. 'Interpreting the New Archival Signals: Nationalities Policy and the Nature of the Soviet Bureaucracy'. *Cahiers du Monde Russe* 40/1–2 (1999): 113–24.
Martin, Terry. *The Affirmative Action Empire: Nations and Nationalism in the Soviet Union, 1923–1939.* Ithaca: Cornell University Press, 2001.
McClelland, James C. 'Utopianism versus Revolutionary Heroism in Bolshevik Policy: The Proletarian Culture Debate'. *Slavic Review* 39, no. 3 (1980): 403–25.
Mihaychuk, George. 'The Role of the 1920s Form and Content Debate in Ukraine'. *Canadian Slavonic Papers/Revue Canadienne des Slavistes* 37, no. 1/2 (1995): 107–26.
Miller, Alexei. *The Ukrainian Question. The Russian Empire and Nationalism in the 19th Century.* Budapest: CEU Press, 2003.
Mintz, Matityahu. 'The Secretariat of Internationality Affairs (Sekretariiat Mizhnatsional'nykh Sprav) of the Ukrainian General Secretariat (1917–1918)'. *Harvard Ukrainian Studies* 6, no. 1 (1982): 25–42.
Mirchuk, Pavlo. *Ukrains'ko-Moskovs'ka Viina 1917–1919.* Toronto: Liha Vyzvolennia Ukrainy, 1957.
Moss, Kenneth, *Jewish Renaissance in the Russian Revolution.* Cambridge: Cambridge University Press, 2009.
Motyl, Alexander J. *The Turn to the Right: The Ideological Origins and Development of Ukrainian Nationalism, 1919–1929.* Boulder; New York: Columbia University Press, 1980.
Movchan, Raisa. *Ukrains'kyi Modernizm 1920-kh: Portret v Istorychnomu Interieri.* Kyiv: Stylos, 2008.
Mudrak, Myroslava. *The New Generation and Artistic Modernism in the Ukraine.* Ann Arbor: UMI Research Press, 1986.
Myronets', Nadiia. 'Ukrains'ka Revoliutsiia v Doli i Tvorchosti Pavla Tychyna'. In Nadiia Myronets', *Dzherela Istorychnoi Pam'iati*, 120–32. Kyiv: NAN Ukrainy, 2008.
Nahaylo, Bohdan. 'Ukrainian National Resistance in Soviet Ukraine during the 1920s'. *Journal of Ukrainian Studies* 15, no. 2 (1990): 1–18.
Naiman, Eric. 'On Soviet Subjects and the Scholars Who Make Them'. *Russian Review* 60, no. 3 (2001): 307–15.
Neumann, Mattias. 'Revolutionizing Mind and Soul? Soviet Youth and Cultural Campaigns during the New Economic Policy (1921–8)'. *Social History* 33, no. 3 (2008): 262–3.
Neumann, Matthias. *The Communist Youth League and the Transformation of the Soviet Union, 1917–1932.* London; New York: Routledge, 2011.
Neumann, Matthias. '"Youth, It's Your Turn!": Generations and the Fate of the Russian Revolution (1917–1932)'. *Journal of Social History* 46, no. 2 (2012): 273–304.
Novacki, Albert. *Myśli pod prąd". Twórczość Mykoły Chwylowego w kontekście ukraińskiej dyskusji literackiej lat 1925–1928.* Lublin: Wydawnictwo KUL, 2013.
Novychenko, Leonid, *Poeziia i Revoliutsiia. Tvorchist' P.Tychyny v Pershi Pisliazhovtnevi Roky.* Kyiv: Dnipro, 1968.
Novychenko, Leonid. 'Tychyna i Ioho Chas: Nezaivi Dopovnennia'. Leonid Novychenko, *Dvadtsiti Roky: Literaturni Dyskusii, Polemiky. Literaturno-Krytychni Statti*, 314–66. Kyiv: Dnipro, 1991.

Nykolyshyn, S. *Kul'turna Polityka Bol'shevykiv i Ukrains'kyi Kul'turnyi Protses*. [s.l.], 1939.
Ohiienko, Ivan. *Narysy z Istorii Ukriins'koi Movy. Systema Ukrains'koho Pravopysu.* Winnipeg: Volyn', 1990.
O'Keeffe, Brigid. *New Soviet Gypsies: Nationality, Performance, and Selfhood in the Early Soviet Union* Toronto: Toronto University Press, 2013.
Ostroverkha, Mykhailo. *Chornoknyzhnyk iz Zubivky: Khvyl'ovyi i khvyl'ovizm*. New-York, [s.l.]: 1955.
Palko, Olena. 'Ukrainian National Communism: Challenging History'. *Journal of Contemporary Central and Eastern Europe* 22, no. 1 (2014): 27–48.
Palko, Olena. 'Between Two Powers: A Soviet Ukrainian Writer Mykola Khvyl'ovyi'. *Jahrbücher für Geschichte Osteuropas* 4 (2016): 575–98.
Palko, Olena. 'Reading in Ukrainian: The Working Class and Mass Literature in Early Soviet Ukraine', *Social History* 44, no. 3 (2019): 343–68.
Palko, Olena. 'Debating the Early Soviet Nationalities Policy: The Case of Soviet Ukraine'. In *The Fate of the Bolshevik Revolution. Illiberal Liberation, 1917–1941*, edited by Lara Douds, James R. Harris and Peter Whitewood. 157–172. London: Bloomsbury, 2020.
Panchenko, Volodymyr, 'Dyptykh pro Vtrachenu Svobodu'. Naukovi Zapysky NaUKMA. Filolohichni Nauky 150 (2013): 55–63.
Parthé, Kathleen.'What Was Soviet Literature?' *The Slavic and East European Journal* 2, no. 38 (1994): 290–301.
Pauly, Matthew D. 'Tending to the "Native Word": Teachers and the Soviet Campaign for Ukrainian-Language Schooling, 1923–1930'. *Nationalities Papers* 37, no. 3 (2009): 251–76.
Pauly, Matthew D. *Breaking the Tongue: Language, Education, and Power in Soviet Ukraine, 1923–1934*. Toronto: Toronto University Press, 2014.
Pavlyshyn, Marko. 'Post-Colonial Features in Contemporary Ukrainian Culture'. '*Australian Slavonic and East European Studies* 2, no. 6 (1992): 41–55.
Petrov, Petre. *Automatic for the Masses: Authorship and Agency in Early Soviet Culture*. Toronto University Press, Scholarly Publishing Division, 2015.
Petrov, Viktor. *Ukrains'ki Kul'turni Diiachi URSR 1920–1940 Zhertvy Bil'shovyts'koho Teroru*. New York: Proloh, 1959.
Petrovsky Shtern, Yohanan. *The Anti-Imperial Choice: The Making of the Ukrainian Jew*. New Haven: Yale UP, 2009.
Pidhayny, Semen. 'Ukrainian National Communism'. *Ukrainian Review* 7 (1959): 45–64.
Pinnow, Kenneth M. 'Violence against the Collective Self: Suicide and the Problem of Social Integration in Early Bolshevik Russia'. In *Histories of Suicide: International Perspectives on Self-Destruction in the Modern World*, edited by John Weaver and David Wright, 201–30. Toronto: Toronto UP, 2009.
Pinnow, Kenneth M. *Lost to the Collective: Suicide and the Promise of Soviet Socialism, 1921–1929*. Ithaca; London: Cornell University Press, 2010.
Pipes, Richard. *The Formation of the Soviet Union. Communism and Nationalism 1917–1923*. New York: Atheneum, 1980.
Plaggenborg, Stefan. *Revolutionskultur: Menschenbilder und Kulturelle Praxis in Sowjetrussland zwischen Oktoberrevolution und Stalinismus*. Köln: Böhlau, 1996.
Pliushch, Leonid. *Ioho Taemnytsia, abo "Prekrasna Lozha" Khvyl'ovoho*. Kyiv: Fakt, 2006.
Pliushch, Vasyl'. *Pravda pro Khvyl'ovizm*. Munich: Spilka Vyzvolennia Ukrainy, 1954.
Plokhy, Serhii. *Unmaking Imperial Russia: Mykhailo Hrushevsky and the Writing of Ukrainian History*. Buffalo, NY: Toronto University Press, 2005.

Prymachenko, Iana. 'Ukrains'ka literaturna dyskusiia 1920-x rr.: vid pytannia profesiinykh standartiv do problemy nacional'noi identychnosti,' *Problemy Istorii Ukrainy: Fakty, Sudzhennia, Poshuky.* Vyp. 23 (2015): 228–46.
Prystaiko, Volodymyr and Shapoval, Iurii. *Mykhailo Hrushevs'kyi: Sprava 'UNTs' i Ostanni Roky.* Kyiv: Krytyka, 1999.
Radziejowski, Janusz. *The Communist Party of Western Ukraine, 1919–29.* Edmonton: The Canadian Library in Ukrainian Studies, 1983.
Rahmannyi, Roman. *Dmytro Dontsov i Mykola Khvyl'ovyi, 1923-1933.* London: Ukrains'ka Vydavnycha Spilka, 1984.
Rakhno, Oleksandr. *Chernihivs'ki Zemtsi (Istoryko-Biohrafichni Narysy).* Chernihiv: Chernihivs'ki oberehy, 2009.
Read, Christopher. *Culture and Power in Revolutionary Russia: The Intelligentsia and the Transition from Tsarism to Communism.* New York: St Martin's Press, 1990.
Reck, Vera T. *Boris Pil'niak: A Soviet Writer in Conflict with the State.* Montreal: McGill-Queen's University Press, 1975.
Remy, Johannes. 'The Valuev Circular and Censorship of Ukrainian Publications in the Russian Empire (1863–1876): Intention and Practice'. *Canadian Slavonic Papers/Revue Canadienne des Slavistes* 49, no. 1–2 (2007): 87–110.
Remy, Johannes. *Brothers or Enemies: The Ukrainian National Movement and Russia from the 1840s to the 1870s.* Toronto: Toronto UP, 2016.
Reshetar, John S. 'National Deviation in the Soviet Union'. *American Slavic and East European Review* 12, no. 2 (1953): 162–74.
Reshetar, John. *The Ukrainian Revolution, 1917–1920: A Study in Nationalism.* New York: Princeton University Press, 1952.
Rév, István. *Retroactive Justice: Prehistory of Post-Communism.* Redwood City: Stanford University Press, 2005.
Robin, Régine, *Socialist Realism: An Impossible Aesthetic.* Stanford: Stanford University Press, 1992.
Romanenko, H. and Sheiko, V. *Evoliutsiia Khudozhnikh i Literaturnykh Obiednan' Ukrainy: Istoryko-Kul'turolohichnyi Vymir.* Kyiv: NAN Ukrainy, 2008.
Rubliov, O. and Cherchenko, Iu. 'Stalinshchyna i dolia zakhidnoukrains'koi intellihentsii'. *Ukrains'kyi Istorychnyi Zhurnal* 1–7 (1991).
Saunders, David. 'Russia and Ukraine under Alexander II: The Valuev Edict of 1863'. *The International History Review* 17, no. 1 (1995): 23–50.
Sawczak, P. 'The Novelazation of the Pamphlet. Aestetic Compromise as Argument: MykolaKhvyl'ovyj's Woodcocks'. *Journal of Ukrainian Studies* 1–2 (1995): 53–60.
Shaitanov, Igor. 'From Avant-Garde to Socialist Realism: How Writers Adapt'. In *In the Party Spirit. Socialist Realism and Literary Practice in the Soviet Union, East Germany and*, edited by Hilary Chung, 44–54. Amsterdam; Atlanta, Rodopi Bv Editions, 1996.
Shakhovskyi, Semen. *V Maisterni poetychnoho slova.* Kyiv: Derzhlitvydav, 1958.
Shakhovs'kyi, Semen. *Pavlo Tychyna.* Kyiv: Dnipro, 1968.
Shapoval, Iurii. *Ukraina 20-50-h Rokiv (Storinky Nenapysanoi Istorii).* Kyiv: Naukova Dumka, 1993.
Sherekh, Iurii. 'Trends in Ukrainian Literature under the Soviets'. *The Ukrainian Quarterly* 2 (1948): 151–67.
Shevel'ov, Iurii. *Ukrains'ka Mova v Pershii Polovyni Dvadtsiatoho Stolittia (1900–1941). Stan i Status.* Chernovtsi: Ruta, 1998.
Sherekh, Iurii. 'Khvyl'ovyi bez Polityky'. In Iurii Sherekh, *Porohy i Zaporizhzhia: Literatura. Mystetstvo. Ideolohiia.* vol. 1, 57–68. Kharkiv: Folio. 1998 [1953].

Shevel'ov, Iurii. 'Lit Ikara (Pamflety Mykoly Khvyl'ovoho)', in Iurii Shevel'ov, *Vybrani Pratsi: Literaturoznavstvo*. vol. II, 287–342. Kyiv: Kyievo-Mohylians'ka Akademiia, 2009 [1977].
Shkandrij, Myroslav. 'U Poshukakh Novoho: Revoliutsiia v Ukrains'komu Mystetstvi 1920- kh'. *Suchasnist'* 25, no. 1 (1986): 41–51; 25, no. 2 (1986): 42–58.
Shkandrij, Myroslav. *Modernists, Marxists and the Nation: The Ukrainian Literary Discussion of the 1920s*. Edmonton: CIUS, 1992.
Shkandrij, Myroslav. *Russia and Ukraine. Literature and the Discourse of Empire from Napoleonic to Postcolonial Times*. Montreal: McGill-Queen's University Press, 2001.
Shkandrij, Myroslav, 'The Ukrainian Reading Public in the 1920s: Real, Implied and Ideal'. *Canadian Slavonic Papers/Revue Canadienne Des Slavistes* 2, no. 5 (2016): 160–83.
Shkandrij, Myroslav and Bertelsen, Olga. 'The Soviet Regime's National Operations in Ukraine, 1929–1934'. *Canadian Slavonic Papers/Revue Canadienne des Slavistes* 55, no. 3–4 (2013): 417–48.
Simonenko, R. 'National'no-kul'turnaia avtonomiia na Ukraine v 1917–1918 godakh'. *Voprosy Istorii* 1 (1997): 50–63.
Slezkine, Yuri. 'The USSR as Communal Apartment, or How a Socialist State Promoted Ethnic Particularism'. *Slavic Review* 53, no. 2 (1994): 414–52.
Slonim, Mark. *Soviet Russian Literature. Writers and Problems*. New York: Oxford University Press, 1964.
Smith, Jeremy. *Red Nations. The Nationalities Experience in and after the USSR*. Cambridge: Cambridge Univesity Press, 2013.
Smolii, Valerii. *Istoriia Ukrainy*. Kyiv: Al'ternatyvy, 1997.
Smolii, Valerii et al. (eds.), *Narysy Istorii Ukrains'koi Revoliutsii 1917–1921 Rokiv*, 2 vols. Kyiv: Naukova dumka, 2011–2.
Smolii, Valerii et al. (eds.), *Ukrainizatsiia 1920-30-kh Rokiv: Peremodumovy, Zdobutky, Uroky*. Kyiv: NAN Ukrainy, 2003.
Snyder, Timothy. *Sketches from a Secret War: A Polish Artist's Mission to Liberate Soviet Ukraine*. New Heaven: Yale UP, 2005.
Soldatenko, Valerii. *Nezlamnyi. Zhyttia i smert' Mykoly Skrypnyka*. Kyiv: Knyha Pamiati Ukrainy, 2002.
Soldatenko, Valerii. *U Poshukah Sotsial'noi ta Natsional'noi Harmonii: Eskizy do Istorii Ukrains'koho Komunizmu*. Kyiv: IPiEND, 2006.
Soldatenko, Valerii. *Ukraina v Revoliutsiinu Dobu*, 4 vols. Kyiv: Svitohliad, 2010.
Somchynsky, Bohdan. 'National Communism and the Politics of Industrialization in Ukraine, 1923–28'. *Journal of Ukrainian Studies* 13, no. 2 (1988): 52–69.
Sontag, John P. 'The Soviet War Scare of 1926–27'. *The Russian Review* 34, no. 1 (1975): 66–77.
Sosnovs'ka, Tetiana. '"Iak Ia Zheniu – Svoho Brata –Riatuvav u Cheka," Malovidome z Zhyttia Poeta Pavla Tychyna'. *Z Arkhiviv VUCHK, GPU, NKVD, KGB* 1 (1994): 163–7.
Soviet Ukraine. Kiev: Editorial office of the Ukrainian Soviet Encyclopedia, Academy of Sciences of the Ukrainian S.S.R, 1969.
Starovoitenko, Inna. *Ievhen Chykalenko: Liudyna na Tli Epokhy*. Kyiv: Tempora, 2009.
Stepun, Fedor. 'The Russian Intelligentsia and Bolshevism'. *Russian Review* 17, no. 4 (1958): 263–77.
Stites, Richard. *Revolutionar Dreams: Utopian Vision and Experimental Life in the Russian Revolution*. New York: Oxford University Press, 1989.
Stites, Richard. *Russian Popular Culture: Entertainment and Society since 1900*. Cambridge: Cambridge University Press, 1992.

Struk, Danylo H. 'Tupyk or Blind-Alley: "Val'dshnepy" of M. Khvyl'ovyi'. *Canadian-American Slavic Papers* II, no. 2 (1968): 239–51.
Stus, Vasyl'. *Fenomen Doby (Skhodzhennia na Holhofu Slavy)*. Kyiv: Znannia Ukrainy, 1993.
Sullivant, Robert. *Soviet Politics and the Ukraine 1917–1957*. New York-London: Columbia University Press, 1962.
Suny, Ronald. *The Revenge of the Past: Nationalism, Revolution, and the Collapse of the Soviet Union*. Redwood City: Stanford University Press, 1993.
Sverstiuk, Ievhen. 'Proshchannia z Madonnoiu'. In Ievhen Sverstiuk, *Bludni Syny Ukrainy*. 196–213. Kyiv: Znannia, 1993.
Tarnavs'kyi, Oleh. 'T. S. Eliot i Pavlo Tychyna'. *Vsesvit* 6 (1990): 130–6.
Tarnawsky, Maxim. 'Modernism in Ukrainian Prose'. *Harvard Ukrainian Studies* 15, nos 3/4 (1991): 263–72.
Tel'niuk, Stanislav. *Pavlo Tychyna. Bibliohrafichna Povist'*. Kyiv: Molod', 1979.
Tel'niuk, Stanislav. 'Mistyfikatsiia Poeta v Totalitarnomu Pekli'. *Dnipro* 1 (1991): 181–97.
Tel'niuk, Stanislav. *'Molodyi ia, Molodyi'. Poetychnyi Svit Pavla Tychyna. 1906–1925*. Kyiv: Dnipro, 1990.
Terence, Emmons and Vucinich, Wayne S. (eds.). *The Zemstvo in Russia: An Experiment in Local Self-Government*. Cambridge: Cambridge University Press, 1982.
Ther, Philipp and Kasianov, Georgiy. *Ukraine: Laboratory of Transnational History*. Budapest: CEU Press, 2009.
Thomson, Boris. *The Premature Revolution, Russian Literature and Society, 1917–1946*. London: Weidenfeld and Nicolson, 1972.
Tsymbal, Iaryna. 'Kharkivs'kyi Tekst 1920-kh.: Obirvana Sproba'. *Ukrains'ka Literatura XX stolittia. Literaturoznavchi Obrii* 18 (2010): 54–61.
Veidlinger, Jeffrey. *In the Shadow of the Shtetl: Small-Town Jewish Life in Soviet Ukraine*. Bloomington; Indianapolis, Indiana University Press, 2013.
Velychenko, Stephen. *State-Building in Revolutionary Ukraine: A Comparative Study of Governments and Bureaucrats, 1917–22*. Toronto: Toronto University Press, 2011.
Velychenko, Stephen. *Painting Imperialism and Nationalism Red: The Ukrainian Marxist Critique of Russian Communist Rule in Ukraine, 1918–1925*. Toronto: Toronto University Press, 2015.
Verstiuk, Vladyslav. *Ukrains'ka Tsentral'na Rada*. Kyiv: Zapovid, 1997.
Verstiuk, Vladyslav. 'Sklad i Struktura Ukrains'koi Tsentral'noi Rady'. *Problemy Vyvchennia Istorii Ukrains'koi Revoliutsii 1917–1921 Rokiv* 4 (2009): 5–30.
Viola, Lynne. *Peasant Rebels under Stalin: Collectivization and the Culture of Peasant Resistance*. New York: Oxford University Press, 1999.
Wade, Rex A. 'Ukrainian Nationalism and "Soviet Power": Kharkiv, 1917'. In *Ukrainian Past, Ukrainian Present*, edited by B. Krawchenko, 70–83. New York: St Martin's Press, 1993.
Waterlow, Jonathan. *It's Only a Joke, Comrade! Humour, Trust and Everyday Life under Stalin*. Oxford: CreateSpace Independent Publishing Platform, 2018.
Westerman, Frank. *Engineers of the Soul: In the Footsteps of Stalin's Writers*. London: Vintage Books, 2011.
Whitewood, Peter. 'The International Situation: Fear of Invasion and Growing Authoritarianism'. In *The Fate of the Bolshevik Revolution. Illiberal Liberation, 1917–1941*, edited by Lara Douds, James R. Harris and Peter Whitewood. London: Bloomsbury, 2020.

Wilson, Andrew. 'The Communist Party of Ukraine: From Soviet Man to East Slavic Brotherhood'. In *The Left Transformed in Post-Communist Societies: The Cases Of East-Central Europe, Russia, and Ukraine*, edited by Leftwich Curry and Joan Barth Urban, 209–44. New York. Oxford: Rowman & Littlefield Publishers, 2003.

Yekelchyk, Serhy. 'Diktat and Dialogue in Stalinist Culture: Staging Patriotic Historical Opera in Soviet Ukraine, 1936–1954'. *Slavic Review* 3, no. 59 (2000): 597–624.

Yekelchyk, Serhy. *Stalin's Empire of Memory. Russian-Ukrainian Relations in the Soviet Historical Imagination*. Toronto: University of Toronto Press, 2004.

Yekelchyk, Serhy. *Ukraine: Birth of a Modern Nation*. New York: Oxford University Press, 2007.

Zadesnians'kyi, Roman [Bzhes'kyi R.]. *Shcho Nam Dav Mykola Khvyl'ovyi*, [s.l.]: 1979.

Zhulyns'kyi, Mykola. 'Talant nezvychainyi i superechlyvyi'. *Vitchyzna* 12 (1987): 144–9.

Zhulyns'kyi, Mykola. *Iz Zabuttia – v Bezsmertia (Storinky Pryzabutoi Spadshchyny)*. Kyiv: Dnipro, 1990.

Zhulyns'kyi, Mykola. *Mykola Khvyl'ovyi*. Kyiv: Znannia, 1991.

Index

All-Russian Constituent Assembly 22–3, 26–7, 29
All-Soviet Congress of Soviet Writers 189
All-Ukrainian Academy of Sciences (*Vseukrains'ka Akademiia Nauk,* VUAN) 43, 132, 161, 163–4, 170
All-Ukrainian Central Executive Committee (VUTsVK) 171
All-Ukrainian Committee of Assistance to Scholars (*Vseukrains'kyi komitet spryiannia vchenym*) 44
All-Ukrainian Congress of Soviets of Workers' and Soldiers' Deputies 29, 51, 53, 56
All-Ukrainian Federation of Proletarian Writers and Artists (*Vseukrains'ka Federatsiia Proletars'kykh Pys'mennykiv ta Myttsiv*) 60
All-Ukrainian Federation of Revolutionary Soviet Writers 166, 167
All-Ukrainian Literary Committee (*Vseukrains'kyi Literaturnyi Komitet, Vseukrlitkom*) 35, 41, 58–9
All-Ukrainian National Congress 25
All-Ukrainian Orthography Conference 157
All-Ukrainian Peasant Writers' Union *Pluh* (Plough) 83, 99, 103, 105, 113, 152, 154, 168
  joining the VUSPP 134
  on mass literature 83–5
  and Tychyna 87
  writers of 102
All-Ukrainian Photo-Cinema Administration (*Vseukrains'ke Foto-Kino Upravlinnia,* VUFKU) 144
All-Ukrainian Publishing House (*Vsevydav*) 58
All-Ukrainian Union of Proletarian Creative Forces 60
All-Ukrainian Union of Proletarian Writers (*Vseukrains'ka Spilka Proletars'kykh Pys'mennykiv,* VUSPP) 113, 132–7, 143–4, 148, 151, 154, 165–6, 168–9, 173, 189
All-Union Resolution on Literature 134
all-Union Soviet culture. *See* Soviet culture
anti-*Ukrainizatsiia* 6, 130–2, 145, 160
Antonenko-Davydovych, Borys 154, 157, 164, 184
Aspanfut (*Komunkul't*) literary organization 220 n.93
The Association of the Proletarian Writers, *Hart* (Tempering) 73, 83–5, 99, 103–4, 133–4
  Bez manifestu (Without a Manifesto) 84
  members of 92, 100, 105
  Nashe siohodni (Our Today) 137
  Tychyna and 87, 92
Association of Revolutionary Art of Ukraine 159
autobiographical writings 11, 61–2
autonomy, Soviet Ukraine's 5, 17, 19, 46, 187–8
  of art 32
  cultural 3, 9–10, 16, 58, 111, 115, 117, 124, 127, 148, 161, 190, 192 n.4
  khvyl'ovizm 165, 168
  KP(b)U 179, 185
  literature 133, 143
  national-personal 27, 201 n.47
  national-territorial 23–6
  Proletkult 60
  VAPLITE 101, 130
Avanhard (Avant-Garde) group 144, 154, 165
avant-garde 88, 122, 159, 199 n.75
  founders of Ukranian 106

Averbakh, Leopold 167
Azarkh, Raisa 147, 223 n.1

Bahrianyi, Ivan 180
Balyts'kyi, Vsevolod 86, 160
Battle of Kruty 30
Bazhan, Mykola 154–5, 182
Bedny, Demian 155
Bila studia (White Studio) literary group 32
Bilets'kyi, Oleksandr 41, 130, 149
Bil'shovyk Ukrainy (The Bolshevik of Ukraine) periodical 58, 143
biographical approach 8, 10–11, 13
Blakytnyi. *See* Ellan-Blakytnyi, Vasyl
Bogdanov, Alexander 59
Boichukisty group. *See* Association of Revolutionary Art of Ukraine
Bolsheviks/Bolshevism 2, 34–8, 42–7, 52, 66, 79, 111–12, 128, 158, 179, 203 n.84
  Bolshevik-led Soviet Republic in Ukraine 5
  Borot'bysty and 35, 52, 56
  and Comintern 57
  Khvyl'ovyi and 11, 13, 52
  and local political forces 53
  nationalism 80
  occupation of Kyiv 30–1, 34
  populism 14, 178
  proletarian culture 17, 28, 82
  against Provisional Government 27
  public support for 55, 67
  revolution 10, 17, 43–4, 49
  revolutionary slogan of 67
  Russian 29–30, 51
  in Ukraine 50–5, 80, 118
  against Ukrainian nationalists 37
  violence 44
Borot'ba (The Struggle) literary group 33, 35
Borot'bysty party 2–3, 34–5, 37, 46, 56–7, 77, 84, 97
  All-Ukrainian Conference of 57
  and Bolsheviks 35, 52, 56–8
  and Comintern 57
  cultural activities in Soviet Ukraine 58–9
  Lenin's Draft Resolution 57

Bourdieu, Pierre 10
bourgeois nationalism/nationalists 6, 52, 55, 119, 121–2, 127, 147, 162, 177
Bukharin, Nikolai 71
Bulgakov, Nikolai, *Belaia Gvardiia* (The White Guard) 157

censorship 11, 24, 125, 171
The Central Committee of the Communist Party of Bolsheviks of Ukraine (*Komitet Komunistychnoi Partii Bil'shovykiv Ukrainy*, TsK KP(b)U)
  Department of Agitation and Propaganda 81
  June Plenum (1926) 118, 120–7, 160
  Politburo Resolution 167
  resolution of 99, 126, 133, 189, 230 n.15
Central Powers 30–1, 50–1
Central State Archive of Literature and Arts of Ukraine (TsDAMLMU) 10–11
chauvinism
  anti-Ukrainian 120
  Russian (Great-Russian) 79, 107, 131, 142, 156, 158
  Ukrainian 142, 162
Cheka. *See* Extraordinary Committee for combating counter-revolution, Sabotage and Speculation
Chekhivs'kyi, Volodymyr 161
Cherniakhivs'ka-Staryts'ka, Liudmyla 161
Cherniakhivs'kyi, Oleksandr 161
Chernihiv, Ukraine 19
  Hromada group 20
  zemstvo reform 20
Chervonyi Shliakh (Red Path) periodical 58, 126, 128, 144, 177
  political significance of 214 n.70
  for Ukrainian literature 90–6
Chubar, Vlas 119, 128–9
  Pro Vyvykhy (On the deviations) 123
  Tychyna, criticism of 128
Chumak, Vasyl' 33, 37, 62
Chykalenko, Ievhen 22–3, 200 n.12
civil war 2, 9, 47, 50–2, 67, 80, 128, 188, 204 n.119
  cultural life of Ukraine 38–9
  end of 66
  in Kyiv 31, 42

project of proletarian culture 82
Russian 31
status of Ukrainian language during 75
Tychyna and 12, 15, 18–19, 35, 39
Ukrainian literature 137
Clark, Katerina 6, 188, 196 n.32
class war 44, 141, 164, 167, 170, 227 n.123, 230 n.2
Commissariat for Education (*Narkomos*) 35–6, 58, 85, 92, 100, 106, 119, 126–7, 140–1, 215 n.8
Communism 57, 61, 73, 81, 110, 112, 118, 151, 171, 174, 177–8, 180
Communist International (Comintern) 57
Communist Party of Bolsheviks of Ukraine (KP(b)U) 2, 5, 8, 11, 16, 29, 73, 80, 98, 100, 147–8, 163, 165, 185, 187, 190
   anti-communist opposition in 178
   and *Borot'bysty* 57–8
   central leadership authority 179
   and Comintern 57
   educational tasks 130
   faction of 77, 115
   on history of 193 n.18
   ideological roots in 97
   Khvyl'ovyi in 53
   meeting in Taganrog 51
   Party Plenum (1926) 16, 115, 145
   resolution of 57
   Third Congress 52
   VIII All-Ukrainian KP(b)U conference 118
Communist Party of Western Ukraine (KPZU) 148
Constitutional Democratic Party 22
counter-revolutionary 12, 44, 73, 125, 132, 149, 162, 167, 170, 176, 195 n.27
cultural development 23, 38, 111, 159, 186
   Moscow 3, 8
   Soviet Ukraine 8, 16, 101, 103, 120–2, 126, 139, 142, 153, 188
   Ukraine 58, 91, 99, 107, 118, 122, 124, 135, 143, 191
cultural diplomacy 91
cultural projects in Soviet Ukraine 2–8, 58, 190
   autonomous 2, 9–10, 16, 58, 111, 115, 117, 124, 127, 148, 161, 190, 192 n.4

during/after Bolshevik revolution 17
   by KP(b)U 77
   Moscow-centred 8
   proletarian 82
   separatist 4–5, 9, 16, 17, 28, 111, 114–15, 159, 190
cultural Sovietization in Ukraine 2, 6–7, 10, 188

Danylenko, Vasyl' 195 n.27
Denikin, Anton 33, 37, 53, 56
Diad'ko Mykola (Uncle Mykola). *See* Khvyl'ovyi, Mykola
Dibrova, Volodymyr 227 n.156
Dniprovs'kyi, Ivan 84, 108, 148, 154, 167
Dni Turbinykh (The Days of the Turbins) play 157–8
Domontovych, Viktor. *See* Petrov, Victor
Dontsov, Dmytro 13
Doroshkevych, Oleksandr 122, 170
Dosvitnii, Oles' 85, 92–4, 100, 105, 133, 140, 154, 166–7
   expulsion from VAPLITE 133
   'On the Development of the Literary Forces' 125
Dovzhenko, Oleksandr 21, 154, 159
   'On the Problem of Arts' 125
Drach, Ivan 197 n.57
Drai-Khmara, Mykhailo 33
DVU. *See* State Publishing House of Ukraine

education 22–3, 54, 72, 84, 187
   campaigns/programme 6, 81
   educational institutes 21, 42–3, 141
   literacy 6, 81–2, 84, 103, 186
   mass education 20
   political 82, 103
Ellan. *See* Ellan-Blakytnyi, Vasyl
Ellan-Blakytnyi, Vasyl 20–1, 33–5, 41, 58, 73, 83, 85–6, 95, 100–1, 104, 171
   Bez manifestu (Without a Manifesto) 84
   death of 89
   and Khvyl'ovyi 58, 73, 101
   and Tychyna 86, 89, 170
emigration, Ukrainian 13, 89, 91–4, 96, 148, 196 n.33
émigrés 46–7, 91, 93–4, 96, 106

Ems decree 200 n.11
English literature 1, 155
Epik, Hryhorii 154, 166-8, 177
executed renaissance (*rozstriliane vidrodzhennia*) paradigm 7, 14, 190, 196 n.33
Executive Committee of the Council of United Community Organizations (*Ispolnitel'nyi Komitet Soveta Ob'edinennykh Obshchestvennykh Organizatsii*, IKSOOO) 22, 24
Extraordinary Committee for combating counter-revolution, Sabotage and Speculation (*Chrezvychainaia Komissia po Bor'be s Kontrrevoliutsiei i Sabotazhem*, Cheka) 44, 64, 66, 86, 131

famine 179-80
　of 1921-2 45, 67
　of 1932-3 174-5, 185
　Khvyl'ovyi on 175
fascism/fascist 73, 123-4, 139, 147, 163, 177, 218 n.35, 223 n.8
February Revolution 23-4, 50, 55, 80
fellow travellers 5, 8, 88, 90, 99-100, 126, 129-30, 152, 162, 168
First All-Ukrainian Congress of Soviet Writers 189, 203 n.90
First All-Ukrainian Military Congress 26, 201 n.36
Fitil'ov, Oleksandr 53
Fitzpatrick, Sheila 44, 160
　class war (soft *vs.* hard line) 230 n.2
Five-Year Plan, first 8, 16, 141, 160, 164, 167, 172-3
Fowler, Mayhill C. 8, 193 n.17, 198 n.72
Free Cossacks units (*vilne kozatstvo*) 29, 52
Friche, Vladimir 155
Frunze, Mikhail 80
Futurism, Ukrainian 216 n.35
Fylypovych, Pavlo 33

Germany 31
　German-backed Ukrainian government 50-1
Gershberg, Semen 179
Gorky, Maxim 20, 155, 159
　Mat' (Mother) 152

Slisarenko and 152-3, 224 n.49
　Ukrainian language and 153
GPU. *See* State Political Directorate
Grabowicz, George 61, 172, 197 n.51, 198-9 n.74
Great-Russian chauvinism 79, 107, 131, 142, 156, 158

Hagen, Mark von 14
Hart (Tempering), journal of VUSPP 136-7, 165
Hermaize, Iosyp 161
Hetmanate, Ukraine 19, 203 n.66
high culture 3, 9, 78, 84, 103, 105, 110
High Stalinism 10, 164, 193 n.14
Hirchak, Ievhen 122
　Na dva fronta v bor'be s natsionalizmom (On Two Fronts in the Struggle with Nationalism) 125
historical identity of Ukraine 230 n.10
Hlobenko, Mykola 12
　on Khvyl'ovyi 192 n.4
Holovko, Andrii 154
Horoshanin, Valerii 160
Hromada group 20
Hrono literary group 213 n.41
Hrushevs'kyi, Mykhailo 22-4, 32, 118, 122, 163, 186
Hryn, Halyna 14
　Ukrainization 195 n.27
Hryn'ko, Hryhorii 58, 90

Iakovenko, Hryts'ko 102
Iakubs'kyi, B. 83
Ialovyi, Mykhailo 90, 100, 105, 126, 133, 140, 147, 167
　accusation and arrest 126, 176
　expulsion from VAPLITE 133
Ianovs'kyi, Iurii 108, 148, 154, 167, 169
Iashek, Mykola 101
　Desiat' rokiv ukrains'koi literatury (Ten years of Ukrainian Literature) 83
Iavors'kyi, Matvii 163-4, 230 n.10
Iefremov, Serhii 34, 42, 92, 122, 161
　and Tychyna 88, 163-4, 170
IKSOOO. *See* Executive Committee of the Council of United Community Organizations
industrialization 80-1, 111, 171, 175, 186

intelligentsia 11, 18, 20, 24, 32
  Kyiv's 23, 42–3
  Soviet bureaucracy and 193 n.14
  toiling intelligentsia (*trudiashcha intelihentsia*) 179
  Ukrainian 23, 34, 38, 52, 89, 102, 109–10, 119, 131–2, 161, 195 n.27
internationalism 80, 93, 120, 133, 135
International Union of Proletarian and Revolutionary Literature (*Mizhnarodna Orhanizatsiia Proletars'koi ta Revoliutsiinoi Literatury*, MOPRL) 169
Iohansen, Maik 41, 60, 84, 149, 154, 166
  on Kharkiv's growth 56
Iura, Hnat 154
Iurynets, Volodymyr 41, 63, 124, 126

Kaganovich, Lazar 119–20, 126, 131, 147
  address to Ukrainian delegates 155–6
  and Shums'kyi 120–1, 130, 148
Katerynoslav, Ukraine 28, 51
Kerensky, Alexander 23, 27
Kerzhentsev, Platon 1, 155
Kharkiv, Ukraine 2–3, 7, 15, 28–9, 41, 43, 46, 48, 66, 133, 179, 195 n.29
  establishment of Soviet government 17
  as industrial centre 55–6
  Iohansen on growth of 56
  Kharkiv orthography 187
  Pilnyak visit to 109
  political capital 55
  Soviet Ukrainian writers in 90
  Ukrainian communists in 6
Khrystiuk, Pavlo 126
Khvylia, Andrii 90, 101, 124, 134, 148, 175
  Iasnoiu Dorohoiu (On a clear path) 123
  Vid ukhylu v prirvu … (From Deviation into Abyss) 125, 139
Khvyl'ovyi, Mykola 1, 3, 5, 8–11, 14–16, 18, 41, 48, 54, 56, 59, 78, 84, 95, 100, 104, 108, 121, 132, 140, 148, 154, 162–3, 166–8, 184
  accusations on 73, 102, 110, 120, 122, 126, 136, 223 n.8
  Apolohety Pysarysmu (Apologists of Scribbling) 101, 107, 117, 120
  Arabesky (Arabesques) 61
  autobiographical nature of 61–2

Chumakivs'ka Komuna (Chumak's Commune) 62
communard 62, 72–3, 118
contribution in Literary Discussion 101–2
  Asiatic Renaissance 101, 111–14
  'Europe' 101, 104–11, 142
  proletarian art 101, 114
  prosvita 101–3, 106, 111, 137
criticism against 110, 122, 124, 139, 147, 211 n.147
Cultural Renaissance 208 n.69
documents on 11
Dumky proty Techii (Thoughts against the Current) 101, 104, 106, 120
early life (and/in politics) 49–50
and Ellan-Blakytnyi 58, 73, 101
in Europe 147–8
expulsion from VAPLITE 133
fictional characters of 62–6, 68–73, 75, 137–9, 173–4
formalism, charges of 73, 82, 136
Free Cossacks by 29, 52
at *Golovpolitosvita* 58, 72
GPU's file on 223 n.17
against hierarchy 103, 114
Ia (Romantyka) (My self (Romanticism)) 64–5, 102
Iakovenko and 102
illness of 147
Ivan Ivanovych 150–1
Iz zhyttiepysu popeliastoi korovy (From the life-story of an ashy-grey cow) 174
Kamo Hriadeshy? (Quo Vadis?) 101, 103, 111, 120
to Kharkiv 58
Kharkivs'kyi Proletar (Kharkiv Proletariat) 161
Khvyl'ovizm 13, 123, 131, 161, 165, 168, 177, 218 n.35
Knyha Sioma (Book Seven) 150
Kolonii, Vily (Colonies, villas) 68
and Koriak 59, 61, 136
Kostiuk on 53, 165, 208 n.70
in KP(b)U 53
Kulish on 140
Lehenda (The Legend) 63
letter to Mohylians'kyi 73–4, 109, 112

Liliuli 63–4
and Liubchenko (Arkadii) 175–6
Maibutni Shakhtari (Future Miners) 173
Moskovski Zadrypanky (Moscow's Dusty Backwaters) 117, 122
Na ozera (To the Lakes) 61
narration (first-person voice) of 61, 63
non-existence of 12–13
Osin' (Autumn) 61
Ostannii Den' (The Last Day) 173
Po barvinkivs'komu raioni (Around the Barvinkove district) 174
Podiaka Pryvatnoho Likaria (Gratitude of the Private Doctor) 66
political campaigns against 185
Povist' pro Sanatoriinu Zonu (A Tale of a Sanatorium) 70, 151
for proletariat 125
Pro Liubov (About Love) 173
recantations 139, 147–9, 161
Redactor Kark 70, 73
in Red Army 53, 55
repentant 133, 148
revolutionary slogans 75, 121, 123, 127, 139, 161
revolution/revolutionary romanticism 8, 61–5, 67–72, 74–5, 138, 188
romantic *vitaism* 61, 109, 112
and Russian Proletkult 216 n.50
Sentymental'na Istoriia (Sentimental Tale) 64, 69
Shchaslyvyi Sekretar (A Happy Secretary) 173
Shliakhetne Hnizdo 68
and Shums'kyi 117–18, 126–7
Stalin and 120, 124
suicide of 9, 11, 175–9, 188
  death note 176, 178
Syliuety (Silhouettes) 62, 72
Syni Etiudy (Blue Etudes) 60, 74
Synii Lystopad (Blue November) 62, 69
trips to Soviet Ukraine's provinces 174
Tvory u P'iat'okh Tomakh 197 n.42, 215 n.16, 223 n.1
and Tychyna 48, 130
Ukraina chy Malorosiia? (Ukraine or Little Russia?) 5, 101, 124, 137, 139–40, 149, 153, 161

on *Ukrainizatsiia* 139
Val'dshnepy (The Woodcocks) 102, 137–40, 147–9, 161
and VAPLITE (*see* VAPLITE)
Vstupna novela (The Introductory Novelette) 61
on VUSPP 136–7
and Zerov 54–5, 74
Zhyttia (Life) 64
Kievlianin newspaper 29, 202 n.58
Klen, Iurii 33, 44
Koliada, Geo (Hryhorii), *Futur Extra* 85–6
kolkhoz (*kolhospna*) 174, 180
Komunist/Kommunist 58, 89, 98, 140, 148–9, 207 n.50
  allegations on Tychyna 128–9
Kopylenko, Oleksandr 149
korenizatsiia policy 3, 6–7, 15, 77, 97–8, 113, 115, 118, 130, 141, 162, 175, 185–7
  and growth 131
  hard-line 131, 185, 230 n.2
  lack of educated speakers 103
  and mass movements 82–5
  soft-line 185, 230 n.2
  in Ukraine 79–82, 121, 145
Koriak, Volodymyr 4, 41, 84, 126, 133, 136
  accusation on 136
  and Khvyl'ovyi 59, 61, 136
  Orhanizatsiia Zhovtnevoi Literatury 193 n.11
  on Tychyna 88–9
  Ukrains'ka Literatura 197 n.58
  V Boiakh: Statti in Vystupy 197 n.58
Korniichuk, Oleksandr 183
Kosior, Stanislav 162
Kostiuk, Hryhorii 53, 165, 208 n.70
Kotsiubyns'kyi, Mykhailo 20
Kovalenko, Borys 133, 182
Kozel's'kyi, Borys 160
KP(b)U. *See* Communist Party of Bolsheviks of Ukraine
KPZU. *See* Communist Party of Western Ukraine
Kratochvil, Alexander 151
Kulish, Mykola 105, 126–7, 133, 140, 154, 165–9, 175
'kul'tura' vs. 'khaltura' 3, 110

Kulyk, Ivan 84, 126, 153, 155, 157, 182
Kurbas, Les' (Oleksandr) 32, 106, 159
Kviring, Emanuel 51
Kyiv Commercial Institute 21
Kyiv State University 42–3, 182
Kyiv, Ukraine 17, 19–20, 22, 24, 28, 38, 46, 55–6, 66, 202 n.55, 205 n.123
   capture of 30–1
   cultural and literary activities in 32
   economic crisis in 42–5
   intelligentsia 23, 42–3
   military parade at St Sophia Square 28
   Tsentral'na Rada (*see* Tsentral'na Rada (Central Council))
   Volunteer Army in 37
   young writers in 24
Kyrylenko, Ivan 154

Lavrinenko, Iurii 33, 73, 182
Le, Ivan 133, 154
Lebed, Dmitrii 98, 122, 126
Left Socialist-Revolutionaries 34
Leites, Oleksander 101, 130, 140
   Desiat' rokiv ukrains'koi literatury (Ten years of Ukrainian Literature) 83
   on Tychyna 88
Leninism 14, 81, 120
Lenin, Vladimir 2, 34, 51–2, 56–7, 72–3, 81, 113, 128, 131, 140, 156, 171, 209 n.107, 212 n.19. *See also* Bolsheviks/Bolshevism
   on art 83
   bureaucracy 67
   civic literacy 82
   death of (commemoration) 73, 87
Leontovych, Mykola 44, 86
   death of 44–5
Liber, George 186, 212 n.11, 230 n.7
liknep campaign 81
literary developments 7, 152, 169, 191, 193 nn.15–16
Literary Discussion of 1925–8 2, 5, 8, 15, 73, 75, 82, 99–102, 115, 118, 122–3, 125–6, 132, 135, 140, 142, 170, 185
literary organization 3–4, 16, 60, 83–5, 104–5, 143, 152, 189. *See also* specific organizations
   independent 133, 165
   mass 84–5, 99, 102–3

   proletarian 75
   state-controlled 83, 133–5
Literatura i Mystetstvo (Literature and Art) 152, 181
Literaturna Hazeta (Literary Gazette) periodical 152, 165
Literaturno-Naukovyi Visnyk journal 20, 22, 24
Literaturnyi Iarmarok (The Literary Fair) 149–52, 161, 165–7, 170
   Khvyl'ovyi, role of 149
Literaturnyi Tsekh (Literary Guild) periodical 167
Little-Russianism (*rozkhliabane malorosiistvo*) 93, 96
Liubchenko, Arkadii 105, 147–8, 154, 166, 175
   Ioho Taiemnytsia (His Secret) 175, 228 n.177
   and Khvyl'ovyi 175–6
Liubchenko, Panas 34, 58, 161, 219 n.71
Lunacharsky, Anatoly 1, 133, 155

Maiorov, Mykhailo 151
Malaniuk, Ievhen 93
   Na mezhi dvokh epokh (At the turn of two eras) 93
   Poslanie (Epistle) 95
   and Tychyna 95
MARS (*Maisternia revoliutsiinoho slova* (The Workshop of the Revolutionary Word)) 137, 221 n.119
Martin, Terry 6, 230 n.2
Marxism/Marxist 14, 34, 82, 111, 124, 126, 139, 156
Marx, Karl 2, 72, 150, 156
mass culture 3, 9, 103, 114, 186
Mayakovski, Vladimir 155, 177
modernism/modernization 7, 9, 15–16, 19, 32, 41, 55–6, 80, 98, 186–7
Mohylians'kyi, Mykola 88–9
   letter from Khvyl'ovyi 73–4, 109, 112
   private collections of 196 n.42
Molodniak (The Union of Komsomol Writers) 152, 154, 168, 224 n.44
Molotov-Ribbentrop Pact 183
Momot, Ivan 166
MOPRL. *See* International Union of Proletarian and Revolutionary Literature

Moscow 13, 16, 34–5, 48, 52, 77, 96–7,
    108, 114, 117, 120, 185, 190
  Bolsheviks in 36, 53, 77
  cultural developments 3, 8
  delegates from Soviet Ukraine 1–3, 152–9
  Kharkiv and 179
  Soviet authorities in 175
Mukhin, Mykhailo 95
Murashko, Oleksandr 44, 86
Muraviov, Mikhail 30
Muzahet (Musagetes) literary group 33
Mykhailychenko, Hnat 4, 33–4, 37, 52, 58
  'Theses on the New Proletarian Art' 60
Mykytenko, Ivan 1, 134, 153, 155, 183
Mystetstvo (Art) journal 33, 35, 58

Nash Universal (Our Universal) 60
National Amateur Choir Chapel 45
national communists 13–14, 52, 56–7, 96,
    132, 178
national cultures 3, 6, 32, 79–81, 136, 156,
    159
national identity 3–6, 9, 79, 97–8, 186
nationalism 130, 132, 139, 143, 149, 158
  bourgeois 6, 52, 55, 119, 121–2, 127,
    147, 162, 177
  local 6, 13, 80, 162
  Ukrainian 89, 130, 165, 185
nationalities policy, Soviet 6–7, 77, 79, 97,
    131–2, 156, 177, 194 n.26. *See also*
    korenizatsiia policy; *Ukrainizatsiia*
    policy
neoklasyky (neoclassicists) group 33, 106,
    122, 135, 154, 189, 203 n.72
New Economic Policy (NEP) 67–72, 74,
    121, 137, 151
Nicholas II 22, 50
Nikovs'kyi, Andrii 161, 170
NKVD commission 11, 182, 185–6
non-Soviet writers 5, 154, 158
Nova Rada journal 24–5, 28, 30, 33
Nova Ukraina (New Ukraine) journal 91–2
Novychynko, Leonid 13
Nytchenko, Dmytro 223 n.13, 226 n.102
  on *Partiia Vede* 181–2

October Revolution 9, 14–15, 41, 108, 152,
    179, 182
Ohloblin, Mykola. *See* Hlobenko, Mykola

Olesha, Iurii 155, 227 n.146
Olympians 101–2, 110, 113, 170
OPOJAZ group (Society for the Study
    of Poetic Language (*Obshchestvo
    izuchenija POeticheskogo JAZyka*))
    208 n.70
Oswald Burkhard. *See* Klen, Iurii

Panch, Petro 100, 167, 183
Panchenko, Mykhailo 58–9, 100
Paparuk, Lidiia 86, 95, 204 n.94
Pauly, Matthew 80, 162, 215 n.8
Pavlyshyn, Marko 193 n.19
peasants/peasantry 34, 49–51, 56, 67, 80,
    134, 185–6
  leaders (*otamans*) 31
  revolutionary 83–4, 202 n.58
  Ukrainian/Ukrainian-speaking 35, 60,
    70, 80–1, 98, 168
  urbanized 114, 186
Pervomais'kyi, Leonid 154
Petliura, Symon 38, 183
Petrenko, Pavlo (O. Gan) 50
Petrograd, Russia 17, 23, 50
  Provisional Government in 22–3,
    26–7, 29, 50
Petrov, Victor 43–4
P'ianov, Volodymyr 86, 183
Piatakov, Georgii 51
Pidmohyl'nyi, Valerian 154, 215 n.22
Pilnyak, Boris 1, 7, 155, 208 n.76
  visit to Kharkiv 109
Pluzhnyk, Ievhen 154
Poland 55, 217 n.12, 219 n.72
polemic 5, 93, 101–2, 117, 125, 136, 165,
    218 n.20
Polishchuk, Valer'ian 59, 83, 92, 94–5, 154,
    157, 165
Polons'ka-Vasylenko, Natalia 43
Poltava, Ukraine 23, 27–8, 175
post-colonial literary criticism 193 n.19
Postyshev, Pavlo 175
Pravda newspaper 179–82
proletarian culture 3–9, 12, 15–16, 17–18, 33,
    35, 41, 44, 46–8, 55–6, 59–61, 75, 82–3,
    99–101, 103, 112, 133, 135–6, 142
  literary front 164–70
Proletkult movement (1917) 59–61, 75,
    82, 84, 136, 207 n.55

PROLITFRONT. *See* The Union of workshops of proletarian literary front
Prolitfront periodical 166–7, 169
pro-Soviet writers 4, 60, 84, 90
prosvita 20, 25, 50, 103, 106
provincial/provincialism 3–4, 6, 16, 19, 55, 110, 113, 124, 138–9
Pylypenko, Serhii 83, 85, 100–1, 153–5
  massivism (*masovizm*) 84
  Nashi 'hrikhy' (Our 'sins') 84
  robsil'kory (worker-peasant correspondents) 84

Radians'ka Osvita (Soviet Education) journal 141, 181
radio-broadcasting, Ukrainian 144
Radnarkom (*Rada Narodnykh Komisariv*, Council of Peoples Commissars) 43, 67, 80
Rakovs'kyi, Khrystian 52, 72
Ravich-Cherkasskii, Moisei 97
Red Army 15, 29–30, 34, 36–7, 50, 52–3, 55, 66, 68, 70, 159, 180, 183
Rév, István 11
Rondeli (Rondels) 38
Rozdolsky, Roman 148
RSDRP. *See* Social-Democratic Labour Party
RSFSR. *See* Russian Soviet Federative Socialist Republic
Rudnyts'kyi, Stepan 119
Rusotiapstvo (mindless Russian chauvinism) 131
Russia (Russian) 1, 2, 5, 7, 9, 13, 17–20, 23–8, 34, 37, 50, 109, 120, 158, 185, 187
  Bolsheviks 29–30, 51
  culture 5, 7, 9, 109, 120–1, 133, 142, 153, 156, 187
  Great Reforms in 199 n.1
  literature 2, 34, 108–9, 112, 143, 155, 209 n.76
  multi-ethnic environment 194 n.26
  Proletkult movement in 59, 136
  revival of Russian patriotism 196 n.37
  revolution/revolutionary movement 35, 49, 97, 112, 200 n.11
  Russian writers to Kharkiv 1

Taganrog 51
Treaty of Brest-Litovsk 51
Ukrainian-Russian relations 193–4 n.19
Russian Communist Party of Bolsheviks (RKP[b]) Congress 6, 8, 50–1, 53, 56, 67
Russian Soviet Federative Socialist Republic (*Rossiiskaia Sovetskaia Federativnaia Sotsialisticheskaia Respublika,* RSFSR) 56, 141, 157, 159
Russification 3–4, 17, 23, 53, 77, 98, 186
  de-Russification 79, 97, 115, 186, 194 n.23
  Russified Ukrainians 80, 98, 113, 119
Ryl's'kyi, Maksym 14, 33, 95, 182

Savchenko, Iakiv 32, 85
Sawczak, Peter 138
Second All-Russian Congress of Political Education Departments 82
Second All-Russian Congress of Soviets of Workers' and Soldiers' Deputies 29
secret services in Ukraine 11, 131–3, 145, 151, 160–1, 170, 175, 177, 195 n.27. *See also* State Political Directorate
Selivanov'skyi, A. 136
Semenko, Mykhailo (Mykhail') 32–3, 85, 154
  Nova Generatsiia (New Generation) 165
  on Tychyna 85
Senchenko, Ivan 148, 167
Serafimovich, Aleksandr 155
Sergeev, Fedor (Artem) 51
Shakhovs'kyi, Semen 13, 41, 171
Shakhty trial in 1928 160–1
Shapoval, Iurii 161
Shapoval, Mykyta 28, 91, 140
Shevchenko, Taras 139, 155
Shidek, V. Ia. 173
Shiller, Friedrich 124
Shkandrij, Myroslav 193 n.19
Shkurupii, Geo 90, 154
Shpol, Iulian 154
Shums'kyi, Oleksandr 16, 100, 109, 118–19, 123, 128, 132, 142, 145, 220 n.77

accusations on 120, 163
and Borot'bysty 34, 52, 57–8
Chervonyi Shliakh, editor 90, 126
'Ideological Struggle in the Ukrainian Cultural Process' 126
and Kaganovich 120–1, 130, 148
and Khvyl'ovyi 117–18, 126–7
NEP 121
political campaigns against 185
proletarian Ukrainization 98, 125
shums'kizm 131, 162, 177
and Stalin 119
Stara in Nova Ukraina (Old and New Ukraine) 91, 93
Skoropads'kyi, Pavlo 30–2
Skrypnyk, Mykola 1, 51, 81, 112, 119, 139, 152, 162, 175, 186
accusation on 175
Do teorii borot'by dvokh kul'tur (On the theory of the struggle of two cultures) 123
literary agenda of 143
opportunities to Soviet Ukraine 130
skrypnykivka 187
skrypnykivshchyna 163, 177
suicide of 179
'The results of the literary discussion' 142
Ukrainizatsiia 141–5
Slisarenko, Oleksa 5, 32, 140, 154
and Gorky 152–3, 224 n.49
'In the struggle for a Proletarian Aesthetics' 125
slavic India 5, 153
Slonim, Marc 190
Smolych, Iurii 21, 101, 148–9, 152–3, 166, 192 n.10
Social-Democratic Labour Party (*Rossiiskaia Sotsial-Demokraticheskaia Rabochaia Partiia*, RSDRP) 28, 50
socialism 3–4, 9, 17, 34, 40, 80, 93, 122, 141, 177, 190
socialist movement 77, 97
socialist realism 4, 10, 15, 171, 173, 189–90, 196 n.40, 199 n.75
Socialist Revolutionary Party (SRs) 22, 28, 52

Society of Ukrainian Progressivists (*Tovarystvo Ukrains'kykh Postupovtsiv,* TUP) 22–3
Sosiura, Volodymyr 41, 60, 84, 100, 104, 127, 154–5
Soviet culture 1–2, 4–5, 6–10, 15–16, 77, 83, 100, 110, 114, 117, 123, 135, 142, 156, 188, 190
ethnonational variants of 192 n.9
'unity in diversity' 127
Soviet literature in Ukrainian 4, 9, 18, 78, 83, 100, 137, 152, 169, 177
Soviet-Polish war 38, 119
Soviet power 15–16, 34, 51, 67–8, 80, 89, 130–1, 160, 179, 189
Soviet republics 1–2, 7, 36, 51, 79, 124, 132–3, 153–5, 159, 177
resolution on literature 135
Soviet Republic in Ukraine 5, 15, 60, 123
Soviet Ukrainian culture 1–3, 6, 8, 20, 187–8, 190–1, 199 n.75
oppositions of agents 3
promoters of 4
Soviet Ukrainian Government (*Radnarkom*) 43, 51, 118
Soviet Ukrainian literature 4, 7–9, 18, 78, 90, 109, 115, 123, 125, 133, 137, 148, 152–3, 158, 170
Soviet-Ukrainian war 29
Soviet Ukrainian writers 7–9, 21, 83, 100, 127, 135. *See also specific writers*
in Artemivs'k 168
in Kharkiv 90
members of VUSPP 173
to Moscow 1–3, 152–9
near Viis'kove village 135
Soviet Union 2, 6, 8, 12, 16, 73, 91, 96, 108–9, 112, 115, 117, 122, 124, 129, 133, 139, 141–2, 145, 153, 156, 159, 179, 183
cultural policies in 194 n.20
suicides in 210 n.119
Sovnarkom decree 67, 204 n.112
Spengler, Oswald 106, 122–3
Der Untergang des Abendlandes (The Decline of the West) 107
Stalinism 10, 188, 195 n.31

Stalin, Joseph 1, 4, 7, 9–10, 13, 16, 57, 99, 120, 136, 141, 147, 156, 170–1, 179, 182, 191, 219 n.43, 227 n.146
   on *Dni Turbinykh* play 158
   'The Foundation of Leninism' 111
   'Great-Russian chauvinism' 79
   and Khvyl'ovyi 120, 124
   nationalism 80, 130
   natsiia and *natsional'nost'* 156–7
   and Shums'kyi 119
   and Soviet Ukrainian writers 156–8
State Political Directorate (*Gosudarstvennoie Politicheskoie Upravleniie*, GPU) 12, 131, 161, 174, 176. *See also* secret services in Ukraine
   file on Khvyl'ovyi 223 n.17
   '*Ob Ukrainskom Separatizme*' (On Ukrainian Separatism) report 131–2, 160
   svodki secret report 132, 149
State Publishing House of Ukraine (*Derzhavne Vydavnytstvo Ukrainy*, DVU/*Derzhvydav*) 58, 147, 160
Stefan Karol'. *See* Khvyl'ovyi, Mykola
Stetsenko, Kyrylo 44
Sturm und Drang group 107
   Geniezeit (the Age of Genius) 113
Stus, Vasyl' 172
   Fenomen Doby (*Skhodzhennia na Holhofu Slavy*) (The Phenomenon of the Age (Ascending to the Golgotha of Fame)) 13
SVU. *See* Union for the Liberation of Ukraine

Taran, F. 140
Tekhnomystetska hrupa A (Techno-artistic group A) group 144, 166, 168
Tel'niuk, Stanislav 13
Tesniak, Oleksa 158
Tobykovets' 100
transnationalism 8
Trotsky, Leon 29, 72, 123
   Literature and Revolution 83
TsDAMLMU. *See* Central State Archive of Literature and Arts of Ukraine
Tsentral'na Rada (Central Council) 23, 25–7, 30, 35, 50, 85, 201 n.47, 202 n.58

First Universal (legal act-declaration) 26
Second Universal 27
Third Universal 27
Fourth Universal 30
TsK KP(b)U. *See* The Central Committee of the Communist Party of Bolsheviks of Ukraine
TUP. *See* Society of Ukrainian Progressivists
Twelfth Russian Communist Party of Bolsheviks (RKP[b]) Congress 6, 8
Tychyna, Pavlo 2, 8–9, 11, 13–16, 18, 32, 35, 40–2, 58, 83, 92, 100, 104, 127–8, 130, 132, 154–5, 163–4, 167, 183, 188
   accusation on 88
   award/honor 183
   Bielyi, i Blok (And Bely and Blok) 33
   and Blakytnyi 86, 89, 171
   Chernihiv 171–3
   Chuttia Iedynoi Rodyny (Feelings of One Unified Family) 183
   Chystyla maty kartopliu (Mother was peeling potato) 128
   on conditions of Kyiv 44
   criticism 85–6, 88–9, 171, 184
   as cultural agent 10, 19
   on death of Leontovych 44–5
   departing Kyiv to Kharkiv 85–7
   documents on 11–12
   Do Koho Hovoryt'? (To Whom to Talk?) 86–7
   Duma pro Triokh Vitriv (A Duma on Three Winds) 28
   early life and education 19–20
   émigrés 46–7, 93–5
   employment 22, 24–5, 87, 90, 96
   Enharmoniine (Enharmonic) 33
   in Europe 91–4
   Hei, Vdarte v Struny, Kobzari (Hey, Strike the Strings, Kobza Players!) 25
   Holod (Famine) 45
   Iak Upav … (When he fell …) 35–6
   and Iefremov 88, 163–4, 170
   intelihent z intelihentiv 130
   international tour for learning 92

Iz Shchodennykovykh Zapysiv 199 n.4
Koriak on 88–9
Lenin, Narody Idut' (The Peoples are Coming) 182
letter to *Komunist* 128–9
Lysty do Poeta (Letters to the Poet) 46
and Malaniuk 95
Mizhplanetni Intervaly (Interplanetary Intervals) 33
and Mohylians'kyi 89
Nadhodylo Lito (Summer is on the Way) 87
Na Maidani … (On the Square …) 35
Na Mohyli Shevchenka II (At Shevchenko's Grave … II) 41
Na zminu (To take the turn) 180
Nenavysti Moiei Syla (Oh Strength of my Hate) 87
Odchyniaite Dveri … (Open the Doors …) 31
official surname of 199 nn.9–10
Oi, shcho v Sofiis'komu Zahraly Dzvony (Oh in Sophia the bells struck) 28
Pam'iaty Trydtsiaty (In Memory of the Thirty) 30
and Paparuk 86, 95, 204 n.94
Partiia Vede (The Party Leads) 9, 180–2
Pisnia Chervonoi Armii (Song of the Red Army) 182
Pisnia Komsomol'tsiv (Song of Komsomol Members) 182
Pisnia Kuzni (Song of a Smithy) 182
Pisnia Traktorystky (Song of a Tractor Girl) 182
Pluh (The Plough) 15, 33, 35, 38–41, 48, 86, 172
Po Blakytnomu Stepu (Along the azure steppe …) 31
poem dedicated to Mykhailychenko 37
poet laureate 179–84
Pokhoron Druha (Funeral of the Friend) 184
Povitrianyi Flot (Air Fleet) 182
to Prague 93–4
Prometei (Prometheus) 46
Psalom Zalizu (Psalm to Iron) 40–2
Rostu (I am Growing) 182

Samosud (Lynch-law) 128
self-portrait of 21
Semenko on 85
Shablia Kotovs'koho (Kotovs'kyi's Sabre) 129
Skorbotna Maty III (Sorrowful Mother III) 31
Skovoroda, review of 93
Soniachni Klarnety (The Clarinets of the Sun) 33–4, 85, 88, 93
Soviet ideology 89
Stara Ukraina Zminytysia Musyt' (Old Ukraine Must Change) 171
transformation 47–8
Tvory u Dvanadtsiaty Tomakh 196 n.42
Velykym Brekhunam (To Big Liars) 86
Vidpovid' Zemliakam (A Reply to my Countrymen) 86–7, 93
Viina I (War I) 30
Viter z Ukrainy (The Wind from Ukraine) 45, 87–9, 93, 171
V Kosmichnomu Orkestri (In Cosmic Orchestra) 46–7, 85, 88
V Tsariakh Znaishly Svoiu Opiku i Ridniu (In Tsars you Found your Support and Kinship) 47
VUAN Academy 164, 170
Vy Znaiete Iak Lypa Shelestyt'? (You Know How Linden Rustle?) 20
Zahupalo v Dveri Prykladom (One Banged on the Door with a Rifle Butt) 45
Zamist' Sonetiv i Oktav (Instead of Sonnets and Octaves) 15, 37–41, 93
Zelene Podillia (Green Podilia) 44
Zerov on 88
Zhyvemo Komunoiu, X (We Live as a Commune, X, 1920) 46, 87, 171
Zolotyi Homin (The Golden Harmony) 26–7, 36

Ukrainian Autocephalous Orthodox Church (UAPTs) 132
Ukrainian Constituent Assembly 27
Ukrainian Freedom Day (*Sviato Svobody*) 24
Ukrainian language 3–4, 7, 17, 20, 23, 37, 53, 60, 80–1, 84, 98, 114
during civil war 75

periodicals of 22, 24
prohibition of 200 n.11
urban space 99
Ukrainian literature 1, 4, 8–9, 13, 15, 18, 23, 32–4, 60, 62, 83, 85, 90–6, 122
  Chervonyi Shliakh (Red Path) for 90–6
  Russian perspective of 109
Ukrainian Military Organization (*Ukrains'ka Viis'kova Orhanisatsiia*, UVO) trial 160, 163
Ukrainian National Centre (*Ukrains'kyi Natsional'nyi Tsentr*, UNTs) trial 160, 163
Ukrainian Party of Socialist Revolutionaries (UPSR) 2, 23, 28–9, 202 n.58
Ukrainian Party of Socialists-Revolutionaries (Communists) (*Ukrains'ka Partiia Sotsialistiv-Revoliutsioneriv (Komunistiv)*) 34
Ukrainian People's Republic (*Ukrains'ka Narodna Respublika*, UNR) 5, 9, 15, 28–31, 36, 38, 46, 50–2, 86, 132, 160, 203 n.90
Ukrainian Revolution 16, 25, 28, 32, 36, 42, 49, 52, 93, 138, 200 n.17
Ukrainian Social-Democratic Workers' Party (*Ukrains'ka Sotsial-Demokratychna Robitnycha Partiia*, USDRP) 23, 26, 28–9
Ukrainian Socialist-Federalist Party (*Ukrains'ka Partiia Sotsialistiv-Federalistiv*, UPSF) 23
Ukrainian Socialist-Revolutionary Party (*Ukrains'ka Partiia Sotsialistiv-Revoliutsioneriv*, UPSR) 23
Ukrainian Socialist Soviet Republic (UkrSSR) 36, 51, 55–6, 80, 183
  anthem of 36
Ukrainization 3, 25, 81, 85, 97–9, 119–20, 123, 142, 144, 186, 194 n.23, 195 n.27
Ukrainizatsiia policy 6, 15–16, 79–80, 85, 90, 96, 102–3, 106, 113, 115, 118–19, 121, 123, 125, 130, 159, 162, 164, 185–7, 194 n.23, 194 n.25
  anti-*Ukrainizatsiia* 130–2, 160
  local agents in promoting 195 n.26
  Skrypnyk's 141–5
  Ukrainian perspective of 97–9

Ukrainka, Lesia 43, 85
Umantseva, Iuliia 66
Union for the Liberation of Ukraine (*Spilka Vyzvolennia Ukrainy*, SVU) trial 160-4, 170
Union of Soviet Writers 7, 16, 189–90
Union of Soviet Writers of Ukraine 189–90
The Union of workshops of proletarian literary front (*Ob'iednannia studii proletars'koho literaturnoho frontu* – PROLITFRONT) 165-9, 173
UNR. See Ukrainian People's Republic
UPSF. See Ukrainian Socialist-Federalist Party
UPSR. See Ukrainian Party of Socialist Revolutionaries
urban-based culture 3, 10, 56, 98–9, 142, 186–7
Urbino, literary group 101, 215 n.13
USDRP. See Ukrainian Social-Democratic Workers' Party
Ushakov, Nikolai 181

VAPLITE (*Vil'na Akademiia Proletars'koi Literatury* (Free Academy of Proletarian Literature)) 3, 101, 104–5, 113–14, 125–7, 133–4, 136, 140, 143–4, 147–9
  Statute of 3, 125, 155, 192 n.10
  Vaplite: Almanakh (*Vaplite*: Almanac) 125
  Vaplite: Zoshyt pershyi (*Vaplite*: First Notebook) 125–6
Vaplite journal 125–6, 136
Velyka Ukraina (Great Ukraine) 157
Vernads'kyi, Volodymyr 43
Viola, Lynn 42
Visti VUTsVK (VUTsVK News) newspaper 58, 109, 133, 152
'The Union for the Liberation of Ukraine (from the SVU accusatory materials)' 160
Volunteer Army of Denikin 37, 52
Voronyi, Mykola 20, 37, 85, 164
  'modernist manifesto' of 1901 32
Vrazhlyvyi, Vasyl' 100
Vseukrlitkom. See All-Ukrainian Literary Committee

Vsevydav. See All-Ukrainian Publishing House
VUAN. See All-Ukrainian Academy of Sciences
VUFKU. See All-Ukrainian Photo-Cinema Administration
VUSPP. See All-Ukrainian Union of Proletarian Writers
VUTsVK. See All-Ukrainian Central Executive Committee
Vynnychenko, Volodymyr 26, 32, 91, 140, 183, 214 n.76
Vyshnia, Ostap 154–5, 167, 169, 223 n.13

War Communism 42–3, 67, 71
Western culture 106–7
West Ukrainian National Republic (*Zakhidno-Ukrains'ka Narodna Respublika*, ZUNR) 37
White Army 37–8, 53
White movement 37
working-class identity 7, 17, 80, 82, 134
  audiences 103, 129
  educated 78
  Russian 35, 113
  Ukraine/Ukrainization 98, 113, 119, 123, 142, 186

Yekelchyk, Serhy 9, 193 n.14
Yesenin, Sergei 95

Zabila, Natalia 154
Zahul, Dmytro 1, 32, 85, 154–5
Zakhidnia Ukraina (Western Ukraine) literary group 144, 168
Zalyvchyi, Andrii 33–4
Zatons'kyi, Volodymyr 81, 90, 121, 126, 129, 175, 207 n.51
  Natsional'na problema na Ukraini (The national problem in Ukraine) 123
  Tychyna, criticism of 129
zemstvo reform, Chernihiv 20, 22, 199 n.2
Zerov, Mykola 33, 44, 48, 56, 101, 107, 122, 196 n.42, 215 n.17
  and Khvyl'ovyi 54–5, 74, 109–11
  on Tychyna 88
Zhdanov, Andrei 189
Zhovten' (October) group 41, 60, 84, 136, 139
Zhuk, Andrii 148, 223 n.11
Zhuk, Mykhailo 20
Zhulyns'kyi, Mykola 178
zminovikhivtsi 160, 162
ZUNR. See West Ukrainian National Republic

www.ingramcontent.com/pod-product-compliance
Lightning Source LLC
Chambersburg PA
CBHW072130290426
44111CB00012B/1848